Social Media and the Law

Social media platforms like Facebook, Twitter, Instagram, YouTube, and Snapchat allow users to connect with one another and share information with the click of a mouse or a tap on a touchscreen—and have become vital tools for professionals in the news and strategic communication fields. But as rapidly as these services have grown in popularity, their legal ramifications aren't widely understood. To what extent do communicators put themselves at risk for defamation and privacy lawsuits when they use these tools, and what rights do communicators have when other users talk about them on social networks? How can people and companies manage intellectual property issues—such as posting copyrighted videos and photographs—consistent with the developing law in this area? How and when can journalists and publicists use these tools to do their jobs without endangering their employers or clients?

Including two new chapters that examine First Amendment issues and ownership of social media accounts and content, *Social Media and the Law* brings together thirteen media law scholars to address these questions and more, including current issues like copyright, online impersonation, anonymity, cyberbullying, sexting, and live streaming. Students and professional communicators alike need to be aware of laws relating to defamation, privacy, intellectual property, and government regulation—and this guidebook is here to help them navigate the tricky legal terrain of social media.

Daxton R. "Chip" Stewart, Ph.D., J.D., LL.M., is an associate professor in the Bob Schieffer College of Communication at Texas Christian University. He has more than fifteen years of professional experience in news media and public relations and has been an attorney since 1998. His recent scholarship focuses on the intersection of media technology and the law.

Social Media and the Law

A Guidebook for Communication Students and Professionals

Second Edition

Edited by
Daxton R. Stewart

Routledge
Taylor & Francis Group

NEW YORK AND LONDON

Second edition published 2017
by Routledge
711 Third Avenue, New York, NY 10017

and by Routledge
2 Park Square, Milton Park, Abingdon, Oxon OX14 4RN

Routledge is an imprint of the Taylor & Francis Group, an informa business

© 2017 Taylor & Francis

First edition published 2013 by Routledge

Library of Congress Cataloging-in-Publication Data
Stewart, Daxton R. Social media and the law : a guidebook for
communication students and professionals / edited by Daxton
R. Stewart.
Second Edition. Online social networks—Law and legislation—
United States. | Social media—Law and legislation—United States. |
Privacy, Right of—United States. | Obscenity (Law)—United States. |
Sexting—Law and legislation—United States. | Cyberbullying—Law
and legislation—United States.
KF390.5.C6 S639 2017 343.7309/944—dc232016032522

ISBN: 978-1-138-69577-1 (hbk)
ISBN: 978-1-138-69578-8 (pbk)
ISBN: 978-1-315-52613-3 (ebk)

Typeset in Bembo
by Swales & Willis Ltd, Exeter, Devon, UK

Contents

Preface

Daxton R. "Chip" Stewart

Bob Schieffer College of Communication
Texas Christian University

When my colleagues and I began work on the first edition of this book back in 2011, we anticipated that new social media platforms would launch and new issues would emerge quickly. We were right. In the months leading up to publication, the photo-sharing app Instagram became one of the world's most popular social tools, while Snapchat had just launched, soon to overtake Instagram and ultimately Twitter in daily users to become the second-most popular social media app behind Facebook.[1] Live-streaming, while technologically plausible, was years away from widespread use; just 5 years later, Periscope made live-streaming not only possible but also an important part of the social media landscape, with 200 million live-stream broadcasts created in its first year after launch.[2]

With these innovations came new challenges. Periscope had to deal with copyright issues when people used it to live-stream new episodes of *Game of Thrones* and the high-profile pay-per-view fight between Floyd Mayweather and Manny Pacquiao.[3] In 2016, a woman live-streamed her suicide in France using Periscope, with nearly 1,500 viewers tuning in, just a month after an American teenager faced criminal charges for live-streaming her friend being raped.[4] While these new technologies showed their dark sides, they also showed potential benefits as tools for shedding light on horrible abuses, as a woman used Facebook Live to broadcast police shooting her boyfriend during a traffic stop, drawing widespread attention to the tragedy.[5] These live-streaming incidents implicate different areas of the law for communication professionals—intellectual property and privacy, for a start—that were largely unthinkable just five years ago. Social media have become an essential part of modern human communications, and as such, their use has proliferated among journalists and other professional communicators as a forum for engaging with their audiences. Using social media for these purposes raises several important legal questions in a variety of areas that professional communicators should be aware of as they do their jobs.

These kinds of questions have become more and more prevalent when I have spoken to professional journalism and public relations groups and have worked with students. New issues arise nearly every day brought on by social media use by media professionals or other citizens, issues that are uncharted terrain for the law. A man is arrested for using Twitter to broadcast police locations, discovered using a police scanner, during G-20 protests in Pittsburgh.[6] A pharmaceutical company receives a warning letter from the FDA because it used a Facebook widget to market one of its prescription drugs.[7] A judge orders a newspaper to stop making posts on Twitter during a high-profile murder prosecution and to delete its previous posts about the trial.[8] Federal investigators issue a subpoena to Twitter for personal information of users suspected of collaborating with WikiLeaks to publish confidential U.S. documents.[9] A high school principal resigned amid allegations that she created a Facebook account under a pseudonym to monitor students.[10] An attorney shuts down her Pinterest boards after reading the terms of use and fearing liability for copyright infringement for photos she posted.[11] State laws against taking selfies in the voting booth were being challenged by Snapchat, arguing that the bans violate the First Amendment guarantee of freedom of speech.[12]

Social media have unquestionably permeated the practice of communicators such as journalists, public relations and advertising professionals. Our audience, our clients, and our colleagues expect that we, as professional communicators, become expert in using all available communication tools to do our respective jobs—and to do so in a way that dodges potential legal and ethical pitfalls.

Centuries of jurisprudence about media law provides a foundation for understanding the particular challenges we face when using social media. However, courts, lawmakers, and regulators have struggled to keep up with these challenges, particularly for media professionals.

The lack of formal guidance from courts and legislators is understandable, of course. New communication tools emerge—and disappear—at a rapid pace, faster than the legal system can evolve to handle the particular issues each presents.

The purpose of this book is to bridge this gap, providing practical guidance for communication students and professionals as they navigate the dangers of daily use of social media tools. To what extent can we use photos users have voluntarily shared on a social media site? Who is responsible when a person's reputation is harmed, or one's privacy is violated, through social media communications? How can social media tools be used to gather information or transmit news and commercial messages? These questions and more are addressed in this volume.

WHAT ARE SOCIAL MEDIA?

Before addressing the particular challenges social media present, it is helpful to understand exactly what social media are.

Communication scholars generally begin with the definition authored by danah boyd and Nicole Ellison in 2007 of social networking sites as "web-based services that allow individuals to (1) construct a public or semi-public profile within a bounded system, (2) articulate a list of other users with whom they share a connection, and (3) view and transverse their list of connections and those made by others within the system."[13] It is the third item—allowing users to make their social networks visible, thus permitting new connections to be made and networks to become larger—that boyd and Ellison say make social networking sites unique.

These core commonalities between social sites are visible in the most trafficked social media sites today.

Whether social tools are used primarily for social networking (such as Facebook and LinkedIn), for sharing videos and photos (YouTube, Instagram, Snapchat), for broadcasting live to the world (Periscope, Facebook Live), or for sharing content and ideas through microblogs (Twitter, Tumblr), they have at their center a transformational way of human interaction.

Social media, as such, are tools that have changed the way people communicate, as noted by Clay Shirky. "The tools that a society uses to create and maintain itself are as central to human life as a hive is to bee life," Shirky wrote in 2008, noting how social tools enable sharing and group formation in new ways.[14] The structure of the tools—individual profiles in bounded systems that can make connections public—has inexorably led to the culture of sharing and voluntariness on social networks.

But sharing and voluntariness are difficult concepts for the law, which often seeks more rigid definitions and boundaries to regulate human affairs. As such, legal definitions of social media often struggle to nail down these concepts. For example, when the Texas legislature sought to outlaw online impersonation—that is, creating a false profile online to harass or defraud another person—it chose the following definition of "commercial social networking site":

> any business, organization, or other similar entity operating a website that permits persons to become registered users for the purpose of establishing personal relationships with other users through direct or real-time communication with other users or the creation of web pages or profiles available to the public or to other users. The term does not include an electronic mail program or a message board program.[15]

Such a definition is so broad as to encompass nearly any online activity, whether publicly available or not, as long as it is not email or message boards—though even message boards, which enable discussion among strangers or friends, have a social aspect to them.

In fact, such statutory definitions have been deemed overbroad by federal courts when it comes to First Amendment concerns. For example, Louisiana's law forbidding sex offenders from using social media was struck down by a federal district court in 2012. The court noted that the term "social media" was not defined in the "Unlawful use of social media" act, though the act did mention "social networking sites, chat rooms, and peer-to-peer networks," a phrase so broad that the court expressed concerns that forbidding access to such sites was tantamount to "a near total ban on internet access."[16] As such, the law infringed some people's rights to express themselves freely, a violation of the First Amendment's mandate that the government "shall make no law . . . abridging freedom of speech, or of the press." A similar law in Nebraska[17] was also deemed overly broad because it encompassed nearly any kind of online communication.[18]

Courts have been a bit less clunky at defining social media. A federal district court in California in 2007, in a case involving MySpace, also described social networking sites in a functional way, as sites that "allow visitors to create personal profiles containing text, graphics, and videos, as well as to view profiles of their friends and other users with similar interests."[19] The court, as such, focused on what users do with social networking sites as a way of defining them. A Maryland state court in 2010 perhaps got closer to the heart of what makes social media challenging:

> Social networking sites and blogs are sophisticated tools of communication where the user voluntarily provides information that the user wants to share with others. Web sites such as Facebook and Myspace, allow the user to tightly control the dissemination of that information. The user can choose what information to provide or can choose not to provide information. The act of posting information on a social networking site, without the poster limiting access to that information, makes whatever is posted available to the world at large.[20]

This definition goes beyond function to consequences. The voluntariness aspect of social tools—users volunteer to share information with the world, perhaps with some limitations—makes them unique.

American courts have been handling disputes involving social media for more than a decade. The first reported opinion I was able to find was in 2004, involving Classmates.com, a site that allowed high school and college acquaintances to register and reconnect. An attorney in Oregon was publicly reprimanded by the state's Supreme Court by posing as a classmate who had become a teacher at their former high school and posting, "Hey all! How is it going. I am married to an incredibly beautiful woman, AND I get to hang out with high school chicks all day (and some evenings too). I have even been lucky with a few. It just doesn't get better than this."[21] Since then, courts have been handling cases involving social media in greater numbers each year. Facebook has been the subject of litigation almost since its founding, with Mark Zuckerberg battling ConnectU LLC, the operation put together by Tyler and Cameron Winklevoss and Divya Narendra, over who owned what intellectual property rights to the site. Just one case— *ConnectU v. Zuckerberg*—was the subject of an opinion in 2006.[22] The caseload has steadily grown. A LexisNexis search found 10 cases mentioning Facebook in 2007; 190 in 2010; 1,410 in 2013; and 2,096 in 2015, with an even greater rate to date in 2016.

Not all of these cases involve issues for media professionals, but many of them have, as is detailed in this book. Beyond the courts, the federal government has become increasingly aware of the impact of social tools on commerce, with regulatory agencies such the Federal Trade Commission and the Food and Drug Administration offering guidelines for making marketing communications via social networks. Professional media organizations such as the Public Relations Society of America, the Institute of Advertising Ethics, and the American Society of News Editors offered updated guidelines and best practices for professional social media use in recent years as well.

LOOKING FORWARD

The particular challenge of a volume like this is to nail down the landscape of social media and the law at a fixed moment in time—as social tools are launching and evolving, as legislatures and regulators are trying to come up with ways to manage the impact of these tools, as professionals are trying to maximize effective use of social tools while minimizing legal risks. All of this is being done in the shadow of the developing culture of social media, one that is rooted in voluntariness, sharing, and group formation rather than legal formalities such as contracts, property, statutes, and regulations.

As such, it may very well be that Lawrence Lessig was right, that "Code is law"—that is, that the hardware and software that make up cyberspace determine its culture and use, so that management of human affairs online is best left to the code, not to legislatures and the courts.[23]

Nevertheless, courts have already handled thousands of cases that involve social media tools, with thousands more on the way. Online human affairs can be and certainly have been the subject of our laws, and those who would use social media tools should be aware of the legal obligations, duties, and expectations created by the law.

Fortunately, we are guided by precedent. While social media may be revolutionary technologies, so were the telegraph, the telephone, the radio, the television, and the Internet. We are guided by the First Amendment and centuries of jurisprudence regarding the law of communication. And the more we understand how social tools work, and how they have fundamentally transformed human interaction, the more we should be able to understand how to use them legally and responsibly.

This volume comprises 13 chapters by media law scholars examining the way the law interacts with social media in their areas of expertise. Media professionals continue to face many of the same challenges they have in the past—defamation, privacy, intellectual property, commercial speech regulations, access to government records and court proceedings— so this volume is organized around these particular challenges. Some areas touch on other aspects of communication—obscenity, cyberbullying, student speech—in which the implications of social media on the law have developed, shedding light on how courts may treat these issues for communicators in the future.

Each chapter opens with an overview of the law in that area, examining how legislatures, courts, and regulators have handled the law in the digital environment. The authors go on to examine the particular challenges that social tools present, and how professionals and the law have responded to them. Finally, each chapter concludes with a "Frequently Asked Questions" section, with answers to five practical questions that professionals and students may most often encounter. The first 10 chapters of this volume focus on areas of substantive law, while the next two examine practical consequences for professionals, offering guidance on developing social media policies for journalism and strategic communication professionals. The final chapter looks forward to some of the potential implications of social media on the free speech and free press guarantees of the First Amendment.

Our hope in writing this book was not to provide a comprehensive, definitive volume on the law of social media as it pertains to media professionals—that would, of course, be impossible in this time of great upheaval to the media landscape. Instead, our goal is to provide professional communicators a foundation of knowledge with practical guidance in what we know to be the most dangerous terrain, with an eye on what is happening now and what is to come. While the law may often seem ill-suited to adapt to technological and social change that have transformed the way people communicate, adapt it has and will continue to do.

NOTES

1 Sarah Frier, Snapchat Passes Twitter in Daily Usage, Bloomberg Technology, June 2, 2016, http://www.bloomberg.com/news/articles/2016-06-02/snapchat-passes-twitter-in-daily-usage.

2 Sarah Perez, Live Streaming App Periscope Touts 200 Million Broadcasts in Its First Year, TechCrunch, March 28, 2016, https://techcrunch.com/2016/03/28/live-streaming-app-periscope-touts-200-million-broadcasts-in-its-first-year/.

3 Nicholas Thompson, Pirates Crash the Mayweather-Pacquiao Fight, The New Yorker, May 4, 2015, http://www.newyorker.com/business/currency/pirates-crash-the-mayweather-pacquiao-fight.

4 Caitlin Dewey, The (Very) Dark Side of Live Streaming That No One Seems Able to Stop, Wash. Post, May 26, 2016, https://www.washingtonpost.com/news/the-intersect/wp/2016/05/26/the-very-dark-side-of-live-streaming-that-no-one-seems-able-to-stop/; Peter Holley, 'She got caught up in the likes': Teen accused of live-streaming friend's rape for attention, Wash. Post, April 19, 2016, https://www.washingtonpost.com/news/morning-mix/wp/2016/04/19/she-got-caught-up-in-the-likes-teen-accused-of-livestreaming-friends-rape-for-attention/?tid=a_inl.

5 Abby Ohlheiser, Is Facebook ready for live video's important role in police accountability, Wash. Post, July 7, 2016, https://www.washingtonpost.com/news/the-intersect/wp/2016/07/07/is-facebook-ready-for-live-videos-important-role-in-police-accountability/.

6 Colin Moynihan, Arrest Puts Focus on Protesters' Texting, N.Y. Times, October 9, 2009, http://www.nytimes.com/2009/10/05/nyregion/05txt.html?_r=2.

7 Katherine Hobson, FDA Dings Novartis for Facebook Widget, WSJ Health Blog, August 6, 2010, http://blogs.wsj.com/health/2010/08/06/fda-dings-novartis-for-facebook-widget/.

8 Dianna Hunt, Judge Restricts Reporting on Capital Murder Trial in Fort Worth, Fort Worth Star-Telegram, January 6, 2012, http://www.star-telegram.com/2012/01/06/3640977/judge-restricts-reporting-on-capital.html.

9 Scott Shane & John F. Burns, U.S. Subpoenas Twitter Over WikiLeaks Supporters, N.Y. Times, January 8, 2011, http://www.nytimes.com/2011/01/09/world/09wiki.html?pagewanted=all.

10 Jessica Bock, Clayton High's Principal Resigns Amid Facebook Mystery, St. Louis Post-Dispatch, May 6, 2012, http://www.stltoday.com/news/local/education/clayton-high-s-principal-resigns-amid-facebook-mystery/article_70bd065a-5912-551a-ac73-746ea58177af.html.

11 Alyson Shontell, A Lawyer Who Is Also a Photographer Just Deleted All of Her Pinterest Boards Out of Fear, Business Insider, February 28, 2012, http://articles.businessinsider.com/2012-02-28/tech/31106641_1_repinning-copyright-entire-image.

12 Daniel Victor, Selfies in the Voting Booth? Snapchat Fights for the Right, N.Y. Times, April 26, 2016, http://www.nytimes.com/2016/04/27/us/politics/voting-booth-snapchat-selfies.html

13 danah m. boyd & Nicole B. Ellison, Social Network Sites: Definition, History, and Scholarship, 13 J. Computer-Mediated Communication 210, 211 (2007).

14 Clay Shirky, Here Comes Everybody 17 (2008).

15 Texas Penal Code § 33.07(f)(1) (2012)

16 Doe v. Jindal, 853 F. Supp. 2d 596, 607 (M.D. La. 2012).

17 Neb. Rev. Stat. § 29-4001.01(13) (2012)

18 See Doe v. Nebraska, 734 F. Supp. 2d 882 (D. Neb. 2010).

19 LifeUniverse v. MySpace, 2007 U.S. Dist. LEXIS 43739 at *1 (C.D. Cal. 2007).

20 Independent Newspapers Inc. v. Brodie, 407 Md. 415, note 3 (Md. Ct. App. 2010).

21 In re Carpenter, 95 P.3d 203 (Oregon 2004).

22 See ConnectU LLC v. Zuckerberg, 2006 U.S. Dist. LEXIS 86118 (D. Mass, 2006); ConnectU LLC v. Zuckerberg, 522 F.3d 82 (1st Cir. 2008).

23 Lawrence Lessig, Code and Other Laws of Cyberspace 6 (1999).

CHAPTER 1

New Boundaries of Free Speech in Social Media

Jennifer Jacobs Henderson, Ph.D.
Trinity University

ABSTRACT

Although the fundamental questions regarding free speech have changed little since the advent of social media, these new ways of connecting and communicating have left judges and legal scholars questioning the shifting boundaries of speech in social digital spaces. To better understand how laws regarding free speech are evolving to address this new medium, this chapter examines three areas of social media law where the boundaries remain contested ground: access, content, and surveillance.

At a time when more people in the United States use social media than vote, what happens in these spaces is becoming increasingly significant—shaping politics, economics, and history. If health care policies, stock market movements, and entertainment franchises are now debated in social networks rather than traditional media, understanding the boundaries of allowable speech in these spaces is essential. The amount of and ability to access digital content means that the potential for disagreement over speech has increased exponentially, and thus the number of legal challenges regarding speech, has increased. The fundamental questions raised, however, are not so different than those posed when people with a podium and a bullhorn spoke a century ago: What kinds of speech should be allowed? When can government intervene? How can someone protect private speech from public eyes? The distributed and participatory nature of social networks, however, have left judges analyzing complex new communication patterns as they attempt to draw the boundaries of free speech, government intervention, user and consumer harms, and privacy rights.

For example, a 2016 lawsuit against the social media app Snapchat alleges it encouraged reckless driving by a Georgia teenager who slammed her car into another while using a Snapchat "lens" that tracks vehicle speed. At the time of impact, her speed was clocked at 107 mph.[1] A 12-year-old girl in Virginia faced criminal charges for emojis of a gun, bomb, and knife, posted to her Instagram that read: "Killing (gun emoji) . . . meet me in the library Tuesday (gun, knife, bomb emojis)."[2] Chanel, the Paris fashion house, filed an intellectual property infringement action against an Indiana salon owner for the use of its logo on the @Chanel Instagram account, which Chanel does not own (Chanel's Instagram handle is @officialChanel).[3]

While the meaning of emojis, @s, likes, and #s will be debated in courts for years to come, like all of the legal battles that arise from this space, the meaning of words and symbols is both an old and a new problem. Judicial interpretation of intention behind speech is and always has been difficult. A slip of the tongue has simply morphed into a slip of the thumb.

ACCESS TO SOCIAL MEDIA

For almost a quarter of a century, public interest organizations have fought for physical access to the most basic Internet services, with scholars noting gaps in access based on race, ethnicity, income, and geographic location. And, while battles against "information redlining" and "the digital divide" might seem to be a relic of another time, the core issue of access still remains. Many individuals in the U.S. and around the world still have limited access to the Internet, and by extension, to social media communities and content. Their speech in these prolific spaces is hampered even before they begin to create.

In the United States, the right to access social media sites has been addressed recently by state courts and attorneys general. In Louisiana, a court ruled in 2012 that a law restricting registered sex offenders from accessing "social networking websites, chat rooms, and peer-to-peer networks," was both unconstitutionally overbroad and vague. The court found that the law as written would make it a crime to access protected content such as online newspapers and had already caused several people to refrain from using the Internet at all for "fear that they may unintentionally and unknowingly violate the law."[4]

In 2012, access was also restricted to online video games through an initiative between Attorney General Eric T. Schneiderman of New York and video game manufacturers such as Microsoft, Apple, Blizzard Entertainment, Electronic Arts, and Disney Interactive Media.[5] The goal of Operation: Game Over was to remove convicted sex offenders from online game interactions with juveniles. Based on data collected from registered sex offenders in New York, 3,500 accounts were deleted or had communication privileges suspended by game companies in the first phase of the operation. While much narrower in scope, Operation: Game Over may also be challenged in court based on the blanket assumption that registered sex offenders are always engaged in criminal activities in online games.

Whether the right to access social media can be taken away from someone after arrest or incarceration is also under debate. In Illinois in 2016, legislators introduced a bill that would ban some juvenile offenders from accessing social media and require them to turn over passwords to law enforcement. Specifically, the legislation would "allow courts to hold pretrial hearings to determine whether to ban a juvenile charged with a crime from accessing social media, and to require him or hire to give the government access to his or her social media accounts."[6]

The freedom to access the Internet and social media sites varies greatly around the world. Freedom House, a non-profit organization concerned with global speech and press freedoms, rated nations based on "obstacles to access," defined as "infrastructural and economic barriers to access; governmental efforts to block specific applications or technologies; and legal, regulatory and ownership controls over internet and mobile phone access providers." In 2015, countries such as China, Syria, and Ethiopia were ranked highest among those who impede access to the Internet.[7]

While outrage against repressive regimes resonated through social media spaces during the Arab Spring in 2011, many governments have pushed back against protestors by implementing new restrictions on Internet and social media use. For example, governments in "14 of 65 countries passed new laws to increase surveillance" in 2014–2015.While Freedom House estimates more than 3 billion people have access to the internet, "58% live in countries where bloggers or ICT users were jailed for sharing content on political, social, and religious issues" in 2014–2015 and "47% live in countries where individuals were attacked or killed for their online activities since June 2014."[8]

It is also important to remember that governments have always attempted to control the flow of information. From the jury verdict convicting Socrates in 339 BC, to the prosecution of U.S. socialists Charles Schenck and Eugene Debs who spoke out against involvement in World War I,[9] to the sentencing of eight youth in Iran for a combined 127 years in prison for anti-government posts on Facebook,[10] governments have sought to suppress speech they find to work against the interests of the state. At this time of unrest worldwide, it is not surprising that government authorities, fearing their loss of power, are turning to access restrictions and censorship for control.

Though the censorship and suppression of speech by government is both common and historically grounded, pressure against oppressive regimes is growing. For example, opposition parties in Russia, dissidents in China, and insurgents in Syria, are all using new technologies to secure access to social media streams. These minority voices have found international support. In May 2011, the United Nations General Assembly's Human Rights Council declared that access to the Internet was a "basic human right" and if restricted, would be a violation of international law.[11]

SOCIAL MEDIA CONTENT

Media content in the second decade of the 21st century has been characterized as "mobile," "ubiquitous," "voyeuristic," and "mean." The most common term used to describe this period, however, has been "social." Social sounds friendly enough, but the content of social media (online participatory sharing communities) has been anything but. Today, media accounts are filled with stories of cyber-bullying, brash examples of defamation, and unauthorized celebrity photos.

Speech in social media is being challenged—along traditional legal lines and in new ways. Obscenity, libel, and copyright cases related to social media are on the rise in many countries. For example, online defamation rose more than 300% from 6 to 26 cases between 2012–13 and 2013–14 in the U.K.[12]

Private Speech

What were once considered private matters, topics such as sex, spousal conflict, personal habits, and finance, are now broadcast 24 hours, 7 days a week via streaming services, podcasts, and on social media sites. Where in past years media attention was focused mainly on those who placed themselves in the public limelight—politicians, celebrities, and athletes—people now have a near-equal opportunity to create their own public stage. While many participants in online social networks behave as if their content is private, these are not "backstage" areas where scandal and intrigue can be revealed to some and kept from others. Instead, content posted on social networking sites such as Facebook is more often than not, searchable, sold, and shared. Concerns regarding private speech were raised in early 2012 when Google announced its new Search Plus Your World feature that combed through both one's personal Google+ social media content and the Internet to return results.[13] Facebook announced a new app in 2014 that would identifying songs or television programs using the iPhone microphone, then incorporate that information into status updates. Facebook, though, never revealed how data collected and "archived as code" through the app would be used.[14] In 2015, LinkedIn settled a class action lawsuit brought by users whose names and likenesses were used to grow LinkedIn's customer base. LinkedIn agreed to pay $13 million to users for the unauthorized use of a service called Add Connections. Through this service, LinkedIn would access user email accounts without their consent, sending user contacts' invitations and reminder emails to join LinkedIn. While the court in this case found LinkedIn users consented (through the Terms of Service Agreement) to accessing their email contacts and sending the initial invitation to join, users did not consent to the sending follow-up emails on their behalf.[15]

Privacy concerns extend beyond the collection and use of personal connections and data. Social media sites have also altered content in users' accounts. In 2012, Facebook allowed researchers to manipulate the news feeds of almost 700,000 users to see if it could alter the mood expressed in posts. Users were never notified of the study or contacted for consent. Findings from the study, published in the *Proceedings of the National Academy of Sciences*, showed that Facebook "could affect the content which those users posted to Facebook. More negative news feeds led to more negative status messages, as more positive news feeds led to positive statuses."[16]

Instead of relying on the hit or miss privacy protections of many social media sites, users are beginning to take privacy into their own hands. As of 2012, 37% of social network users had untagged photos, 44% had deleted comments, and 63% had "unfriended" someone. In addition, 58% of users "restrict access" to their social media sites by setting privacy controls so "only friends can see."[17] In fact, a 2016 study found U.S. respondents have very nuanced opinions regarding privacy and information sharing, noting that they take into account "the company or organization," "how trustworthy or safe they perceive the firm to be," what happens to their data after they are collected," and "how long the data are retained."[18]

Many privacy cases hinge on whether the person had an expectation of privacy in the particular forum in which the utterance was made. The courts have long held there is no expectation of privacy in public. On the user-side, this is where confusion reigns. Private companies (or publicly traded ones) run these sites. A user must register and agree to terms of service. How, then, can these sites not be private?

Political Speech

Over the course of 350 years, the idea of a free and open venue for speech has percolated. John Milton wrote: "Where there is much desire to learn, there of necessity will be much arguing, much writing, many opinions; for opinion in good men is but knowledge in the making."[19] It was 1644. John Stuart Mill's "marketplace of ideas," where the best ideas rise to the fore through free and open debate[20] resounded in 1859, and Justice Oliver

Wendell Holmes, Jr. contended, "the best test of truth is the power of the thought to get itself accepted in the competition of the market" in 1919.[21] The maxim exhorted is just as applicable today. When they work well, social media encourage a wide range of often competing voices. When they work poorly, they are they are an echo chamber of one-sided, often offensive, commentaries rejecting all opposing ideas.

For almost 100 years in the United States—from 1920 at the dawn of radio to 2010 and the rise of social media—the biggest concern among free speech activists was how individual citizens could be heard. Due to the cost of production and distribution, media remained solidly in the hands of the few.[22] Beyond the states, ownership also resided in the hands of the few, though often in the hands of a few government officials.

"The marketplace theory justifies free speech as a means to an end," writes Professor Rodney Smolla, "But free speech is also an end itself, an end intimately intertwined with human autonomy and dignity."[23] In this theoretical vein, the UN's 2011 declaration regarding access to the Internet is a part of a larger report "on the promotion and protection of the right to freedom of opinion and expression" and begins by outlining the rights provided for in article 19 of the International Covenant on Civil and Political Rights. They are: "the right to hold opinions without interference," "the right to seek and receive information and the right of access to information," and "the right to impart information and ideas of all kinds."[24]

These basic rights are clearly consistent with First Amendment protections, however, even in the United States political expression in social media is being squelched. Currently, there are 17 states that have some kind of law that makes it a crime to state a falsehood in an election campaign.[25] These laws have been put to use in silencing a key vehicle for political speech—Twitter messages. Mark W. Miller, a Cincinnati resident concerned with how the city was allocating funds for a new streetcar project, sent regular tweets voicing his complaints. For example, "15% of Cincinnati's Fire Dept browned out today to help pay for a streetcar boondoggle. If you think it's a waste of money, VOTE YES on 48." When charged with a crime under the Ohio law forbidding such speech as a lie, his non-profit, the Coalition Opposed to Additional Spending of Taxes (COAST), sued the Ohio Election Commission, claiming the law was unconstitutional restriction on free speech.[26] Miller's tweet suit inspired a similar case challenging the same Ohio law. In 2014, the U.S. Supreme Court unanimously found that the restriction of speech violated free speech rights and remanded to the lower courts for reconsideration.[27] In 2016, the Sixth Circuit Court of Appeals agreed, stating, "Ohio's political false-statements laws are content-based restrictions targeting core political speech that are not narrowly tailored to serve the state's admittedly compelling interest in conducting fair elections."[28]

Political speech in Facebook posts have also led to First Amendment cases. In Hampton, Virginia, the Sheriff fired six employees who supported an opposing candidate during his re-election campaign. One of these workers contended in federal court that he was fired for expressing his support of the other candidate by "liking" him on Facebook. Essentially, he was being punished for expressing his protected political speech. The district court judge in this case ruled that the firing could not be linked to the employee's support of the opposition candidate because clicking the "like" button on Facebook was not equivalent to writing a message of support for the opposition candidate. The "like" button, the court found, was not expressive speech. In 2013, the Fourth Circuit overruled the lower court decision, siding with the employee against the Sheriff. Here, the court ruled that "liking" was protected by the First Amendment because it was the "Internet equivalent of displaying a political sign in one's front yard, which the Supreme Court has held is substantive speech."[29]

During the 2016 elections, "ballot selfies," photos of ballots or voters filling out ballots, in polling places, became an issue. Laws governing picture-taking in voting locations and individual voting booths vary by state. In Pennsylvania, for example, taking a photo inside a voting booth can lead to $1,000 fine and up to 12 months in jail. Showing someone else a completed ballot is a felony in Wisconsin.[30] In 2015, the U.S. District Court for the District of New Hampshire struck down a New Hampshire law that prohibited ballot selfies.[31] Snapchat argued that these selfies were important to young voters and compared them to "I Voted" stickers, noting in their brief that the ballot selfie "dramatizes the power that one person has to influence our government."[32]

These election laws, especially as they have been applied to social media, restrict speech that has always been afforded the highest protection under the First Amendment. In challenges involving the limitation of political speech, courts rule the law constitutional only if (1) a compelling government interest is articulated, (2) the law is narrowly tailored to meet that interest, and (3) it is the least restrictive means necessary to address the government interest.[33] This strict scrutiny test should protect political speech in social media as it does in traditional media, erecting a legal firewall between government and the opinions of the people.

Government Regulation of Media Content

A quite debate is raging between those who believe the Wild West of the Internet Age supports free speech and democracy and those who argue that the new "vast wasteland" of hate, violence, and porn is delivered via the Internet rather than television. These rumblings are growing louder as politicians are pressured to regulate and public interest organizations are preparing to defend freedom online.

It all began when the Internet first started worrying elected officials, way back in the days of BBBs systems. In 1996, Congress, concerned about the potential for the Internet to become a "red light district,"[34] passed the Communications Decency Act (CDA), Title V of the Telecommunications Act. Section 223 of the CDA regulated access by minors to indecent material on the Internet. In June of 1997, the Supreme Court ruled on the constitutionality of the Communication Decency Act in *Reno v. ACLU*.[35] The Court unanimously agreed that Section 223 of the CDA was unconstitutional. Here, Justice Stevens writing for the Court contended that the CDA, as written, was overbroad and vague. When considering the issue of over-breadth, the Court found that Act's use of the term "indecency" was not consistent with the First Amendment protection of all but "obscene" materials when adult audiences were considered. In addition, the Court said the CDA was a content-based restriction, which "raises special First Amendment concerns because of its obvious chilling effect on free speech."[36]

The lasting effect of *Reno* was the blanket of First Amendment protection placed on the Internet by the Supreme Court. Eight years earlier in the *Sable* decision,[37] the Court had made clear that each telecommunication medium should be considered individually when determining the breadth of First Amendment protection. In *Reno*, the Justices gave the widest possible berth to the fledgling Internet, comparing its First Amendment rights to that of traditional press such as newspapers and not broadcasters, whose regulation had been upheld due to the passive nature of the audience in relation to the medium.

The regulation and censorship of speech in social media by government organizations continues to be a concern. In 2014, in Rapides Parish, Louisiana, a teacher was reprimanded by the principal when she posted comments critical of Louisiana's Common Core school curriculum on her personal Facebook page from her home computer. The principal ordered the teacher to delete the remarks that suggested parents remove their children from the schools "until we get rid of this." The teacher sued the principal and the school district for a violation of her First Amendment rights.[38]

Students at public colleges and universities have also been punished for commentary on social media sites. A mortuary science student at the University of Minnesota posted comments on Facebook in 2009 regarding her coursework. In one post, she wrote about the cadaver she was working on: "(I get) to play, I mean dissect, Bernie today." She also wrote of her ex-boyfriend that she would like to use an embalming tool "to stab a certain someone in the throat." In response to her Facebook posts, the University of Minnesota gave her an F in the course and required her to complete an ethics class and undergo a psychiatric exam. The woman has appealed the university's decision in court saying that the actions violated her right to free speech.[39] Similarly, a nursing student at the University of Louisville was kicked out of college for violating the Honor Code and a Course Confidentiality Agreement when she posted a description of a live birth on her MySpace page. The student, in turn, brought suit against the university for a violation of her First and Fourteenth Amendment rights as well as injunctive relief and damages under the Civil Rights Act.[40] The U.S. District Court for the Western District of Kentucky found that this was not a free speech issue, but a contractual one, and that Yoder did not violate the contract of the Honor Code or the Confidentiality Agreement with her post. The court ruled that the woman must be reinstated as a student.[41]

On the other hand, the Eighth Circuit Court of Appeals found that twin brothers did not have their rights violated when they were expelled for using school computers to create a blog about their Lee's Summit, Missouri, high school. On the blog, they posted "a variety of offensive and racist comments as well as sexually explicit and degrading comments about particular female classmates, whom they identify by name." In response, the brothers were expelled from school for 180 days. They filed suit against the school district alleging that their First Amendment rights had been violated. Ruling on a preliminary injunction against the expulsion, the Eighth Circuit Court of Appeals found that the school's actions to be constitutional, explaining that the speech was "targeted at" Lee's Summit North High School and "could reasonably be expected to reach the school or impact the environment."[42] In sum, these cases show that courts are apt to allow school punishment of offensive student speech when the content is created on campus, using school technology, or causes disruption to student learning at a specific school.

There is currently a battle raging on college campuses regarding the kind and extent of speech encouraged and allowed. Trying to find a balance between spaces of open inquiry and discussion and hateful, derogatory comments, many private colleges and universities have come down on the side of restriction while many public universities have walked a very fine line between civility and censorship.

For example, at Texas Christian University, a 19-year-old student was placed on probation and not allowed to live on campus or attend on-campus sporting events after posting offensive comments on Twitter. Remarking on the shooting death of Freddie Gray and following riots in Baltimore, he tweeted, "#Baltimore in 4 words: poor uneducated druggy hoodrats."[43] A disciplinary panel upheld a finding that the student had violated two conduct code violations, "infliction of bodily or emotional harm" and "disorderly conduct." Ultimately, the punishment was reversed by university administrators.

Many comments causing concern on college and university campuses have been posted anonymously on the social media site Yik Yak. Yik Yak is a mobile app that allows users to post anonymous comments to anyone within a five-mile radius, based on the user's location. These posts, known as "Yaks," have created substantial controversy and several legal cases surrounding issues of free speech. For example in 2015, a 19-year-old Western Washington University student was arrested for first-degree malicious harassment for Yaks he posted that threatened students of color. In response to a suggestion that the university reconsider its Viking mascot because it was not representative of all students, he posted: "Let's lynch her." School officials took "her" to mean the university's African American student president. If found guilty, the student could face up to five years in jail.[44]

Following protests at the University of Missouri regarding racial inequality and police brutality, three students on Missouri campuses were arrested for posting threatening comments on Yik Yak. University of Missouri police arrested one student at Missouri University of Science and Technology in Rolla for "making a terrorist threat" via Yik Yak[45] after the student posted: "I'm going to stand my ground tomorrow and shoot every black person I see."[46] A second student at Missouri University of Science and Technology in Rolla was prosecuted for "posting online threats to attack a college campus" after writing "I'm gonna shoot up this school" on Yik Yak. A third student, also 19, was arrested in his dormitory at Missouri State University for "making racist threats on social media."[47]

In cases such as these, law enforcement may seek an emergency subpoena for social media posts that "poses a risk of imminent harm."[48] In these instances, Yik Yak will turn over information they "believe would prevent the harm" which "may include a user's IP address, GPS coordinates, message timestamps, telephone number, user-agent string and/or the contents of other messages from the user's posting history."[49] This was the procedure used when Texas A&M police obtained an emergency subpoena to arrest at student for posting, "This is not a joke! Don't go to campus between 7 and 7:30. This will be my only warning!"[50]

Law enforcement officials, however, are having a very difficult time determining what is a true threat, what is a hoax, and what is simply a poorly executed joke in social media. At the extreme end of social media harassment, "swatting" is also on the rise. Swatting is when those watching livestream videogame players call or hack into 911 systems with a terror threat to send the SWAT team to the home of the player so the reaction of the gamer is caught on webcam.[51] Officials have estimated that a single Swatting episode can cost more than $25,000 law enforcement agencies.[52] For these "pranks," Swatters have received up to 11 years in jail.[53]

Student athletes, even at public universities, are in a unique position in regards to free speech. While they are protected from state interference as students, by agreeing to participate in extracurricular athletic activities, they also agree to special rules and regulations governing their behavior.[54] Many of these regulations involve social media. For example, in the 2014–15 season, men's basketball teams at Minnesota, Purdue, Iowa and Louisville banned their players from tweeting.[55] At Mississippi State, basketball coach Rick Stansbury banned the use of Twitter after student athletes criticized his performance and the team's fans following a loss.[56] Western Kentucky University went a step further when they suspended a football player in October 2011 after he posted comments critical of fans on Twitter.[57] A student athlete at Lehigh University was suspended for retweeting a racial slur,[58] and a Boston College female soccer athlete was suspended from the team during the 2012 NCAA tournament when she posted multiple insensitive tweets about Penn State's locker room where young boys were molested by Jerry Sandusky.[59]

In response to concerns regarding social media posts, some athletic programs have either banned the use of social media or required athletes turn over passwords to the coaching staff. While legislation in many states forbids this kind of social media monitoring, the outright ban of social media use is acceptable in athletic programs as participation is seen as a privilege rather than a right.[60]

Personal Threats, Revenge and Social Media

In addition to general threats of terrorism and harm, individual threats via social media have been at the center of free speech case law in recent years. The most high-profile case involving online personal threats, *Elonis v. United States*, was decided by the Supreme Court in 2015. In this case, Anthony Elonis posted threats on his personal account and as his rap persona "Tone Dougie" to Facebook. These comments threatened his estranged wife ("I'm not going to rest until your body is a mess, soaked in blood and dying from a thousand tiny cuts"), local schools ("Enough elementary schools in a ten mile radius to initiate the most heinous school shooting ever imagined/Hell hath no fury like a crazy man in a kindergarten class"), and a female FBI agent working on his case ("Pull my knife, flick my wrist, and slit her throat").[61] For these posts and others, Elonis was convicted under a federal law and sentenced to 44 months in prison. The Supreme Court ruled in favor of Elonis, reasoning that to be convicted under this law, the state must prove Elonis made his statements "for the purpose of issuing a threat, or with knowledge that the communication will be viewed as a threat."[62] While this decision certainly did not limit the boundaries of free speech allowed in social media, the actual court decision relied heavily on the criminal law requirements of intent rather than First Amendment arguments related to speech.

Three years earlier, courts ruled on a similar case and offered a very different solution to social media threats. Mark Byron, engaged in a bitter divorce and custody suit over his young son, wrote on his Facebook page, "If you are an evil, vindictive woman who wants to ruin your husband's life and take your son's father away from him completely—all you need to do is say you're scared of your husband or domestic partner and they'll take him away." Based on these comments, a magistrate found Byron in contempt of a protective order. To avoid a 60-day jail sentence and a $500 fine, the magistrate said Byron could post an apology on his Facebook page every day by 9 a.m. between February 13, 2012, and March 16, 2012, when he returned to court. Byron contended that the apology, which stated he was placing his ex-wife in "an unfavorable light" and "attempting to mislead" his friends, was untrue.[63] Many free speech advocates found this court-compelled speech to be concerning as government-forced speech is equivalent to restricting free speech.

Social media posts that cause personal harm also include revenge porn and doxing. Revenge porn is the posting of nude or intimate photographs or videos via social media or websites. Most revenge porn targets women. By 2016, 34 states and the District of Columbia had laws criminalizing revenge porn.[64] For example, the Arizona revenge porn law states that "Unlawful distribution of images depicting states of nudity or specific sexual activities. If disclosed by electronic means, Class 4 felony. If threatens to disclose but does not disclose, Class 1 Misdemeanor."[65] This law and others were challenged by the ACLU and a coalition of bookstores, journalists, and librarians for being overbroad. They argue that these laws restrict not only revenge porn, but all nude and sexual images, including art and historical images, which are clearly protected by the First Amendment.[66]

Doxing is the posting of a dossier of your private information online for anyone to see. It is often used as a threat or revenge against those online with whom you disagree. Most of the time, doxing cases involve the legal collection of information, often from users' own social media posts or voluntarily disclosed data on the Internet. However, doxing can become illegal when information such as social security or credit card numbers, often bought from the deep web (the portion of the Internet not discoverable through standard search engines), are released.[67]

Government Requested and Court-Ordered Information

The most high-profile government information request case in recent years involved Apple and the FBI. In 2015, the Department of Justice obtained a court order instructing Apple to unlock the security code and provide backdoor access to the iPhone of a man who committed a terrorist attack in San Bernardino. Apple refused to comply with the order, citing privacy promises made to its users. While this case did not involve social media directly, it was one of the first to acknowledge that access to a users' phones would provide instant access to any social media accounts set to remain open. As Apple explained in its Open Letter to Customers in 2015: "We built strong security into the iPhone because people carry so much personal information on our phones today."[68]

Requests for user identification and account information are regularly issued to social media companies. A very large percentage of these requests are fulfilled. For example, between July 1 and December 31, 2015, there were 862 U.S. Criminal Legal Requests involving 1,819 accounts made to Snapchat. In turn, Snapchat complied with the request, producing at least "some data," in 80% of the cases.[69] During this same period, 2,673 requests for information specifying 7,435 accounts were made to Twitter. Of those, Twitter produced "some information" 79% of the time.[70] Facebook received the most government requests for user information during the July to December 2015 period—19,235 requests involving 30,041 accounts—and provided information in 81.41% of the cases.[71]

The information provided in most cases does not include message content, only user account information or account metadata. For example, law enforcement subpoenas for documentation from Snapchat allow access to basic account information such as "account name, email address, phone number and when the account was created." To get a log of metadata, when messages were sent and to whom, requires a state or federal search warrant. The only time content of snaps would be released is if the receiving party had not opened them within 30 days of the original message being sent. After 30 days, Snapchat says, unopened snaps are "wiped from their servers."[72]

SURVEILLANCE OF SOCIAL MEDIA

Surveillance of social media networks and the messages created in them in is increasing daily. In many ways, social media sites are now more like a fish tank than a lock box. Government agencies, employers, site operators, and advertisers are all peeking into the aquarium of social media to see what's up. Users of social networks, just now realizing that everyone is a Peeping Tom, are beginning to close their blinds.

Government Agencies

Security agencies for governments around the world are reading, watching, and listening in social media networks. The ultimate "lurkers," these agencies are tracking conversations, looking for clues to crimes and other misdeeds. As law enforcement agents link social media to terrorist recruitment efforts and plots of violence,[73] additional oversight is inevitable. For example, the National Security Agency (NSA), a long-time surveillant of private citizen information, stated in March 2012 that it would begin storing digital information collected on U.S. citizens even when they were not under investigation. Information, once only stored for those suspected of terrorist activities and only for 18 months, would not be held for anyone caught in the net of surveillance for up to five years.[74]

After Edward Snowden's unauthorized release of U.S. government surveillance program details, many Americans took action to protect their online information. The Pew Research Center reported in 2015 that "34% of those who are aware of the surveillance programs (30% of all adults) have taken at least one step to hide or shield their information from the government." These steps included "changing their privacy settings on social media," using "social media less often," and avoiding or installing certain apps to help with privacy.[75]

Since the revelation in December 2015 that one of the San Bernardino attackers had sent private messages on Facebook "pledging her support for Islamic jihad and saying she hoped to join the fight one day,"[76] the Department of Homeland Security (DHS) has come under growing pressure from Congress to increase surveillance of the social media accounts of individuals applying for visas, work permits, and citizenship. In January 2016, the DHS began searching for social media analytics software to aid in their investigations.[77]

Government agencies in many nations also monitor social media sites for material that is deemed inappropriate for its citizens. Because social media companies are private corporations, they must abide by the laws of each country in order to expand and secure customers. As an illustration, between January and June 2015, India submitted 227 requests for 1,037 individual "offending" items to be removed from Google-owned sites. Of those, 41% requested by court order and 6% requested by government agencies or law enforcement were granted.[78] Google offered this as one example of content removed on the Indian government's request: "Following a protest at Google Mumbai office regarding the appearance in Google Search of allegedly obscene and defamatory photos of Shri Balasaheb Thackrey, founder of the regional political party Shiv Sena, we received a request from police to delist pages containing the photos." Google's response: "We delisted the URLs from google.in under local obscenity laws."

Other nations are more concerned with monitoring messages that disagree with government leaders or policies. In Eritrea, for example, the government surveyed social networking sites for criticisms, then launched online attacks, including disinformation campaigns against those posting these concerns.[79] Reporters Without Borders' 2015 *Enemies of the Internet* report summed up the state of international government surveillance this way:

In practice, surveillance of communications networks continues to grow. It allows governments to identify Internet users and their contacts, to read their email and to know where they are. In authoritarian countries, this surveillance results in the arrest and mistreatment of human rights defenders, journalists, netizens and other civil society representatives. The fight for human rights has spread to the Internet, and more and more dissidents are ending up in prison after their online communications are intercepted.[80]

Employers

While employers have always known that applicants selectively construct resumes, with multiple data points of information displayed through social networking sites, those who make hiring decisions are now able to construct their own, more comprehensive, profiles of potential employees. A 2016 survey found that 60% of employers use social media to screen job candidates, an increase of 500% over the last decade. Most often, hiring managers want to "see if the candidate has a professional persona," and are "looking for information that supports their qualifications for the job."[81] Employer surveillance of applicants is commonly conducted by compiling publicly accessible information available to everyone through search engines such as Google. A separate survey found that 75% of all human resource professionals have been instructed to search the Internet for public information on applicants.[82]

Some firms, however, have moved into more legally dangerous territory, demanding that applicants turn over the passwords to their social media accounts. These requests have become so commonplace that in March 2012 Facebook made a formal announcement to employers telling them to stop demanding the passwords of users looking for a job with their organizations and reminding employers that practice goes against Facebook's privacy policy which forbids the exchange of account password information to a third party. In 2012, the state of Maryland became the first to prohibit employers from requesting user names and passwords for social media sites as a requirement for employment[83] and by 2016, 14 states had similar legislation pending.[84] The U.S. Congress has also taken note of this practice and has drafted a bill, the Social Networking Online Protection Act (SNOPA), to forbid it. SNOPA would extend protection of user names and passwords to employers, K-12 schools, and universities, outlawing the punishment of users based on refusal to comply.[85]

Surveillance on the job goes far beyond the hiring process. While employers have the right to sift through email messages stored on their own servers, for example, the National Labor Relations Board (NLRB) has come down on the side of the employees in a series of cases involving negative messages posted on blogs and personal social media accounts. In January 2012, the NLRB issued a memo outlining more than a dozen instances in which employers went too far in punishing employees for personal speech.[86] In one case, a woman used her cell phone at work to post sexist comments made by a supervisor and her disapproval of a co-worker's firing to her Facebook page. She continued to post Facebook messages that criticized management and ignored a supervisor's warning to "not get involved in other worker's problems" even after being asked to refrain from such activity. In this case, the NLRB found that by punishing the woman for discussing wage and working conditions with fellow employees via Facebook, the employer had unlawfully terminated her employment.[87] Similarly, in 2016, an administrative law judge in Havertown, Pennsylvania, ordered Chipotle to rehire an employee who had been fired for tweeting about the company's "cheap" labor policies. The judge found the firing violated the National Labor Relations Act.[88]

In many of these cases outlined in the report, as in the ones above, social media policies prohibited "discussions of wages or working conditions," a violation of Section 7 of the National Labor Relations Act. These NLRB regulations, which originally ensured face to face deliberations among employees and with labor union representatives regarding working conditions and salaries, are now being applied to online communications to multiple, diverse parties. What was once a whisper in the break room to a colleague is now a Twitter or LinkedIn post to hundreds or thousands of "friends" or "followers." The challenge for the NLRB and other regulatory agencies is how to best balance the protection of employee rights with the potential scope and power of social media messages.

As with many other legal questions, laws about employee termination for out-of-work speech varies from state to state. In Texas, for example, you can be fired for private conduct at home that is legal but does not align with the values of the employer. Much of this private conduct is on public display for employers to see through Facebook, Instagram, and Twitter.

In recent years, many broadcasting professionals have been fired for posting inappropriate comments – often racist, sexist, or homophobic – that have nothing to do with their jobs, wages, or working conditions. For example, CNN analyst Roland Martin was suspended from his job for a homophobic tweet during the 2012 Super Bowl that read, "If a dude at your Super Bowl party is hyped about David Beckham's H&M underwear ad, smack the ish out of him!"[89] In 2016, Curt Shilling, analyst for *Monday Night Baseball*, was fired from ESPN for a Facebook post reacting to North Carolina's transgender bathroom law.[90]

Arguments that their First Amendment rights had been violated were obviously incorrect as CNN and ESPN are private businesses, not government entities that trigger First Amendment protections for individuals.

Advertisers

Social media users may be unaware that advertisers and media companies are tracking their movements online, paying close attention to keywords, hashtags, and "likes." Gone are the days of simple cookies deposited on one's computer through an Internet browser. Today, advertisers track mouse movements, widget use,[91] online purchases, GIS location data, and even your latest prescription refill. They compile this information in real time and often sell it to the highest bidder.[92]

When users find out about these practices, they are often astonished, then appalled. For example, a *USA Today/Gallup* poll from December 2010 found that 67% of U.S. Internet users surveyed believed advertisers should not be able to target messages based on "your specific interests and web-sites you have visited."[93] A 2014 survey confirmed that social media users do not want their data aiding advertisers. It found that "only 35 percent of respondents agreed with the statement "I use free services online and on smartphones/tablets and don't mind if my data is potentially also used for advertising purposes.""[94]

Currently, there are no government regulations limiting to the kind or amount of information that can be collected by advertisers online. Recent media attention in the United States, however, has encouraged the Federal Trade Commission, in conjunction with the nation's largest advertising associations, to support federal Do Not Track legislation. Beginning in 2009, advertisers and media companies could voluntarily offer users the "do not track" option on their sites. In 2012, the White House announced the development of a "Consumer Bill of Rights" in concert with the Digital Advertising Alliance's (DAA) self-imposed "do not track" policies. The Consumer Privacy Bill of Rights would assure individuals had control over their personal information online including easy-to-use privacy settings. Through such a bill, consumers would be given access to all of the informa-tion collected by companies as well as notification of how that information would be collected, used, or disclosed.[95]

Site Surveillance

Those who own, and thus control, social media sites are also key surveillants of content. For example, Facebook employs a team of "User Operations Analysts" who act upon complaints regarding content and behavior vio-lations and determine whether users have violated the terms of service agreement. In many ways, these Facebook staff and those of other social media sites are asked to determine the outcome of free speech issues usually decided in the courtroom.

While everyone accepts the terms of social media user agreements with little consideration for the contractual obligations set forth, each of these agreements has restrictions on free speech. At their most basic (for an extensive examination of Terms of Service Agreements, see Chapter 3), user agreements for social media sites contain two kinds of restrictions: those courts have ruled are acceptable limits on free speech (copyright, defamation, etc . . .) and restrictions that would be ruled on as violations of free speech rights such as "hateful" or "objectionable" language. An example of this first category, LinkedIn does not allow material that "infringes upon patents, trademarks, trade secrets, copyright, or other proprietary rights." In the second category of extra-legal restrictions, Facebook will not allow "hateful, threatening, or pornographic" material or content that "contains nudity" or "graphic violence."[96] LinkedIn reminds users that their accounts can be shut down if they participate in "discriminatory" discussions.[97]

Moderators in online gaming communities monitor real-time in-game chat. Offending remarks made in these chat logs can get players removed indefinitely for speech that would otherwise be protected on the sidewalk outside their door. X-Box Live has a Code of Conduct that bans "topics or content of a sexual nature" and immediate suspension can be applied for "severe racial remarks."[98] The online social bulletin board, Pinterest, has an even more restrictive speech policy, banning speech with may be "racially or ethnically offensive," or "profane," or "otherwise objectionable."[99] Pinterest notes in its Terms of Service agreement that "we have the right, but not the obligation, to remove User Content from the Service for any reason."[100] YouTube, one of the most popular social media sites with more than a billion users,[101] has very specific limits on expression outlined in its Community Guidelines. YouTube will remove any videos that violate the Community Guidelines including those that feature "pornography," "child exploitation," "bad stuff like animal abuse, drug abuse, under-age drinking and smoking, or bomb making," "graphic or gratuitous violence," "predatory behavior, stalking threats, harassment, intimidation, invading privacy, revealing other people's personal information, and inciting others to commit violent acts."[102] YouTube also reminds users on the Community Guidelines website that videos are screened for unseemly content 24 hours a day.

In 2016, Twitter formed a "Trust & Safety Council" to "ensure people can continue to express themselves freely and safely on Twitter." The Council, a response to CEO Dick Costolo's memo the year before stating that "we suck at dealing with abuse and trolls on the platform," is one of several remedies being implement by the company.[103] Twitter's policy on "Abusive Behavior" states: "In order to ensure that people feel safe expressing diverse opinions and beliefs, we do not tolerate behavior that crosses the line into abuse, including behavior that harasses, intimidates, or uses fear to silence another user's voice."[104] These rules, revised and implemented by Twitter in 2015, led to the removal of Breitbart contributor and conservative rabble-rouser Milo Yiannopoulos' verified account status.[105]

Self-Surveillance

When Facebook was a shiny new social media platform, just out of the box, users friended with abandon. High school boyfriend? Friend. College roommate? Friend. Random woman you met at a conference? Friend. Don't really recognize the person but somehow they found you online? Friend.

In recent years, however, the "friendzy" has subsided. Over the past decade, we have read thousands of status updates, viewed hundreds of cats playing piano videos, and given a big "thumb's up" to more news articles than we can count. Just as users learned Second Life and MySpace no longer contributed positively to their online identities, users of contemporary social media platforms have become savvier through self-surveillance. Now, people are removing those they once considered "friends" from social networks. A 2012 survey on social media privacy found that 63% of those surveyed had removed someone as a friend from their social network.[106] In the process, these "unfrienders" have limited the kinds of number of voices they are willing to hear.

The power to pick and choose whom to hear was granted by the Supreme Court in the 1943 case *Martin v. City of Struthers*.[107] In this case, a city ordinance forbade the distribution of handbills door-to-door. The ordinance, challenged by the Jehovah's Witnesses who delivered literature door-to-door as part of their ministry, was found to be an unconstitutional restriction on free speech. Here, the Supreme Court ruled that individuals should have the right to listen to or turn away speech at their own door. It was unconstitutional, the court concluded, for the government to take on this role of speech gatekeeper. This decision was reaffirmed almost 60 years later in *Watchtower Bible and Tract Society v. Village of Stratton*,[108] when the Court again found door-to-door distribution of literature constitutional. Many people who found these rulings more nuisance than fundamental right as politicians, solicitors, and religious adherents rang their doorbells are now using this power to control their personal information online. Each time a person is "unfriended," it is as if a homeowner has said "no thank you. Please don't knock on my door again."

In recent years, legislatures and courts have extended the right not to listen to the Internet. For example, the CAN-SPAM Act of 2003 (Controlling the Assault of Non-Solicited Pornography and Marketing Act) banned false, misleading, or deceptive messages from being sent via email and gives email recipients an opt-out option for receiving commercial messages (spam) via email. [109] In 2011, a federal district court in California expanded the interpretation of the CAN-SPAM Act to include social media sites such as Facebook, concluding that deceptive commercial messages posted on Facebook walls, sent as messages to "friends," or included on newsfeeds were also "electronic mail messages" and illegal under the act.[110] By opting-out of advertising on social media sites, users now have additional control over their participation in social media.

In an effort to protect young people from cyberbullying (a laudable interest), Facebook created a Network of Support that encourages users to "block bullies," "report harassment," "stick up for others," "think twice before posting," and "get help if you feel overwhelmed." While this is an important initiative, some of the suggested actions clearly encourage self-censorship. For example, the Network of Support guidelines suggest, "it's also important to be aware of how your own behavior can harm others, even unintentionally. Before you post a comment or a photo that you think is funny, ask yourself [if] it could embarrass or hurt someone. If in doubt, don't post it."[111]

Users of social media are more aware than ever that their comments and photos follow them. To help reconstruct (or rescue) their digital identities, users are now self-censoring across social media. A 2012 Pew study on social media use found that 44% of respondents reported that they removed comments from their Facebook profile.[112] This social media spring cleaning may not be enough to scrub the past, however. Photos deleted from Facebook may linger on the Internet for months or years,[113] and snaps on Snapchat, once promised to "disappear," are no longer "ephemeral." In 2014, Snapchat settled a suit brought by the Federal Trade Commission for false, misleading, and deceptive advertising. The FTC found that users could save messages in many ways, including through third party applications. Following the settlement, Snapchat can no longer legally claim that photos sent via its social media app are "ephemeral," "disappear forever" and "aren't saved."[114]

Self-surveillance also involves online reputation control, otherwise known as getting rid of past mistakes. Whether it is photos from a drunken night in Las Vegas, a sweet love note to a past boyfriend, or a heated rant in a refrigerator repair forum, past imperfections can be erased. You can now hire "cleaners" to help you lose your online memory. Just like the mafia version of cleaners from your favorite detective novel, online reputation companies such as reputation.com, eliminate what's following you.

People are not the only ones trying to control their social media reputations. Businesses, non-profits, and even government agencies are doing all they can to control the front stage face of their organizations. For example, in 2012 the U.S. Department of Homeland Security contracted with General Dynamic for $11 million to monitor social media for any information that could reflect negatively on the department, the Federal Emergency Management Agency (FEMA) or the Central Intelligence Agency (CIA).[115] Analysts in the Department of Homeland Security were instructed in a department manual to monitor policy debates in social networks related to their agency. Although agency officials say the program was never initiated, the 2011 manual instructed employees to monitor discussions in social media such as Facebook and Twitter related to "policy directives, debates and implementations related to DHS."[116] The 2013 DHS Analysts Desktop Binder still considers "policy directives, debates and implementations related to DHS," "Items of Interest" (IOI) but clarifies the extent and kind of monitoring that are acceptable, noting that "Analysts are to refrain from generating IOI reports "including public reaction to DHS programs, policies, or procedures" or "focus on individuals' First Amendment protected activities" unless "they are operationally relevant."[117]

An even more egregious attempt at controlling social media content was made public in 2012, when the Department of Defense was accused of creating fake Twitter and Facebook accounts and altering the Wikipedia pages of a *USA Today* journalist and editor who were investigating the department's payment of hundreds of millions of dollars to outside contractors to improve the image of the military in Iraq and Afghanistan.[118] This "attempt at intimidation,"[119] may be the first of many brought to light as government agencies, businesses, and individuals scramble to control information flow and protect their reputations in social media.

The rise of social media surveillance adds another dimension of concern to the narrowing boundaries of free speech in social media. While these spaces are often praised as opening up debate, they may in fact be on the front lines of future censorship efforts by governments, employers, and the sites themselves. To ensure a breadth of discourse in social media, all users must be aware of the limits placed on them and speak up with the walls of free speech close in.

FREQUENTLY ASKED QUESTIONS

1. Can I be fired for making a Facebook post?

It depends. The National Labor Relations Board finds employee termination to be unlawful if the social media message discusses "working conditions or wages" and the firing is a punishment for discussion of these issues with co-workers. So, if you are criticizing your employer for the work environment, job expectations, or salary, you should keep your job. If you comment on the boss' pattern of dating very young women or repeatedly post material during working hours, probably not.

Your employer can set guidelines for your use of social media related to work—whether it is time spent on sites or what information you are allowed to post. This is especially true if your employer is one in which federal regulations apply to the distribution of information (such as in the financial services industry). Businesses that create new products or services are also likely to have a restrictive social media policy as leaking information regarding the newest product before the launch date can have disastrous consequences for the company's profits and image.

2. What kinds of statements on social media could get me arrested or charged with a crime?

Both website managers and law enforcement officials are concerned with what you post on social media sites. Guidelines for acceptable content are outlined on each site's Community Standards or Terms of Use pages. In general, you can have your membership in social networking sites revoked for a number of content categories that are protected under the First Amendment but not acceptable in these privately owned spaces such as hate speech, pornography, the use of humiliating or bullying language or images, and derogatory statements dealing with race, ethnicity, sexual orientation, and disabilities. Law enforcement officials are much more concerned with illegal content: terror and other national security threats, images of drug production or use, obscenity, child pornography, stalking, or physical abuse. Several courts have accepted evidence from social media sites to support other claims. For example, a woman on probation for drinking and driving had her probation revoked after evidence was submitted showing her intoxicated in a Facebook post.[120] Social media messages and images are also being used regularly in divorce and child custody cases to show infidelity or parenting ability.[121] Civil suits involving injuries are now commonly challenged by evidence of activities shown on social media sites.

The most common legal concern on social media sites, though, is copyright infringement. You could be notified by either the site manager or the lawyer for a copyright holder to take down copyrighted material from social media sites.

3. Can my anonymous posts on social media be tied to me in real life?

Yes. Depending on the content of the post, courts or law enforcement officials may request your account information including user name, address, and contact information from the social media company. If a court order is issued, more specific information regarding your account, including how often and what kind of additional posts were made, may be obtained.

4. How are American laws and policies about social media different than the rules in other countries?

Many countries have laws that allow for surveillance, censorship, and restriction of content on social network sites. When using social media sites in other countries it is very important to know the boundaries of speech in those nations. If you are traveling or studying abroad you should assume that you do not have the same breadth of freedom allowed here—even on the most restrictive sites. In many countries, journalists, activists, and citizens have been arrested and jailed for comments made in social media.

It is also important to remember that social media companies are private corporations and set their own terms of service for users. While these vary, they all contain detailed policies regarding what is acceptable and unacceptable content on the site for each country of service.

5. Are social media sites private or public spaces?

To date, social network sites have been treated as private spaces rather than public ones. For example, in *Noah v. AOL Time Warner, Inc.,*[122] the court ruled that Google's search engine was not a place of public accommodation under Title II of the Civil Rights Act because it was located in a virtual rather than a physical space. Places of public accommodation cannot discriminate on basis of race, gender, ethnicity would be applied. This means that social media websites are allowed to make their own rules, even if those rules are more restrictive or more offensive than allowed under the constitution or U.S. law.

NOTES

1 Katie Rogers, Snapchat at 107 M.P.H.? Lawsuit Blames Teenager (and Snapchat). N.Y. Times, May 3, 2016, http://www.nytimes.com/2016/05/04/us/snapchat-speeding-teenager-crash-lawsuit.html?_r=0

2 Jusin Jouvenal, A 12-year-old girl is facing criminal charges for using certain emoji. She's not alone. Wash. Post, February 27, 2016, https://www.washingtonpost.com/news/local/wp/2016/02/27/a-12-year-old-girl-is-facing-criminal-charges-for-using-emoji-shes-not-alone/

3 Chanel May Have Just Won a Battle for the Chanel Instagram Account, The Fashion Law, January 8, 2016, http://www.thefashionlaw.com/home/chanel-may-have-just-won-a-battle-for-the-chanel-instagram-account

4 Doe v. Jindal, 852 F. Supp. 2d 596, 606 (M.D. La. 2012).

5 A.G. Schneiderman's "Operation: Game Over" Purges Thousands of Sex Offenders from Online Video Game Networks, Office of the New York Attorney General, April 5, 2012, http://www.ag.ny.gov/press-release/ag-schneidermans-operation-game-over-purges-thousands-sex-offenders-online-video-game

6 Austin Berg, Illinois Bill Allows Courts to Ban Social Media and Demand Access to Accounts for Juveniles Charged with Crimes, Illinois Policy, April 7, 2016, https://

www.illinoispolicy.org/illinois-bill-allows-courts-to-ban-social-media-and-demand-access-to-accounts-for-juveniles-charged-with-crimes/

7 Freedom House, Freedom on the Net 2015: Privatizing Censorship, Eroding Privacy 3 (2015), https://freedomhouse.org/sites/default/files/FOTN%202015%20Full%20Report.pdf

8 Id. at 8, 15.

9 Schenck v. U.S., 249 U.S. 47 (1919); U.S. v. U.S. v. Debs, 249 U.S. 211 (1919).

10 Freedom House, supra note 7, at 3.

11 United Nations General Assembly Human Rights Council, Report of the Special Rapporteur on the promotion and protection of the right to freedom of opinion and expression, Mr. Frank LaRue (May 16, 2011), http://www2.ohchr.org/english/bodies/hrcouncil/docs/17session/A.HRC.17.27_en.pdf

12 Ian Burrell, Libel Cases Prompted by Social Media Posts Rise 300% in a Year, The Independent, October 19, 2014, http://www.independent.co.uk/news/uk/home-news/libel-cases-prompted-by-social-media-posts-rise-300-in-a-year-9805004.html

13 Danny Sullivan, Google's Results Get More Personal with "Search Plus Your World," Search Engine Land, January 10, 2012, http://searchengineland.com/googles-results-get-more-personal-with-search-plus-your-world-107285

14 Optional Facebook app upgrade captures audio through smartphone microphone, CityNews, May 26, 2014, http://www.citynews.ca/2014/05/26/optional-facebook-app-upgrade-captures-audio-from-smartphone-microphone/

15 Perkins v. LinkedIn Corp., 2016 U.S. Dist. LEXIS 18649 (N.D. Cal. 2016).

16 Robinson Meyer, Everything We Know about Facebooks Mood Manipulation Experiment, The Atlantic, June 28, 2014, http://www.theatlantic.com/technology/archive/2014/06/everything-we-know-about-facebooks-secret-mood-manipulation-experiment/373648/

17 Mary Madden, Privacy Management on Social Media Sites, Pew Research Center, February 24, 2012, at 2, http://www.pewinternet.org/2012/02/24/privacy-management-on-social-media-sites/

18 Lee Rainie & Maeve Duggan, Privacy and Information Sharing, Pew Research Center, January 14, 2016, http://www.pewinternet.org/2016/01/14/privacy-and-information-sharing/

19 John Milton, The Areopagitica (1644)

20 John Stuart Mill, On Liberty (1859).

21 Abrams v. U.S., 250 U.S. 616, 630 (1919).

22 See, e.g., Robert W. McChesney, Rich Media, Poor Democracy: Communication Politics in Dubious Times (1999); Ben Bagdikian, The Media Monopoly (1997); Edward S. Herman & Noam Chomsky, Manufacturing Consent (2002).

23 Rodney A. Smolla, Free Speech in an Open Society 9 (1992).

24 United Nations General Assembly Human Rights Council, supra note 11, at 5.

25 Adam Liptak, Was That Twitter Blast False, or Just Honest Hyperbole? N.Y. Times, March 5, 2012, at A12.

26 Id.

27 Susan B. Anthony List v. Driehaus, 134 S. Ct. 2334 (2014).

28 Susan B. Anthony List v. Driehaus, 814 F.3d 466 (6th Cir. 2016).

29 Bland v. Roberts, 2013 U.S. App. LEXIS 19268, 46 (4th Cir. 2013).

30 Heather Kelly, Snapchat Fights Ban on 'Ballot Selfies,' CNN Money, April 22, 2016, http://money.cnn.com/2016/04/22/technology/snapchat-ballot-selfie/

31 Rideout v. Gardner, 123 F. Supp. 3d (D.N.H. 2015).

32 Kelly, supra note 30.

33 United States v. Carolene Products 304 U.S. 144, note 4 (1938).

34 141 Cong. Rec. S1953 (daily ed. Feb. 1, 1995).

35 521 U.S. 884 (1997).

36 Id. at 871–872.

37 Sable Communications of California, Inc. v. FCC, 492 U.S. 115 (1989).

38 Terry L. Jones, Free Speech Limits Tested When Louisiana Public Agencies Restrict Employees' Social Media, The Advocate, April 22, 2016, http://theadvocate.com/news/15387448-123/attempts-to-restrict-social-media-posts-of-employees-are-tricky-for-public-agencies-in-louisiana

39 Sarah Brown, Student Free Speech Case Concerning Social Media Arises in Minnesota, The Daily Tar Heel, February 13, 2012, http://www.dailytarheel.com/index.php/article/2012/02/student_free_speech_case_concerning_social_media_arises_in_minnesota

40 42 U.S.C. § 1983 (2016).

41 Yoder v. University of Louisville, 2012 U.S.Dist LEXIS 45264 (6th Cir. 2012).

42 S.J.W. v. Lee's Summit R-7 School District, 696 F.3d 771 (8th Cir. 2012)

43 Deanna Boyd, TCU, Student at Odds over Comments on Social Media, Fort Worth Star-Telegram, July 30, 2015, http://www.star-telegram.com/news/local/community/fort-worth/article29592781.html

44 Jack Broom, Bail set at $10,000 for WWU Student Accused of Racist Threats, Seattle Times, December 1, 2015, http://www.seattletimes.com/seattle-news/crime/bail-set-at-10000-for-wwu-student-accused-of-racist-threats/

45 Edwin Rios, Everything You Need to Know about Yik Yak, the Social App at the Center of Missouri's Racist Threats, Mother Jones, November 11, 2016, http://www.motherjones.com/media/2015/11/yik-yak-anonymous-app-missouri-explainer

46 Robert A. Cronkleton, Jason Hancock & Ian Cummings, Student Charged with Allegedly Making Online Threat Targeting African-American Students on MU Campus, Kansas City Star, November 10, 2015, http://www.kansascity.com/news/local/crime/article44216625.html

47 Ian Cummings, Third Missouri Man Charged with Posting Yik Yak Threats against College Campus, Kansas City Star, November 12, 2015, http://www.kansascity.com/news/local/crime/article44216625.html

48 Edwin Rios, Everything You Need to Know About Yik Yak, the Social App at the Center of Missouri's Racist Threats, 11 November 2015, Mother Jones, http://www.motherjones.com/media/2015/11/yik-yak-anonymous-app-missouri-explainer

49 Yik Yak, Yik Yak Guidelines for Law Enforcement (2016), https://www.yikyak.com/guidelines

50 Dan Solomon, A Texas A&M Student Was Arrested for Posting an Anonymous Shooting Threat on Yik Yak, Texas Monthly, October 22, 2015, http://www.texasmonthly.com/the-daily-post/a-texas-am-student-was-arrested-for-posting-an-anonymous-shooting-threat-on-yik-yak/#sthash.dxm5gHaN.dpuf

51 Jason Fagone, The Serial Swatter, N.Y. Times Magazine, November 24, 2015, http://www.nytimes.com/2015/11/29/magazine/the-serial-swatter.html?_r=0

52 Alan Gathright, 'Swatting' Hoax Cost $25,000 for Law Enforcement Response to Bogus Hostage Taking Incident in Greeley, Denver ABC 7, 15 June 2015, http://www.thedenverchannel.com/news/front-range/greeley/swatting-hoax-cost-25000-for-law-enforcement-response-to-bogus-hostage-incident-in-greeley

53 Federal Bureau of Investigation, The Crime of 'Swatting,' September 3, 2013, https://www.fbi.gov/news/stories/2013/september/the-crime-of-swatting-fake-9-1-1-calls-have-real-consequences

54 Meg Penrose, Outspoken: Social Media and the Modern College Athlete, 12 J. Marshall Rev. Intell. Prop. L. 509, 514 (2013).

55 Mina Kimes, Social Media Bans May Violate College Athletes' First Amendment Rights, ESPN The Magazine, September 14, 2015.

56 Brandon Marcello, Rick Stansbury Bans Mississippi State from Twitter after Criticism, USA Today, February 3, 2011, http://usatoday30.usatoday.com/sports/college/mensbasketball/sec/2011-02-03-mississippi-state-twitter-ban_N.htm

57 Ken Paulson: Free Speech Sacks Ban on College-Athlete Tweets, USA Today, April 15, 2012, http://usatoday30.usatoday.com/news/opinion/forum/story/2012-04-15/twitter-social-media-college-sports-coaches-ban/54301178/1

58 Id.

59 Josh Moyer, BC's Stephanie McCaffrey Punished, ESPN, November 16, 2012, http://espn.go.com/college-sports/story/_/id/8637607/stephanie-mccaffrey-boston-college-eagles-soccer-player-suspended-tweets-penn-state-nittany-lions-jerry-sandusky

60 Penrose, supra note 54, at 526.

61 Elonis v. United States, 135 S.Ct. 2001, 2006–07 (2015).

62 Id. at 2004.

63 Deborah Netburn, Court Orders Man to Apologize to Estranged Wife on Facebook, L.A. Times, February 23, 2012, http://articles.latimes.com/2012/feb/23/business/la-fi-tn-court-ordered-facebook-apology-20120223

64 Cyber Civil Rights Initiative, 34 States + DC have revenge porn laws (2016), http://www.cybercivilrights.org/revenge-porn-laws/

65 Ariz. Rev. Stat. § 13–1425 (2016).

66 Bookstores, Publishers, News Media, Librarians, and Photographers Charge Law Violates Freedom of Speech, American Civil Liberties Union, September 23, 2014, https://www.aclu.org/news/first-amendment-lawsuit-challenges-arizona-criminal-law-banning-nude-images

67 Paige Miles Feldmann, Doxing: A Legal Violation of Privacy, Campbell Law Observer, December 31, 2014, http://campbelllawobserver.com/doxing-a-legal-violation-of-privacy/

68 Apple, Answers to Your Questions about Apple and Security (2016), http://www.apple.com/customer-letter/answers/

69 Snapchat, Transparency Report (March 29, 2016), https://www.snapchat.com/transparency

70 Twittter, Transparency Reports: Information Requests: July 1–December 31, 2015 (2016), https://transparency.twitter.com/information-requests/2015/jul-dec

71 Facebook, Government Requests Report: July 2015–December 2015 (2016), https://govtrequests.facebook.com/

72 Ian Hoppe, Does law enforcement have access to your Snapchat photos? A simple guide, Al.com, November 14, 2014, http://www.al.com/business/index.ssf/2014/11/snapchat_subpeona.html

73 Dina Temple-Raston, Terrorists Struggle to Gain Recruits on the Web, National Public Radio, December 29, 2011, http://www.npr.org/2011/12/29/144342062/terrorists-struggle-to-gain-recruits-on-the-web

74 Jaikumar Vijayan, Privacy Tussle Brews over Social Media Monitoring, Computerworld, February 16, 2012, http://www.computerworld.com/article/2501725/data-privacy/privacy-tussle-brews-over-social-media-monitoring.html

75 Lee Raine & Mary Madden, Americans' Privacy Strategies Post-Snowden, Pew Research Center, March 16, 2015, http://www.pewinternet.org/2015/03/16/americans-privacy-strategies-post-snowden/

76 Richard A. Serrano, Tashfeen Malik Messaged Facebook Friends about Her Support for Jihad, L.A. Times, December 14, 2015, http://www.latimes.com/local/lanow/la-me-ln-malik-facebook-messages-jihad-20151214-story.html

77 Molly Bernhart Walker, DHS Begins Hunt for Social Media Monitoring Technology, Fierce Government IT, January 27, 2016, http://www.fiercegovernmentit.com/story/dhs-begins-hunt-social-media-monitoring-technology/2016-01-27

78 Google, Government Requests to Remove Content (2015), https://www.google.com/transparencyreport/removals/government/?hl=en

79 Reporters Without Borders, Enemies of the Internet (2012), http://12mars.rsf.org/2016-en/

80 Reporters Without Borders, Enemies of the Internet 10 (2014), https://12mars.rsf.org/wp-content/uploads/EN_RAPPORT_INTERNET_BD.pdf

81 Amy McDonnell, 60% Employers Use Social Media to Screen Job Candidates, The Hiring Site Blog, April 28, 2016, http://thehiringsite.careerbuilder.com/2016/04/28/37823/

82 Bidhan Parmar, Should You Check Facebook Before Hiring? Wash. Post, January 22, 2011, http://www.washingtonpost.com/wp-dyn/content/article/2011/01/22/AR2011012203193.html

83 Catherine Ho, Maryland Becomes First State to Prohibit Employers for Asking for Facebook Logins, Wash. Post., May 3, 2012, https://www.washingtonpost.com/blogs/capital-business/post/maryland-becomes-first-state-to-prohibit-employers-from-asking-for-facebook-logins/2012/05/03/gIQAsE1GzT_blog.html

84 National Council of State Legislatures, Access to Social Media Usernames and Passwords, April 6, 2016, http://www.ncsl.org/research/telecommunications-and-information-technology/employer-access-to-social-media-passwords-2013.aspx

85 H.R. 5107, 114th Congress (2016).

86 Office of the General Counsel, Division of Operations-Management, National Labor Relations Board, Report of the General Counsel Concerning Social Media (January 24, 2012).

87 Id. at 18-20.

88 An Administrative Judge Has Ordered Chipotle to Rehire a Philadelphia-Area Employee Who Was Fired after Criticizing the Company on Twitter Last Year, US News & World Report, March 16, 2016, http://www.usnews.com/news/technology/articles/2016-03-16/judge-orders-chipotle-to-rehire-worker-fired-after-tweets

89 Nedra Rhone, Social Media; With Iffy Tweets, Job Can Delete, Atlanta Journal-Constitution, February 11, 2012, at 1D.

90 Richard Sandomir, Curt Shilling, ESPN Analyst, Is Fired over Offensive Facebook Post, N.Y. Times, April 20, 2016, http://www.nytimes.com/2016/04/21/sports/baseball/curt-schilling-is-fired-by-espn.html?_r=0

91 Amir Efrati, "Like" Button Follows Web Users, Wall Street J., May 18, 2011, http://online.wsj.com/article/SB10001424052748704281504576329441432995616.html

92 Getting to Know You, The Economist, September 13, 2014, http://www.economist.com/news/special-report/21615871-everything-people-do-online-avidly-followed-advertisers-and-third-party

93 Lymari Morales, U.S. Internet Users Ready to Limit Online Advertisers Tracking for Ads, Gallup.com, December 21, 2010, http://www.gallup.com/poll/145337/Internet-Users-Ready-Limit-Online-Tracking-Ads.aspx

94 Jack Marshall, Do Consumers Really Want Targeted Ads? Wall Street J., April 17, 2014, http://blogs.wsj.com/cmo/2014/04/17/do-consumers-really-want-targeted-ads/

95 Brian Wassom, White House and Advertisers Announce New Consumer Privacy Standards, Augmented Legality, February 29, 2012, www.wassom.com/white-house-and-advertisers-announce-new-consumer-privacy-standards.html

96 Facebook, Statement of Rights and Responsibilities (Updated January 30, 2015), http://www.facebook.com/legal/terms

97 LinkedIn, User Agreement (2016), http://www.linkedin.com/static?key=user_agreement

98 Microsoft's Code of Conduct Explained for Xbox Live Customers (Updated August 2015), http://www.xbox.com/en-US/Legal/CodeOfConduct

99 Pinterest, Acceptable Use Policy (2016), http://pinterest.com/about/use/

100 Pinterest, Terms of Service (2016), http://pinterest.com/about/terms/

101 YouTube, Statistics (2016), https://www.youtube.com/yt/press/statistics.html

102 YouTube, YouTube Community Guidelines (2016), http://www.youtube.com/t/community_guidelines

103 Natasha Lomas, Twitter Forms A "Trust & Safety Council" To Balance Abuse vs Fee Speech, Tech Crunch, February 9, 2016, http://techcrunch.com/2016/02/09/twitter-forms-a-trust-safety-council-to-balance-abuse-vs-free-speech/

104 Twitter, The Twitter Rules (2016), https://support.twitter.com/articles/18311

105 Emily Bell, Twitter Tackles the Free Speech Conundrum, The Guardian, January 10, 2016, http://www.theguardian.com/media/2016/jan/10/twitter-free-speech-rules-hostile-behaviour

106 Madden, supra note 17.

107 319 U.S. 141 (1943).

108 Watchtower Bible and Tract Society of New York v. Village of Stratton, 536 U.S. 150 (2006).

109 15 U.S.C. 103 (2016).

110 Facebook, Inc. v. MaxBounty, Inc., 2011 U.S. Dist. LEXIS 32343 (N.D. Cal. 2011).

111 Facebook Safety, Facebook's' Network of Support (October 19, 2010), http://www.facebook.com/note.php?note_id=161164070571050

112 Madden, supra note 17.

113 Joann Pan, Deleted Facebook Photos May Still Lurk on the Internet, Mashable, February 6, 2012, http://mashable.com/2012/02/06/deleted-facebook-pictures-still-exist/

114 Jill Scharr, Snapchat Admits Its Photos Don't "Disappear Forever," Yahoo News, May 9, 2014, https://www.yahoo.com/news/snapchat-admits-photos-dont-disappear-124756882.html?ref=gs

115 Vijayan, supra note 74.

116 Charlie Savage, Hearing Held on Program Monitoring Social Media, N.Y. Times, February 22, 2012, at A17.

117 Department of Homeland Security, Analysts Desktop Binder 12–13, (August 2013).

118 Gregory Korte, Misinformation Campaign Targets USA Today Journalist, Editor, USA Today, April 19, 2012, http://www.usatoday.com/news/washington/story/2012-04-19/vanden-brook-locker-propaganda/54419654/1

119 Id.

120 State of Connecticut v. Altajir, 33 A.3d 193 (Conn. 2012).

121 Leanne Italie, Divorce Lawyers: Facebook Tops in Online Evidence in Court, USA Today, June 29, 2010, http://www.usatoday.com/tech/news/2010-06-29-facebook-divorce_N.htm

122 261 F. Supp. 2d 532 (E.D. Va. 2003).

CHAPTER 2

Defamation

Derigan Silver

University of Denver

ABSTRACT

Defamation is a false statement of fact that is harmful to another's reputation. Because defamation is a tort that allows individuals to sue for monetary damages, it creates a risk for journalists, other professional communicators, and average people. However, in the United States, defamation law also attempts to balance an individual's interest in maintaining his reputation with our society's commitment to freedom of expression. This chapter explains how the law applies to traditional media and online media and explores the many ways the law has adapted to—or struggled to adapt to—the new world of social media.

Since according libel protection under the First Amendment in 1964, the U.S. Supreme Court has attempted to find the "proper accommodation" between society's interest in the free dissemination of information and the state's interest in protecting an individual's reputation. However, with its roots in feudal times, the law of defamation often has trouble keeping up with both society and technology. Global networks such as the Internet have made reputation "more enduring and yet more ephemeral."[1] Reputation has become more enduring because in many ways the Internet is "forever." Information tends to lurk in the dark corners of the Internet for years and years. It is more ephemeral because maintaining one's reputation in a networked society, replete with anonymous postings that can be instantly updated from nearly anywhere in the world, is becoming no easy task. Although, as one author noted, the invention of the Internet and the spread of online speech have not required the formulation of a new area of "cyberspace tort law,"[2] Internet defamation and the advent of social media have forced courts to apply old laws to new situations.

Already called one of the most complicated areas of communication law, with many tenets that run counter to common sense, the law of defamation is even more complicated when online communication is at issue. For example, because of ambiguity in several Supreme Court decisions, lower courts are divided over whether there is or should be a different standard of review for media and non-media defendants, an issue much more likely to be raised in situations involving social media because of the ability of average citizens to widely spread information via sites such as Twitter and Facebook. In addition, since 1996, qualified "Internet service providers" have been immune from defamation suits under Section 230 of the Communication Decency Act[3] for the postings of third-party content providers.

This chapter explains both how the law for traditional media and online media are the same and explores the many ways the law has adapted to—or struggled to adapt to—the new world of social media. First, the traditional elements needed to successfully prove a libel claim and the various options available to defendants with an emphasis on the Internet and digital media are explored. Each section also explains some of the particular challenges presented by social media. The chapter concludes by discussing some emerging issues that courts are beginning to deal with and will continue to deal with as social media sites become even more prevalent.

THE LAW OF DEFAMATION

Traditional defamation law recognizes that our society considers reputation to be one of a person's most valuable possessions and an individual has an interest in preserving his good name. Defamation is a tort, or a civil wrong, that attempts to redress damages to reputation.[4] Written or printed defamation is libel, while spoken defamation is slander. Although the law used to treat libel and slander distinctly, the introduction of broadcasting blurred the distinction between the two over time. Some jurisdictions, however, still make the distinction with most considering defamation on the Internet to be libel.

Because they allow individuals to sue for reputational damages, libel and slander create financial risks for journalists, other professional communicators, and average people posting on sites such as Facebook and Twitter. However, defamation law also tries to balance an individual's interest in maintaining his reputation with our society's deep commitment to freedom of expression. In some situations, then, defamation law subordinates a person's reputational interest to freedom of expression.

Any living individual, business, non-profit corporation, or unincorporated association can sue for defamation. While government organizations cannot sue, government officials may file a suit. Dead people cannot sue for reputational damage in the United States.[5] In some states there are laws designed to protect particular products from harm by false allegations, typically known as "veggie libel laws." For example, Oprah Winfrey was sued in Texas for statements she made during a show about mad cow disease. Following a drastic drop in cattle prices after the show aired, Texas cattle ranchers sued Winfrey for violating the state's False Disparagement of Perishable Food Product Act, although the jury eventually ruled in Winfrey's favor.[6]

A person who files a defamation complaint becomes the plaintiff. The person being sued becomes the defendant. The burden of proof in defamation is typically on the plaintiff. That is, to win a defamation suit, the plaintiff must establish certain claims or satisfy individual "elements." They include:

1. publication
2. identification
3. defamation
4. fault
5. falsity
6. injury or harm.

Most plaintiffs have to satisfy all six elements of a defamation suit in order to win. Even if a plaintiff can prove all six elements, the defendant may present a defense based on the First Amendment or common law. Defamation is state common law and often varies by jurisdiction. All jurisdictions are similar in some regards, however, and it is these similarities this chapter will focus on.

Publication

Publication, in legal terms, requires at least three people—one to communicate the defamatory statement, the person being defamed, and at least one other person to hear, see, or read the defamatory statement. A false statement made directly to an individual, but no one else, cannot be the subject of a defamation claim because there has been no reputational damage. No third party thinks less of the individual because no third party received the message. Any article that appears in a printed medium or online or any story that is distributed via broadcast, cable, satellite, or the Internet is considered published. Libel can also be published in press releases, advertisements, letters, and other personal communications. Information is also considered published when it appears in a blog, a personal website, a social media website—such as Facebook or Twitter—or in an email. While very few libel cases involving Twitter have made it to trial, several cases have been settled out of court. In 2010, Courtney Love, the musician and actress, used Twitter to accuse her former attorney Rhonda Holmes of bribery. Love posted the tweet after Holmes declined to help Love bring a fraud case against individuals managing the estate of Love's late husband, Kurt Cobain, the lead singer of the band Nirvana. Love tweeted, "I was f——devestated [sic] when Rhonda J. Holmes esq. of san diego was bought off @FairNewsSpears perhaps you can get a quote."[7] Holmes and her law firm sued Love for defamation. When the case went to trial in 2014, Love prevailed when the jury ruled that while the statement was false and defamatory, Holmes could not prove the required level of fault to prevail in the case. The jury's decision was upheld on appeal in 2016.[8] This was not the first time Love got herself into legal trouble over a tweet. In 2011, Love paid $430,000 to settle a libel action by a fashion designer she referred to as a "nasty lying hosebag thief."[9] As long as the communication is consumed by a third person, the information is considered published.

You are also liable for repeating—or "republishing"—defamation if the defamatory statement does not come from a "privileged" source, which is explained below. Under the common law of libel a person who repeats a libel is just as responsible for the damaged caused as the original publisher. This includes a journalist who accurately quotes a source or media organizations that publish or broadcast defamatory advertisements. However, this doctrine is limited by several factors.

First, the republication rule is typically limited to situations where the publisher controls the content. Media companies are responsible for the republication of libelous statements because their employees write, edit, select, or are otherwise responsible for the content of the communication, even if the content did not originate with the media company. Common carriers—such as telephone companies, libraries, book stores, newsstands, and others who provide content but do not edit it—are not typically liable for the defamatory content they distribute. Asking a bookstore to review the content of every book offered for sale for defamatory material would hinder the flow of information.

Second, in the United States every distribution of a libelous statement does not constitute a separate publication. Under the "single publication rule," a libel plaintiff may only sue once, eliminating the possibility of multiple suits across multiple jurisdictions for the same defamatory statement. The single publication rule also applies to text and videos on the Internet. Thus, a plaintiff may sue in only one jurisdiction even if a defamatory statement published on Facebook was accessible in every state where the defendant had a friend.

Third, under federal statutory law, operators of websites, blogs, online bulletin boards, and discussion groups are not considered publishers and are thus not liable for statements posted on their sites by third parties. This is true even if the website's operator attempts to edit or screen material for defamatory content. Section 230 of the Communication Decency Act, enacted as part of the Telecommunications Act of 1996, provides a safe harbor that protects online service providers from liability for their users' posts. Intended to encourage "interactive computer services" to restrict the flow of objectionable content Section 230 states, "No provider or user of an interactive computer service shall be treated as the publisher or speaker of any information provided by another information content provider."[10]

The law was passed in reaction to the idea that by editing material on the Internet, an ISP could be held liable under the republication rule. In *Stratton Oakmont, Inc. v. Prodigy Services Co.*,[11] a New York court held that Prodigy, an online service provider that appeared to be exercising editor control over its service by using software to screen out offensive language and a moderator to enforce content provisions, was liable for its users' posts. Thus, in an effort to encourage interactive service to make good-faith attempts to control indecency on the Internet, Congress provided Internet Service Providers (ISPs) with immunity from libel suits. After all, if policing content had made Prodigy libel for defamatory content posted by a third party, few providers would want to exercise editorial control over content. Thus, ISPs were granted immunity in order to encourage them to edit indecent material.

Section 230 attempts to distinguish between ISPs and Internet information content providers. Section 230 defines "an interactive computer service" as "an information service, system, or access software provider that provides or enables computer access by multiple users to a computer server, including specifically a service or system that provides access to the Internet and such systems operated or services offered by libraries or educational institutions."[12] The interactive computer service is protected from defamatory statements made by other information content providers, or "any person or entity that is responsible, in whole or in part, for the creation or development of information provided through the Internet or any other interactive computer service."[13] Since Section 230 was passed, courts have interpreted "interactive service providers" quite broadly. Section 230 has been applied to interactive websites, forums, listservs, and blogs. Courts have also ruled that Section 230 applies to social media sites. For example, in February 2009, a New York teenager sued four former high school classmates, their parents, and Facebook for a private Facebook group called "90 Cents Short of a Dollar." The teenager alleged the site contained defamatory statements that she "was a woman of dubious morals, dubious sexual character, having engaged in bestiality, an 'IV drug user' as well as having contracted the H.I.V. virus and AIDS."[14] In September 2009, the court dismissed the case against Facebook, ruling the site was protected under Section 230 as an "interactive computer service."[15] Section 230 has also been used to protect sites such as the now defunct JuicyCampus, even though these sites encourage anonymous gossips that are often full of vitriol.[16] In 2013, numerous commentators questioned the future of section 230 when a federal jury awarded $338,000 to a former Cincinnati Bengals cheerleader for postings made by a third party to thedirty.com. In that case, the trial judged ruled in 2012 that thedirty.com was not protected by section 230, a decision that was initially upheld on appeal.[17] However, in 2014, the Sixth Circuit Court of Appeals ruled thedirty.com was protected under section 230 because the website did not materially contribute to the statements posted on the site about the former cheerleader.[18] In addition, Section 230 has been invoked to bar claims of invasion of privacy and other areas of law.[19]

An additional area of concern that may arise regarding publication and Internet defamation relates to statutes of limitations. All states have a statute of limitations on defamation claims, typically ranging from one to three years from the date of publication. Courts have nearly uniformly ruled that the continuous nature of online publications does not indefinitely extend the statute of limitations for Internet libel. In 2002, for example, a New York court ruled that a defamatory statement that was posted to a website in 1996 was no longer actionable in 1998, one year after the state's statute of limitations had passed.[20] Instead, the statute of limitations for Internet material begins when the information is first published. In addition, courts have ruled that updating a website does not constitute a new publication unless the defamatory statement itself is altered or updated.[21]

Identification

Plaintiffs must establish that a published communication is about them. This requires a plaintiff to prove a defamatory statement was "of and concerning" them. That is, they must show that someone else could identify them as the subject of the defamatory statements. A plaintiff can be identified by name, picture, description, nickname, caricature, cartoon, and even a set of circumstances. Any information about the individual may identify them. Some defamation suits arise because of the naming of the wrong person. For example, reporting that Adam Smith of 123 Main St. was arresting for murder could lead to a defamation suit if the Adam Smith arrested lived at 456 First Ave. For this reason, some media lawyers recommend identifying subjects in several ways—for example by full name, including a middle name or initial if available, address, and occupation. Some commentators have argued, however, that the ability of Internet publications to reach a very large audience reduces the likelihood that a plaintiff can be identified by "mere commonality of a name or other shared attribute."[22] After all, if there are millions of Adam Smiths within the reach of the Internet, it is difficult to say your friends assumed you were *the* Adam Smith who was identified in an Internet post.

Although persons who are part of a large group are usually not able to prove identification, in some situations members of a small group may be able to prove they have been identified by reference to the group as a whole. Under the group libel rule, large groups, such as all college professors, could not sue for libel based on statements such as "All college professors are lazy and most are unqualified to teach." However, members of smaller groups might be able to sue depending on the size of the group and the language used. The smaller the group, the more likely it is that a statement identifies members of the group. While there is no definitive size or "magic number," in an oft-cited example, the Oklahoma Supreme Court ruled an article published in *True* magazine that said team "members" of a university football team used an amphetamine nasal spray to increase aggressiveness libeled all 60 members of the team. Although the article did not name any team member by name or position, a jury awarded fullback Dennit Morris $75,000, an award held up on appeal by the Oklahoma Supreme Court.[23]

Defamatory Content

Defamation is a communication that exposes a person to hatred, ridicule, or contempt, lowers him in the esteem of others, causes the person to be shunned, or injures him in his business or profession. The New York Court of Appeals defined a defamatory statement as one which "tends to expose a person to hatred, contempt or aversion, or to induce an evil or unsavory opinion of him in the minds of a substantial number of the community, even though it may impute no moral turpitude to him."[24] Whether a statement has a defamatory meaning ultimately depends on how a community responds to it. The general rule in the United States is that a statement conveys a defamatory meaning if it would harm a person's reputation to "a substantial and respectable minority" of the community. In every case the court must determine the particular words or phrases that were used and determine if those words lower the individual's reputation among a significant number of "right minded" people in the community. Words should be considered in light of their ordinary meaning. A judge is responsible for determining as a matter of law if the words are capable of being defamatory. It is then up to the jury to determine if the words actually conveyed a defamatory meaning.

The term libel *per se* refers to statements that are defamatory on their face. This typically includes accusations of criminal conduct or activity; attacks on one's character traits or lifestyle, including claims of sexual promiscuity, sexual behaviors that deviate from accepted norms, and marital infidelity; allegations that a plaintiff has a communicable or loathsome disease; and allegations that tend to injure a person in his business, trade, profession, office, or calling. While the inclusion of statements regarding unchaste behavior or deviant sexual behavior may seem anachronistic because community mores about appropriate sexual conduct vary dramatically, statements relating to such conduct may be the subject of lawsuits, particularly when published on the Internet, which effectively distributes such statements internationally.[25]

Libel *per quod* refers to statements where the defamatory meaning of a statement results from extrinsic knowledge. Libel *per quod* is akin to libel by implication or innuendo. Libel *per quod* can be difficult for a plaintiff to prove. Typically, you cannot be held liable for statements that are defamatory because of facts you had no reason to know. In addition, as discussed below, in many jurisdictions, plaintiffs alleging libel *per quod* must prove actual monetary loss, or "special" damages. In some jurisdictions, lawsuits involving libel *per se* proof of defamation itself establishes the existence of damages. Other jurisdictions, however, have abandoned the *per se/per quod* distinction. In addition, the distinction between the two was weakened by the U.S. Supreme Court in *Gertz v. Robert Welch, Inc.*, when the Court ruled in matters of public concern all plaintiffs must prove statements are made negligently or recklessly.[26]

Fault

Fault is perhaps the most complicated area of defamation, and the element has changed dramatically over time. As Justice Byron White noted in *Gertz v. Robert Welch, Inc.*, the Supreme Court's "consistent view" before *New York Times v. Sullivan*[27] was that defamatory statements "were wholly unprotected by the First Amendment."[28] Thus, prior to 1964, a defendant was held strictly liable unless she could prove her statement was either true or privileged.[29] Under strict liability, if a defendant commits an act, even if by accident or in ignorance, they are liable for damages. Today, however, based on a series of decisions by the Supreme Court the level of fault a plaintiff must prove depends on the identity of the plaintiff, the subject matter of the defamatory statement, and the type of damages, or monetary awards, the defendant is seeking.

In *Sullivan*, the Court held that a public official could not recover damages for a defamatory falsehood relating to his official conduct unless the defendant acted with "actual malice,"[30] that is, with knowledge of the statement's falsity or reckless disregard for the truth. In addition, the Court provided added protection for defamatory speech by requiring the plaintiff prove actual malice with "convincing clarity" rather than the normal preponderance of evidence.[31] In *Curtis Publishing Co. v. Butts*,[32] the Court extended the protection afforded by the actual malice standard to "public figures."[33] The court reasoned that the distinction between public officials and public figures in 1960s America was artificial.

In *Gertz v. Welch, Inc.*,[34] the Court ruled while public officials and public figures must prove actual malice to win their libel lawsuits, private figure plaintiffs had to prove some degree of fault, at least negligence.[35] The Court, however, also made a distinction between winning a defamation suit and the ability to recover presumed and punitive damages. Because presumed and punitive damages are typically large, the Court ruled that the states could not permit their recovery unless the plaintiff could show actual malice, regardless of their status as a public official, public figure, or private individual.[36] The Court wrote presumed damages invited "juries to punish unpopular opinion rather than to compensate individuals for injury sustained by the publication of a false fact."[37] The plurality opinion in *Gertz*, it is also important to note, consistently referred to the need to protect "publishers," "broadcasters," and "the media" from juries who might award large presumed and punitive damages.[38] As discussed below, some lower courts have interpreted these statements to mean that the Constitution requires a different standard for media and non-media defendants, a move that causes concern given the ability of non-media defendants to publish information on blogs and social media sites with relative ease.

In 1976, in *Dun & Bradstreet v. Greenmoss Builders*, the Court continued to refine the law of defamation. In the case, the Court backtracked, concluding that the limitation on the recovery of presumed and punitive damages established in *Gertz* did not apply "when the defamatory statements do not involve matters of public concern."[39] In a plurality opinion, Justice Lewis F. Powell, Jr. characterized the Court's defamation decisions as attempts to balance the state's interest in compensating individuals for injury to their reputations with First Amendment interests in protecting speech.[40] Powell wrote that *Gertz*'s ban on recovery of presumed and punitive damages absent a showing of actual malice appropriately struck a balance between this strong state interest and the strong First Amendment interest in protecting speech on matters of public concern.[41] However, according to Justice Powell, there was nothing in *Gertz* that "indicated that the same balance would be struck regardless of the type of speech involved."[42] Thus, in addition to suggesting non-media defendants don't receive the same protections as media defendants in *Gertz*, the Court has also used language that has led some courts to conclude private speech by private individuals deserves little or no constitutional protection, making such libel lawsuits much easier for plaintiffs to win.

In sum, public officials and public figures must prove actual malice to win their lawsuits. Private persons must prove at least negligence to win their lawsuits and collect compensatory damages. All plaintiffs, both public and private, must prove actual malice to collect punitive damages if the subject of the report is a matter of public concern. The Supreme Court has never ruled if private figures must prove fault if the subject matter of the defamatory statement does not involve a public concern. Different jurisdictions have reached different conclusions.[43]

A public official is not simply any individual who works for the government. The Supreme Court has determined that the public official category includes "at the very least . . . those among the hierarchy of government employees who have, or appear to the public to have, substantial responsibility for or control over the conduct of governmental affairs."[44] Courts look at number of indicators to determine if a plaintiff is a public official. Courts consider if the individual controls expenditure of public money, or has the ability to set government policy or make governmental decisions, or if they have control over citizens or are responsible for health, safety, or welfare. Public officials do not have to wield great power or occupy lofty positions. For example, law enforcement personnel, even beat cops, are typically categorized as public officials. According to one scholar, school superintendents, a county medical examiner, and a director of financial aid for a public college have all been ruled public officials.[45]

In *Gertz*, the Court ruled there were several types of public figures. All-purpose public figures are individuals who "occupy positions of such pervasive power and influence that they are deemed public figures for all purposes."[46] This can include an individual with widespread fame or notoriety or individuals who occupy a position of continuing news value. The distinction between the fault level required of public and private figures has been justified by the distinction that public figures have the resources and media access to refute defamatory content.

In *Gertz*, the Court also ruled that an individual could be a limited-purpose public figure. Limited-purpose public figures are individuals who have "thrust themselves to the forefront of particular public controversies in order to influence the resolution of the issues involved."[47] Like all-purpose public figures, limited-purpose public figures are assumed to have access to the media based on their involvement in the public controversy and can rebut false statements about themselves. When considering Internet defamation, a court might consider independent chat room discussions about the same controversy or extensive or multiple postings on a blog by a plaintiff to support a finding that an individual has thrust themselves into the controversy in an effort to affect public opinion.[48]

In contrast to public officials and public figures, a private individual is an average person who has not voluntarily injected themselves into a public controversy. Many individuals who allege a defamatory statement was made about them on a social media site would probably fall into this category of plaintiff.

Proving actual malice can be very difficult for a plaintiff. As noted above, actual malice is publishing with knowledge of falsity or reckless disregard for the truth, and plaintiffs must prove actual malice with clear and convincing evidence, a higher burden than most civil cases, which only require proof by a preponderance of the evidence, a more-likely-than-not standard. While knowledge of falsity is easily understandable—the defendant knew what they published was false—reckless disregard for the truth can be a more nuanced concept.

Reckless disregard has been described by the Supreme Court as "the purposeful avoidance of the truth,"[49] "serious doubts as to the truth of the publication,"[50] and "a high degree of awareness of probable falsity."[51] The crucial focus of actual malice is the defendant's state of mind or attitude about the allegedly defamatory statement at the time the statement was made. Neither ill will nor even "extreme departure from professional standards"[52] qualifies as actual malice, although along with other factors these might contribute to a finding of actual malice. Actual malice is usually either a knowingly false statement or a combination of reckless behaviors that led someone to publish a story even if there were obvious reasons to doubt its veracity. In addition to inquiring into the state of the mind of the defendant at the time of publication,[53] courts consider the source(s) that were used or not used, the nature of the story—especially whether the story was "hot news" or time-sensitive—and the inherent probability or believability of the defamatory statement.

Negligence is the fault standard most states have adopted for defamation involving a private individual and a matter of public concern. Widely used in tort law, negligence is a failure to act as a reasonable person would in similar circumstances. In libel cases, courts sometimes use the "professional" standard rather than the reasonable person standard. For journalists, this standard asks if they failed to follow accepted professional standards and practices. When the professional standard is used, a journalist's behavior is measured against what is considered acceptable behavior within the profession. While there is no set definitive list of what practices are considered negligent, negligence by a journalist might include failure to check public records, failure to contact the subject of the defamatory statement unless a thorough investigation had already been conducted, failure to contact multiple sources or verify information from more than one source, or a failure to address a discrepancy between what a source says he told the journalist and what the journalist reported. As with actual malice, courts consider the source(s) that were used or not used, whether the story was time-sensitive, and the inherent probability or believability of the defamatory statement.

Courts do not usually demand that a story is investigated exhaustively before publication, so long as a communicator contacts the subject of the defamation directly and checks all information carefully with reliable sources. In addition, many jurisdictions hold that it is not negligent to publish a wire service story without checking the facts in the story. The so-called "wire service defense," which is not really a defense, but rather is simply considered to be an absence of negligence, is recognized by numerous states because wire services are normally considered trustworthy.[54]

Falsity

A defamatory communication must be harmful to someone's reputation and false. To be protected, a defamatory statement does not have to be absolutely accurate in every aspect. Minor flaws are not actionable, so long as the statement was "substantially true." Mistakes in a statement that do not harm a plaintiff's reputation cannot be the subject of a defamation suit.

Under American law, public officials, public figures, and private persons involved in matters of public concern must prove falsity. Put another way, anytime a matter of public concern is involved the plaintiff must prove falsity. Writing for the majority in *Philadelphia Newspapers, Inc. v. Hepps*,[55] Justice Sandra Day O'Connor said *Sullivan* and its progeny reflected "two forces" that had reshaped the common law of libel: the plaintiff's status and "whether the speech at issue is of public concern."[56] The Court ruled that whenever the speech involved a matter of public concern the Constitution required that the plaintiff bear the burden of proving falsity as well as fault in a suit for libel.[57]

Because both fault and falsity deal with determining what is a matter of public concern, both elements raise some difficult questions regarding the subject matter of defamatory speech, particularly as it applies to Internet defamation. As online speech becomes more ubiquitous in our culture, it has replaced other means of communication. However, much of the speech on Facebook, Twitter, and blogs may interest a relatively small number of people, and it may be difficult to determine whether it is a matter of public or private concern. This is particularly troublesome because in some situations the conclusion that a statement is merely a matter of private concern may ultimately determine the outcome of a defamation suit. Further, it's unclear if the public nature of social media publications—unless you have protected your account, you can publish to the whole world—may cause problems. While some may argue this could serve to elevate private speech into public speech, numerous courts have ruled expression is private even when widely distributed.[58]

Complicating matters, the U.S. Supreme Court has never defined "matters of public concern" although the phrase appears in a wide variety of cases, including cases involving speech by government employees,[59] intentional infliction of emotional distress,[60] and false light invasion of privacy,[61] as well as others.[62] Recently, in *Snyder v. Phelps*, a case involving the tort of intentional infliction of emotional distress, the Court explicated the concept. After writing that the Court itself had admitted "'the boundaries of the public concern test are not well defined,'"[63] Chief Justice John Roberts nonetheless set out to articulate some principles. Roberts began by noting that speech on a matter of public concern can "'be fairly considered as relating to any matter of political, social, or other concern to the community' or when it 'is a subject of legitimate news interest; that is, a subject of general interest and of value and concern to the public.'"[64] Private speech, on the other hand, "'concerns no public issue.'"[65] Roberts said one factor that "confirmed" the credit report at issue in *Dun & Bradstreet* was private speech was that it "was sent to only five subscribers."[66] Roberts then contrasted that with the speech at issue in *Snyder v. Phelps*, which was "designed, unlike the private speech in *Dun & Bradstreet*, to reach as broad a public audience as possible."[67]

Unfortunately, adding audience size to the public interest calculus is especially problematic in today's Internet environment as it would appear to require courts to take into account how large an audience or how many "followers" a speaker might have in a forum like Facebook or Twitter. In addition, as noted above, while some users have elected to enact privacy settings on Twitter, others have not, which makes publication on Twitter in effect publication to the whole world regardless of the number of followers you have. Blogs also might become problematic forums for expression. Would, for example, a blog post by an unknown writer be treated differently than a blog post on the widely read *Volokh Conspiracy*[68] even if the topic of both posts was similar? Finally, what does this say about email? The U.S. Court of Appeals for the First Circuit upheld a lower court's determination that an email sent to approximately 1,500 employees detailing the firing of a fellow employee for violating company policies was a matter of private concern involving a private plaintiff.[69] Surely 1,500 people is a fairly large "intended audience." And what if the expression in question goes viral? In the age of the Internet, even the most private video, picture, or Facebook post can quickly have an audience of thousands, if not millions.[70] As discussed below, this is further complicated by the fact that some courts treat media and non-media defendants differently.

Injury or Harm

In libel suits, plaintiffs must prove damages that go beyond embarrassment or being upset. Plaintiffs must show harm, sometimes called injury to reputation.

Harm can be intangible: loss of reputation, standing in community, mental harm, emotional distress, etc. However, sometimes harm may include loss of income. Not all defamatory statements bring about harm, while with other statements harm to reputation may be "presumed." For states that still recognize the difference, damage may be presumed in cases of libel *per se*, but not in libel *per quod*. In some states, in cases of libel *per quod* plaintiffs must prove the special circumstances of the defamation—that the audience understood the defamatory connotation—and actual monetary loss before a plaintiff can recover for damages based on emotional distress, damage to reputation, or other intangible harm.

Thus, libel plaintiffs may sue for presumed damages or harm that loss of reputation is assumed to cause. They may also sue for compensatory damages, awards designed to compensate for proven loss of a good name or reputation (called actual damages in libel law) or awards designed to compensate for lost revenue or other monetary loss (called special damages in libel law). Finally, plaintiffs may sue for punitive damages, awards imposed to punish the plaintiff rather than compensate the defendant.

The system for calculating damages awards is complex, even before courts begin to consider harm as it applies to Internet communications.[71] Public officials and public figures can only be awarded damages if they prove actual malice. Private figures in matters of public concern must show actual malice if they wish to collect presumed or punitive damages, and at least negligence if they wish to collect compensatory damages. States vary greatly in how they approach the defamation of private individuals who are not involved in a matter of public concern. In some states they are allowed to collect presumed and punitive damages without a showing of actual malice or are allowed to collect compensatory damages without a showing of negligence. Some jurisdictions have even ruled that defamation involving a private plaintiff and a matter of private concern are completely governed by state common law, and do not implicate the Constitution whatsoever.[72]

DEFENSES TO DEFAMATION

In a defamation suit, defendants have a number of defenses they can actively assert. It is widely recognized in American law that truth is an absolute defense to libel claims.[73] As noted above, in all cases involving a matter of public concern, the plaintiff has the burden of proving falsity. In these cases, if a plaintiff fails to prove a statement was false, the defendant will win without having to prove the statement was true. However, defendants can also use truth as a proactive defense.

The truth of a statement rests on the overall gist of a statement or story. Minor inaccuracies will not destroy a truth defense, and "substantially" true statements will be considered true for a defamation suit. In addition, the U.S. Supreme Court has ruled that intentionally changing quotes in a story does not equate to actual malice unless the changes substantially increase damage to the plaintiff's reputation or add to the defamatory meaning of the words.[74]

Opinion, Hyperbole, and Fair Comment and Criticism

Some statements are incapable of being true or false. Thus, while in 1990, in *Milkovich v. Lorain Journal Co.*[75] the U.S. Supreme Court declined to establish separate constitutional protection for opinion, the Court has ruled that some statements are not actionable in a libel suit because they are not false statements of fact.

First, exaggerated, loose, figurative language, rhetorical hyperbole and parody are all protected by the First Amendment. For example, calling a worker who crossed picket lines "a traitor to his God, his country, his family and his class" does not literally mean the worker was guilty of treason and no one would take the statement to imply it.[76]

Second, statements incapable of being proven true or false—such as imprecise evaluations like good, bad, or ugly—cannot be proven true or false. However, this does not mean there is a wholesale exemption for anything labeled "opinion" or using the phrase "in my opinion" (or IMHO for those familiar with Twitter) will automatically protect a speaker. Writing "In my opinion John Jones is a child molester" on a blog or "IMHO: John Jones is a liar when he says he doesn't know where his wife's body is" in a tweet would most certainly not be protected opinion. Furthermore, even unverifiable statements of opinion can lose their protection if they imply the existence of false, defamatory but undisclosed facts, or the statement is based on disclosed but false or incomplete facts, or the statement is based on an erroneous assessment of accurate information.

Statements of opinion are also protected under the common law defense of fair comment and criticism. This privilege protects non–malicious statements of opinion about matters of public interest. The opinion must be "fair," and many courts have stated this means the opinion must have a factual basis that has either been provided by the plaintiff, is generally known to the public, or is readily available to the public. Thus food critics, movie reviewers, and other commentators who might post a scathing review of a new restaurant, film, or music album are generally protected. For example, posting that a restaurant's new sauce tasted "like rotten garbage" is not an actionable statement, whereas "in my opinion the restaurant regularly uses expired food products" would be actionable because it implies a statement of fact—that the restaurant uses unsafe food in the preparation of its dishes. This is particularly important given the proliferation of websites on which individuals can share their opinions about everything from the restaurant down to the street,[77] the reliability of a plumber,[78] or the quality of a tour guide[79] to the suitability of miniature ponies as guide animals for the vision-impaired.[80]

Privileges

Some false defamatory statements of fact are still protected by law. An absolute privilege protects a speaker regardless of the speaker's accuracy or motives. In other situations, a speaker may have a qualified privilege. A qualified privilege protects a statement only when certain conditions are met that vary from jurisdiction to jurisdiction. The U.S. Constitution provides an absolute privilege from libel litigation for members of Congress when making remarks on the floor of either house.[81] Federal legislators are also protected when communicating in committee hearings, legislative reports, and other activities. Statements made beyond the legislative process, however, are not protected.[82] The official statements of executive branch officers and all comments made during judicial proceedings—whether by judges, lawyers, or witnesses—also have absolute privilege from libel litigation.

Similarly, the fair report privilege, sometimes called the reporter's privilege, is a common law qualified privilege that protects reports of official government proceedings and records if the reports are: (1) accurate; (2) fair or balanced; (3) substantially complete; and (4) not motivated by malice or ill will. Under common law, courts recognize that the public needs access to information regarding the workings of government and reporters should be free to communicate what happens at public meetings and the contents of public documents. Thus, someone who reports a defamatory comment made in an official government proceeding or a defamatory statement from an official government document cannot be sued for libel as long as the conditions of the privilege are met. Courts in some states have said the report must be attributed to the official record or meeting for the privilege to apply, while other states have ruled the privilege can only be claimed by a member of the press. In addition, the privilege does not extend to comments made by government officials outside of official proceedings. A reporter's privilege also extends to any and all statements made during official judicial proceedings by judges, witnesses, jurors, litigants, and attorneys and any information obtained from most official court records and documents filed with a court.

Privileges for communications of mutual interest protect a communication between two individuals when those individuals have a common or shared interest. In these situations a statement is privileged if: (1) it is about something in which the speaker has an interest or duty; (2) the hearer has a corresponding interest or duty; (3) the statement is made in protection of that interest or performance of that duty; and (4) the speaker honestly believes the statement to be true. Thus an email between business partners or corporate employees that defamed a third party might be protected under this privilege. The privilege also protects members of religious organizations, fraternities, sororities, and educational institutions.

Some jurisdictions recognize a privilege known as neutral reportage. This privilege allows third parties to report statements by reliable sources even if the third party doubts the accuracy of the statement. The privilege is based on the idea that the accusation itself is newsworthy, even if the accusation might not be true. The privilege has not been widely recognized by courts and has never been recognized by the U.S. Supreme Court.[83] Those courts that have recognized the privilege typically require the charges must be: (1) newsworthy and related to a public controversy; (2) made by a responsible person or organization; (3) made against a public official or public figure; (4) accurately reported with opposing views; and (5) reported impartially.

SLAPP Lawsuits

In some situations, libel suits can be filed in an attempt to silence criticism or stifle political expression. These suits are referred to as Strategic Lawsuits Against Public Participation, or SLAPP suits, a term coined by two University of Denver professors in articles that described lawsuits to silence opposition to a developer's plan to cut trees or suits meant to stifle reports of police brutality.[84] The purpose of a SLAPP suit is not necessarily to win damages. Rather, the goal is to discourage criticism because libel suits can be time-consuming and costly. As Professor Robert D. Richards wrote, "[T]he SLAPP filer does not have to win the lawsuit to accomplish his objective. Indeed, it is through the legal process itself—dragging the unwitting target through the churning waters of litigation—that the SLAPP filer prevails."[85] A proliferation of SLAPP suits led many states to pass anti-SLAPP laws. According to one source, 29 states have anti-SLAPP statutes designed to protect political speech and criticism by stopping SLAPP suits.[86]

In recent years SLAPP suits have become an increasingly popular way for business and professionals to silence criticism on the Internet or made via social media.[87] For example, in 2010 a woman was sued for defamation over negative comments she made on Yelp.com about her dentist,[88] while another man was sued for negative reviews of his chiropractor.[89] Other suits have come from postings on Twitter[90] or Facebook.[91] In one case that received wide media attention, Justin Kurtz, a student at Western Michigan

University, was sued for $750,000 by a towing company after he created a Facebook page called "Kalamazoo Residents Against T & J Towing." T & J Towing sued after the page attracted 800 followers in just two days.[92] In addition, SLAPP suits can also be designed simply to unmask anonymous and pseudonymous posters to social networking sites, blogs, and consumer gripe sites.[93] When applied to anonymous and pseudonymous social media and blogs, these suits are sometimes called CyberSLAPP cases.

Fortunately, online commentators have several remedies for SLAPP suits. First, citizens can countersue and contend a lawsuit was filed from spite or maliciousness rather than on legitimate legal concerns. Second, defendants in states with anti-SLAPP statutes can have the cases dismissed and, in some states, can recover court costs and attorneys' fees. In addition, some anti-SLAPP statues allow defendants to recover compensatory damages if they can show a suit was filed against them in an attempt to harass, intimidate, punish, or inhibit free speech.

EMERGING ISSUES IN SOCIAL MEDIA

In addition to the many ways defamation has adapted to the Internet discussed above, there are a number of ways the law might adapt to—or struggle to adapt to—social media specifically. Because there is little case law dealing specifically with social media and defamation, there are many questions about how the law might be applied to this quickly growing means of communication.

One of the biggest issues facing non-media users of social media is the distinctions some courts have created between the constitutional protections afforded the media and those afforded to average individuals. As noted above, in effect, lower courts are removing a wide range of speech from constitutional protections at the very time new communication technologies such as email, Facebook, Twitter, and blogs are giving non-media individuals the power to reach wider and wider audiences.

From the outset, it is important to note that the Supreme Court has never explicitly stated there should be a difference between media and non-media defendants. The confusion comes from a series of cases in which the Court appeared to be making the distinction without directly saying so and the Court's unwillingness to directly answer the question since then. While clarifying the rules about which plaintiffs would have to prove which level of fault to win their libel cases, the majority opinion in *Gertz* also introduced uncertainty as to whether the fault rules applied to all defendants. Justice Powell defined the issue in *Gertz* as "whether *a newspaper or broadcaster* that publishes defamatory falsehoods about an individual who is neither a public official nor a public figure may claim a constitutional privilege against liability for the injury inflicted by those statements."[94] In addition, when limiting presumed and punitive damages to showings of actual malice, Powell repeatedly referred to the need to protect "publishers," "broadcasters," and "the media" from juries,[95] words that led some courts to conclude that constitutional limits did not apply in cases involving non-media defendants.[96] Indeed, it was the Vermont Supreme Court's decision that *Gertz* did not apply to non-media defendants that brought *Dun & Bradstreet v. Greenmoss Builders*[97] to the Court in the first place. After acknowledging lower court confusion over the media–non-media issue and citing six state supreme court decisions to illustrate the disagreement,[98] Justice Powell's plurality opinion ignored the issue altogether, even though it would have been the perfect opportunity to settle the question.

The following year, in *Hepps*, while Justice Sandra Day O'Connor cited only "two forces" determining constitutional requirements in libel cases—the plaintiff's status and "whether the speech at issue is of public concern"[99]—her opinion served to further fuel confusion over whether defendant's status was a third force to be considered. In discussing various issues the Court was not required to address, O'Connor stated, "Nor need we consider what standards would apply if the plaintiff sues a nonmedia defendant."[100] Finally in 1990, in *Milkovich v. Lorain Journal Co.*, the Court continued to keep alive the possibility of a media–non-media distinction by declaring that provable falsity was required "at least in situations, like the present, where a media defendant is involved."[101] That statement was followed by a footnote stating, "In *Hepps* the Court reserved judgment on cases involving nonmedia defendants, and accordingly we do the same."[102]

Based on these statements, and lower courts that have definitively held them to mean non-media defendants are not entitled to the same level of protection as media defendants, private individuals posting on social media sites need to be particularly wary of what they post. Numerous lower courts have been willing to treat media and non-media defendants differently in defamation cases.[103] In late 2011, the question of whether non-media libel defendants enjoy constitutional protection drew renewed attention—especially in the online world—when the U.S. District Court for the District of Oregon held that a blogger did not qualify as a media defendant and, therefore, was not entitled to the protections of *Gertz v. Robert Welch, Inc.*[104] because the blogger was "not media."[105] Judge Marco Hernandez's ruling led to a jury verdict of $2.5 million against blogger Crystal Cox, who a jury found had libeled Obsidian Finance Group and its co-founder, Kevin Padrick, in one of her posts.[106]

While Twitter has created a great deal of speculation in the legal community, besides Courtney Love's lawsuit, discussed above, few defamation cases involving Twitter have made it to court. Most have been settled without litigating the details of how the law of defamation applies to the micro-blogging site. For example, on January 24, 2011, Associated Press (AP) sportswriter Jon Krawczynski was covering a National Basketball Association (NBA) game between the Minnesota Timberwolves and the Houston Rockets when he thought he overheard a comment between referee Bill Spooner and Minnesota Coach Kurt Rambis. Krawczynski tweeted, "Ref Bill Spooner told Rambis he'd 'get it back' after a bad call. Then he made an even worse call on Rockets. That's NBA officiating folks." The referee denied making the comment and sued Krawczynski and the AP, seeking at least $75,000 in damages. The parties settled, however, after the AP agreed to pay $20,000 and Krawczynski agreed to delete the tweet.[107]

Despite this lack of case law, lawyers and scholars are currently speculating how the courts should treat social media posts such as tweets. One author, for example, has suggested social media's characteristics should lend courts to treat posts on these mediums as opinion rather than fact. Noting that courts have consistently considered the context of a statement when determining if a statement was fact or opinion, attorney William Charron argued the nature of tweets should cause courts to mitigate the otherwise libelous nature of a tweet. Charron wrote, "Twitter is a 'buyer beware' shopping mart of thoughts, making it an ideal public forum to spark imagination and further discussion. In and of itself, however, Twitter should be viewed as a dubious medium through which to spread libel."[108] Because of the speed in which one can communicate over Twitter, the medium, even more so than blogs or other online forums, "provides a context to more readily perceive and excuse seemingly defamatory statements as emotional, unguarded, and imprecise 'opinions,'" wrote Charron.[109] To support his argument, Charron relied on numerous cases in which courts have found that blog readers expect to read informal and personal content akin to opinion rather than statements of fact. Based on this, Charron proposed a wholesale exemption for Twitter under current defamation law.

Others have suggested the unique nature of Twitter calls for new statutory or common law approaches to libel via Twitter. Legal commentator Julie Hilden, for example, wrote that current libel law is not a good fit for social media because much of it was crafted for a time when newspapers reigned supreme. According to Hilden, Twitter is unlike traditional mass media for a number of reasons. First, Twitter followers are easy to number and identify. This makes it easier for potential plaintiffs to determine who has enough followers to create a worthwhile suit, although because of Twitter's scrolling feed it might make it difficult to know just how much reputational damage was done by a tweet or subsequent retweets. Conversely, it also makes it easier to determine the effectiveness of retractions. Second, the

140-character nature of tweets makes it very difficult to apply the traditional protection for opinion supported by fact. It is difficult to describe both an opinion and the facts supporting it in 140 characters. Hilden also agreed that the shoot-from-the-hip nature of most tweets makes it likely tweets are opinion or hyperbole rather than fact. Finally, Hilden contended that the nature of tweets actually make them more like slander, even though some jurisdictions have blurred the distinction between the two torts while others have typically ruled Internet defamation is libel. Unless changes are made to libel law, Hilden predicted many, many more defamation suits based on Twitter.[110]

Another author has questioned how a retweet would be treated under the republication rule. Noting Krawczynski's tweet was retweeted by 14 people, Professor Daxton Stewart wrote lawyers were divided over the question of whether a retweet could constitute a defamatory republication. Stewart reasoned that while Twitter itself would clearly be protected under Section 230, a Twitter user who retweets the content of others is making the conscious decision to repeat content which would appear to make them acting more like classic republishers rather than classic distributors. The question under Section 230, however, would boil down to whether a retweeter was an "information content provider." According to Stewart's analysis, current case law makes it unlikely a retweeter would be held liable for a defamatory retweet, although a user might be liable for adding defamatory content to a modified retweet.[111] Similarly, while social media users who provide a link to a defamatory statement are unlikely to be liable for defamation, providing a defamatory comment with the link or using defamatory hypertext to create the link may make you liable.

In 2013, attorney Ellyn Angelotti Kamke wrote that traditional legal approaches to libel law did not translate well to online speech and proposed numerous solutions to help libel law deal with the novelties presented by sites like Twitter. Angelotti Kamke focused on non-legal remedies to online defamatory speech, including focusing on counter-speech (or fighting "bad speech" with "good speech") and private sector reputation management tools. She also suggested online dispute resolution was a less expensive and more convenient option than litigation.[112]

An additional question regarding social media and defamation is how courts should handle damages. In 2012, a Texas jury awarded $13.78 million in damages to a Texas couple, Mark and Rhonda Lesher, for statements made by multiple individuals on Topix.com, self-described as "the world's largest community news site." The case involved 1,700 separate posts—which began after the Leshers were accused of sexual assault—that describe the couple as sexual deviants, molesters, and drug dealers.[113] Such a large award directed at multiple defendants raises numerous questions about social media and damages related to the number of negative posts, how spread out the posts are over time, and how audience reaction and the mob mentality of some social media sites should factor into damages.

Although the case raises far more questions than it answers about how juries will deal with defamation on social networks, it is clear this jury took the number and viciousness of posts to heart, and the already difficult process of determining harm is only going to be complicated by social media. It's also unclear how the privacy settings of a social media account might affect damages. It is also unclear how a jury would view the lack of a definable mass audience of sites like Twitter. Should my total number of followers, the number of followers who read the tweet, the number of followers who retweeted the defamatory statement, or the number of followers who know the plaintiff be determinative? In addition, as mentioned above, the scrolling nature of Twitter makes audience size difficult to determine. As Professor Amy Kristin Sanders noted, given the unique character of the Internet, it is more important than ever that courts carefully consider how to award damages in order to ensure that freedom of expression is protected.[114]

In 2012, when this book was first published it was unclear how the law would handle cases involving social media and defamation. Since then, only a handful of cases have made their way to the courts. As was predicted, these courts have had a great deal of difficulty handling these cases and it is still unclear how courts are going to handle social media. As this book goes to press, reality TV star and president-elect Donald Trump, is being sued for defamation by a longtime Republican consultant for tweets in which Trump called the consultant "a real dummy" who had "begged my people for a job."[115] This is just one example of the many defamation cases involving social media that will soon reach the courts. As noted above, the law of defamation is centuries old, yet typically, little libel law is created specifically for a new medium. Although Section 230 stands out in contrast, most libel law has simply had to adapt to new technologies over time. Thus, only time will tell how defamation and social media will coexist as the courts continue to attempt to strike a balance between reputational interests and freedom of expression.

FREQUENTLY ASKED QUESTIONS

1. Can I get in trouble for posting a vicious lie about somebody on Facebook?

Yes, if the lie damages the person's reputation. Posting something on Facebook is considered "publishing." If you post a vicious lie about somebody on Facebook and as a result people think less of them, you've damaged their reputation with a false statement of fact. You can be sued for defamation for a Facebook post, a tweet, a blog, or a video posted to the Internet.

2. If I repeat something I thought was true but turned out to be wrong on Twitter, will I be responsible for it?

It depends. Generally, anyone who repeats someone else's statements is just as responsible for the defamatory content as the original speaker. This is sometimes described as "The bearer of tales is as guilty as the teller of tales." However, simply posting a link to a defamatory statement or retweeting someone else's defamatory tweet will probably not make you liable. On the other hand, if you create your own tweet based on a false defamatory tweet, modify the original tweet in a defamatory way, or add you own defamatory statement to the tweet, you can be liable.

3. Is it libelous to record something in public and post it on YouTube?

Not if it's true. Defamation is a false statement of fact. Recording a real event can't be defamatory unless you misidentify the individuals in the video, suggest the video is something that it is not, or add some sort of false connotation to the video. For example, videotaping two people kissing in the street is not defamatory. Suggesting the two are engaging in an adulterous relationship when they are in fact happily married to each other or falsely identifying the two individuals in the video could be defamatory.

4. What should I do if somebody sues me for libel for posting an opinion on a site such as Yelp?

You should consult a lawyer who is familiar with your state's laws regarding defamation. It's possible your statement will be protected because it is constitutionally protected opinion, it is considered fair comment and criticism under common law, or because the lawsuit is actually designed to stifle your speech rather than win damages against you. Many states have anti–SLAPP statutes that are designed to protect people who are sued just to keep them quiet. If you qualify for protection under an anti–SLAPP statute, you can have the case dismissed before trial and, in some states, you can be awarded attorney fees from the plaintiff.

5. Why don't anonymous gossip sites get in trouble for libel?

In 1996, in an effort to get Internet Service Providers (ISPs) to police indecent sexual content, Congress passed a law that granted immunity to websites that contain defamatory content posted by third parties. Prior to this law, ISPs would not edit content on their websites because doing so made them liable for the defamatory postings of third parties. In the years after the law was passed courts interpreted its protections broadly, granting blanket immunity to almost all websites that host the content of others. This allows websites like CollegeACB and anonymous chat apps like Yik Yak to host vicious, untrue, defamatory statements without having to worry about being sued.

NOTES

1 David S. Ardia, Reputation in a Networked World: Revisiting the Social Foundations of Defamation Law, 45 Harv. C.R.-C.L. L. Rev. 261, 262 (2010).
2 See Frank H. Easterbrook, Cyberspace and the Law of the Horse, U. Chi. Legal F. 207 (1996) for a discussion of the application of real space laws to cyberspace situations.
3 47 U.S.C. 230 (1996).
4 Historically, libel law was criminal law. Governments punished libelous speech to prevent breaches of the peace and prevent criticism of the government. Today, however, most libel cases in the United States are civil suits. This does not mean that criminal libel has disappeared. Although the prevailing view of criminal libel among communication law scholars in the United States is that there are only a handful of criminal libel prosecutions per year, a recent empirical study of all Wisconsin criminal libel cases from 1991 through 2007 suggests that criminal libel might be prosecuted far more often than realized. See David Pritchard, Rethinking Criminal Libel: An Empirical Study, 14 Comm. L. Pol'y 303 (2009). In addition, bloggers and tweeters who do not deal with public issues should be wary of criminal libel laws that might exist in their state. Professor Pritchard concluded that criminal libel is especially likely to be used when expression harms the reputations of private figures in cases that have nothing to do with public issues.
5 Reputation is a personal right and cannot be inherited. Friends, relatives, or associates of a person may only sue for defamation if they have been defamed personally.
6 Texas Beef Group v. Winfrey, 11 F. Supp. 2d 858 (1998), aff'd, 201 F.3d 980 (5th Cir. 2000).
7 Ellyn Angelotti, How Courtney Love and U.S.'s First Twitter Libel Trial Could Impact Journalists, Poynter.org, Jan. 14, 2014 available at http://www.poynter.org/2014/how-courtney-love-and-u-s-s-first-twitter-libel-trial-could-impact-journalists/235728/ (last visited Apr. 20, 2016).
8 Gordon & Holmes v. Courtney Love, No. B256367, Court of Appeals. Cal. Feb. 1, 2016. The jury ruled that while the statement was false and could damage Holmes in her profession, Love did not publish the statement with knowledge of falsity or reckless disregard for the truth.
9 Anthony McCartney, $430k Love Settlement Shows Tweets can Be Costly, Associated Press, March 5, 2011.
10 47 U.S.C. 230 (1996).
11 1995 WL323710 (N.Y. Sup. Ct. 1995).
12 47 U.S.C. 230 (f) (2).
13 47 U.S.C. 230 (f) (3).
14 Finkel v. Facebook, No. 102578 (N.Y. Sup. Ct. filed Feb. 16, 2009), http://www.citmedialaw.org/sites/citmedialaw.org/files/2009-02-16-Finkel%20Complaint.pdf.

15 Finkel v. Facebook, No. 102578 (N.Y. Sup. Ct. filed Sept. 16, 2009)(order granting motion to dismiss), http://www.citmedialaw.org/sites/citmedialaw.org/files/2009-09-15-Finkel%20v.%20Facebook%20Order%20to%20Dismiss.pdf.

16 JuicyCampus, although infamous, was never sued for defamation, perhaps because of Section 230. The company went out of business because of an inability to generate revenue. After spending $1 million of investor's money the site shut down in February 2009. Its founder has since gone on to write a book about online reputation management. See From Gossip Site Founder to Web Reputation Manager, Forbes.com, October 12, 2011, http://management.fortune.cnn.com/2011/10/12/from-gossip-site-founder-to-web-reputation-defender/.

17 Jones v. Dirty World Entertainment Recordings, LLC., 840 F.Supp.2d 1008 (2012), *appeal dismissed*, No. 12-5133 (6th Cir. May 9, 2012).

18 Jones v. Dirty World Entertainment Recording, LLC. No. 13-5946 (6th Cir. Jun. 16, 2014)

19 But see Fair Housing Council of San Fernando Valley v. Roommates.com, LLC, 521 F.3d 1157 (9th Cir. 2008) (holding immunity under Section 230 did not apply to an interactive online operator whose questionnaire violated the Fair Housing Act); Federal Trade Commission v. Accusearch, 570 F.3d 1187 (10th Cir. 2009) (holding that section 230 did not grant a website immunity from prosecution under federal wiretapping law for providing access to phone records by virtue of the the fact that the information was provided by third parties).

20 Firth v. State, 98 N.Y.2d 365 (2002). See also, Nationwide Biweekly Administration, Inc., v. Belo Corp., 512 F.3d 137 (5th Cir. 2007).

21 Firth, 98 N.Y.2d at 371.

22 Madeleine Schachter & Joel Kurtzber, Law of Internet Speech 424 (2008).

23 Fawcett Publications, Inc. v. Morriss, 377 P.2d 42 (Okla.).

24 Nichols v. Item Publishers, Inc., 309 N.Y. 596, 600–601 (1956).

25 For example, some courts continue to hold that a false statement that an individual is gay is defamatory and some still view this characterization as defamatory per se. Other courts have held that changing moral attitudes toward homosexuality have made such rulings outdated and some recent cases have questioned whether an allegation of homosexuality should ever be construed as defamatory. For a discussion of these cases, see Matthew D. Bunker, Drew E. Shenkman, & Charles D. Tobin, Not That There's Anything Wrong with That: Imputations of Homosexuality and the Normative Structure of Defamation Law, 21 Fordham Intell. Prop. Media & Ent. L.J. 581 (2011).

26 388 U.S. 130, 347–348 (1967).

27 376 U.S. 254 (1964).

28 418 U.S. 323, 384–385 (1974) (White, J., dissenting).

29 Nat Stern, Private Concerns of Private Plaintiffs: Revisiting a Problematic Defamation Category, 65 Mo. L. Rev. 597, 599 (2000).

30 Sullivan, 376 U.S. at 279–280 (1964).

31 Id.

32 388 U.S. 130 (1967).

33 Id. at 164 (Warren, C.J., concurring).

34 418 U.S. 323 (1974).

35 Id. at 347–348.

36 Id. at 349.

37 Id.

38 See, e.g., id. at 350.

39 472 U.S. 749, 763 (1985).

40 Id. at 756–757.

41 Id.

42 Id. at 756–757.

43 See Ruth Walden & Derigan Silver, Deciphering Dun & Bradstreet: Does the First Amendment Matter in Private Figure-Private Concern Defamation Cases?, 14 Comm. L. & Pol'y 1 (2009).

44 Rosenblatt v. Baer, 383 U.S. 75, 85 (1966).

45 Bruce Stanford, Libel and Privacy § 7.2.2.2, at 260–264 (2d ed. 1999).

46 Gertz v. Robert Welch, Inc., 418 U.S. 323, 345 (1974).

47 Id.

48 See, e.g., Ellis v. Time, Inc., WL 863267 (D.D.C. 1997) (holding a plaintiff's multiple postings on CompuServe about a public controversy made him a limited-purpose public figure).

49 Harte-Hanks Communications, Inc. v. Connaughton, 491 U.S. 657, 692 (1989).

50 St. Amant v. Thompson, 390 U.S. 727, 730 (1968).

51 Garrison v. Louisiana, 379 U.S. 64, 74 (1964).

52 Harte-Hanks Communications, Inc., 491 U.S. at 664.

53 In Herbert v. Lando, 441 U.S. 153 (1979), the Supreme Court ruled that the First Amendment did not bar examining the editorial process and a reporter for *60 Minutes* could be asked how he evaluated information prior to publication of a story about a controversial retired Army officer. The Court held that the actual malice standard made it important for public officials and public figures to know both the actions and state of mind of defendants.

54 See Kyu Youm, The "Wire Service" Libel Defense, 70 Journalism Q. 682 (1993).

55 475 U.S. 767, 771 (1986).

56 Id. at 775.

57 Id. at 776.

58 See, e.g., Roffman v. Trump, 754 F. Supp. 411, 418 (E.D. Pa. 1990) (holding statements published in the Wall Street Journal, Business Week, Fortune, and the New York Post were "of no concern to the general public"); Katz v. Gladstone, 673 F. Supp. 76, 83 (D. Conn. 1987) (statements made in book reviews which appeared "in a number of periodicals" lacked "public concern").

59 See, e.g., Connick v. Myers, 461 U.S. 138 (1983); Pickering v. Bd. of Educ., 391 U.S. 563 (1968).

60 See, e.g., Snyder v. Phelps, 562 U.S. 443 (2011).

61 See, e.g., Time, Inc. v. Hill, 385 U.S. 374 (1967).

62 See, e.g., Bartnicki v. Vopper, 532 U.S. 514 (2001).

63 131 S. Ct. 1207, 1216 (2011) (quoting San Diego v. Roe, 543 U.S. 77, 83 (2004)).

64 Id. (quoting Connick, 461 U.S. at 146; and San Diego v. Roe, 543 U.S. at 83–83).

65 Id. (quoting Dun & Bradstreet, 472 U.S. at 762).

66 Id.

67 Id. at 1217.

68 See http://volokh.com/ (last visited April 20, 2016).

69 Noonan v. Staples, 556 F.3d 20, 22 (1st Cir. 2009) (holding that an email sent to 1,500 Staples employees regarding the firing of a fellow employee for violating the company's travel and expense policy and code of ethics was a matter of private concern).

70 For a detailed discussion of this approach to defamation law and its potential problems, see Derigan Silver & Ruth Walden, A Dangerous Distinction: The Deconstitutionalization of Private Speech, 21 CommLaw Conspectus 59 (2012).

71 For a discussion of harm and the unique nature of defamation in American tort law, see David Anderson, Reputation, Compensation & Proof, 25 Wm. & Mary L. Rev. 747 (1984). For a discussion of the concept of harm in the context of Internet-based defamation, see Amy Kristin Sanders, Defining Defamation: Evaluating Harm in the Age of the Internet, 3 UB J. Media L. & Ethics 112 (2012).

72 See Walden & Silver, supra note 43 for a discussion of how different jurisdictions have handled the Supreme Court's decision in Dun & Bradstreet v. Greenmoss Builders.

73 There is at least one anomaly to this statement. In Noonan v. Staples, 561 F.3d 4, 7 (1st Cir. 2009) the U.S. Court of Appeals for the First Circuit refused to hold unconstitutional a Massachusetts law that allowed liability for true defamatory statements. It is important to note, however, the First Circuit apparently never addressed the constitutionality of the 1902 Massachusetts statute in its opinion because the defendant's attorneys never raised the issue.

74 Masson v. New Yorker Magazine Inc., 501 U.S. 496 (1991).

75 497 U.S. 1 (1990).

76 National Ass'n of Letter Carriers v. Austin, 418 U.S. 264 (1974).

77 See, e.g., http://www.yelp.com.

78 See, e.g., http://www.angieslist.com/AngiesList/.

79 See, e.g., http://www.tripadvisor.com/.

80 See, e.g., Burleson v. Toback, 391 F. Supp. 2d 401 (M.D.N.C. 2005).

81 U.S. Const., art. 1, § 6.

82 Hutchinson v. Proxmire, 443 U.S. 111 (1979).

83 Several states and the District of Columbia have accepted neutral reportage in some form, as have several U.S. Circuit Courts of Appeal. The inconsistent manner in which it has been applied, however, makes it an unreliable defense.

84 See Penelope Canan & George W. Pring, Strategic Lawsuits Against Public Participation, 35 Soc. Prob. 506 (1988); George W. Pring & Penelope Canan, SLAPPs: Getting Sued For Speaking Out (1996).

85 Robert D. Richards, A SLAPP In the Facebook: Assessing the Impact of Strategic Lawsuits Against Public Participation on Social Networks, Blogs and Consumer Gripe Sites, 21 DePaul J. Art Tech. & Intell. Prop. L 221, 231 (2011).

86 California Anti-SLAPP Project, http://www.casp.net/ (last visited).

87 Richards, supra note 85 at 221–242.

88 Want to Complain Online? Look Out. You Might Be Sued, USA Today, June 9, 2010, at 8A.

89 Elinor Mills, Yelp User Faces Lawsuit Over Negative Review, CNET News, January 6, 2009, http://news.cnet.com/8301-1023_3-10133466-93.html.

90 See, e.g., Lisa Donovan, Tenant's Twitter Slam Draws Suit, Chicago Sun-Times, July 28, 2009; Dan Frosch, Venting Online, Consumers Can Land in Court, N.Y. Times, June 1, 2010, at A1.

91 Rex Hall, Jr., Western Michigan University Student Sued in Battle with Towing Company: Facebook Group Airing Complaints about T & J Towing Takes Off, Kalamazoo Gazette, April 14, 2010.

92 Id.

93 See Richards, supra note 85 at 242–253.

94 418 U.S. 323, 332 (1974) (emphasis added).

95 See, e.g., id. at 340–341.

96 See, e.g., Rowe v. Metz, 579 P.2d 83, 84 (Colo. 1978); Harley-Davidson Motorsports, Inc. v. Markley, 568 P.2d 1359, 1363 (Ore. 1977); Greenmoss Builders v. Dun & Bradstreet, 461 A.2d 414, 417–418 (Vt. 1983); Denny v. Mertz, 318 N.W.2d 141, 153 (Wis. 1982).

97 472 U.S. 749 (1985).

98 Id. at 753 n.1.

99 Id. at 775.

100 Id. at 779 n.4.

101 497 U.S. 1, 19–20 (1990).

102 Id. at 20 n.6 (citation omitted).

103 For further discussion, see Walden & Silver, supra note 43; Silver & Walden, supra note 70; Rebecca Phillips, Constitutional Protections for Non-media Defendants: Should There Be a Distinction Between Larry King and You?, 33 Campbell L. Rev. 173 (2010).

104 Obsidian Finance Group LLC v. Cox, No. CV-11-57-HZ, 2011 WL 5999334 (D. Ore. November 30, 2011).

105 2011 WL 5999334, at *5.

106 Douglas Lee, Troubling Rulings Paved Way for Blogger's Libel Conviction, First Amendment Center (December 19, 2011), http://www.firstamendmentcenter.org/troubling-rulings-paved-way-for-bloggers-libel-conviction.

107 Spooner v. Associated Press, Inc. Case 0:11-cv-00642-JRT-JJK (D.C. Minn. 2011); Lauren Dugan, The AP Settles Over NBA Twitter Lawsuit, Pays $20,000 Fine, AllTwitter, December 8, 2011, http://www.mediabistro.com/alltwitter/the-ap-settles-over-nba-twitter-lawsuit-pays-20000-fine_b16514.

108 Michael Charron, Twitter: A "Caveat Emptor" Exception to Libel Law, 1 Berkley J. Ent. & Sports L. 57, 58 (2012).

109 Id. at 60.

110 Julie Hilden, Should the Law Treat Tweets the Same Way it Treats Printed Defamation? Justia.com, http://verdict.justia.com/2011/10/03/should-the-law-treat-defamatory-tweets-the-same-way-it-treats-printed-defamation (last accessed May 21, 2012).

111 Daxton R. "Chip" Stewart, When Retweets Attack: Are Twitter Users Liable for Republishing the Defamatory Tweets of Others? 90 Journ. & Mass Comm. Q (Summer 2013, in press).

112 See Ellyn M. Angelotti, Twibel Law: What Defamation and Its Remedies Look Like in the Age of Twitter, 13 J. High Tech. L. 430, 487–500 (2013).

113 Plaintiff's First Amended Petition, Leshers v. Does, No. 348-235791-09, http://www.citmedialaw.org/sites/citmedialaw.org/files/2009-07-28-First%20Amended%20Petition.pdf (last accessed May 21, 2012).

114 See Stephen Kruiser, GOP Consultant Jacobus Files Libel Suite against Trump and Lewandowski, PJ Media, April 18, 2016. Available at https://pjmedia.com/trending/2016/04/18/gop-consultant-jacobus-files-libel-suit-against-trump-and-lewandowski/?utm_source=twitterfeed&utm_medium=twitter

115 Sanders, supra note 71 at 117.

CHAPTER 3

Privacy and Terms of Use

Woodrow Hartzog

Cumberland School of Law
Samford University

ABSTRACT

Privacy is one of the most important social media concepts. The doctrine surrounding privacy and social media is fraught with uncertainty despite being increasingly governed by terms of use agreements and privacy policies. What information, if any, is private on social media? Courts and lawmakers have struggled to determine whether and to what degree personal information disclosed on social media is private under traditional tort remedies and online agreements. This chapter will examine privacy law in the social media environment, including the ineffectiveness of the privacy torts and the ascent of privacy policies and terms of use agreements.

Users of social media must disclose personal information in order to receive the benefits conferred by these online communities. This personal information is extremely valuable to social media companies and other social media users. Indeed, personal information is the fuel that powers the social media engine. However, the disclosure of personal information on social media leaves users vulnerable to privacy violations. This vulnerability has raised the question of whether privacy can even exist in online social networks.

Courts have struggled in trying to determine whether and to what degree personal information disclosed on social media is private under common law, administrative regulations, and statutes. However, the weaknesses inherent in the privacy torts, regulations, and statutes might not remain a problem for very long, because privacy disputes are increasingly governed by contracts between the user and the website.

In some respects, the ascension of contract law in the area of privacy might be useful. The traditional privacy torts are not well-suited to protect users of social media. In their place, a dubious patchwork of administrative and statutory laws ostensibly protects users from unauthorized disclosure by other users and the website itself. If clearly drafted and consistently enforced, contracts in the form of terms of use agreements and privacy policies can bring some degree of clarity to a great deal of, if not nearly all, self-disclosed online information implicating privacy. Yet this clarity can have unintended consequences for users who rarely understand or even read these dense, boilerplate agreements.

The current legal landscape of privacy, contracts, and social media is fraught with uncertainty. What information, if any, is private in online social networks? What laws protect this information? Is it reasonable for users to expect privacy in self-disclosed information? This chapter will examine privacy law in the social media environment, including the ineffectiveness of the privacy torts and the increasingly dominant role of contracts in the form of privacy policies and terms of use agreements.

PRIVACY LAW IS STRUGGLING WITH SOCIAL MEDIA

The proper legal response to the issue of social media and privacy has proven elusive because there is no fixed conceptualization of privacy.[1] Daniel Solove called privacy "a concept in disarray" that encompasses, among other things, the "freedom of thought, control over one's body, solitude in one's home, control over personal information, freedom from surveillance, protection of one's reputation, and protection from searches and interrogations."[2] The law's struggle to conceptualize privacy has often stunted its ability to adapt to rapid technological change.[3] That has been especially true with the Internet's rapid rise as courts grapple to define the contours of privacy in cyberspace.[4]

While privacy for social media users who cannot stop sharing information might seem contradictory, it is clear that users consider it important.[5] Today, people are disclosing very personal information on a wide array of websites. Commentators frequently argue that people who expose their deep secrets online do not value their privacy. Courts find they have no expectation of privacy.[6] The unprecedented sharing of private information on the Internet is leading some to herald the demise of privacy.[7]

It is far too easy, however, to conclude that because people are sharing private data online, they should expect no privacy. Many social media websites have elaborate privacy settings. Members of various online communities take considerable effort to manage the degree of exposure of their information.[8] Consider Facebook. Many individuals set their privacy settings so that only people they have designated as friends can see their information.[9] People using dating websites often set their profiles only to be visible to other members of the particular online dating community.[10] Members of online support communities for substance abuse problems also expect exposure only to other members of the community.[11] The emergence of Snapchat, for example, illustrates the importance that users place on privacy. People are attracted to apps like Snapchat because they promise more privacy by having the photos vanish after they are shared, making them more ephemeral than things shared on Facebook. Breaches of that promise of privacy and security, such as hacks that led to unauthorized access to user identities and phone numbers as well as several thousands of stored photos that dumped online in 2014, led to widespread criticism and intervention by the Federal Trade Commission (FTC).[12]

What happens when information leaks outside these communities? In short, privacy law has yet to figure out how to properly address the collection, use, and dissemination of personal information on social media. These practices on the Internet as a whole, which have been well-addressed by scholars,[13] leave Internet users such as those using social media vulnerable to a panoply of harms including excessive government and commercial entity surveillance, breach of confidentiality, misuse of personal information for such things as denial of employment or insurance benefits, damage to reputation, blackmail, loss of anonymity, chilled speech or association, and extreme emotional distress.[14]

Our current privacy protection regime is a patchwork of laws and remedies that are often muddled or in conflict with other laws and evolving technology. Privacy laws that limit the collection or disclosure of certain kinds of information or laws that are based on particular kinds of technology—for example, by classifying all communications into either wire, oral, or electronic communications—seem to create the most confusion.[15]

Many regulatory schemes governing privacy and social media inconsistently apply standards of "private" information or subjective tests such as one's "reasonable expectations of privacy."[16] Approaches that focus on the nature of the information are problematic because personal information is usually not seen as strictly private or public.[17] The same piece of information collected from social media can be considered sensitive in some circumstances and completely benign in others. For example, a Facebook user might post her new cell phone number to a discrete group of "friends," yet she might not want that information to be posted on her publicly available and widely read blog. Additionally, any law aimed at the suppression of a particular kind of expression is suspect under the First Amendment. These are just some of the many problems that inhibit the traditional tort-based approach to the protection of privacy.

THE GROWING IRRELEVANCE OF THE PRIVACY TORTS IN SOCIAL MEDIA

The traditional remedy for harms resulting from the publication of private information is the tort of pub lic disclosure of embarrassing private facts, also known as "the disclosure tort." The disclosure tort generally prohibits giving publicity to a matter concerning the private life of another, if the matter publicized is of a kind that would be highly offensive to a reasonable person and is not of legitimate concern to the public.[18] The flaws in the disclosure tort, including a difficulty in deciding when expectations of privacy are reasonable and when First Amendment concerns take precedence, have rendered it largely toothless to privacy harms occurring via social media.

The disclosure tort was extensively criticized before the Internet.[19] From its inception, the tort was troubled, and its faults became magnified over time. Joseph Elford noted in 1995 that "[t]he private facts tort is a mess. It has disappointed those who hope it would enhance individual privacy while it has exceeded all estimations of its chilling effect on speech."[20]

Several scholars claim the disclosure tort was rendered ineffective in 1989 in the case *Florida Star v. B.J.F.*[21] In this case, the U.S. Supreme Court declared that defendants cannot be punished for publishing matters of public significance without the claimant proving that punishment is necessary to advance a state interest of the highest order.[22] Andrew McClurg argued that this declaration almost guarantees defeat for plaintiffs pursuing claims based on the disclosure tort.[23] McClurg actually found that "[f]or the most part, the privacy torts as defined in the Second Restatement have functioned inadequately and fared poorly in the courts."[24]

However, the increased threat to privacy resulting from the technological destruction of any meaningful barriers to surveillance and publishing has rendered the disclosure tort nearly inert.[25] One scholar has argued that "[a]ttempts to apply traditional public disclosure jurisprudence to online social networking demonstrate the incoherence of this jurisprudence" because the disclosure tort is centered around keeping information from people and social networking is centered around disclosure and sharing of information.[26]

One of the main reasons the disclosure tort has been inconsistently applied and often unsuccessful for social media users is the amount of speculation the tort requires from judges. Judges regularly are called upon to make normative and subjective judgment pertaining to concepts like privacy, public concern, and offensiveness.[27] Critics assert that the cases often hinge on judges' imperfect estimates as to what society should expect.[28]

The tort also calls upon judges to determine what information is "private" and what information is public or at least "of public concern." Other scholars commenting on the tort have noted the practical and constitutional difficulty in defining the term "public" in order to determine whether information is worthy of privacy protections.[29] Dianne Zimmerman noted that "to distinguish private facts from 'public' information about an individual, courts often look either to the location of the action or to the nature of the subject matter. Courts using the 'location' analysis commonly state that information individuals reveal about themselves in public places is by definition not private."[30] Courts using the subject-matter analysis "rule that the subject matter is private even though the locus is not."[31] Zimmerman found that both approaches are practically unfeasible and threaten freedom of speech.

Perhaps the most significant failure of the privacy tort's application to social media is that the tort typically fails to protect self-disclosed information. Unlike Samuel Warren and Louis Brandeis, who worried in the late 1800s about tabloids publishing their private moments, the most likely publisher of personal information in the Internet age is the person herself.[32] In light of the mass adoption of social media and pervasiveness of electronically-mediated communication, Internet users have become their own worst enemy.

Online self-disclosure lies at the heart of the problem posed by social media. The rampant self-disclosure of personal information concomitant with an expectation of privacy is a problem because courts have struggled to determine whether and to what degree self-disclosed information is private.[33] Professor Lior Strahilevitz stated, "Despite the centrality of this issue, the American courts lack a coherent, consistent methodology for determining whether an individual has a reasonable expectation of privacy in a particular fact that has been shared with one or more persons."[34]

It is becoming increasingly clear that the privacy torts, particularly the disclosure tort, are ineffective in many scenarios involving social media. For practitioners, then, the main issue of concern is that of contract.

PRIVACY IN AN AGE OF CONTRACTS

Contracts have had a curious, bipolar relationship with privacy. As negotiated confidentiality agreements, contracts can be effective tools that help individuals control the flow of personal information. As standard-form contracts of adhesion, they can extract consent to practices that threaten the privacy of individuals who likely did not understand or even read the proposed terms. This schism rendering contracts as a cause of, and solution for, privacy problems has been magnified in a networked world, where individuals have more privity of contract than ever. Due to the ubiquity of terms of use agreements and privacy polices, the schism is widening. The erosion of privacy can be measured in standard-form contracts.

How did contracts come to have such a disparate impact on privacy? After all, in their famous article "The Right to Privacy," which influenced modern privacy law, Warren and Brandeis explicitly deemed contracts inadequate to protect individuals from the new privacy violations wrought by the technology of the late 1800s. Although the scholars recognized the utility of contracts, they asserted that because "modern devices afford abundant opportunities for the perpetration of [privacy harms] without any participation by the injured party, the protection granted by the law must be placed upon a broader foundation."[35] They went on to state:

> While, for instance, the state of photographic art was such that one's picture could seldom be taken without consciously "sitting" for the purpose, the law of contract or trust might afford the prudent man sufficient safeguards against the improper circulation of his portrait; But since the latest advances in photographic art have rendered it possible to take pictures surreptitiously, the doctrines of contract and of trust are inadequate to support the required protection, and the law of tort must be resorted to.[36]

Intimate and confidential information previously could have been contained by the injured party through trust and contracts, since those who most commonly obtained such information were dealt with at arm's length. Yet new technologies at the time, such as the Kodak handheld camera, enabled complete strangers to capture and disclose intimacies otherwise held in confidence.

Radio and television further frustrated an individual's ability to use contracts to protect their privacy. Because these technologies were one-way broadcast media, listeners and viewers were inundated with information about other people, yet the medium's audience had no discernible connection with each other. Initially, the Internet appeared to obliterate a user's ability to control collection and use of their information.[37] As personal information went viral online, the always-on convergence of text, photographs, audio, and video seemed to render contracts ineffective as a means of protecting privacy. After all, most Internet users are strangers to each other, and contracts provide no remedy against people with whom we have no connection.

Yet, the primary function of the Internet is to connect people. These connections can create a privity of contract between websites and users. Privity, an essential element for a binding contract, is defined as "The connection or relationship between two parties, each having a legally recognized interest in the same subject matter."[38] Contracts between websites and users are typically seen in the form of terms of use. These omnipresent online agreements have come to significantly govern the privacy of Internet users. With online agreements seemingly on every website, the 74% of Americans online each day likely enter into dozens of contracts that impact the flow of their personal information.[39] These agreements are adjudicated under standard-form contract doctrine because they are perceived as non-negotiable. This means users are regularly bound by terms they didn't read or understand—a common critique of all standard-form contracts. The mass proliferation of standard-form contracts[40] has significant consequences for information privacy on social media.

STANDARD FORM CONTRACTS AND SOCIAL MEDIA

Fundamentally, a contract is "a promise or a set of promises that the law will enforce."[41] Thus contracts exist to bind parties to promises by creating legal obligations. Some of these obligations can protect an individual's privacy. For example, confidentiality agreements prohibit the disclosure of information that at least one of the parties to a contract wishes to keep private.

Yet the enforceability of many social media agreements also might prohibit a user from denying "consent" to practices regarding the disclosure of personal information even if he or she failed to read the relevant terms. In any event, for good or bad, contracts that address privacy issues provide a degree of clarity.[42]

The traditional rule holds that in order for a contract to be valid the parties must reach a "meeting of the minds." In other words, both parties to the contract must agree to be bound by mutually understood terms.[43] In recent years, some critics have asserted that the traditional rules of contract law, "based on the ideal of two humans meeting in person to agree to terms, have been modified almost to the point of non-existence."[44]

As evidence, these critics cite the fact that courts do not consider the actual state of mind of the parties, but rather what they objectively conveyed to each other when forming the contract—known as "the objective theory of contract."[45] The emergence of online agreements has only hastened this evolution to objectivity by flooding the market with contracts.

Online contracts have traditionally been categorized as "browsewrap" or "clickwrap" agreements, although that distinction can be blurred at times.[46] "A clickwrap agreement is electronically transmitted and requires clicking on a button indicating an assent prior to downloading software or accessing a web site."[47] Browsewrap agreements dictate that additional "browsing" past the homepage constitutes acceptance of the contract, regardless of whether the user knows it or not.[48] The most important kinds of browsewrap and clickwrap contracts for the purposes of this chapter are terms of use agreements.

Wayne Barnes asserted that:

> [t]hrough a few clicks of the mouse, consumers are agreeing in record numbers to unfavorable, one-sided terms in adhesion contracts. These include many of the standard favorite terms of businesses, such as arbitration clauses, damage limitations, and warranty disclaimers. But, in the online and software contract context, it also increasingly includes new creations such as spyware clauses and severe license restrictions.[49]

Some of the most problematic areas of online contracting are the noticeable presentation of offers and formation of assent. "Courts presented with the issue [of online agreements] apply traditional principles of contract law and focus on whether the plaintiff had reasonable notice of and manifested assent to the online agreement."[50] Specifically regarding browsewrap agreements, courts "have held that 'the validity of a browsewrap turns on whether a website user has actual or constructive knowledge of a site's terms and conditions prior to using the site.'"[51] Thus, in order to be bound, parties need not have a "meeting of the minds." Rather, a "reasonable communication" of the terms will suffice.[52]

The reasonable communication requirement is a combination "of reasonable notice of the contractual nature of the offered terms and the opportunity to review those terms[,]" which serves as a "proxy for the offeree's clear manifestation of assent."[53] A reasonable communication of terms gives rise to what is commonly referred to as the offeree's "duty to read."[54] In other words, if the terms of a contract are reasonably communicated, the offeree cannot then absolve herself from liability for failing to read them, because she had a legal duty to do so.

The notice requirement is fulfilled differently for clickwrap and browsewrap agreements.[55] While notice for clickwrap agreements can be satisfied by prohibiting a user through code from proceeding without first having the opportunity to review the contract, notice in browsewrap agreements "is given through conspicuous display of the contract."[56]

Mutual assent to a contract is typically manifested in the process of offer and acceptance.[57] Both offer and acceptance are categorized by an outward manifestation of intent to be bound.[58] Related to the requirement of assent, traditional contract doctrine also imposes on the parties a "duty to read."[59] Edith Warkentine noted that the practical result of this duty is that "if a party objectively manifests assent to be bound to a contract (for example, by signing a written contract document), a court will almost automatically find assent to all terms contained in the writing."[60] Thus, parties will find little relief in defenses like "I didn't read it" or "I didn't understand it."[61]

Yet, notwithstanding all of the academic attention paid to the problems with terms of use,[62] courts seem to be struggling less than scholars regarding their enforceability. A recent survey of online boilerplate cases concluded that:

> [a]n offeree who "signs" an agreement by hitting the "I accept" button is bound to its terms just as much as will someone who signs a paper contract. Repeat and sophisticated players will be more likely bound by more ambiguous forms of assent than will innocent ones.[63]

Thus, standard-form contract doctrine on the Web, while controversial, is largely stable. Courts relying on this doctrine give great weight to the specific language of the terms, often with little regard to other understandings and representations that arise within relationships. Thus, these terms have great significance for user privacy.

PROBLEMS RELATED TO PRIVACY AND TERMS OF USE IN SOCIAL MEDIA

Privacy Policies

Seemingly every social media website has a privacy policy. Privacy policies explain how a website will use a visitor's personal information.[64] Allyson Haynes has found that these policies "have appeared all over the Internet both in response to increases in legislation requiring such disclosure, and as a voluntary measure by websites to appeal to consumers by emphasizing the care with which they treat consumer information."[65] These policies are perhaps most significant as tools by which the FTC can regulate unfair and deceptive trade practices. Courts have recognized the power of the FTC in this area, making the agency a key player in regulating privacy and data security on behalf of Internet users.[66]

While privacy policies, on their face, are often simply statements of a website's practices, many websites incorporate the policy into their terms of use as, according to Haynes, "binding upon visitors, using the language of contract and assent."[67] Most dictate that a user manifests assent to the policy by simply using the website, which is a form of a "browsewrap" contract. Haynes found that "the typical privacy policy includes, or incorporates by reference, a slew of terms both relating to privacy (and often allowing sharing and multiple uses of personal information) and relating to other rights of the consumer."[68] However, in some of the most prominent court decisions addressing breach of contract claims arising from privacy policies, courts have not enforced the privacy policy against the website owner.[69]

Pamela Samuelson found promise in the binding nature of privacy policies. She argues that:

> [a]s between the website and the user, a privacy policy bears all the earmarks of a contract, but perhaps one enforceable only at the option of the user. It is no stretch to regard the policy as an offer to treat information in specified ways, inviting a user's acceptance by using the site or submitting the information. The website's promise is sufficient consideration to support a contractual obligation, as is the user's use of the site and submission of personal data.[70]

However, Haynes argued that such binding policies can actually provide a liability shield for companies looking to take advantage of a user's failure to read by selling or sharing that user's personal information.[71]

As applied to most commercial websites, the existing legislation requires that a privacy policy be posted, and that the entity abide by that policy, but does not regulate the substance of that policy. No law prevents a website operator from sharing or selling personal information it has lawfully been given, although a website can be held liable for failing to notify its customers of its practice of selling or sharing such information. As long as they comply with the disclosure requirement, websites are free to state in their privacy policies that they will treat a visitor's personal information virtually any way they wish, arguably immunizing themselves from liability for such treatment.[72]

Others have noted that privacy policies and other online agreements included provisions that permitted websites to track and exploit user information.[73] Nancy Kim stated that "even those users that have some knowledge of website customer privacy practices may not have an accurate perception of the nature or extent of such practices. Websites may respond to customer ignorance by inserting increasingly more aggressive and intrusive terms in 'wrap contracts'."[74]

Thus, the true effect of privacy policies on an individual, like standard-form contracts in general, is dependent upon the drafter of the contract. A number of lawsuits have been filed by website users claiming breach of contract and promissory estoppel resulting from a website's violation of their privacy policy.[75] However, applying a strict standard-form contract analysis, a number of courts have denied any meaningful recovery for a website breaking promises it made in a privacy policy.[76]

Behavioral Restrictions

Many of the privacy threats created by the actions of other individuals are explicitly prohibited by online contracts. For example, in September 2007, a cheerleading coach at Pearl High School in Mississippi required the members of her cheerleading squad to reveal the usernames and passwords of their Facebook accounts.[77] With this information, school officials could access the private profiles of all of those students' "friends." However, as part of the registration process, Facebook requires a promise that "[y]ou will not share your password . . . let anyone else access your account, or do anything else that might jeopardize the security of your account."[78]

These requests for access to protected information are seemingly on the rise. The Florida Board of Bar Examiners and the city of Bozeman, Montana, have also implemented policies requesting an individual's username and password for online services.[79] Indeed, the trend is not even limited to state action—employers have now begun to request access to their employees' profiles in order to access private content.[80] Terms of use, like those proposed by Facebook, often explicitly prohibit this activity. Yet it remains to be seen what effect that prohibition might have. Maryland has responded to these requests by passing legislation explicitly prohibiting the practice of employers asking current employees as well as job applicants for access to their social media accounts.[81]

Restrictions on behavior in terms of use could be beneficial to others using the same website. For example, the social network website Facebook encourages millions daily to share personal information as a part of the site. Unsurprisingly, its terms of use prohibit certain kinds of user activity that could deter the disclosure of information.[82] Users might not disclose information if they feel their privacy is threatened. These terms are representative of terms commonly found on social network sites,[83] and are useful examples of terms of use that specifically address privacy issues.

Information harvesting by third parties also threatens individuals' privacy,[84] and is typically governed via terms of use. A number of entities have employed "web scraper" software to systematically and automatically access and download ownership information from websites.

Facebook mandates that visitors "will not collect users' content or information, or otherwise access Facebook, using automated means (such as harvesting bots, robots, spiders, or scrapers) without our permission."[85] It goes on to state that "[i]f you collect information from users, you will: obtain their consent, make it clear you (and not Facebook) are the one collecting their information, and post a privacy policy explaining what information you collect and how you will use it."[86] Thus, terms of use can regulate both automated and non-automated collection of information from social media.

Behavior restrictions can be beneficial terms for website users. Typically, they attempt to keep an online community civil and relatively safe while protecting their users from abuse. Yet, under traditional contract analysis, the restrictions only indirectly benefit website users. Only the website, not the users, can enforce these restrictions. Could users ever invoke these terms in a cause of action against other users who violate the behavior restrictions?

Contracts and Reasonable Expectations of Privacy

Social media terms of use and privacy policies can also affect whether users have a reasonable expectation of privacy. The Fourth Amendment only protects individuals from a governmental search of information if society recognizes that an expectation of privacy in that information was reasonable. Orin Kerr stated "[t]he 'reasonable expectation of privacy' test governs Fourth Amendment law, and it is up to the courts to determine when an expectation of privacy is 'reasonable'."[87] Regarding a determination of "reasonable," a number of courts have found that "the terms of service agreement or subscriber agreement . . . are relevant to characterizing objective privacy interests."[88]

Courts have typically found that terms of use can dispel an expectation of privacy regardless of whether the user actually read the terms.[89] In *United States v. Hart*,[90] the government sought and obtained personal information from an email the defendant allegedly used to commit a crime. As part of the email registration process, the defendant consented to terms of service that required the user to acknowledge that his personal information might be disclosed to comply with legal process.[91] The court found that given the defendant consented to the terms of use, "it is difficult to conclude that [the defendant] has an actual expectation of privacy in the contents of any communications sent or received with his Yahoo! accounts."[92]

Fourth Amendment cases are not the only ones to consider the effect of terms of use on a user's expectation of privacy.[93] Courts grappling with issues of anonymity and the public disclosure of private facts have tackled the issue, with results that—if not inconsistent—are highly dependent upon the terms of the contract.

Social Media Contracts and the Maintenance of Anonymity

Social media terms of use and privacy policies can also affect the anonymity of the user. The Supreme Court has repeatedly held that the First Amendment protects anonymous speech and expressive activity.[94] Yet anonymous speech can also cause harm that results in lawsuits that aim to expose the speaker's identity.[95] In order to balance the interest of the speaker with the interest of the harmed person or entity, courts often employ a balancing test. This determines whether a court will compel the exposure of an individual's identity. One of the factors a court considers when determining whether to compel identity disclosure is "the expectation of privacy held by the Doe defendants, as well as other innocent users who may be dragged into the case (for example, because they shared an IP address with an alleged infringer)."[96]

While a court's decision whether contract terms establish an expectation of privacy is naturally dependent upon the text of the agreement, interpretation of what a user should expect from the language varies. Some have interpreted the vague nature of online agreements to mean that users naturally expect privacy if the website offers general promises of confidentiality.

For example, in *McVicker v. King*,[97] the United States District Court for the Western District of Pennsylvania in 2010 considered whether to grant a motion to compel the disclosure of records that could identify seven anonymous users who commented on a website's message board. The website objected to the motion as an "attempt to strip anonymity from those who choose to engage in political discussion and debate on its website."[98]

The plaintiff asserted, among other things, that the terms of use of the blog did not create any expectation of privacy because they didn't explicitly provide that the identity of the user would be protected.[99]

The court disagreed. Instead, the court found that "[t]he Privacy Policy clearly reflects that Total Trib Media will disclose its users' personally identifiable information only in very limited situations. Thus, the Court finds that the terms of service of the blog create an expectation of privacy for any registered user."[100]

Other courts provide no such benefit to contract adherents. In *London-Sire Records v. Doe 1*,[101] record companies brought copyright infringement claims against several unnamed defendants using peer-to-peer file-sharing software to download music. The United States District Court for the District of Massachusetts attributed great importance to the ISP's (Boston University) terms of use agreement, stating the "agreement could conceivably make a substantial difference to the expectation of privacy a student has in his or her internet use."[102]

The court foreshadowed what it was seeking by requesting additional evidence of the terms of use agreement when it stated "many internet service providers require their users to acknowledge as a condition of service that they are forbidden from infringing copyright owners' rights, and that the ISP may be required to disclose their identity in litigation."[103]

Although it would later be reversed on other grounds, the United States District Court for the District of Columbia in *In re Verizon Internet Services*[104] had similar strong words for a plaintiff's expectation of privacy in light of terms of use:

> In the end, Verizon's customers should have little expectation
> of privacy (or anonymity) in infringing copyrights. Subscribers to
> Verizon's Internet services are put on clear notice that they cannot
> use Verizon's service or network to infringe copyrights. In fact, as
> part of its corporate policy, Verizon alerts its subscribers at the
> outset that it will "disclose individual customer information to an
> outside entity . . . when Verizon is served with valid legal process
> for customer information." And if an individual subscriber opens
> his computer to permit others, through peer-to-peer filesharing, to
> download materials from that computer, it is hard to understand
> just what privacy expectation he or she has after essentially
> opening the computer to the world.[105]

Thus, terms of use can also be used as evidence to destroy a social media user's pseudonymity.[106]

Courts have split when dealing with unmasking anonymous or pseu-dononymous social media users, typically looking to balance the harms to people suing for injury with the harms to free speech of posters. For example, in 2015, the federal court for the Northern District of California refused to enforce subpoenas against multiple Twitter users in a defamation case, expressing concern that requiring Twitter to identify its users would "unduly chill speech" in what appeared to be a questionable libel suit.[107]

Contracts and Unfair or Deceptive Trade Practices

The Federal Trade Commission (FTC) has recently taken a keen interest in the privacy practices of social media, particularly focusing on adherence and changes to social media privacy policies.[108] Social media could be found liable for a deceptive or unfair trade practice even if the website's terms of use and privacy policies purportedly gained the consent of their users for collection and use of their personal information.[109]

Susan Gindin noted that the

> FTC has long required that businesses clearly and conspicuously
> disclose material facts, and that an act or practice is deceptive
> and therefore a violation of the FTC Act if it is: likely to mislead
> consumers acting reasonably under the circumstances; and is
> "material"—that is, important to a consumer's decision to buy or
> use the product.[110]

However, Gindin noted that "while the FTC has become increasingly active in requiring that companies provide conspicuous notice of material terms, the courts have almost unanimously enforced online contracts against consumers—even those with so-called 'hidden terms.'"[111]

An excellent example of the role of the FTC in contractual privacy disputes is its 2009 action against Sears. Here, Sears distributed a software application that allowed Sears to track consumers' online behavior, as well as some offline activities.[112] Sears included a Privacy Statement and licensing agreement with the software that "described the Tracking Application in detail, and before a consumer agreed to have the Tracking Application installed, the consumer was required to check a box"[113] acknowledging those terms had been read. Yet, in a move that potentially renders the standard practices for obtaining consent ineffective, the FTC argued that the disclosures made by Sears were not adequate to avoid deceiving consumers.[114]

Similarly, the FTC took action in 2014 against Goldenshores Technologies, a developer that created the Brightest Flashlight application for Android devices, because the privacy policy was deceptive. The FTC found that the policy misrepresented how personal data, including geolocation information, was being gathered from users by the flashlight app. As part of a settlement with the FTC, Goldenshores was required to delete personal information it had collected. Further, the company had to make disclosures that fully informed users "when, how, and why their geolocation information is being collected, used, and shared," and it was required to obtain affirmative consent from users before gathering and sharing this information.[115]

Some states have also acted under "mini-FTC" statutes to bring actions against entities that mislead consumers about the confidentiality of their personal information.[116]

Terms of Use and Liability as an Unauthorized Social Media User

Breaching a social media website's terms of use agreement could result in more than just contractual liability. A number of statutes that were designed to prevent computer fraud and misuse revolve around the concept of an "unauthorized user." If a user breaches the proposed terms of use, are they still authorized to use the website?

As previously discussed, restrictions on user behavior in online agreements can protect other user's privacy. These restrictions on behavior are common, so statutory penalties for breaching these contracts could be pervasive. Recall the Facebook prohibitions on soliciting login information, disclosing passwords, providing false personal information, and information harvesting.[117]

Some of the most recent relevant attempts to leverage terms of use violations have been through application of the Computer Fraud and Abuse Act

(CFAA). The CFAA is a statute that criminalizes the unauthorized access, or use in excess of authorization of, a computer.[118] The CFAA permits a website owner in its terms of use to "spell out explicitly what is forbidden" or unauthorized on its site.[119] Breaches of these contracts can then be used to demonstrate a lack of authorization for site use under the CFAA.[120] The statute provides that "whoever . . . intentionally access[es] a computer without authorization or exceeds authorized access, and thereby obtains [. . .] information from any protected computer if the conduct involved an interstate or foreign communication" is in violation of the statute.[121] For example, the Second Circuit Court of Appeals allowed a woman's case under the CFAA to proceed after she alleged that her ex-boyfriend had unlawfully accessed her Facebook account, changed her password, and posted malicious statements about her sex life.[122]

In *United States v. Lori Drew*,[123] the prosecution relied upon the theory that Drew's cyberbullying of another user violated the MySpace terms of use. According to the prosecution, these violations negated MySpace's authorization for Drew to access MySpace's networked computers, thus violating the CFAA. However, U.S. District Court Judge Wu largely rejected this interpretation, stating

> if any conscious breach of a website's terms of service is held to be sufficient by itself to constitute intentionally accessing a computer without authorization or in excess of authorization, the result will be that section 1030(a)(2)(C) becomes a law 'that affords too much discretion to the police and too little notice to citizens who wish to use the [Internet].'[124]

This theory was also unsuccessful in *A.V. v. iParadigms*[125] and *Southwest Airlines Co. v. BoardFirst*[126] largely due to findings of insufficient damages alleged by the plaintiffs.

Yet the issue of whether violation of terms of use can be considered a violation of the CFAA is still a point of contention. Courts have relied upon terms of use violations to support liability under the CFAA in other contexts, most notably to enforce prohibitions on junk electronic communication.[127]

However, in *Facebook v. Power Ventures*,[128] the United States District Court for the Northern District of California ruled that merely violating a website's terms of use cannot constitute a violation of the CFAA.[129] Thus, the issue has not been definitively resolved. Given the availability of statutory damages and injunctive relief available under the CFAA,[130] this statute has emerged as a potential amplifier of the impact of contracts on privacy disputes stemming from the use of social media.

User Consent to Surveillance

Finally, social media terms of use agreements might even serve as consent to surveillance under a few statutes. Numerous electronic surveillance or privacy of commercial and personal data statutes deal with some form of "unauthorized" activity. The Stored Communications Act[131] (SCA) prohibits accessing without authorization or exceeding authorization digital or electronic technology to access an electronic communication.[132] The Wiretap Act as part of the Electronic Communications Privacy Act (ECPA) does not apply if one of the parties to an electronic communication consents to surveillance.[133]

Orin Kerr has questioned whether clicking through presented terms can constitute notice sufficient to satisfy the "consent" exceptions to these statutes. He discussed the use of "banners" or "messages that greet computer users when they log on to a network" informing them their communications might be monitored.[134] He noted that while banners can generate consent to monitoring, he questioned whether it was "sufficient if the notice of monitoring can be found somewhere in the Terms of Service or an employee manual."[135] While it is unclear exactly what constitutes consent under these statutes, it is possible that terms of use could play an important role.

WHAT DOES ALL OF THIS MEAN FOR PRIVACY?

Unfortunately, privacy in social media remains a vague and constantly evolving concept. Social norms and context play a large role in any such determination, thus standardized rules must be largely displaced with factually-specific determinations. To that end, the best strategy for social media users is to take a full stock of what context and cues are available when trying to determine whether to disclose personal information or determining if the disclosures of others are private.

Such context and cues can come primarily from three sources:

1. the terms of use;
2. technological protections such as privacy settings; and
3. the nature of the information itself in (and out) of context.

Beause most social media websites mandate respect for the privacy of others and personal information in their terms of use, users must be aware that the information posted is likely not a free-for-all.

Instead, consider whether the user utilized privacy settings. If so, how restrictive are they? How many people were potentially privy to the same information? How sensitive is the information? Did the user hide his or her identity with a pseudonym, initials, or only his or her first name? Would the information make sense devoid of the context in which it was disclosed, or could extraction from context distort the message?

Also, while the terms of use might be dense and lengthy, they are also consequential. Although the enforceability of many of these terms is questionable, as is the viability of a breach of contract claim by Facebook for their violation, what is clear is that Facebook will rely on the violation of these terms to justify suspension or deletion of a user account. This is true even though most violations of these terms go unpunished because the violations are too vague or too numerous.

Ultimately, it is important to consider that while it may seem that another user's disclosure of personal information online is public, in many instances that user would disagree. Empirical research demonstrates that social media users regularly consider information disclosed on the website as private to some degree.[136] Only a careful consideration of context and cues will help you navigate the grey area of privacy within online communities.

FREQUENTLY ASKED QUESTIONS

1. If a social media user posts information to their profile, can I assume that it is not private information and thus free to use?

There is no categorically absolute answer to this question. Context, the nature of the information, the role of the user and your relationship with that user, the privacy settings, and any other implied or explicit terms of disclosure are all relevant in determining if information shared within a social network site can be appropriately shared or used elsewhere.

In any event, it is important to remember that all users are bound by both the terms of use and the other relevant duties such as those arising from tort law such as the duty to refrain from public disclosure of privacy facts and intentional infliction of emotional distress.

2. If someone posts an embarrassing picture of me on a social network site, what are my legal rights to remove it or collect damages?

Legal protection in these circumstances can vary. Your rights to have a photograph or piece of information about you removed or to collect damages are entirely dependent upon the context in which the photo was taken, the content of the photo, the extent of disclosure, the terms of use of the website, the technological allowances and dispute resolution procedures of the website, and your relationship to the poster of the photograph or piece of information.

Little *ex ante* advice can be given here, given the variables that can determine your rights. For example, was the photo taken in public? The term "public" itself has no fixed definition and is difficult to determine in practice. Additionally, a number of safeguards protect hosts and disclosers of information such as the First Amendment and Section 230 of the Communications Decency Act, which insulates websites from liability for hosting potentially harmful material that was posted by a third party.

Did you take the photo yourself? If so, you might be able to assert your copyright to take the photo down using the "notice and takedown" procedure provided for in the Digital Millennium Copyright Act. (See any social media website's terms of use for more information.)

The most efficient and low-cost method to have embarrassing photographs and information removed from social media is to utilize their internal technological controls or dispute resolution mechanisms. For example, Facebook and other social media provide users with the option of "tagging" certain photos as inappropriate, which could lead to their removal.

3. Am I bound by terms of use and privacy policies if I don't read them?

Yes. While not all terms of use agreements are enforceable, courts have almost uniformly rejected the "I didn't read or understand them" defense. This is known as "the objective theory of contracts."

4. Are all terms of use agreements enforceable? What about if I am just browsing a website?

It appears as though most courts are willing to enforce agreements where you "click" a button to indicate your agreement. Because most social media require such an action during the registration process, social media users with a registered profile are likely bound by the terms of use.

However, courts have been more reluctant to enforce agreements where the terms stipulate mere "use" (e.g., browsing) of the website constitutes acceptance of the terms. These so-called "browsewrap" agreements must be prominent and clearly noticeable (e.g., not at the bottom of the page) to be enforceable.

5. Is each term within the agreement enforceable?

Even if a terms of use agreement is found to be binding, not every term in the agreement is automatically enforceable. While many of the standard terms, including many behavioral restrictions and user consent to common information practices have been found to be enforceable, some terms such as "we reserve the right to modify this agreement at any time without notice" have been ruled unenforceable.[137] Additionally, the doctrine of "unconscionability" limits the enforceability of some contractual terms such as some one-sided arbitration agreements.

Unconscionability is the main tool used by courts to reject some or all terms in standard-form contracts.[138] While "substantive unconscionability" supports the invalidation of fundamentally "unfair" or one-sided terms, procedural unconscionability focuses on deficiencies in the actual formation of the contract resulting from lack of knowledge of some or all of the terms or lack of voluntariness.[139] Thus, if a term stipulated that you promise to give up your kidney in exchange for use of a social media website, that term would likely not be enforceable because it was substantively unconscionable. Likewise, if a social media website tricked you into clicking "I Agree" by designing the "Cancel" button to indicate acceptance to the terms, then that agreement would likely be procedurally unconscionable.

NOTES

1 See, e.g., Daniel Solove, Understanding Privacy 1 (2008); see also Julie C. Innes, Privacy, Intimacy, and Isolation 3 (1992); Hyman Gross, The Concept of Privacy, 43 N.Y.U. L. Rev. 34, 35 (1967); Ruth Gavison, Privacy and the Limits of Law, 89 Yale L. J. 421 (1980); Alan Westin, Privacy and Freedom (1967); Daniel Solove, A Taxonomy of Privacy, 154 U. Penn. L. Rev. 477 (2006); Robert C. Post, Three Concepts of Privacy, Geo. L. Jour. 2087, 2087 (2001).

2 Solove, Understanding Privacy, supra note 1 at 1.

3 See, e.g., Neil Richards & Daniel Solove, Prosser's Privacy Law: A Mixed Legacy, 98 Cal. L. Rev. 1887 (2010); Daniel Solove, Conceptualizing Privacy, 90 Cal. L. Rev. 1087 (2002); Neil Richards, The Limits of Tort Privacy, 9 J. on Telecomm. & High Tech. L. 357 (2011).

4 See, e.g., Moreno v. Hanford Sentinel, 172 Cal. App. 4th 1125, 1128 (Cal. Ct. App. 2009); cf Pietrylo v. Hillstone Restaurant Group, 2008 WL 6085437 (D.N.J.).

5 See Patricia Sanchez Abril, A (My)Space of One's Own: On Privacy and Online Social Networks, 6 Nw. J. Tech. & Intell. Prop. 73, 77 (2007).

6 See Moreno v. Hanford Sentinel, 2009 WL 866795 (Cal. App. Ct. 2009); see also, Diane Zimmerman, Requiem for a Heavyweight: A Farewell to Warren and Brandeis's Privacy Tort, 68 Cornell L. Rev. 291 (1983); Solveig Singleton, Privacy Versus the First Amendment: A Skeptical Approach, 11 Fordham Intell. Prop. Media & Ent. L.J. 97 (2000).

7 Eve Fairbanks, The Porn Identity, New Republic, February 6, 2006.

8 Emily Christofides, Amy Muise, & Desmarais Serge, Information Disclosure and Control on Facebook: Are They Two Sides of the Same Coin or Two Different Processes?, 12(3) CyberPsychology & Behavior 341 (2009); Zeynep Tufekci, Can You See Me Now? Audience and Disclosure Regulation in Online Social Network Sites, 28(1) Bulletin of Science, Technology & Society 20 (2008).

9 Christofides et al., supra note 8.

10 Jennifer Gibbs, Nicole Ellison, & Rebecca Heino, Self-Presentation in Online Personals: The Role of Anticipated Future Interaction, Self-Disclosure, and Perceived Success in Internet Dating, 33(2) Communication Research 152 (2006).

11 See, e.g., Alcoholics Anonymous, A.A. Guidelines – Internet, http://www.aa.org/en_pdfs/mg-18_internet.pdf.

12 Federal Trade Commission, Snapchat Settles FTC Charge That Promises of Disappearing Messages Were False (May 8, 2014), https://www.ftc.gov/news-events/press-releases/2014/05/snapchat-settles-ftc-charges-promises-disappearing-messages-were

13 See, e.g., Daniel Solove, The Digital Person (2004).

14 See, e.g., Solove, Taxonomy, supra note 1; M. Ryan Calo, The Boundaries of Privacy Harm, 86 Ind. L.J. 1131 (2011).

15 See, e.g., Electronic Communications Privacy Act of 1986, 18 U.S.C. §§ 2510–2522, 2701–2709 (2011).

16 See, e.g., Daniel Solove, Fourth Amendment Pragmatism, 51 B.C. L. Rev. 1511 (2010) (arguing that the "reasonable expectation of privacy" test should be abandoned).

17 See, e.g., Helen Nissenbaum, Privacy in Context (2009); Sharon Sandeen, Relative Privacy: What Privacy Advocates Can Learn from Trade Secret Law, 2006 Mich. St. L. Rev. 667, 694 (2006).

18 Restatement (Second) of Torts § 652 D.

19 See, e.g., Harry Klaven, Jr., Privacy in Tort Law – Were Warren and Brandeis Wrong?, 31 L. & Contemp. Probs. 326, 327 (1966).

20 Joseph Elford, Trafficking in Stolen Information: A "Hierarchy of Rights" Approach to the Private Facts Tort, 105 Yale L. J. 727 (1995).

21 491 U.S. 524 (1999).

22 491 U.S. at 533.

23 Andrew J. McClurg, Kiss and Tell: Protecting Intimate Relationship Privacy Through Implied Contracts of Confidentiality, 887 U. Cincinnati L. Rev. 877, 899 (2006).

24 Id. at 908.

25 Abril, supra note 5.

26 Id. at 3.

27 Id. at 10.

28 Id. at 10 (citing Albert W. Alschuler, Interpersonal Privacy and the Fourth Amendment, 4 N. Ill. U. L. Rev. 1, 8 n. 12 (1983)).

29 Zimmerman, supra note 6; Singleton, supra note 6.

30 Zimmerman, supra note 6 at 347.

31 Id. at 349.

32 Daniel Solove, The Slow Demise of Defamation and Privacy Torts, Huffington Post, October 12, 2010, http://www.huffingtonpost.com/daniel-j-solove/the-slow-demise-of-defama_b_758570.html; Lauren Gelman, Privacy, Free Speech, and Blurry-Edged Social Networks, 50 B.C. L. Rev. 1315 (2009); James Grimmelmann, Saving Facebook, 94 Iowa L. Rev. 1137, 1197 (2009).

33 Lior J. Strahilevitz, A Social Networks Theory of Privacy, 72 U. Chi. L. Rev. 919, 920–921 (2005).

34 Id.

35 Samuel D. Warren & Louis D. Brandeis, The Right to Privacy, 4 Harv. L. Rev. 193 (1890).

36 Id. at 211.

37 See, Daniel Solove, The Future of Reputation (2007); Helen Nissenbaum, Privacy in Context (2009).

38 Black's Law Dictionary (8th ed. 2004).

39 74% of Americans Online, Pew Internet & American Life Project (2009), http://pewresearch.org/databank/dailynumber/?NumberID=948.

40 Friedrich Kessler, Contracts of Adhesion—Some Thoughts About Freedom of Contract, 43 Colum. L. Rev. 629, 640 (1943).

41 E. Allan Farnsworth, Farnsworth on Contracts § 1.1, at 4 (Little, Brown & Co. 1999); see also Restatement (Second) of Contracts § 1 (1981) (defining contracts as "A contract is a promise or a set of promises for the breach of which the law gives a remedy, or the performance of which the law in some way recognizes as a duty").

42 See, e.g., Pamela Samuelson, Privacy As Intellectual Property?, 52 Stan. L. Rev. 1125 (2000); Peter P. Swire & Robert E. Litan, None of Your Business: World Data Flows, Electronic Commerce, and the European Privacy Directive 8 (1998).

43 Juliet Moringiello, Signals, Assent and Internet Contracting, 57 Rutgers L. Rev. 1307, 1311 (2005).

44 Id.

45 Id.

46 See, e.g., Hotels.com v. Canales, 195 S.W.3d 147 (Tex. Ct. App. 2006).

47 Nancy Kim, Clicking and Cringing, 86 Or. L. Rev. 797, 799 (2007).

48 See Specht v. Netscape Comm. Corp., 306 F.3d 17 (2d Cir. 2002); Register.com, Inc. v. Verio, Inc., 356 F.3d 393 (2d Cir. 2004); Pollstar v. Gigmania Ltd., 170 F. Supp2d 974 (E.D. Cal. 2000).

49 Wayne Barnes, Toward a Fairer Model of Consumer Assent to Standard Form Contracts: In Defense of Restatement Section 211(3), 82 Wash. L. Rev. 227, 228 (2007).

50 Burcham v. Expedia, 2009 U.S. Dist. LEXIS 17104 (citing Feldman v. Google, Inc., 513 F. Supp. 2d 229, 236 (E.D. Pa. 2007); Specht v. Netscape Comm. Corp., 306 F.3d 17, 28-30 (2nd Cir. 2002)).

51 Id. at *8 (citing Register.com, Inc. v. Verio, Inc., 356 F.3d 393, 429 (2d Cir. 2004)).

52 See, e.g., Register.com, Inc. v. Verio, Inc., 356 F.3d 393, 429 (2d Cir. 2004).

53 Moringiello, supra note 43 at 1314.

54 Id.

55 Ian Rambarran & Robert Hunt, Are Browse-Wrap Agreements All They Are Wrapped Up To Be?, 9 Tul. J. Tech. & Intell. Prop. 173, 176 (2007).

56 Id.

57 Edith Warkentine, Beyond Unconscionability: The Case for Using "Knowing Assent" as the Basis for Analyzing Unbargained-For Terms in Standard Form Contracts, 31 Seattle U. L. Rev. 469, 475 (2008).

58 Id.

59 Id. at 476.

60 Id.

61 Id.

62 See Richard Craswell, Property Rules and Liability Rules in Unconscionability and Related Doctrines, 60 U. Chi. L. Rev. 1, 9–10 (1993).

63 Id.

64 Allyson Haynes, Online Privacy Policies: Contracting Away Control Over Personal Information?, 111 Penn St. L. Rev. 587, 594 (2007).

65 Id.

66 FTC v. Wyndham Worldwide Corp., 799 F.3d 236 (3rd Cir. 2015); see also Woodrow Hartzog & Daniel J. Solove, The Scope and Potential of FTC Data Protection, 83 George Wash. L. Rev. 2230 (2015).

67 Haynes supra note 64 at 598.

68 Id.

69 In re Northwest Airlines Privacy Litigation, 2004 WL 1278459 (D. Minn. 2004) (finding that the privacy statement did not constitute a unilateral contract and that plaintiff must have read the policy to rely on it); Dyer v. Northwest Airlines Corp., 334 F. Supp. 2d 1196 (D.N.D. 2004) (finding that plaintiffs failed to allege that they read, understood or relied upon the privacy policy and failed to allege contractual damages); In re Jet Blue Airways Corp. Privacy Litigation, 379 F. Supp. 2d 299 (E.D.N.Y. 2005).

70 Samuelson, supra note 42 at 1164–1165.

71 Haynes, supra note 64 at 594.

72 Id. (citations omitted).

73 Nancy S. Kim, Wrap Contracts and Privacy, Association for the Advancement of Artificial Intelligence Press Technical Report SS-10-05, 2010, at 1, http://papers. ssrn.com/sol3/papers.cfm?abstract_id=1580111.

74 Id. at 1.

75 Saffold v. Plain Dealer Publishing Co., CV 10 723512, Cuyahoga County Court of Common Pleas (filed April 7, 2010); McVicker v. King, No. 09-cv-436 (W.D. Pa. March 3, 2010); Sedersten v. Taylor, 2009 U.S. Dist. LEXIS 114525 (Case No. 09-3031-CV-S-GAF) (W.D. Mo. December 9, 2009).

76 In re Northwest Airlines Privacy Litigation, 2004 WL 1278459 (D. Minn. 2004) (finding that the privacy statement did not constitute a unilateral contract and that plaintiff must have read the policy to rely on it); Dyer v. Northwest Airlines Corp., 334 F. Supp. 2d 1196 (D.N.D. 2004) (finding that plaintiffs failed to allege that they read, understood, or relied upon the privacy policy and failed to allege contractual damages); In re Jet Blue Airways Corp. Privacy Litigation, 379 F. Supp. 2d 299 (E.D.N.Y. 2005).

77 Student Files Lawsuit After Coach Distributed Private Facebook Content, Student Press Law Center, July 22, 2009, http://www.splc.org/newsflash.asp?id=1938.

78 Statement of Rights and Responsibilities, Facebook, http://www.facebook. com/terms.php?ref=pf.

79 Andrew Moshirina, Florida Nukes the Fridge: Facebook, the Bar, and the Latest Entry in the Social Network Hijacking Saga, Citizen Media Law Project, September 2, 2009, http://www.citmedialaw.org/blog/2009/florida-nukes-fridge-facebook-bar-and-latest-entry-social-network-hijacking-saga; Molly McDonough, Town Requires Job Seekers to Reveal Social Media Passwords, ABA Journal Law News Now, June 19, 2009, http://www.abajournal.com/news/town_requires_job_seekers_to_reveal_social_media_passwords/. Bozeman quickly abolished its policy after public outcry.

80 Andrew Moshirina, Employee Privacy and Social Networks: The Case for a New Don't Ask Don't Tell, Citizen Media Law Project, July 2, 2009, http://www.citmedia law.org/blog/2009/employee-privacy-and-social-networks-case-new-don%E2%80%99t-ask-don%E2%80%99t-tell.

81 Emil Protalinski, Maryland Bans Employers Asking for Your Facebook Password, ZDNet, May 3, 2012, http://www.zdnet.com/blog/facebook/maryland-bans-employers-asking-for-your-facebook-password/12509.

82 Statement of Rights and Responsibilities, Facebook, supra note 78.

83 See, e.g. Myspace.com Terms of Use Agreement, MySpace, http://www.myspace. com/help/terms.

84 See Solove, supra note 13.

85 Statement of Rights and Responsibilities, Facebook, supra note 78.

86 Id.

87 Orin S. Kerr, The Fourth Amendment and New Technologies: Constitutional Myths and the Case for Caution, 102 Mich. L. Rev. 801, 802 (2004).

88 Lukowski v. County of Seneca, 2009 WL 467075 (W.D.N.Y. 2009) (finding that the "terms of service agreements between customers and businesses have been considered relevant to characterization of privacy interests"); United States v. Hart, 2009 WL 2552347 (W.D.Ky. 2009); Warshak v. United States, 532 F.3d 521 (6th Cir. 2008).

89 See, e.g., United States v. Hart, 2009 WL 2552347 (W.D.Ky. 2009); Warshak v. United States, 532 F.3d 521 (6th Cir. 2008); Lukowski v. County of Seneca, 2009 WL 467075 (W.D.N.Y. 2009).

90 2009 WL 2552347 (W.D.Ky. 2009).

91 Id.

92 Id. at *25.

93 See, e.g., Freedman v. America Online, 412 Supp. 174 (D. Conn. 2005) (finding AOL's privacy policy relevant in the scope of a user's Fourth Amendment rights).

94 London-Sire Records v. Doe, 542 F. Supp. 2d 153, 163 (D.Mass. 2008) (citing McIntyre v. Ohio Elections Comm'n, 514 U.S. 334 (1995); NAACP v. Alabama ex rel. Patterson, 357 U.S. 449 (1958)).

95 See Solove, supra note 37.

96 London-Sire Records v. Doe, 542 F. Supp. 2d 153, 179 (D.Mass. 2008).

97 No. 02:09-cv-00436 (W.D. Pa. 2010).

98 Id. at 7.

99 Id. at 9.

100 Id. at 10.

101 542 F. Supp. 2d 153 (D.Mass. 2008).

102 Id.

103 Id.

104 257 F. Supp. 244 (D.C.D.C. 2003), rev'd, Recording Industry Ass'n of America v. Verizon Internet Services, 351 F.3d 1229 (D.C. Cir. 2003).

105 Id. at 268.

106 See, Sony Music Entm't v. Does 1-40, 326 F. Supp. 2d 556 (S.D.N.Y. 2004) (finding there was only a minimal expectation of privacy under the ISP's terms of service).

107 Music Group Macao Commercial Offshore Ltd. v. Does, 82 F. Supp. 3d 979, 986 (N.D. Cal. 2015).

108 See, e.g., FTC, Exploring Privacy: A Roundtable Series (2010), http://www.ftc. gov/bcp/workshops/privacyroundtables/index.shtml.

109 See, e.g., Susan Gindin, Nobody Reads Your Privacy Policy or Online Contract? Lessons Learned and Questions Raised by the FTC's Action Against Sears, 8 Nw. J. Tech. & Intell. Prop. 1 (2009), http://www.law.northwestern.edu/journals/njtip/v8/n1/1/; Marcia Hofmann, The Federal Trade Commission's Enforcement of Privacy, in Proskauer on Privacy: A Guide to Privacy and Data Security Law in the Information Age (2010).

110 Id.

111 Id.

112 In the Matter of Sears Holdings Management Corp., FTC File No. 082 3099 (June 4, 2009) (available at http://www.ftc.gov/os/caselist/0823099/index.shtm). The final consent order was issued on September 9, 2009; FTC, Press Release, Sears Settles

FTC Charges Regarding Tracking Software: Sears Failed to Disclose Adequately that Software Collected Consumers' Sensitive Personal Information, June 4, 2009, http://www.ftc.gov/opa/2009/06/sears.shtm.

113 Gindin, supra note 109 at 1.

114 Id.

115 Federal Trade Commission, FTC Approves Final Order Settling Charges Against Flashlight App Creator, April 9, 2014, https://www.ftc.gov/news-events/press-releases/2014/04/ftc-approves-final-order-settling-charges-against-flashlight-app

116 Jonathan K. Sobel, et al., The Evolution of Data Protection as a Privacy Concern, and the Contract Law Dynamics Underlying It, in Anupam Chandler et al., eds., Securing Privacy in the Internet Age 56 (2008).

117 Statement of Rights and Responsibilities, Facebook, supra note 78.

118 18 U.S.C. §1030(a)(2) (2001); see, e.g., Orin Kerr, Computer Crime Law 478 (2nd ed. 2009).

119 EF Cultural Travel B.V. v. Zefer Corp., 318 F.3d 58, 63 (1st Cir. 2003).

120 United States v. Phillips, 477 F.3d 215, 220 (5th Cir. 2007).

121 18 U.S.C. §§1030(a)(2), (a)(2)(C).

122 Sewell v. Bernardin, 795 F.3d 337 (2nd Cir. 2015).

123 U.S. v. Drew, 2009 WL 2872855 (C.D. Cal. 2009).

124 Id. at ★17 (citing City of Chicago v. Morales, 527 U.S. 41, 60, 119 S.Ct. 1849, 144 L.Ed.2d 67 (1999)).

125 544 F. Supp. 2d 473, 486 (E.D.Va. 2008), aff'd in part, rev'd in part, 562 F.3d 630 (4th Cir. 2009) (remanded to determine actual amount of damages).

126 2007 U.S. Dist. LEXIS 96230, at ★46 (N.D.Text. Sept. 12, 2007).

127 America Online v. LCGM, 46 F. Supp. 2d 444 (E.D. Va. 1998). Craigslist v. Naturemarket, 2010 WL 807446 (N.D. Cal. 2010).

128 NO. C 08-05780 JW (N.D. Cal. July 20, 2010).

129 Id. at 8–22.

130 18 U.S.C. §1030(e) (2001).

131 18 U.S.C. §§ 2701–2711 (2008). Similar to the Wiretap Act, The Stored Communication Act has a specific consent exception (§ 2702(b)).

132 18 U.S.C. § 2701 (2008).

133 18 U.S.C. § 2511(2)(c) (2008).

134 Kerr, supra note 118.

135 Id.

136 See, e.g., Frederic Stutzman and Woodrow Hartzog, Boundary Regulation in Social Media, ACM Conference on Computer Supported Cooperative Work (CSCW 2012); Robert Wilson, Samuel D. Gosling, & Lindsay T. Graham, A Review of Facebook Research in the Social Sciences, 7 Persp. Psychol. Sci. 203 (2012).

137 See, e.g., Harris v. Blockbuster, 622 F. Supp. 2d 396 (N.D.Tex. 2009).

138 Id.

139 Bank of Indiana, N.A. v. Holyfield, 476 F. Supp. 104, 109-10 (S.D. Miss. 1979).

CHAPTER 4

Intellectual Property

Kathleen K. Olson

Lehigh University

ABSTRACT

The collaborative nature of social media challenges traditional notions of ownership of content online. This chapter summarizes the law of copyright, "hot news," trademark and publicity rights as applied to social media and discusses current case law and legislative proposals. Copyright issues include fair use, linking and embedding video, Creative Commons licenses, liability for infringement by others and the "safe harbor" provisions of the Digital Millennium Copyright Act. The application of the hot news doctrine and trademark law to social media is examined, including liability for news aggregators and fake corporate and celebrity Twitter accounts.

Digital technology and the rise of social media have challenged the ability of existing legal rules to manage intellectual property online. Social media users engage with content in new ways: They create it, share it, curate it, remix it and collaborate with others to create new works from it. Questions about authorship and ownership arise that challenge traditional conceptions of intellectual property law and may require a re-examination of the law to determine ways to cope with these and future challenges.

For now, however, copyright and other intellectual property laws generally apply to content on social media sites in much the same way as other contexts, both with regard to original content and to the use of material that belongs to others. While the billions of pieces of content copied and distributed on sites such as Facebook, Twitter, Flickr, Pinterest and YouTube may make it impossible for copyright owners to fully enforce their rights, those rights are not forfeited. Because social media users are both creators and users of works, they need to understand both the rights and the limitations of intellectual property. This chapter discusses the basic rules of copyright, "hot news," trademark and publicity rights and describes the current state of the law governing content on social media platforms.

COPYRIGHT

Most content on social media sites is governed by copyright law. Copyright refers to ownership rights given to those who produce creative expression, whether it is text, photographs, video, music, software, works of art or other creative works. Among these ownership rights are the right to reproduce the work; to prepare "derivative" works based on the original, such as a translation or movie version; to distribute copies; and to perform or display the work. Copyright protection begins as soon as the work is "fixed in a tangible medium of expression," which includes material posted online.

Copyright is governed exclusively by federal law and has as its source the Copyright Clause of the U.S. Constitution, which gives Congress the power to grant authors exclusive rights in their works, for a limited time, in order to "promote the progress of science and useful arts."[1] Copyright provides creators with a limited monopoly right in their works so they can profit economically from them. This helps promote the progress of science and the arts because it gives authors the incentive to create and disseminate political, social, and artistic expression that adds to the free flow of information and ideas. In return, their works will eventually become part of the public domain, free for others to use and build upon as material for new creative works.

Copyright protects original works of authorship created from an individual's own efforts and not by copying existing works, although originality requires only a minimal level of creativity. Facts are not copyrightable, however, so tweeting a piece of information from a news story is not infringement (although breaking news may be protected by the "hot news" doctrine, which is described in more detail later in this chapter). Recipes—a popular item on sites such as Pinterest—are not copyrightable if they consist mainly of a list of ingredients.

Copyright also does not protect ideas. The law limits property rights to the particular expression of an idea, but not the idea itself. In some cases, the idea and the expression can't be separated. Under the "merger doctrine," if an idea can be expressed only in a limited number of ways, the idea and its expression "merge" and the expression also will not be protected. Whether a post on a social media platform is protected by copyright depends, therefore, on the level of original expression it contains. Posts that consist of personal updates or other statements of fact or that express an opinion or idea without the level of creative expression necessary to escape the merger doctrine are not copyrightable and are free for others to copy and share.

The length of the post may also preclude copyright protection because short posts are less likely to fulfill the originality requirement. Historically, titles and short phrases or expressions have not been copyright-protected (they may be protected by trademark if used commercially, however). Given Twitter's 140-character limit, most tweets do not rise to the required level of creativity, although no bright-line rule exists: A haiku or other short work that is sufficiently creative may be protected. In 2015, Twitter deleted tweets that copied a joke tweeted by a comedy writer after she filed a takedown request under the Digital Millennium Copyright Act ("DMCA"), a law that will be discussed in more detail later in this chapter. No legal conclusion can be drawn from Twitter's actions, however, and a court would have to determine the copyrightability of jokes on a case-by-case basis. Compilations of tweets – such as the 2010 *New York Times* bestseller *Sh*t My Dad Says*, derived from the popular Twitter account – can be copyright-protected if there is creativity in the selection or arrangement of the tweets and if there is additional text that meets the originality requirements for copyrightability.

If content shared on social media is copyrightable, it is automatically protected as soon as it is "fixed" by being posted on a site. Written expression, sound recordings, photographs and videos retain their copyright when uploaded to a social media or photo-sharing site and do not become part of the public domain just by being freely available online. An artist named Richard Prince was sued for copyright infringement in December 2015, for example, because his artwork consisted of blown-up "screen saves" of other people's Instagram posts. Even music heard in the background of user-generated videos is copyright-protected, as beauty blogger Michelle Phan found out when she was sued in 2014 over songs used in her makeup tutorials on YouTube.

Most social media sites' terms of service specify that you must be the copyright owner of content you post or have permission to post it. While the terms of service generally give those sites a blanket license for use of your content, that license applies only to that site and does not give others the right to use your content without permission. A federal court recognized this in 2013 when it ruled in favor of professional photographer Daniel Morel in his copyright infringement lawsuit against the French wire service Agence France Press and Getty Images for copying and distributing photos of the Haitian earthquake he had taken and uploaded to Twitter. The defendants argued that their use of Morel's photos was authorized because Twitter's terms of service granted third parties a license to use the site's content, but the judge ruled that the license extended only to Twitter and its partners.[2] After appeal, a federal jury awarded Morel $1.2 million in damages, the maximum statutory penalty available under the Copyright Act.

To win a copyright infringement suit, the plaintiff must prove he owns a valid copyright in the work and that the defendant copied the original elements in the work without permission. If there is no direct proof that the defendant copied the work, the plaintiff must prove that the defendant had access to the work and that the two works are "substantially similar." Access may be proven by showing the defendant had a reasonable opportunity to see the original work—if it was posted on the Internet, that may be enough. The similarity standard is based on whether an average observer would see the two works as similar enough to recognize that the alleged infringing work was copied from the original.

While copyright infringement may be prosecuted as a criminal offense, most cases are civil proceedings. Remedies in civil infringement lawsuits may include an injunction to stop the infringement, attorney's fees, and actual damages and profits. Statutory damages may also be available, and they can be as high as $30,000 per work for innocent infringement and $150,000 for willful infringement.[3] In the past decade, juries awarded substantial statutory damages in lawsuits brought by record companies against individuals who downloaded songs from file-sharing sites. In the most well-known case, a college student named Joel Tenenbaum was found liable in 2009 for statutory damages of $22,500 per song, for a total of $675,000. Although the judge reduced the damages award, it was later reinstated and upheld by the court of appeals.[4] In 2015, Tenenbaum filed for bankruptcy.

Linking and Embedding Content

If copying without permission is infringement, what about linking to copyrighted material without permission? A simple hyperlink to content on another site does not generally raise intellectual property concerns. When content from one site is "framed"—embedded on a second site and displayed through a scrollable window or frame—claims of unfair competition and trademark infringement or dilution may arise if the defendant attempts to "pass off" the embedded content as its own or otherwise causes confusion as to its source. In 1997, for example, news organizations including *The Washington Post* and CNN sued a website called TotalNews for its use of framing to embed stories from the plaintiffs' servers and display them surrounded by TotalNews advertising rather than that of the original news sites. The suit alleged unfair competition, trademark infringement and dilution, as well as copyright infringement, but the suit was settled before going to trial.

A finding of copyright infringement is unlikely if the framing or embedding is done by "inline linking," the most commonly used method to display images or embed videos on a site. It allows a video to be played and viewed on a website while the actual video file remains on another server, such as YouTube. Visitors viewing the video on the website have no indication that it is not part of that site, but since no copying is involved—only linking—the reproduction right of the copyright owner is not infringed.

The U.S. Court of Appeals for the Ninth Circuit affirmed that position in a 2007 ruling in a case involving Google's visual search engine. In *Perfect 10 v. Amazon.com,* Google was sued for copyright infringement because the search engine used inline links to display the images that matched search terms, while the actual image files remained on their original servers. The court ruled in favor of Google and adopted the "server test," which turned on whether the defendant's server housed an actual copy of the infringing content. If it did not and the site merely embedded the content on another site using inline linking, there was no infringement of either the copyright owner's reproduction rights or its display rights.[5] On the other hand, when Google altered the images to create smaller "thumbnail" versions, it created derivative works of the originals. Because the right to create derivative works belongs to the copyright owner, Google would have been liable for infringement if the court hadn't ruled the thumbnails were protected by fair use, a concept explained in the next section.

Limitations on Copyright Protection

Along with the threshold copyrightability requirements, other rules further the goals of copyright by putting limits on the monopoly copyright owners hold over their works. Copyright terms ensure that their monopoly does not last forever, for example, and the fair use doctrine ensures that their control over the use of their works is never absolute.

Because copyright terms limit the period during which a copyright owner has exclusive rights to the work, they foster the growth of the public domain by making material available for future authors to draw on to create new works. Congress has the power to give authors the exclusive right to their writings "for limited times," and this has been consistently interpreted to prohibit perpetual copyrights. In 1998, the Copyright Term Extension Act extended copyright terms by 20 years, so that today, the copyright term for a work of individual authorship is the life of the author plus 70 years, and for a work of corporate authorship, it is 120 years after its creation or 95 years after its publication, whichever is shorter.[6]

The fair use doctrine is one of the most important tools in copyright law to maintain the proper balance between an individual's property rights and the social benefits that come from a free flow of information. By allowing the use of material without the permission of the copyright owner, fair use helps resolve some of the potential conflicts that may arise between copyright and free speech. Fair use is an exception to the exclusive rights of a copyright owner; it allows creative works to be used by others for certain purposes that are socially beneficial. To determine fair use, courts examine and weigh four different factors, which are found in Section 107 of the 1976 Copyright Act. These are:

1. the purpose and character of the use, including whether such use is of a commercial nature or is for non-profit educational purposes;
2. the nature of the copyrighted work;
3. the amount and substantiality of the portion used in relation to the copyrighted work as a whole; and
4. the effect of the use upon the potential market for or value of the copyrighted work.[7]

The first factor requires an examination of the purpose of the secondary use. News reporting, comment, criticism, research, scholarship, and teaching are all listed in Section 107 as protected purposes under the fair use doctrine, although this is not an exclusive list. While non-profit uses are favored, a commercial use does not preclude a finding of fair use; the Supreme Court has said that other characteristics, such as "transformativeness," may be more important. This factor is an important one for social media users, so it will be discussed in more detail below.

The second factor looks at whether the original work is highly creative or primarily factual; a factual work is given less copyright protection, while artistic works such as fiction or music have more protection. The third factor looks at how much of the original work was taken, and is measured in proportion to the entire work—secondary users should take only as much of the original as is needed for their purpose. Generally, only a small portion of the original work needs to be borrowed: When commenting on a news story, for example, excerpts may be quoted, but not the entire article. Sometimes using the entire work is necessary, however, as when commenting on a photograph or using a journal article for classroom use, and this will not prevent a finding of fair use.

The fourth factor, the effect of the use on the value of or potential market for the original work, is regarded by some as the most important factor. It measures the economic harm that may be caused by the secondary use of the work, which is often closely tied to the purpose of that use—if a secondary use serves mainly as a replacement for the original in the marketplace, for example, neither the first nor the fourth factor will weigh in favor of fair use. Secondary uses that go beyond merely substituting for the original work and instead create something new are less likely to harm the market for the original, and they also do more to further the goals of copyright. Because of this, the concept of "transformativeness" has come to have added weight in fair use analysis, particularly with regard to the first factor.

The Purpose and Character of the Use

While news reporting, comment, criticism, research, scholarship, and teaching are listed as protected purposes under the fair use doctrine, even they may not be fair use if a secondary work serves the same purpose as the original. Instead, the law favors a use that transforms the original or "adds something new, with a further purpose or different character, altering the first with new expression, meaning, or message."[8]

The protected categories found in Section 107 are often themselves transformative, however; examples include copying a short video clip for a movie review and quoting excerpts from a political speech in a scholarly biography or news story. Parody is generally considered transformative as a humorous form of comment or criticism, as the Supreme Court ruled in a landmark case in 1994 involving a parody of Roy Orbison's hit "Oh, Pretty Woman" by 2 Live Crew.[9] The importance of transformativeness to the Court in that case led lower courts to make it a central issue in subsequent fair use cases, even as they retained the four-factor analysis required by Section 107. Thus in *North Jersey Media Group, Inc. v. Pirro*, a 2015 case involving Fox News' Facebook pages, the court denied the network's motion for summary judgment after an extensive analysis of transformativeness. North Jersey Media Group was the copyright owner of the iconic 9/11 photo depicting firefighters raising the American flag at Ground Zero. On the anniversary of 9/11, the photo was posted on the Facebook pages of two Fox News shows next to a photo of Marines raising the flag at Iwo Jima during World War II and the hashtag "#neverforget." The court said that even though the photo had been cropped, resized and combined with the other elements, it could not conclude as a matter of law that it was transformed sufficiently to be fair use.[10]

To be transformative, then, the use must do more than simply repackage or republish the original work—it must change it in some way. At the same time, the change may be less in the appearance of the original work than in its expressive purpose. In *Prince v. Cariou*, a Second Circuit case decided in 2013, the court ruled in favor of an artist named Richard Prince who had incorporated copyrighted photos into his paintings and collages with minor alterations to the photos themselves.[11] The court ruled that the artist had added something new to the photos and had presented them with a "fundamentally different aesthetic," which was enough to make the new works transformative and therefore protected by fair use.[12]

Even using a copyrighted work for a different purpose, without altering or adding to it to make it into something new, may be transformative. In the *Perfect 10* case discussed earlier in the chapter, the Ninth Circuit ruled that thumbnail copies of images made by Google's visual search engine were protected by fair use because the images were used for a different purpose—indexing the Web, rather than aesthetics—that benefitted the public.[13] Courts that adopt an expanded reading of what is transformative are more likely to find fair use.

How does all of this apply to social media? While no bright-line rules apply, a variety of fair use defenses may be available for those who use the works of others. Material that is posted on social media sites is frequently done so for purposes of comment or criticism, whether it's a news story commented on in a blog or the latest "Avengers" movie trailer posted and critiqued on Facebook. Parodies, wikis, and creative remixes of works, such as mashups and certain kinds of fan fiction, may be highly transformative. Compilations of photos or other copyrighted material on social curation sites like Pinterest and Storify may be protected by fair use, depending on the degree to which the aggregation of individual pieces of content transforms the material into something new or uses it for a different purpose, such as comment or criticism, or for a different aesthetic. Curating material just to compile it or share it, without adding something extra that transforms it or otherwise gives it a new purpose, is not fair use.

While the purpose or character of the use is central to a finding of fair use, the other fair use factors are still part of the analysis, and they may outweigh the first factor, even when the use is transformative. Posts that include comment or criticism of a work should copy only the amount of material needed to make the point. Fan fiction is more likely to be fair use if it borrows relatively little material and does not harm the market for the original. Noncommercial uses are favored under both the first and fourth factors.

Finally, practices such as attribution and linking back to the original source may be helpful to demonstrate good faith on the part of the secondary user. Although neither necessary nor sufficient for a finding of fair use, these practices may have some bearing on a judge's determination of the equities of the particular case. A lack of good faith on the part of a copyright plaintiff may also affect the outcome: Several district court judges in Nevada and Colorado sided with secondary users in infringement cases filed by the profit-driven "copyright troll" Righthaven LLC in 2010 and 2011, and the company's questionable business model and litigation tactics may have played a role. After transferring the rights to content from clients such as the *Las Vegas Review-Journal* and the *Denver Post*, the company filed more than 200 infringement suits against bloggers and other non-profit websites for using the content without permission. The suits were filed without issuing the customary cease-and-desist letters or takedown notices, and maximum statutory damages were sought in each case.

While many of the suits were settled or dismissed for lack of standing, several judges ruled for the defendants based on fair use, in one case even when an entire article had been copied on a non-profit site.[14] Apart from the merits of the fair use argument, some judges made clear in their rulings their disapproval of Righthaven's aggressive legal strategy, which one opinion characterized as an "abuse" of the copyright law.[15] Righthaven's failures in court led to its insolvency, and in March 2012, its copyright registrations were transferred to a court-appointed receiver to be auctioned off to pay the company's creditors.[16]

Because fair use analysis accounts for the individual facts and equities of each case, specific guidelines for what is permissible are difficult to provide. The American University's Center for Social Media has created codes of best practices regarding fair use in different contexts, including one for online video, that may be helpful in some cases.[17] A use that is noncommercial, that transforms the original work or otherwise has some public benefit, that doesn't take more than is needed and that doesn't replace the original in the market has a plausible claim of fair use. Still, generalities such as these cannot predict the outcome in a particular case. The fair use doctrine, because it is meant to be flexible, can also be frustratingly unclear.

Fair use may provide a legal defense for some uses of copyrighted material on social media sites, but the fact is that many social media practices, even if infringing, are likely to be tolerated. In practice, most copyright disputes never make it to court, and an individual blogger or other social media user may at most receive a cease-and-desist letter from an attorney asking for infringing material to be removed. Social networking, because it has been used more for personal sharing than for commercial purposes, is a setting in which copyright owners have so far practiced a good deal of forbearance with regard to infringement.

Why have individual social media users been spared the draconian legal action that people like Joel Tenenbaum experienced? Most importantly, illegal file-sharing of digital music caused direct and significant economic harm to the music industry in a way that most people's social media uses of copyrighted content do not. In the end, however, the record companies found that suing individual file-sharers was both ineffectual, given the scope of the problem, and a public relations disaster. Rather than trying to control social media, most copyright owners have realized they are better off embracing it as a marketing and promotional tool.

As the use and sharing of content through social networking continues to grow, and as copyright owners continue to tolerate certain social uses of their material, standards will develop for acceptable practices in the social media context that may also shape what is permissible in other environments. The law, especially the fair use doctrine, reflects contemporary social norms. As social media becomes an integral part of the culture, the norms that govern it will begin to shape legal norms as well, especially for judges trying to make equitable decisions in fair use cases.

Liability for Infringement by Others

If an individual using a social media platform infringes copyright, the site itself may also be liable on the theory of contributory infringement, which occurs when the defendant has knowledge of the infringing activity and induces, causes or materially contributes to the infringement. Social media sites receive statutory protection from secondary liability for content they host under the Digital Millennium Copyright Act of 1998 ("DMCA"), a federal statute that was aimed at addressing the unique copyright concerns of content online. The Act's primary purpose was to combat online piracy, and the statute raised the penalties for copyright infringement online and made it illegal to gain unauthorized access to a copyrighted work by circumventing anti-piracy protections.

For online service providers such as social media platforms, the DMCA provides protection against secondary liability for copyright infringement when they act simply as hosts of the content of others and do not play a role in determining its content. Without this protection, Web hosts would be forced to actively monitor their sites for possible infringement, but the vast amount of material makes it impossible to do this effectively. Instead, sites might simply bar or severely limit the ability of users to post content to their sites. Without DMCA protection, the explosion of social networking and user-generated content never would have occurred.

Section 512 of the statute provides a "safe harbor" for online service providers and other web-based hosts of content against liability for contributory infringement if they follow certain procedures to safeguard copyrights on their sites. In order to be protected, an online service provider providing a forum for material to be posted at the direction of its users must not have "actual knowledge" that the material is infringing or, in the absence of such knowledge, must not be aware of "facts or circumstances from which infringing activity is apparent." The host site must also establish certain "notice and takedown" procedures, including designating an agent to receive notices of copyright infringement in order to remove infringing material when notified of its existence on the site by a copyright owner. While the DMCA does not require an online service provider to actively monitor its service for infringing activity, it must act "expeditiously" to remove or disable access to the material once it is made aware of it.[18]

Although the Act requires that a copyright owner provide a statement of a "good faith belief" that the material is infringing when it issues a takedown notice, critics contend that copyright owners can overreach by issuing takedown notices that are unwarranted or when the use of their content is fair use. One user fought back when YouTube, after receiving a takedown notice from Universal Music, removed a 30-second home video of her toddler dancing to the Prince song "Let's Go Crazy." Stephanie Lenz filed a counter-notification to challenge the removal, but then went further and sued the copyright owner in federal court for misrepresenting its claim of infringement under the Act. The trial court's denial of Universal's motion to dismiss was affirmed on appeal by the Ninth Circuit, which held that a copyright owner must consider fair use before it issues a takedown notice and must have a subjective good faith belief that the use was not protected or it may be held liable for damages under the DMCA.[19]

Litigation focusing on secondary liability under Section 512 has centered on what level of knowledge of infringing activity is sufficient for an online service provider to be disqualified from safe harbor protection. A site that has actual knowledge of infringing material and does nothing will lose its protection. On the other hand, it is not enough that a site merely knows infringement is possible: The Ninth Circuit ruled in 2013 that a video-sharing site did not lose its immunity under the safe harbor provision based solely on its general knowledge that some of its users might use the site to infringe copyrights.[20] Instead, courts use a "red flag" test: To lose the safe harbor protection of Section 512, the online service provider must be aware of facts and circumstances that raise a "red flag" that would indicate to a reasonable person that specific infringing activity has occurred on the site.

At the same time, the service provider "cannot willfully bury its head in the sand" to avoid specific knowledge of an infringement.[21] This theory of "willful blindness" was considered in a $1 billion lawsuit filed in 2007 by media giant Viacom against YouTube, in which Viacom accused YouTube of encouraging users to upload *The Daily Show* and other copyrighted content to its site. YouTube won summary judgment at the district court level in 2010 when the court ruled that it qualified for protection under the safe harbor provision. The lower court found that YouTube quickly removed infringing material once it was notified of its existence by copyright owners, and that while YouTube may have had a "general awareness" that users were posting videos that may be infringing, that awareness did not rise to the level of knowledge required to disqualify YouTube from safe harbor protection.[22]

On appeal, however, the Second Circuit reversed the lower court's ruling. The court agreed that Section 512 requires not just general awareness but knowledge of specific instances of infringement. The court ruled, however, that in this case, a reasonable jury could find that YouTube did have actual knowledge of instances of specific infringing activity that would disqualify it from safe harbor protection. In addition, the court instructed the district court to examine whether YouTube had exercised "willful blindness" to avoid knowing about specific infringing clips on its site, which it suggested would jeopardize its immunity under the DMCA.[23] On remand, the district court ruled in favor of YouTube on these issues and prior to appeal, the parties settled the case.

Some online service providers have implemented technological measures to supplement their notice and takedown procedures and limit their liability for user infringement. Since 2007, YouTube has used Content ID, a content management tool that allows the site not only to identify copyrighted material but to take action, at the request of the copyright owner, to block it, track it and provide viewing statistics, or monetize it by linking to an official website or inserting advertising. Critics charge that the identifications are not always accurate, however, and that the system does not sufficiently protect fair use.

While technological tools may alleviate some of the uncertainty about the extent of safe harbor protection, they do not replace statutory protection. Some online service providers fear that the "willful blindness" standard has made it harder for them to enjoy the protection of DMCA's safe harbor and requires them to be more proactive about monitoring possible infringement on their sites. At the same time, copyright owners have grown tired of the "whack-a-mole game" they must play in dealing with widespread posting of their content.[24]

Legislation introduced in Congress in 2011 would have significantly changed the safe harbor provision of the DMCA in a way that critics feared would have discouraged innovation on the Web. The Stop Online Piracy Act ("SOPA") and the PROTECT IP Act ("PIPA")[25] were companion bills introduced in the House and Senate in 2011 that opponents say would require online service providers to become responsible for their users' content. The purpose of the legislation was to target foreign websites that exist primarily to distribute pirated content such as movies and music, but analysts said the language of the bill was so broad that it would undo the safe harbor protections of the DMCA for American online service providers and would stifle investment in online start-ups.

According to the Center for Democracy & Technology, online service providers would be required to take measures to prevent access to infringing sites, and the law would make social media sites liable for "facilitating" infringement merely by hosting content, contrary to the provisions of the DMCA. Content hosts would be forced into the role of "content police" to avoid being liable for their users' content, which would chill free expression on the Internet and stifle online innovation. Opposition led by Internet and technology companies culminated in the biggest online protest in history on January 18, 2012, and the House and Senate quickly tabled consideration of the bills. In 2016, the Copyright Office began a review of Section 512 in order to evaluate its effectiveness in today's online world and to consider "the costs and burdens of the notice-and-takedown process on large- and small-scale copyright owners, online service providers and the general public."[26] Initial public comments on the study numbered over 92,000.

Creative Commons

Some copyright owners would like to voluntarily give up some or all of their property rights with regard to their creative works. In 2001, in order to promote "universal access to research, education and culture," Lawrence Lessig and other copyright activists founded Creative Commons, a non- profit organization that encourages the sharing of information online by providing "a free, public, and standardized infrastructure that creates a bal- ance between the reality of the Internet and the reality of copyright laws."[27] Creative Commons sets up a "some rights reserved" system of licenses that allows copyright owners to permit certain uses of their work by others without forfeiting the entire bundle of rights that come with copyright.

The system lets copyright owners indicate up front whether they will permit others to use their works and for what purposes. Copyright owners can waive all of their rights and indicate that they have chosen to place the work in the public domain, or they can choose from a number of different licenses represented on their websites by symbols indicating different levels of permission. The most permissive license is an "Attribution" or "CC BY" license, which allows others to copy, distribute, remix or "tweak" the work, even for commercial purposes, as long as the original author is credited. The "Attribution-ShareAlike" (CC BY-SA) license adds the requirement that anyone who creates a derivative work by changing or building upon the original must make the new work available under the same licensing terms. This type of license is used by open source software projects and by Wikipedia and its affiliated Wikimedia sites.

Flickr, the online photo-sharing community, was one of the first social media sites to make Creative Commons licensing available as part of its user interface, and it is the single largest source of Creative Commons-licensed content on the Web, with more than 200 million images available. In 2011, YouTube added Creative Commons licensing as an option for users who upload video and created a library of CC BY-licensed videos from sources such as C-SPAN and Al Jazeera.

A Creative Commons license presumes, of course, that the licensor actually owns the copyright in the first place. Secondary works that are created from copyrighted works cannot be licensed under a Creative Commons license unless the permission of the original copyright owner is obtained, either expressly or through an existing Creative Commons license, unless the secondary work is protected by fair use.

The most restrictive license reserves all rights other than the right to download the work and to share it by copying, distributing, and transmitting it, with attribution and for non-commercial purposes only. Indicating even this level of permission is useful, however, because otherwise sharing it would most likely be infringement. The utility of the Creative Commons licensing system is that it eliminates the often-difficult task of identifying and contacting a copyright owner in order to ask permission and the uncertainty that comes with guessing if something is protected by fair use. It allows the free use of copyrighted works for everything from simple sharing on social media sites to incorporating images or music into new creative works without the fear of liability for infringement.

THE HOT NEWS DOCTRINE

Social media has become a significant source for news: When Osama bin Laden was killed in May 2011, more people learned about it through social networking than from a news site or blog.[28] What happens when breaking news is reported—do news organizations have a legal right to control access to their "scoop"? Since the facts of the news report are not copyrightable, any such right must come from another area of the law. The Supreme Court created such a right in 1918 and based it on the tort of unfair competition. Called "hot news misappropriation," it was developed to prevent competitors from free-riding on the time and effort required to report time-sensitive news and other information and preserve the economic incentive for companies to invest in those efforts.[29]

No one who tweeted the news of bin Laden's death was liable for repeating that fact, of course—the tort is available only in very limited circumstances. The public has the right to tell others about breaking news on Facebook or to live-tweet a basketball game. In some circumstances, however, if done repeatedly by a competitor for commercial advantage, those activities may be actionable.

The 1918 Supreme Court case that produced the hot news doctrine, *INS v. Associated Press*, featured a battle between competing wire services during World War I. The Associated Press sued the International News Service for rewriting AP dispatches and calling them their own. The Court granted the AP an injunction against this practice and created a limited quasi-property right in the news—in facts—based on a theory of unfair competition to protect the labor and expense required to gather and disseminate the news.[30]

Hot news misappropriation still exists, but only in the common law of a handful of states, and its scope was narrowed to avoid overlapping with and being pre-empted by federal copyright law. One important limitation is that the property right is strictly limited by time—the news must still be "hot" to be protected—in order to avoid First Amendment concerns. In 1997, the Second Circuit outlined the elements that are generally required in order for a hot news case to avoid copyright pre-emption. *NBA v. Motorola* centered on whether the transmission of "real-time" scores and statistics from NBA games via pagers constituted hot news misappropriation. The district court granted the NBA an injunction, but the Second Circuit reversed, holding that while the NBA and other sports leagues may own the copyright in the broadcast descriptions of their games, they do not own the underlying facts, which include statistical information and updated scores. The court held that, unlike INS, the pager service did not act as a substitute or direct competitor with the league's "product," which the court defined as the experience of watching the game in person or on TV. The pager service also did not free-ride on the effort required to provide the information because the service hired its own freelancers to watch the games and send out the score updates. The court set out some general guidelines for what would constitute an actionable hot news case. Although state laws differ to some degree, hot news appropriation has generally required that:

1. a plaintiff generates or gathers information at a cost;
2. the information is time-sensitive;
3. a defendant's use of the information constitutes free-riding on the plaintiff's efforts;
4. the defendant is in direct competition with a product or service offered by the plaintiffs; and
5. the ability of other parties to free-ride on the efforts of the plaintiff or others would so reduce the incentive to produce the product or service that its existence or quality would be substantially threatened.[31]

Using these guidelines, fans or even commercial ventures that live-tweet a sporting event would not be liable under the hot news doctrine if they are monitoring the games themselves and unless they pose direct competition sufficient to threaten the viability of the event itself. In the news context, the doctrine has undergone something of a revival as news organizations have fought aggregators, such as Google News, that reuse headlines and lead paragraphs or summaries on the Web. The Associated Press entered into a licensing agreement with Google in 2006, but it and other media companies continue to pursue hot news claims against other news aggregators.

In 2011, the Second Circuit affirmed the continuing survival of hot news claims but limited its future applicability in a case involving an online newsletter that regularly reported investment banks' time-sensitive analysis and stock recommendations. In *Barclays Capital v. TheFlyOnTheWall.com*, the court ruled the banks could not state a hot news claim because TheFly did not free-ride on the banks' efforts by making its own recommendations—it reported the banks' recommendations as news, not as its own product the way INS did. The court also indicated that the guidelines in the *NBA* case were not binding, and that future hot news claims would need to involve facts that closely parallel those in the *INS* case in order to be successful.[32] Twitter and other Internet companies submitted amicus briefs urging the court to throw out hot news as obsolete. Public interest groups urged the court to renounce the doctrine because it restricts free speech, but the court did not reach the First Amendment issue.

Calls by news organizations for federal hot news legislation have so far been unsuccessful. Any such legislation would have to be strictly limited to avoid limiting free speech, and it should retain most of the restrictive elements from the *NBA* case in order to limit claims to those that would have a direct and substantial anti-competitive effect and lead to long-term harm to the business of news- and information-gathering.

TRADEMARKS

A trademark can be a word, phrase, symbol or design, or a combination of words, phrases, symbols or designs that identifies and distinguishes the source of the goods of one party from those of others. The purpose of a trademark or a service mark, which protects services rather than goods, is to protect businesses from the unauthorized use of their corporate or product names, slogans or logos for commercial purposes.

Unlike copyright, which is exclusively federal law, trademarks may be governed by both the federal Lanham Act and state trademark laws. To qualify for protection, a trademark cannot be deceptive or confusingly similar to another mark and it must be distinctive—it must be capable of identifying the source of a particular good or service.

Infringement occurs when a trademark is used in a commercial context in a manner that is likely to cause consumer confusion as to the source of the product or service. Trademark "dilution" occurs when the distinctive quality of the mark is diminished, even though consumer confusion is not likely. A trademark may be diluted by "blurring," when it becomes identified with goods that are dissimilar to what made it famous, or by "tarnishment," when the mark is portrayed negatively, such as being associated with inferior or disreputable products or services. To bring a dilution claim under federal law, a trademark must be "famous"—one that is widely known, such as Xerox or Exxon.

As with copyright, free speech considerations require that a company's trademark may be used for descriptive purposes if necessary to accurately identify the product or service. As a result, a Facebook post that describes a celebrity's outfit at an awards ceremony using trademarks ("Zooey Deschanel wore Prada to the Golden Globes") infringes neither Prada's nor the Golden Globes' trademark. Parodies of trademarks are generally protected as critical commentary, although the degree to which the parody involves a commercial use of the mark may determine whether the use crosses the line into infringement or tarnishment. Editorial uses are favored over uses in commercial products such as posters or T-shirts, so a trademark parody posted on a social networking site would most likely be protected, although no bright-line rules apply.

In 2013, the U.S. Patent and Trademark Office began to allow hashtags to be registered as trademarks. Hashtags, which started on Twitter but are now seen across social media, are words or phrases preceded by the hash or pound sign (#) that are used to label or tag the messages they accompany. The PTO allows the registration of a hashtag as a trademark as long as it functions, like any trademark, as an identifier of the source of goods or services. Company and product names, for example, can be registered as hashtags ("#IBM," "#Coke"), as can slogans, such as Nike's "#justdoit." The hashtag must be shown to have been used in commerce to be registrable.

Use of another's trademarked hashtag in commerce may be infringement if it is likely to confuse the public about the source of the goods or services. In 2015, clothing maker Fraternity Collection sued its former designer for trademark infringement over her use on social media of the tags "#fratcollection" and "#fraternitycollection." The court dismissed the defendant's motion to dismiss, ruling that the inclusion of the hashtag of a competitor's name or product in a social media post could lead to consumer confusion.[33] At the same time, the free speech protections given to descriptive purposes and parodies for trademarks also extend to trademarked hashtags.

On Twitter, the use of corporate trademarks for fake accounts has resulted in controversy, but not much litigation to date. Twitter allows users to sign up under another's name as long as the account profile makes clear that the account is an impersonation and they do not pretend to be someone else "in order to mislead or deceive"—if they do, their account will be suspended.[34] The guidelines also advise users to differentiate their account name from that of their parody subject; accounts such as "Google Brain,"

"AT&T Parody Relations," and "The Fake CNN" make clear to consumers that the account is meant as an exercise in free speech, not commerce.

Fake accounts on social media sites may be actionable if they use trademarks for commercial purposes and if consumer confusion is likely to occur. Some have argued that confusion may be more likely on fast-moving and de-contextualized Twitter feeds than on a static website. The fake Twitter account @BPGlobalPR brought wide attention to the practice when it satirized the oil company's attempts at public relations after the massive 2010 Gulf Coast oil spill (example: "The ocean looks just a bit slimmer today. Dressing it in black really did the trick! #bpcares"). Although the account did not contain a disclaimer, a spokesman for the real BP indicated the company would not take legal action, saying, "People are entitled to their views on what we're doing and we have to live with those."[35]

In 2011, a viatical life insurance firm called Coventry First sued an anonymous Twitter user over a fake account that sent out tweets such as, "Praying to Jesus for an earthquake in the North Eastern US!!" The lawsuit included claims for trademark infringement and dilution. The account's user profile indicated it was meant as a parody, and the user subsequently changed the account name slightly to comply with Twitter's guidelines for parody accounts, which forbid use of the exact name of the parody's subject. The suit was eventually dropped.[36]

Celebrity Impersonation and Trademark

Impersonation is not limited to corporate identities on social media sites. In 2009, St. Louis Cardinals manager Tony La Russa sued Twitter over a fake account that used his name and image. Tweets were posted in his name that referred to team-related incidents such as the death of pitcher Josh Hancock and La Russa's own DUI arrest: "Lost 2 out of 3, but we made it out of Chicago without one drunk driving incident or dead pitcher," read one tweet. The only disclaimer was in the user profile, which stated, "Bio parodies are fun for everyone."

Although other celebrities had also had their names "twitterjacked," this was the first reported instance of a celebrity suing Twitter over a fake account. The complaint listed a number of claims against Twitter, including trademark infringement and dilution.[37]

The case is interesting for what it reveals about the limits federal law has put on plaintiffs hoping to hold online service providers responsible for harm caused by posts on social media sites. La Russa's real complaint about the fake account was that the tasteless statements in the tweets would be ascribed to him and would hurt his reputation. La Russa could not easily sue the actual impersonator because the person who set up the account was unknown, and Twitter deleted the fake account the same day the suit was filed.

Although his harm had more to do with false light or defamation, he also would have been barred from suing Twitter on those claims, because the federal Communication Decency Act immunizes online service providers from liability for damages caused by offensive or harmful content posted by its users. Section 230 of the CDA gives sites like Twitter a safe harbor against secondary liability for a variety of state claims, which different courts have held to include defamation, misappropriation, obscenity, invasion of privacy, and state trademark dilution claims.[38]

Federal intellectual property claims are not included in the CDA's safe harbor provision but are covered by Section 512 of the DMCA and by a similar provision in the Lanham Act that protects online service providers from secondary liability for federal trademark infringement claims.[39] La Russa had little choice, then, but to sue Twitter for direct trademark infringement. He did so by claiming that the fake account falsely implied a personal endorsement of Twitter because of statements that said, "Tony La Russa is using Twitter" and "Join today to start receiving Tony La Russa's updates." To win, he would have had to show that the statements were likely to confuse consumers into thinking he had personally endorsed the site, and that as a result, he had been harmed. This may have been especially difficult to prove—according to news reports, the fake account had only four followers.[40]

In 2010, California passed an "e-personation" law that made online impersonation a crime. While its purpose was to combat fraud and cyberbullying, critics charge that it undermines First Amendment rights and chills protected speech such as parody and satirical commentary.[41] Today, Twitter protects celebrity accounts with a verification policy that authenticates the identities of public figures and attaches a blue checkmark next to the profile name on verified accounts, although in at least one case it has authenticated the wrong account—due to a copy-editing error, an account spoofing Wendi Deng Murdoch, the wife of News Corp. CEO Rupert Murdoch, was authenticated instead of the real account.[42]

THE RIGHT OF PUBLICITY

Twitterjacking may also violate a celebrity's right of publicity if the account is used for commercial purposes. The right of publicity protects against the commercial use of a person's name, likeness or other aspect of his identity, including voice, signature or persona. Most lawsuits concern unauthorized use of a person's name or likeness in advertising or by putting a celebrity's name or image on commercial products such as T-shirts or coffee mugs without permission. The publicity right, which is governed by state law, is rooted in both privacy law—to safeguard a person's privacy from being exploited commercially—and intellectual property law—to protect the economic value a person has established in his name, likeness, and persona.

First Amendment concerns arise when a person's name or likeness is used for descriptive purposes or for criticism, parody, news reporting or art. A number of tests have been developed by the courts to balance free speech and publicity rights, with First Amendment protections yielding when the primary purpose of the use is commercial exploitation. This is not always clear: Can a restaurant report on its Twitter feed that a celebrity was spotted there, or does that imply endorsement? What about tweeting a photo? In 2014, actress Katherine Heigl sued the New York drugstore chain Duane Reade in 2014 for $6 million for tweeting a paparazzi photo of her carrying a Duane Reade shopping bag with the comment, "Love a quick #DuaneReade run? Even @KatieHeigl can't resist shopping #NYC's favorite drugstore." While Heigl quickly settled with Duane Reade without going to trial, the case served to warn companies of the potential for future litigation in this area.

Finally, although most cases involve celebrities, it is not necessary to be well known to win a right of publicity lawsuit. In 2013, Facebook settled a class action lawsuit over its inclusion of users' names and likenesses in advertisements it called "sponsored stories." A user's "likes" triggered the creation of a sponsored story—an ad—that included the user's name and image. In 2016, the Ninth Circuit upheld the settlement, which awarded class members $15 each and imposed changes to Facebook's disclosure policies.[43]

INTELLECTUAL PROPERTY: THE NEED FOR REFORM

Intellectual property is a complex issue and an increasingly important one in the digital age. The tension between protecting property rights in works and promoting creativity and the free flow of ideas is evident in the controversies and cases discussed in this chapter. Social networking highlights this tension, because traditional copyright rules, which emphasize exclusive authorship and ownership, are not well suited to fostering a system based on collaborative and interactive creation.

While activists and copyright scholars have called for changes in the law to encourage this new means of creative production and reduce the uncertainty surrounding social media sharing, others have created their own guidelines. The Center for Social Media's development of fair use standards in their Codes of Best Practices is just one example of the kind of "bottom-up" rulemaking practiced by creative communities today. Self-regulation can be effective because it reflects pre-existing social norms and therefore has automatic moral authority and "buy-in" from the community, and because it can adapt to changes that occur in community practices and norms. At the same time, it risks tilting too much towards the interests of the community at the expense of copyright owners' property rights or the public interest.

Technology also provides a way for copyright owners to control their works online, as examples like YouTube's Content ID system show. These tools also have the capability to create an imbalance of interests, however. In 1999, Lawrence Lessig contrasted the two types of "code" that regulate cyberspace: "East Coast Code," or the code that Congress enacts, and "West Coast Code," which is "the code that code writers 'enact' – the instructions imbedded in the software and hardware that make cyberspace work."[44] Lessig warned that as copyright owners increasingly turned to regulation by computer code—cheaper, more efficient and more flexible than East Coast Code—society must ensure that fundamental values like fair use are protected.

Finally, private ordering through contract can give social media sites the means to regulate their own sites with the flexibility needed to respond to changing circumstances—Twitter's terms of service, for example, give it the authority to regulate the use of its site and shut down a user's account without resorting to legal action. Here, too, however, default legal rules that try to strike a fair balance give way to whatever realignment of rights the private parties have bargained for. In the case of most terms of service agreements on social media sites, these rights are not truly bargained for and tend to favor the site rather than its users or the public interest.

Legislation—East Coast Code—can be slow, cumbersome, and complex. At the same time, while private ordering through self-regulation, technology, or contract can fill in some of the gaps in the law, it can never completely replace it. When it comes to regulating the diverse and fast-changing social media environment, the challenge for Congress and the courts will be to strike the proper balance between private interests and public benefits so that intellectual property rights continue to be protected without limiting the future possibilities for expression that social networking represents.

FREQUENTLY ASKED QUESTIONS

1. Can I use a photo I find on Facebook?

It depends. The absence of a copyright notice does not mean the photo isn't copyrighted, and you should generally get permission unless you believe your use would be protected by the fair use doctrine. Non-commercial uses that are transformative or otherwise productive, such as comment, criticism, news reporting, research, scholarship, or teaching, may be fair use. Copying the photo for the same purpose as, or to substitute for, the original is not fair use. Attribution without permission ("Photo courtesy of CNN.com") is still infringement.

2. Can I embed a video from someone else's website on my Facebook page?

Probably. The Ninth Circuit has ruled that because embedding works by linking to a file that resides on another server, rather than by making a copy, it does not infringe copyright. Making changes to the video or trying to "pass off" the video as your own content may violate the rights of the video owner, however. Commenting on the video in the post would also make a fair use defense possible.

3. Can I be sued if someone posts a copyrighted photo on my blog?

You could be, but generally you will not be if you take the photo down when notified by the copyright owner. Because you host content on your blog that you do not control, you may be protected from secondary liability as an online service provider under Section 512 of the Digital Millennium Copyright Act. In order to take advantage of the safe harbor provision, you should include a notice to your readers not to post infringing content and file a form with the Copyright Office (http://www.copyright.gov/onlinesp/agent.pdf) to designate an agent for takedown notification.

4. Can I be sued for trademark infringement for creating a parody Twitter account?

Maybe, but you would most likely be protected by the First Amendment. In addition, trademark infringement requires commercial use of a trademark and the likelihood of consumer confusion. If you made clear your account was a parody, it would be hard for the subject of your parody to show it caused consumer confusion or that it caused any real harm to its trademark.

5. What is a Creative Commons license?

Creative Commons licenses give copyright owners a way to give permission in advance for certain uses of their content. Most of the licenses include some restrictions on use, such as requiring attribution or forbidding commercial use. Look for the CC logo on sites that use the licenses.

NOTES

1 U.S. Const, art. I, § 8.
2 Agence France Presse v. Morel, 769 F. Supp. 2d 295 (S.D.N.Y. 2011).
3 17 U.S.C. §§ 502–506.
4 Sony BMG Music Entertainment v. Tenenbaum, 719 F.3d 67 (1st Cir. 2013).
5 Perfect 10, Inc. v. Amazon.com, Inc., 508 F.3d 1146 (9th Cir. 2007).
6 17 U.S.C. § 302.
7 17 U.S.C. § 107.
8 Campbell v. Acuff-Rose Music, Inc., 510 U.S. 569, 579 (1994).
9 Id.
10 74 F. Supp. 3d 605 (S.D.N.Y. 2015).
11 725 F.3d 1170 (9th Cir. 2013).
12 Id. at 708. The court ultimately concluded Prince's use of the photographs was fair use in all but five instances.
13 Perfect 10 v. Amazon.com, Inc., 508 F.3d 1146 (9th Cir. 2007).
14 Righthaven, LLC v. Jama, 2011 U.S. Dist. LEXIS 43952 (D. Nev. Apr. 22, 2011).
15 Righthaven, LLC v. Wolf, 813 F. Supp. 2d 1265, 1273 (D. Colo. 2011).
16 For more on Righthaven, see Righthaven Stories, VegasInc, http://www.vegasInc. com/news/legal/righthaven/
17 Codes, Center for Social Media, http://www.centerforsocialmedia.org/fair-use/ related-materials/codes
18 Digital Millennium Copyright Act, 17 U.S.C. § 512 (1998).
19 Lenz v. Universal Music Corp., 801 F.3d 1126 (9th Cir. 2015) *opinion amended and superseded on denial of reh'g*, 815 F.3d 1145 (9th Cir. 2016).
20 UMG Recordings, Inc. v. Shelter Capital Partners LLC, 667 F.3d 1022 (9th Cir. 2011).
21 Id.
22 Viacom Int'l, Inc. v. YouTube, Inc., 718 F. Supp. 514 (S.D.N.Y. 2010).
23 676 F.3d 19(2d Cir. 2012).
24 Section 512 of Title 17: Hearing Before the House Judiciary Committee, Subcommittee on Courts, Intellectual Property, and the Internet, 113th Cong., 2d Sess. (2014) (opening remarks by Chairman Goodlatte).
25 Stop Online Piracy Act, H.R. 3261, 112th Cong. § 2(a)(2) (2011); Protect IP Act of 2011, S. 986,112th Cong. § 6(b) (2011).
26 http://copyright.gov/policy/section512/
27 About, Creative Commons, http://creativecommons.org/about
28 Public "Relieved" by bin Laden's Death, Obama's Job Approval Rises, Pew Research Center for the People & the Press (May 3, 2011), http://pyewresearch.org/pubs/1978/ poll-osama-bin-laden-death-reaction-obama-bush-military-cia-credit-first-heard-news.
29 See Victoria Smith Ekstrand, Hot News in the Age of Big Data (2015).
30 Int'l News Serv. v. Associated Press, 248 U.S. 215, 236 (1918).
31 Nat'l Basketball Ass'n v. Motorola, Inc., 105 F.3d 841, 844–45 (2d Cir. 1997).
32 Barclays Capital, Inc. v. TheFlyOnTheWall.com, Inc., 650 F.3d 876 (2d Cir. 2011).
33 Fraternity Collection, LLC v. Fargnoli, 2015 WL 1486375 (S.D. Miss. Mar. 31, 2015).
34 Impersonation Policy, Twitter, https://support.twitter.com/articles/18366#

35 Paulina Reso, Imposter BP Twitter Account That Parodies Oil Giant Left Untouched, N. Y. Daily News, May 27, 2010, http://articles.nydailynews.com/2010-05-27/news/27065593_1_bp-spokesman-toby-odone-gulf-oil-spill.

36 Complaint, Coventry First, LLC v. Does 1–10, No. 1 1-cv-03700-JS (E.D.Va. June 7, 2011); Jeff Roberts, Insurer Sues Twitter Imposter Who Cheers Death, Mayhem, Reuters (June 9, 2011), http://www.reuters.com/article/2011/06/09/us-coventiy-idUSTRE7586ST20110609.

37 Complaint, La Russa v. Twitter, Inc., No. CGC09488101 (Cal. Sup. Ct. May 6, 2009).

38 Mark A. Lemley, Rationalizing Internet Safe Harbors, 6 J. on Telecomm. & High Tech. L. 101,101 n. 2 (2007) (listing cases).

39 15 U.S.C. § 1114(2).

40 William McGeveran, Celebrity Impersonation and Section 230, Info/Law (June 25, 2009), http://blogs.law.har-vard.edu/infolaw/2009/06/25/impersonation-and-230/.

41 Cal. Penal Code § 528.5 (West 2011).

42 Adam Clark Estes, How Twitter Accidentally Verified the Wrong Wendi Deng, The Atlantic Wire (Jan. 4, 2012), http://www.theatlanticwire.com/technology/2012/01/how-twitter-accidentally-verified-wrong-wendi-deng/46991/.

43 Fraley v. Batman, 2016 U.S. App. LEXIS 518 (9th Cir. Cal. Jan. 6, 2016).

44 Lawrence Lessig, Code and Other Laws of Cyberspace 53 (1999).

CHAPTER 5

Commercial Speech in a Social Space

Courtney Barclay

Jacksonville University

ABSTRACT

Online and mobile communications, including social media, provide new and valuable opportunities for interaction between an organization and its publics. The increased use of these media, however, presents significant concerns for consumer protection. Congress and key regulatory agencies—the Federal Trade Commission, the Food and Drug Administration, and the Securities and Exchange Commission—have worked to ensure consumers continue to be protected in the new media environment. These laws continue to focus on long-standing values of commercial speech regulation: truth, accurate disclosure, and fairness. This chapter discusses the legislative and regulatory developments essential to advertising and public relations professionals.

Historically, commercial speech—that speech which promotes financial transactions—received no protection under the First Amendment. However, this approach shifted in the 1970s, when the U.S. Supreme Court recognized that society "may have a strong interest in the free flow of commercial information."[1] The protection the Court recognized is limited, classifying commercial speech, such as advertising and public relations communications, as deserving lesser protection than other forms of protected expression.

In 1980, the Court established a four-part test for reviewing government restrictions on commercial speech.[2] In *Central Hudson Gas & Electric Corporation v. Public Service Commission*, the Court ruled that for a commercial speech regulation to be upheld, a court must first find that the speech is eligible for First Amendment protection; false or misleading advertising, or the promotion of an illegal product or service, is not protected expression. If the speech is lawful and truthful commercial expression, the government must prove that there is a substantial government interest in restricting the speech and that the regulation directly advances that interest. Finally, the government must prove that the regulation is narrowly tailored, and thus not so broad as to prevent valuable speech.

This test demonstrates the lower status afforded commercial speech. Even truthful speech can be strongly regulated to serve an important government interest. A variety of federal agencies have been granted the authority to regulate commercial speech in an effort to protect consumers. In 1914, the federal government passed the Federal Trade Commission Act, which charges the Federal Trade Commission (FTC) to protect consumers from unfair and deceptive practices.[3] The FTC has exercised its authority on a variety of issues, including monopolistic practices, advertising directed to children, health-related claims, and consumer privacy.

While the FTC is the agency primarily responsible for regulating general business practices and advertising messages, other federal agencies focus on particular consumer products and practices. For example, the Food, Drug, and Cosmetic Act charges the Food and Drug Administration (FDA) with regulating the advertising and labeling of prescription drugs and medical devices.[4] The FDA has promulgated rules on the advertising of tobacco products, direct-to-consumer advertisements for prescription drugs, and off-label marketing of pharmaceuticals.

Another key agency in the regulation of commercial speech is the Securities and Exchange Commission, created by the Securities Exchange Act of 1934. The SEC ensures that investors receive truthful information about securities offered for sale.[5] For example, companies are required to accurately report, among other things, changes in the command structure of the company, changes in significant assets, and any bankruptcy filings.[6]

Americans are using social media sites in rising numbers. As consumers have turned more attention to social media, advertisers have increased spending to reach them in this new space. Social advertising provides new methods to target and analyze messages. In 2014, digital marketing accounted for $50 billion in advertising revenue, with $24 billion spent on social media platforms such as Facebook.[7] Throughout this growth of online and mobile brand communications, existing laws have been extended to these paid messages, shared content, and social media interactions. However, several new challenges have been presented by these media platforms. However, the growth of online communications, including social media, has posed several new challenges for these regulatory agencies. This chapter will discuss key developments in the rules and regulatory actions of the Federal Trade Commission, the Food and Drug Administration, and the Securities and Exchange Commission that impact commercial speech.

TRUTH IN ADVERTISING AND UNFAIR PRACTICES

The Federal Trade Commission is the federal agency primarily responsible for protecting consumers from deceptive or misleading messages and unfair business practices. In discharging this duty, the FTC has maintained advertisers must have a reasonable basis for all claims, either expressed or implied, for reasonable consumers.[8] The FTC works to ensure truthful information in advertising through the requirement of disclosures, substantiation, and enforcement actions. The FTC has applied these rules to online communications in the same way they have been applied to traditional media in print, radio, and television.

For example, in 2011, the FTC settled deceptive advertising charges with the marketers of AcneApp and Acne Pwner, mobile applications sold in the Apple iTunes store and Google Android Marketplace. The FTC charged the marketers with making unsubstantiated health claims, such as the ability for the smart phone apps to treat acne by emitting colored lights. In the complaint documents for both cases, the FTC relied on the requirement that advertisers have a reasonable basis to substantiate representations made to consumers. Such substantiation was lacking in these cases.

Although the FTC has held that online communications will be subjected to the same standards as traditional media, the development of new technologies, delivery methods, and user-generated content has pushed the FTC to focus on certain issues specific to protecting consumers online.

Deceptive Endorsements

In 1975, the FTC issued the first Guides Concerning Use of Endorsements and Testimonials in Advertising, which set out rules for advertisements using testimonials and endorsements. Specifically, these Guides define endorsement relationships, require that certain standards are met in all endorsement communications, and mandate that all "material connections" between an advertiser and an endorser be disclosed to the public.

An endorsement is defined as "any advertising message that consumers are likely to believe reflects the opinions, beliefs, findings, or experiences of a party other than the sponsoring advertiser, even if the views expressed by that party are identical to those of the sponsoring advertiser." In general, the FTC Endorsement Guides require that endorsements "reflect the honest opinions, findings, beliefs, or experience of the endorser."[9] The Guides specifically address rules for endorsements by consumers, organizations, and experts. In all of these cases, the Guides require that where the audience would not reasonably expect it, any material connection between the endorser and the advertiser must be "fully disclosed."[10] The public generally expects that celebrity statements endorsing a product or service represent a relationship between the advertiser and the celebrity; no disclosure needs to be made in that instance. However, individuals unknown to the public would not raise similar expectations for the audience. In those situations, a clear disclosure must be made regarding payment or other compensation received for the endorsement.

These word-of-mouth campaigns were expensive and required a great deal of effort before the technological advancements of interactive media. Social media "amplifies" consumer reviews and provides unique opportunity for brands to monitor consumer opinions.[11] However, it was unclear how sponsored word-of-mouth campaigns online would be regulated under the Deceptive Trade Practices Act.[12] To answer these questions, the FTC in 2009 revised existing endorsement and testimonial guidelines to include examples that specifically address these kinds of commercial messages online. In one example provided in the Guides, the FTC considers a tennis player who provides information on her social networking site about the results of her laser eye surgery. In the post, the tennis player names the clinic where the surgery was performed. Because her followers on the social network may not realize that she is a paid endorser for the clinic, the relationship needs to be disclosed.[13]

In the revised Guides, the FTC was careful to include examples of online endorsements by consumers, as well. One such example discusses a college student blogger who posts a review of a video game and system he has received for free from the hardware manufacturer. The FTC states, "the blogger should clearly and conspicuously disclose that he received the gaming system free of charge." Further, the FTC requires that the manufacturer advise the blogger that the relationship be disclosed, and that the manufacturer monitor the blogger's posts for compliance.[14]

In the first regulatory action under these Guides, the FTC found that Reverb Communications, Inc., had engaged in misleading advertisements when it failed to disclose its relationships with reviewers.[15] Reverb provides marketing and public relations services to clients selling gaming applications via the Apple iTunes store. As part of these marketing efforts, employees of Reverb posted public reviews on iTunes with account names that did not disclose the relationship they had to the game developers. All of the reviews provided four- and five-star ratings as well as written accolades. The FTC found that these reviews misled consumers to believe independent users of the applications wrote them. Reverb was ordered to remove all reviews that violated the disclosure requirements.[16]

The FTC has also ruled that a contractual requirement for compliance is not enough to preclude an advertiser from being held responsible for the nondisclosures of its advertising affiliates. In 2011, the FTC fined Legacy

Learning Systems $250,000 for failing to disclose material connections with online reviewers.[17] Legacy Learning Systems manufactures and sells instructional courses on DVD through a website. An affiliate program is the primary advertising method for these courses. Affiliates of the program work to direct traffic to Legacy's website and then receive between 20 and 45% commission for each course sold. Some of the affiliates are "Review Ad" affiliates, who place positive reviews in articles, blogs, and other online content. The reviews include hyperlinks to Legacy's website. Many of these reviews give the impression that they have been written by ordinary consumers. Although the contracts for the program mandated that the affiliates "comply with the FTC guidelines on disclosures," the FTC found that Legacy had not instituted a compliance-monitoring program, resulting in consumers receiving deceptive and misleading information.

One step that advertisers can take to promote compliance with the FTC Guides is to develop an established social media policy that addresses under what circumstances disclosures must be made.[18] In 2011, the FTC determined not to pursue an enforcement action against Hyundai Motor America, in part due to the fact that such a policy was in place.[19] The FTC staff reviewed a blogging campaign executed in the lead up to the 2011 Super Bowl broadcast. Some of the bloggers were given gift certificates, but not all of them disclosed that information. The question was whether any of the bloggers were instructed to *not* disclose the gift certificates. The FTC staff determined that any such actions were the efforts of an individual working for a media firm hired by Hyundai to conduct the blogging campaign. Those actions conflicted with the social media policies at both Hyundai and the media firm, which specifically directed bloggers to disclose any compensation. Therefore, the FTC closed the investigation with no action against the media firm or Hyundai.[20]

A particular concern in social media has been the amount of space that may be required to make these disclosures. For example, the FTC Bureau of Consumer Protection (BCP) received questions about how to effectively make disclosures via the 140-character limit on Twitter's social media platform. The BCP has suggested that users may disclose an endorsement relationship by appending a hashtag identifier, such as #paid or #ad. This should provide readers sufficient information to evaluate the message.[21]

Deceptive Advertising Format

The FTC has found that one measure of deceptive or misleading advertising is the format it takes. Native advertising is content that "bears similarity to the news, feature articles, product reviews, entertainment, and other material that surrounds it online."[22] For example, in its 2016 Guide, the FTC considers a feature story in an online lifestyle magazine that features and promotes the sponsor's products.[23]

Advertising in news format is not new to online media. In the 1960s, the FTC found that what appeared to be a newspaper column offering unbiased reviews of local restaurants was, in fact, a misleading advertisement.[24] Although the column did not include pricing information, the FTC determined that it would not change the effect on readers. Instead, the FTC recommended clear labels for advertising messages. Since then, the FTC has continued to find advertising messages disguised as independent content to be misleading.[25]

In 2016, the FTC found that not only had a retailer failed to disclose paid relationships with social media posters, but it also engaged in misleading native advertising. Lord & Taylor paid *Nylon*, an online fashion magazine, to publish an article about a new Lord & Taylor apparel line including a feature photo of the single piece of apparel in the new line. The retailer reviewed the article prior to publication, but did not instruct *Nylon* to include any disclosure statement. The FTC further defines the disclosure necessary for native advertising in the consent agreement reached with Lord & Taylor. Such disclosure must be "clear and conspicuous," meaning (1) it must be made in the same medium as the overall message; (2) visual disclosures must stand out so that they are easily noticed; (3) audible disclosures must be easily heard and understood; and (4) interactive media message must include unavoidable disclosures. Additionally, the disclosure must generally be in "close proximity" to the triggering message, meaning it must be simultaneously viewed. A link or popup is not considered in "close proximity."[26] In 2013, the FTC issued a guidance document providing specific application of the "clear and conspicuous" disclosure requirements, as well as illustrative examples.[27]

Spamming

"Spam" generally refers to unsolicited commercial emails.[28] Since the mid-1990s, the FTC has worked to protect consumers from spam-related unfair practices.[29] In 2003, the U.S. Congress granted the FTC special jurisdiction over spamming practices when it passed the Controlling the Assault of Non-Solicited Pornography and Marketing Act (CAN-SPAM Act). The CAN-SPAM Act places certain requirements on marketers to protect consumers against unfair practices. For example, marketers may not use deceptive subject lines, they must include a valid return address, and the messages must include a method for the recipient to opt-out of future messages.

The FTC has been particularly vigilant against spam that contains fraudulent content, malware, and links to phishing websites—a form of identity theft that uses emails to get consumers to provide personal and financial information.[30] In *FTC v. Hill*, Zachary Hill was charged—and pleaded guilty—to fraudulently acquiring credit card numbers and Internet account information through email ostensibly sent to users from AOL and PayPal.[31]

One of the difficulties of controlling spam and the related fraudulent practices is the constant development of new delivery methods. For example, botnets, or networks of hijacked computers, allow spammers to send bulk messages anonymously and remotely. The FTC continues to pursue these cases. In 2010, a district court judge permanently enjoined the operation of an Internet Service Provider that shielded and assisted botnet spammers.[32] The ISP, which the FTC estimated controlled nearly 5,000 malicious soft-ware programs, also was ordered to pay more than $1 million to the U.S. Treasury for disgorgement of ill-gotten gains.

In 2011, the FTC filed the first spam action for deceptive Short Message Service (SMS) ads sent to mobile phones.[33] In the complaint, the FTC charged Phil Flora, a California resident, with sending "at least 5 million unsolicited commercial electronic text messages." Many of the messages advertised mortgage and debt relief programs, referring recipients to a website, loanmod-gov.net. The inclusion of "gov" as part of the website address misled consumers to believe that these programs were government-sponsored. The FTC settled the case for a judgment of nearly $60,000. The settlement also includes a prohibition on Flora sending any unsolicited commercial text messages or making any misrepresentations that he, or anyone else, is affiliated with a government agency.[34] The FTC also enforces spam actions against companies misleading message recipients as to the source of the emails, such as in 2016, when it investigated a marketing firm that was paid for emails to be sent from hacked email accounts, misleading consumers to believe emails were sent from their friends or family members. The emails linked to fake news stories about a weight-loss product and included fake testimonials about weight loss.[35]

In addition to case-by-case enforcement, the FTC and Congress have explored preventative options to protect consumers on a larger scale. Most significantly, Congress charged the FTC with establishing a national Do-Not-Email Registry.[36] Upon investigation, the FTC reported that such a registry would be largely ineffective at reducing the incidence of spam. Rather, a registry of email addresses may pose privacy and security risks.[37] However, the FTC does work with a variety of federal agencies, industry associations and consumer groups to lead consumer education efforts through an interactive site launched in 2005.[38] OnGuardOnline.gov provides tips for consumers in the form of articles, games, and videos.[39] Additionally, the FTC hosts a spam-reporting service that allows consumers to forward unsolicited messages, including phishing scams, to be stored in a law enforcement database for further investigation. However, the FTC continues to urge the industry to develop technological solutions, such as authentication systems, to combat these issues.[40]

Online Behavioral Advertising

The Federal Trade Commission has also urged stringent self-regulation to address the consumer privacy concerns raised by behavioral advertising methods. These methods use tracking devices, such as cookies, to scan web activity in real time to assess a user's location, age, income, and, in some instances, medical conditions. The *Wall Street Journal*, in an investigative series on behavioral tracking, identified certain trackers that scanned the content of health-related pages on sites such as Encyclopedia Britannica that would allow companies to serve related ads to those users for diseases including bipolar disorder, bladder conditions, and depression.[41]

The use of these tracking methods, particularly for commercial purposes, has raised significant privacy concerns for consumers. Advertisers using behavioral tracking are able to analyze a person's web viewing habits "to predict user preferences or interests to deliver advertising to that computer or device based on the preferences or interests inferred from such Web viewing behaviors."[42] Approximately 80% of all online advertisements are served as a result of behavioral targeting.[43] Behavioral advertising revenues for 12 advertising networks were approximately $598 million.[44]

The FTC has recognized the serious concerns these practices raise for consumers, including loss of privacy, fraud, and deceptive marketing.[45] In 1996, the FTC staff recommended that the Commission continue to monitor issues of online privacy, but concluded that self-regulation and technological solutions may be sufficient to protect consumers' privacy in the marketplace.

However, in 2000, the FTC reported to Congress on online profiling and recommended that Congress legislate online profiling to mandate compliance with established fair information practices.[46] Although the FTC praised industry efforts at self-regulation, the Commission noted that not all advertisers and website owners were allied with the organizations issuing these guidelines.[47] Federal legislation would mandate compliance for all websites and advertising networks and provide an agency with the authority to enforce privacy protections.[48] Congress failed to pass any such law.

In 2009, the FTC released a statement supporting a policy of industry self-regulation, including proposed principles to guide the industry's efforts.[49] These principles focused on transparency, data security, changes in privacy policies, and sensitive data.[50] In response, the industry, represented by two key groups—the Network Advertising Initiative (NAI) and the Digital Advertising Alliance (DAA)—released a series of guidelines and tools to advance privacy protections for online consumers.[51] These guidelines have focused on improving the transparency and clarity of privacy notices, educating consumers about behavioral or interest-based advertising techniques, and providing consumers with user-friendly opt-out tools.[52]

The NAI completed compliance reviews of member companies in 2009 and 2010.[53] These reports indicate that member companies have improved their notices in various ways, including specific data retention period information, increasing visibility and readability of notices, using more prominent "privacy" or "opt-out" labels, and using an industry developed advertising option icon on served advertisements.[54]

However, in December 2010, the FTC issued a report stating that these efforts "have been too slow and up to now have failed to provide adequate and meaningful protection."[55] The report called for a Do-Not-Track mechanism that would allow consumers to opt out of data collection for ad targeting with one simple, easy-to-use tool.[56] Following this report, privacy issues became a hot commodity in Congress, with more than 10 privacy-related bills introduced to the 112th Congress in 2011. Among them was the Do Not Track Me Online Act to authorize the FTC to adopt regulations requiring companies to use an online opt-out tool.[57] Despite these efforts, no federal law has been passed to regulate data collection for targeted advertising practices.

The FTC has engaged in enforcement actions against companies for failing to protect consumers' personal information.[58] For example, in 2011, the FTC settled complaints against social networking sites Facebook and Twitter that focused on the failure of those companies to protect users' personal information. A settlement against Google Buzz alleged inadequate privacy policies and ordered the company to implement a "comprehensive privacy policy." The settlement agreement also orders the company to submit to independent privacy audits for 20 years.

The agency also has pursued cases specifically dealing with behavioral targeting.[59] Chitika, an online advertising company, engages in behavioral tracking and reportedly delivers three billion ad impressions a month. In a complaint against the ad company, the FTC alleged that Chitika deceptively offered consumers an "opt-out" mechanism that only stored the consumer's preference to not be tracked for 10 days. After 10 days had passed, Chitika would begin tracking those consumers again until they opted out again. The settlement agreement requires that every targeted ad served by Chitika include a hyperlink to a clear opt-out tool that allows consumers to opt out of tracking for at least five years.[60]

The FTC has continued to focus on consumer choice, specifically broad opt-out schemes, especially as marketers have focused more on cross-device tracking and messaging. According to former FTC Commissioner Julie Brill, the FTC found that much of the cross-device tracking was done without notifying consumers. Brill noted that consumers do not have "adequate" ability to opt out of tracking, cross-device or otherwise, despite nearly two decades of the FTC pushing for more consumer control.[61]

Children's Privacy Online

Since Congress and the FTC began monitoring behavioral advertising, a key concern has been protecting information collected on minors using online services. In 1998, Congress passed the Children's Online Privacy Protection Act (COPPA).[62] This delegated to the FTC the authority to regulate websites targeting children under the age of 13. COPPA requires that these websites limit collection to information that is necessary for the child to use the websites' functions. Additionally, these sites must notify parents about the type of information being collected from children and get consent from the parents before collection, use or disclosure begins. These sites must develop procedures to reasonably secure the personally identifiable data and allow parents access to any data collected about their children.

The FTC has engaged in enforcement actions against smartphone app developers and social network sites for their deceptive practices in collecting information from children. For example, in 2011 the FTC settled with a mobile app developer for failing to provide notice and gain consent before collecting information from children using games such as Emily's Girl World, which included games and a journal for users to record "private" thoughts.[63] In response to children's increasing use of mobile technology and social networks, the FTC made several key changes to the COPPA rule in 2013, including expanding the definition of personal information to include IP addresses and geolocation information, as well as persistent identifiers placed on a computer for tracking purposes, requiring websites to obtain parental consent for these practices.[64]

PHARMACEUTICAL ADVERTISING

Although the FTC is the agency that protects consumers in the general marketplace, the Food and Drug Administration polices the labeling, advertising, and public relations efforts for prescription medications and medical devices.[65] In addition to general requirements of truth and accuracy, the FDA requires that commercial messages for pharmaceuticals include the generic or "established" name of the drug, a detailed list of ingredients, and a summary of side effects and contraindications.[66] These mandates commonly are enforced through the use of notices of violation and warning letters sent to pharmaceutical companies, describing the offending conduct, asking for remediation, such as removal or corrective advertising, and threatening further legal action.

Despite significant delays in issuing guidance for online communications, the FDA in 2014 began issuing draft guidance documents for pharmaceutical companies engaging with the public on online and mobile platforms, including company websites, online videos, online advertising, and social media. Generally, the concerns expressed by the FDA are that pharmaceutical companies either overstate the efficacy of a drug, omit or minimize the risks associated with the drug, or fail to correct inaccurate third-party information about a drug. These common concerns are the subject of the first two draft guidance documents on social media. Additional guidance documents provide direction for specific concerns, including how pharmaceutical companies can comply with the requirement to include the established drug name in all marketing materials and under which circumstances the companies must report adverse drug effects reported on the Internet.

Presenting Risks and Benefits

The Food, Drug and Cosmetic Act requires that all prescription drug advertisements include a "true statement" of information relating to the drug's effectiveness.[67] FDA regulations require that this information include specific indications for the drug use being advertised.[68] In its enforcement actions, the FDA has consistently held that "promotional materials are misleading if they represent or suggest that a drug is more effective than has been demonstrated by substantial evidence or substantial clinical experience."[69] For example, in 2010, the FDA issued a Warning Letter to Axcan Pharma stating that the company's web page for Photofrin, a drug therapy for patients with certain kinds of lung and esophageal cancer, presented misleading information about the drug's efficacy. According to the FDA, patient and physician videos on the web page presented Photofrin as helping patients live symptom free, or even providing a cure. However, the studies on the efficacy of this drug therapy do not support these claims.[70] It is important that claims made by pharmaceutical companies are supported by "substantial" evidence or clinical experience.

The Food, Drug and Cosmetic Act requires that all prescription drug advertisements include a "true statement" of information relating to the drug's side effects.[71] FDA regulations require that advertisements broadcast through media like radio and television include the side effect information in the audio and video portions of the advertisements.[72] The information must disclose each specific side effect or other warning or contraindication. For example, in a 2009 Warning Letter, the FDA found that web pages for the drug Sotradecol were misleading to consumers because they failed to communicate the risks associated with the drug, as well as overstating the indication and efficacy of the drug.[73] The FDA did note that the pages included links for "further information . . . including its approved indication and possible side effects."[74] However, these links were "not sufficient to provide appropriate qualification." To meet this standard, the risk and indication information must appear within the main body of any promotional materials that communicate information on the effectiveness of a drug.[75]

In applying this standard to online videos, the FDA alleged that Pfizer had omitted risk information in a promotion for the drug Viagra.[76] The video, which portrayed a group of men playing instruments and singing a song ending with "Viva Viagra," appeared on CNN's website as a video advertisement. Although the video included text at the beginning that directed viewers to "see important safety information on this page," the FDA noted that the page on cnn.com did not contain any such information.[77]

The FDA also requires that information relating to side effects be presented in "fair balance" with information about the drug's efficacy and benefits. Advertisements that fail to provide "sufficient emphasis" on side effect information or fail to present the side effect information with "prominence and readability reasonably comparable" to the information on efficacy will be found false or misleading.[78] In a seven-minute webcast video, Johnson & Johnson only devoted the last minute to including specific risk information about a drug that manages chronic pain. Additionally, the risk information was presented only in "rapidly scrolling text in small type font." The FDA found that the inclusion of risk and indication information presented in the text alone is not sufficient.[79]

Although the FDA has applied these requirements to a variety of new media, including web pages, online videos, and online sponsored advertisements, there is little guidance for advertisers online beyond this general application of existing rules. Most of the guidance documents—in the form of notices of violation and warning letters—have focused on product websites, rather than social media tools. There are a variety of notices of violation that address some of these tools. However, in 2014, the FDA issued a draft guidance specifically discussing the use of character-limited social media. In that document, the FDA states that risk information should be presented together with benefit information, and should at the least contain the most serious risk information. The FDA provides examples of how a company can communicate about a drug, including its names, benefits, risks, and more information. One example is specific to a platform like Twitter, using 134 characters:

NoFocus (rememberine HCl) for mild to moderate memory loss-May cause seizures in patients with a seizure disorder www.nofocus. com/risk

In the draft guidance document, the FDA notes that in this example the company has established the brand, offered accurate information about the benefit and use, as well as provided the serious risk information. The link is a direct link to more safety information about the drug.[80]

The link alone would not be sufficient based on a Notice of Violation issued to Novartis Pharmaceuticals in 2010 regarding the company's use of Facebook Share widgets.[81] The widget appeared on a variety of Novartis product web pages. Clicking on the widget allowed a user to share on his or her Facebook news feed customized information or comments about the drug. However, the user comments were accompanied by Novartis-created content about the drug, which the user could not edit. An example the FDA supplied in the Notice was a Facebook Share for the drug Tasigna, which is approved to treat certain chronic conditions in adults.

> Treating Your PH+ CMP with Tasigna | Tasigna (nilotnib) 200-mg capsules
>
> http://www.us.tasigna.com
>
> In addition to taking Tasigna (nilotnib) 200-mg capsules, talking to your doctor and receiving health tips can help you treat your CML.

Like the sponsored links, the FDA noted that the shared content linked to more in-depth product information, including side effects and other risks. However, this linking was again found "insufficient to mitigate the misleading omission of risk information."[82]

Product Name Promotion

The FDA requires that when promotions for a drug include the proprietary name—or trademark name—of the drug, the established name of the drug must also be presented.[83] In 2012, the FDA issued a guidance document providing more specific information on the placement, size, and prominence requirements for inclusion of the established name as related to the proprietary name.[84] For all media, the FDA mandated that the established name be

1. placed in "direct conjunction" with the proprietary name;
2. presented in the same text and font as the proprietary name when used in the body of the promotion;
3. be presented in text "at least half as large" as the proprietary name when used in a headline; and
4. be presented with "a prominence commensurate with the prominence of the proprietary name."[85]

Although the FDA applied consistent measures, regardless of media outlet, for the juxtaposition, size, and prominence of the established name, the required frequency of the established name was treated differently in online media than in traditional print and broadcast communications. The FDA recognized that online media might not be presented through traditional text pages. Therefore, the FDA recommended that if the proprietary name appears in a headline or other element outside the main body of text, the established name should appear each time the proprietary name appears. However, if the proprietary name appears in the main text of a website, for example, the established name need appear only at least once per screen span.[86]

This guidance seems to group all online communications for purposes of compliance with the required disclosure of the established name. The recommendations, though seemingly written from the perspective of the traditional web page format, would apply equally to shorter online messages, such as sponsored links and Twitter posts. This significantly restricts the information that can be distributed through those tools.

Reporting Adverse Drug Events

Pharmaceutical companies are required to report to the FDA any adverse drug events they receive, including information obtained from commercial marketing efforts.[87] In 2001, the FDA released a draft guidance further addressing this concern, but provided very little comment on online tools beyond traditional web pages. As more pharmaceutical companies began to take advantage of online and social media tools, industry professionals began to question to what extent pharmaceutical companies would be responsible for reporting adverse events reported via these formats.

The FDA requires that pharmaceutical companies monitor websites sponsored by the company.[88] Companies are not responsible for sites sponsored by third parties unless the company is notified of adverse event reports appearing on third-party sites. Companies must review the adverse drug experiences to determine whether they need to be submitted to the FDA. Events must be reported only if the pharmaceutical company can gather the basic information required for a safety report including an identifiable patient, an identifiable reporter, a suspect drug or biological product, and an adverse experience or fatal outcome suspected to be due to the suspect drug or biological product. This does not require that the patients be identifiable by name, only that there is specific enough information to "suspect that specific patients were involved." For example, the FDA suggests that a report that "an elderly woman had anaphylaxis" constitutes identifiable patient information.

Seemingly, pharmaceutical companies would be required to review and report information submitted via social media platforms for which the company has some ownership. For example, if a user comment made directly on the company's Facebook page recounts an adverse drug event, and contains the requisite information, that would be reportable.

User-Generated Off-Label Marketing and Misinformation

Pharmaceutical companies are prohibited from marketing any prescription drug for any purpose not approved by the FDA, or "off-label uses." However, the FDA has recognized that individuals may make unsolicited requests for off-label information, and that information may be helpful to certain individuals researching medical treatments.[89] Therefore, the FDA permits companies to respond to these requests "by providing truthful, balanced, non-misleading, and non-promotional scientific or medical information that is responsive to the specific request."[90] The response should only be provided to the initial requestor, regardless of whether the request was made in a non-public or public forum.

Special concerns arise when requests are made in a public forum. Online and social media platforms have potentially increased the visibility of such user-initiated, public requests for off-label information. The FDA noted that an area of concern is the broad audience and indefinite availability of any information that pharmaceutical companies may provide in response.[91] Therefore in 2011, the FDA provided specific recommendations for responding to unsolicited requests through online forums.

First, companies should only respond when a request "pertains specifically to its own named product." Second, public responses should not be promotional in any way. A public response should use an objective tone to inform the audience that the request refers to unapproved uses of the drug and provide easy access to FDA-approved information on the drug, such as labeling or other patient information. These links should not lead to product websites or any other promotional materials. The response also should provide direct contact information for interested individuals to seek follow-up information. Once a private request has been made, the company may respond with "truthful, balanced, non-misleading, and non-promotional scientific or medical information" in a one-on-one communication.[92]

In its 2014 draft guidance on the topic, the FDA indicated that pharmaceutical companies also should correct any misinformation provided on public forums by third parties for which the company is not otherwise responsible. The FDA provides an example of a company that becomes aware of an independent blogger posting inaccurate information about the company's drug product. In this situation, the FDA states that the company may consider correcting the information, but is not obligated to do so. Should a company wish to correct the information, the FDA suggests using official accounts to provide a link to the FDA labeling information online; the FDA specifically prohibits linking to any kind of promotional page, even if the correct information is present. The draft guidance provides other ways of correcting information depending on the medium, the type of error, and technological limitations of the platforms.[93]

INVESTOR RELATIONS

Investors are increasingly turning to the Internet as a source of information. Brokerage firms such as TD Ameritrade and Charles Schwab are devoting resources to provide their clients with social media access and tools. As online communications have become increasingly important to investors, the Securities and Exchange Commission (SEC) has encouraged companies to use these new platforms, while underscoring the importance of compliance with existing securities regulations.

The SEC was established in 1934 to ensure the public received timely, complete and truthful information about publicly traded securities.[94] This is accomplished through the requirement for and oversight of specific financial filings, such as corporate registration forms, annual and quarterly filings, annual reports to shareholders and other corporate financial communications.[95] An industry self-regulatory agency—the Financial Industry Regulatory Authority (FINRA)—works both independently and in coordination with the SEC to offer guidance to securities firms on a variety of regulatory issues, and act to penalize firms that violate these regulations. Both the SEC and FINRA have released documents addressing the application of existing regulations to online communications.

Online Communications to the Public

Publicly traded companies are required to disclose to the public information relevant to investment decisions. Additionally, companies must ensure that the information disclosed is truthful and accurate.[96] The SEC has ruled that these disclosure requirements apply equally to any online disclosures as well as those made through traditional print and broadcast media.

In 2008, the SEC issued an interpretive release to provide guidance to companies on how to comply with SEC disclosure regulations when posting information to company websites.[97] The guidance provides that when a company's website is recognized by the public as a channel of information, posting material information on the site would satisfy the requirement of disclosing information to the public at large, as opposed to a more selective group.[98] This encourages companies to develop their websites in the marketplace. The 2008 interpretive release also addresses concerns with preventing fraudulent communications. For example, the SEC recommends carefully explaining the context of any link to third-party content that the company is not adopting. This will ensure that consumers do not rely on the information found at the linked page as information directly from the company. In 2013, the SEC also stated in a report that social media platforms, including Facebook and Twitter, can be used to announce "key information . . . so long as investors have been alerted about which social media will be used to disseminate such information."[99]

The SEC also recognized the contribution that certain interactive features of a website, such as a blog, can make to the "robust use" of company websites. The SEC encourages the use of these technologies but cautions companies to educate any company representative using these blogs, or other forums, that they are acting "on behalf of the company." Companies should, therefore, develop procedures for monitoring these communications. The guidance provides that responsibility transfers to statements made on behalf of the company via third-party websites, as well. This indicates that companies should rely on the SEC recommendation for sponsored Twitter and Facebook accounts as well as traditional owned website content.

In 2010, FINRA released guidance more specific to social media. FINRA has categorized online communications tools as advertisements, correspondence, sales literature, and public appearance.[100] For example, information posted on publicly available websites and feeds, such as a Twitter profile, is considered an advertisement. However, password-protected websites and social media feeds are considered sales literature. Content posted in real-time that allows for consumer interaction, such as a chat or a Twitter post, is considered a public appearance. FINRA's 2010 guidance document addressed the recordkeeping and pre-approval requirements for these various communications to the public.[101]

Advertisements, or static content on social media sites, such as profile information, requires pre-approval by a principal in the company. Interactive elements, or public appearances, do not require pre-approval, but companies should archive all communications through these media for record retention. This should be considered as the company determines which technologies and social networks to use for public communication. Additionally, companies must develop a method to supervise these communications to ensure content regulations are not violated.

FINRA has also addressed third-party statements. Generally, FINRA does not consider a post by a consumer to represent the company. Therefore, approval and recordkeeping rules would not apply. However, if a company republishes the comment through a Facebook Share or a retweet on Twitter, the company can be found to have endorsed the statement.[102]

Some statements online may constitute investment fraud, as individuals have used social media to manipulate the stock market by posting false or misleading information about a company. For example, in 2015, the SEC filed charges against James Craig for tweeting false statements that publicly traded companies were under investigation, allowing Craig to purchase stock in the company when the price dropped, while in another case, posters illegally published false information to increase the stock price in order to profit from the sale of their shares.[103]

"Crowd Funding"

Social media tools also have enabled companies to raise funds in new ways. For example, "crowd funding" allows companies to solicit small investments from thousands of investors.[104] In 2011, the SEC settled with two entrepreneurs over an "experiment" to raise funds online to purchase Pabst Brewing Company. The SEC stated that the entrepreneurs violated securities law when they launched a website seeking pledges of money in exchange for ownership shares. This online offering triggered requirements for security registration and financial information disclosures.[105]

This case demonstrated the fundraising opportunities available for small companies via online communication tools. Other crowd-funding websites, such as Kickstarter, allow entrepreneurs to raise capital without triggering SEC investigation because the capital is considered a donation; investors do not receive an ownership share of the company. Pebble, a start-up company developing a digital watch that links to smartphones to run and control apps, has set a new record for money raised through Kickstarter. The company offered returns including exclusive updates, prototypes of the watch, and the opportunity to vote on the fourth color option for the watch. The company raised more than $10 million from more than 65,000 backers.

In 2012, the JOBS Act created an exception to traditional securities requirements for small companies going public via online offerings.[106] The JOBS Act exception would allow companies to raise up to $1 million within a 12-month period through the online issuance of stock shares. In 2015, the SEC adopted new rules to address the impact of this law on existing crowdfunding rules. These rules permit companies to engage in equity crowdfunding without registering with the SEC as brokers, meaning that individual investors can now invest in startups in exchange for a share of the company rather than a non-monetary return.

FREQUENTLY ASKED QUESTIONS

1. Can bloggers and Twitter users endorse products?

Yes. The FTC defines an endorsement as "Any advertising message . . . that consumers are likely to believe reflects the opinions, beliefs, findings, or experiences of a party other than the sponsoring advertiser, even if the views expressed by that party are identical to those of the sponsoring advertiser." Bloggers and social media users can endorse commercial products and services through online and social media posts. However, if the poster has any relationship to the company that offers the product or service for sale, that relationship must be disclosed in a clear and prominent way. For example, if a blogger receives a free gaming system to test, he or she must disclose in any blog post about the performance of that system that he or she received the product for free.

The FTC's Bureau of Consumer Protection has noted that such disclosures can be made via social media short cuts. For example, on Twitter, users were concerned that the limit of 140 characters to a post would make the required disclosures too difficult. The FTC Bureau of Consumer Protection has suggested that including such hashtags as #paidad or #paid or #ad may be sufficient to help consumers evaluate the usefulness of the sponsored statements.

2. Does engaging in behavioral targeting online run afoul of FTC regulations?

Currently, the only FTC documents on behavioral targeting are principles for self-regulation. These principles address the need to protect consumer privacy and data security. Companies collecting or maintaining consumer data should ensure reasonable data security measures are in place. Additionally, online consumers should receive adequate notice of the data collection and use, as well as a meaningful opportunity to opt out of targeting.

3. Are pharmaceutical companies liable for third-party comments on Facebook about off-label uses of drugs?

Pharmaceutical companies are not liable under FDA regulations for unsolicited comments regarding off-label uses of drugs. However, companies can respond to individual questions about these uses in a truthful and accurate way using one-on-one communications. Companies may also respond publicly by providing non-promotional materials that clarify the FDA-approved uses of a drug. For example, the company could post to a public forum a statement that the drug is not approved for the related use with a link to the FDA-approved drug packaging or patient information sheet.

4. Do Twitter posts, and other interactive social media posts, trigger SEC scrutiny?

If the posts are on behalf of a publicly traded company, they are subject to securities law requirements. Companies must ensure that the communications are truthful and accurate. Additionally, companies should develop methods to archive these communications to the public under SEC record-keeping requirements.

5. Can companies use online website and social media platforms to seek investments for startup companies?

Yes, but these efforts are subject to securities regulations. In 2012, President Obama signed into the law the JOBS Act, which does allow companies to raise up to $1 million within a 12-month period through the online issuance of stocks without triggering many of the existing SEC requirements. However, the SEC has not yet drafted the required regulations for this provision. There may be additional requirements triggered by this practice. All investments exceeding $1 million per year trigger traditional SEC registration and disclosure requirements.

NOTES

1 Virginia State Board of Pharmacy v. Virginia Citizens Consumer Council, Inc., 425 U.S. 748, 764 (1976).
2 Central Hudson Gas & Elec. Corp. v. Public Serv. Comm'n, 447 U.S. 557, 564 (1980).
3 15 U.S.C. §§ 41 et seq.
4 21 U.SC. §§ 301 et seq.
5 15 U.S.C. 78d; 17 C.F.R. § 200.1.
6 17 C.F.R. § 240.13a-11.
7 Christopher Heine, Mobile Ads Skyrocketed 76% in 2014, Making Digital Advertising a $50 Billion Business, AdWeek, Apr. 22, 2015, http://www.adweek.com/news/technology/mobile-ads-skyrocketed-76-2014-making-digital-advertising-50-billion-business-164222; Steven Perlberg, Social Media Ad Spending to Hit $24 Billion This Year, The Wall Street Journal, Apr. 15, 2015, http://blogs.wsj.com/cmo/2015/04/15/social-media-ad-spending-24-billion/.
8 Advertising Substantiation Policy Statement, appended to Thompson Med. Co., 104 F.T.C. 648, 839 (1984), aff'd, 791 F.2d 189 (D.C. Cir. 1986).
9 16 C.F.R. § 255.1.
10 16 C.F.R. 255.5.
11 William McGeveran, Disclosure, Endorsement, and Identity in Social Marketing, 2009 Univ. Ill. L. Rev. 1105, 1112 (2009).
12 15 U.S.C. § 45 (2016).
13 16 C.F.R. § 255.5, Example 3.

14 Id. at Example 7.

15 In the Matter of Reverb Communications, Inc., FTC Docket No. C-4310 (November 22, 2010).

16 Id.

17 In the Matter of Legacy Learning Systems, Inc., FTC Docket No. C-4323 (June 1, 2011).

18 See, e.g., In re: Hyundai Motor America, FTC File No. 112-3110 (November 16, 2011); In re: AnnTaylor Stores Corp., FTC File No. 102-3147 (April 20, 2010).

19 Hyundai Motor America, FTC File No. 112-3110.

20 Id.

21 The FTC's Revised Endorsement Guides: What People are Asking, FTC Bureau of Consumer Protection (June 2010), http://business.ftc.gov/documents/bus71-ftcs-revised-endorsement-guideswhat-people-are-asking.

22 Federal Trade Commission, Native Advertising: A Guide for Businesses (2015).

23 Id.

24 FTC, Enforcement Policy Statement on Deceptively Formatted Advertisements (2016) (citing Statement in Regard to Advertisements That Appear in Feature Article Format, FTC Release (Nov. 28, 1967); Advisory Opinion No. 191, Advertisements which appear in news format, 73 F.T.C. 1307 (1968)).

25 Id. at 3.

26 In Re Lord & Taylor, FTC Docket No. C-4576 (May 20, 2016).

27 Federal Trade Commission, Dot Com Disclosures: How to Make Effective Disclosures in Digital Advertising (March 2013).

28 See Black's Law Dictionary 1430 (8th ed. 2004).

29 Spam Summit: The Next Generation of Threats and Solutions, Federal Trade Commission, Division of Marketing Practices (November 2007).

30 Id.

31 CV No. H 03-5537 (S.D. Tex. Filed December 3, 2003), http://www.ftc.gov/os/caselist/0323102/0323102zkhill.htm.

32 FTC v. Pricewert, No. C-09-CV-2407 (N.D. Cal. April 8, 2010).

33 FTC v. Flora, No. 11-CV-00299 (C.D. Cal. August 16, 2011).

34 Id.

35 FTC v. Tachht, No. 8:16-cv-01397 (M.D. Fla., filed June 2, 2016).

36 15 U.S.C. § 7708.

37 Federal Trade Commission, National Do Not Email Registry, Report to Congress (June 2004).

38 Federal Trade Commission, Protecting Consumer Privacy in an Era of Rapid Change, Preliminary FTC Staff Report 14 note 32 (December 2010).

39 See generally, OnGuardOnline.gov.

40 Spam Summit, supra note 20 at 19.

41 Julia Angwin, The Web's New Gold Mine: Your Secrets, The Wall Street Journal, July 30, 2010.

42 American Association of Advertising Agencies, the Association of National Advertisers, the Better Business Bureau, the Direct Marketing Association, and the Interactive Advertising Bureau, Self-Regulatory Principles for Online Behavioral Advertising (July 2009) [hereinafter Coop Principles], http://www.iab.net/media/file/ven-principles-07-01-09.pdf.

43 IAB Tells Congress Privacy Bills May Harm Business and Consumers, Interactive Advertising Bureau, http://www.iab.net/public_policy/1296039 (last accessed March 28, 2011); see also Omar Tawakol, Forget Targeted Ads—I'd Rather Pay for Content, MediaPost.com, February 15, 2011, http://www.iab.net/public_policy/1296039.

44 Howard Beales, The Value of Behavioral Targeting, Network Advertising Initiative, March 24, 2011, http://www.networkadvertising.org/pdfs/Beales_NAI_Study.pdf. The report states that total ad revenues for the 12 companies equaled $3.32 billion; 17.9% of that was attributed to behavioral targeting.

45 Federal Trade Commission, Staff Report: Public Workshop on Consumer Privacy on the Global Information Infrastructure (Federal Trade Commission 1996).

46 Federal Trade Commission, Privacy Online: Fair Information Practices in the Electronic Marketplace: A Report to Congress (2000).

47 Id. at 35.

48 Id. at 36.

49 Online Behavioral Advertising: Moving the Discussion Forward to Possible Self-Regulatory Principles, FTC (December 2007), http://www.ftc.gov/os/2007/12/P859900stmt.pdf.

50 Id.

51 See generally NAI website, http://www.networkadvertising.org; The Self Regulatory Program for Online Behavioral Advertising, http://www.aboutads.info (last accessed March 2, 2012).

52 See, e.g., Understanding Online Advertising, Interactive Advertising Bureau, http://www.iab.net/privacymatters/; Self-Regulatory Principles for Online Behavioral Advertising, July 2009, http://www.aboutads.info/resource/down load/seven-principles-07-01-09.pdf; Self-Regulatory Principles for Online Behavioral Advertising Implementation Guide, October 2010, http://www.aboutads.info/resource/download/OBA%20Self-Reg%20Implementation%20Guide%20-%20Full%20Text.pdf; NAI, Opt Out of Behavioral Advertising, http://www.networkadvertising.org/managing/opt_out.asp.

53 NAI 2009 Annual Compliance Report, December 30, 2009, http://www.networkadvertising.org/pdfs/2009_NAI_Compliance_Report_12-30-09.pdf; NAI 2010 Annual Compliance Report, February 18, 2011, http://www.network advertising.org/pdfs/2010_NAI_Compliance_Report.pdf.

54 NAI 2010 Annual Compliance Report, id. at 13–15. For more information on the icon, see Advertising Option Icon Application, http://www.aboutads.info/participants/icon/.

55 Federal Trade Commission, Protecting Consumer Privacy in an Era of Rapid Change: A Proposed Framework for Businesses and Policymakers, Preliminary FTC Staff Report iii (December 2010).

56 Id. at 63.

57 H.R. 654, 112th Cong. (2011).

58 See Federal Trade Commission, supra note 45 at 39–68.

59 In the Matter of Chitika, Inc., FTC File No. 1023087 (Complaint filed March 14, 2011).

60 In the Matter of Chitika, Inc., FTC Docket No. C-4324 (June 7, 2011).

61 Mike Shields, FTC Commissioner Urges Ad Industry to Let Consumers Opt Out of Tracking; Julie Brill also warns publishers and advertisers to make sure native ads are clearly labeled, Wall Street Journal, January 21, 2016.

63 15 U.S.C. §§6501–6506.

62 U.S. v. W3 Innovations, CV11–03958 (N.D. Cal. 2011).

64 Children's Online Privacy Protection Rule, 16 C.F.R. Part 32, 78 Fed. Reg. 3927 (Jan. 17, 2013).

65 Food, Drug and Cosmetic Act, 21 U.S.C. §§ 352–353.

66 Prescription Drug Advertisements Rule, 21 CFR 202.1 (2008).

67 21 U.S.C. § 352(n).

68 21 CFR § 202.1(e3ii)

69 See, e.g., FDA Notice of Violation to Dow Pharmaceutical Sciences, Inc. (June 16, 2011); FDA Warning Letter to Hill Dermaceuticals, Inc. (December 3, 2010); FDA Warning Letter to Abbot Laboratories (July 14, 2009).

70 Id.

71 21 U.S.C. § 352(n).

72 21 C.F.R. § 202.1(e)(1).

73 FDA Warning Letter to Bioniche Pharma USA LLC (September 14, 2009). See also FDA Warning Letter to BioMarin Pharmaceutical, Inc. (October 11, 2006).

74 FDA Warning Letter to Bioniche Pharma, supra note 62.

75 Id. See also 21 C.F.R. §201.1(e)(3)(i)(2011).

76 FDA Warning Letter to Pfizer, Inc. (April 16, 2008). See also FDA Warning Letter to Warner Chilcott, LLC (May 5, 2011); FDA Warning Letter to Shire Dev., Inc. (September 25, 2008).

77 FDA Warning Letter to Pfizer, supra note 65.

78 21 C.F.R. § 202.1(e)(7).

79 FDA Warning Letter to Johnson & Johnson (May 12, 2009). See also FDA Notice of Violation to Cephalon, Inc. (June 21, 2011).

80 Food and Drug Administration, Internet/Social Media Platforms with Character Space Limitations—Presenting Risk and Benefit Information for Prescription Drugs and Medical Devices, Draft Guidance (June 2014).

81 FDA Notice of Violation to Novartis Pharmaceuticals Corporation (July 29, 2010).

82 Id.

83 21 C.F.R. § 202.1(b)(1).

84 FDA, Guidance for Industry: Product Name Placement, Size, and Prominence in Advertising and Promotional Labeling (January 2012).

85 Id.

86 Id.

87 Postmarketing Reporting of Adverse Drug Experiences, 21 C.F.R. § 314.80 (2009).

88 FDA, Guidance for Industry: Postmarketing Safety Reporting for Human Drug and Biological Products Including Vaccines (March 2001).

89 FDA, Guidance for Industry: Responding to Unsolicited Requests for Off-Label Information About Prescription Drugs and Medical Devices (December 2011).

90 Id.

91 Id.

92 Food and Drug Administration, Responding to Unsolicited Requests for Off-Label Information About Prescription Drugs and Medical Devices, Draft Guidance (December 2011).

93 Food and Drug Administration, Internet/Social Media Platforms: Correcting Independent 5 Third-Party Misinformation About Prescription Drugs and Medical Devices, Draft Guidance (June 2014).

94 15 U.S.C. § 78gg.

95 SEC, The Investor's Advocate: How the SEC Protects Investors, Maintains Market Integrity, and Facilitates Capital Formation, http://www.sec.gov/about/whatwedo.

96 17 C.F.R. § 240.10b-5.

97 Commission Guidance on the Use of Company Web Sites, 73 Fed. Reg. 45,862 (August 7, 2008), codified at 17 C.F.R. pt. 241 (2008).

98 Id.

99 Report of Investigation Pursuant to Section 21(a) of the Securities Exchange Act of 1934: Netflix, Inc., and Reed Hastings, SEC, Release No. 69279, April 2 2013.

100 FINRA, Guide to the Web for Registered Representatives, http://www.finra.org/industry/issues/advertising/p006118.

101 FINRA, Guidance on Blogs and Social Networking Web Sites, Reg. Notice 10-06 (2010).

102 Id.

103 See SEC v. Craig, 15-cr-00517 (N.D. Cal. filed Nov. 5, 2015); SEC v. McKeown, Civil Action 10-80748-CIV-Cohn (S.D. Fla. June 23, 2010).

104 Jean Easglesham & Jessica Holzer, SEC Boots Up for Internet Age, The Wall Street Journal, April 9, 2011 at B1.

105 Michael Migliozzi, II and Brian William Flatow, SEC No. 3-14415 (June 8, 2011).

106 Jumpstart Our Business Startups Act, Pub. L. No. 112-106 (2012).

CHAPTER 6

Account Ownership and Control

By Jasmine McNealy

University of Florida

ABSTRACT

Social media's popularity has attracted businesses, including news and strategic communication organizations, interested in using the established connections to consumers to market their brands. This use of social media often goes beyond the company's official account to include the public accounts of its employees or those with whom it has contracted. This chapter explores the possible legal conflicts that may arise related to the access and ownership of social media accounts and the related properties.

S ocial capital is a concept with many iterations. Some scholars have called it the goodwill, fellowship, sympathy, and the social intercourse that happens in families or close-knit groups. Others have likened it to the function of networked relationships or social structures.[1] Whichever way it is defined, nowhere is the concept of social capital more exemplified than on social networking sites. From followers to friends to likes and shares, the connections inherent in social media are valuable to both individuals and businesses.

Odds are, you have created an account on some social media platform. Actually, you probably have not stopped after creating the account, but have gone about the business of creating a presence on that platform. On Twitter, this would involve choosing an account handle and associated name, uploading a photo or other avatar, choosing a background image, and curating your timeline. Timeline curation is the most time-consuming facet of your social media use because it requires careful (or not so careful) selection of other accounts to follow or friend.

Whereas timeline curation may be the most time-consuming activity, arguably the most important activity is posting to the account. An important decision to make before posting concerns the types of posts that will come from your account. On the most basic level, this decision may be as simple as whether the account will be personal or professional, or whether you will separate the two purposes at all. You must also decide the kinds of things you will post. Will it be strictly news, personal thoughts, topic specific information, etc.? Whatever your choices, in making these decisions—from which avatar to use, to what things to post—you are constructing an online identity, or persona, connected with that social media account (or accounts), and ultimately yourself.

Now, imagine that your account becomes popular, perhaps not Justin Bieber levels of popularity, but you amass a large number of followers and your posts are shared often. Your account becomes so popular that it helps you land a job, a job that requires you to post information related to your position to your social media account, and to maintain and increase the number of followers. Once the account becomes a part of the job, what are the rules with respect to who may access, control or otherwise use the account? And what happens to the account when you leave that job?

The need for answers to these and related questions has become more urgent as the use of social media as a tool for marketing continues to grow. Organizations have discovered the benefits of leveraging online personal networks and relationships. And certain industries use of the number of social media connections as a measure of the qualifications of prospective job applicants. Certainly, the use and management of social media accounts, both personal and business related, are now important parts of corporate culture. And businesses believe that the corporate brand and consumer base may grow with the addition of employees with strong social media presences. This chapter examines the legal issues arising or that may emerge in connection to the creation and use of personal and business social media accounts.

BRING YOUR OWN PERSONA

As businesses tell employees to "bring your own device" to the workplace, the phenomenon at issue in the use and ownership of social media accounts can be thought of as "bring your own persona" (BYOP), an evocation of the marketing practices from which business social media gets its foundation. Within the context of a social media account, BYOP describes two possibilities. First is a requirement that employees have and maintain an online presence. An example of this would be when a company hires a "(whatever social media site)-famous" person, and requires that they post about company products and/or content. Beauty and style bloggers, for instance, may be hired to promote the products of a particular company. In this situation, brands are attempting to capitalize on the established, and potential, following of a known social media personality. With millions of followers across many social media sites including Instagram, Twitter, and Snapchat, the Kardashian/Jenner sisters (and their current and former relations) are a good example of this. Brands recognize the influence that the family has with certain demographics, and hire them to use/promote products on social media.

A second BYOP scenario is that of an organization hiring an individual and placing them in charge of a social media account, though this may not be the firm's official account. An example of this is when an individual specifies their affiliation in the account name. An account created for an employee of a news station may be, for instance, @janedoe_WXXX. If not as explicit, the account may also indicate affiliation in the description and/ or biography. In both cases, the expectation is that the employee use social media in such a way so as to attract an audience of current and potential consumers. To do this, the employee creates an online persona. Before leaving the *New York Times*, then-assistant managing editor Jim Roberts, for example, used @NYTJim as his Twitter handle. When Roberts joined Reuters in 2013, he changed his handle to @NYCJim, indicating that he was no longer with the newspaper.

The creation of a persona, for business or other purposes, is not uncommon at all. One of the first things that occurs when a person begins using a social networking site is the creation of a persona. That is, the creation of the personality or the identity to be shared with friends, followers, and the rest of the world. From Facebook to Tumblr, Soundcloud to Twitter, whenever a new user signs up, the social media site prompts them to create a profile, to tell a little about themselves, to tell others what makes them unique. But a persona is not a profile, although the profile certainly is a part of the persona, along with the avatar or profile pictures and background images, among other things. The persona is made up of all of the items from which an identity or reputation, online or otherwise, is constructed. The definition of "persona" has a Latin origin and means the face the individual wears in public or during social interaction. Carl Jung described the persona as a kind of mask, designed on the one hand to make a definite impression upon others, and on the other to conceal the true nature of the individual.[2] The persona was how the individual represented themselves to other members of society.

Businesses have used what's called "persona marketing" since the 1990s.[3] The concept of persona marketing finds its foundation in customer or market segmentation, the practice of dividing a pool of potential customers based on demographic information, i.e., race, gender, education, and spending habits. Persona marketing, used also in user experience design, takes the customer segmentation concept further and constructs and tells the story of a fictional character, providing their name, age, race, gender, and lifestyle characteristics. The fictionalization also establishes that persona's motivation for purchasing and or using certain products or services, and the times at which they do so.

Personas are thought to be beneficial because they visualize the humans behind the data, cluing in marketers and user experience designers to the needs and wants of their product customers. Fujitsu, for example, was able to improve its Fujitsu for kids site after creating three different personas, including that of "Misaki Sato," a virtual 9-year-old. A case study of the Fujitsu for kids site by Fujitsu brand designer Yumi Hisanabe found that the Misaki persona allowed designers to ask and answer questions about the usability of the site from the perspective of a child, a specific child.[4] A similar rationale is at play when individuals decide which portions of their personality or professional identity to display on social media. The goal is to attract as many consumers as possible using points of interest attractive to a selected audience. In this way a social media account becomes a tool for marketing a personality and the connected organization.

WHO OWNS THE PERSONA?

A question that arises with the creation of a persona is that of who owns that persona. Though created and maintained on third-party platforms, it is easy to think of social media personas and accounts as personal property. Designating something as "property" infers that the owner is provided with a "bundle of rights" that allows her to control its use and access. As intangible objects, social media property ownership issues would fall into the area of intellectual property, specifically in the areas of copyright, trade secret, and trademark.

Copyright

In a general sense, copyright law protects original, creative works. This includes fictional or fictionalized characters. Copyright protection for fictional persons was established in 1930 by Judge Learned Hand in *Nichols v. Universal Pictures Corp.*, in which the court found that the more developed or distinctive a character, the more it can be copyrighted. This is not to say that online personas are the same as characters like Mickey Mouse or Goku. But the combination of a social media account profile, timeline curation, and aggregation of tweets from the account may be enough to reach the originality requirement for copyright. Copyright protects the expression of ideas. It is not a stretch to conclude that copyright protects the combination of choices above, all of which are made to express the user's ideas about her social media identity.

Assuming that the combination of elements that create a persona are enough for copyright protection, the issue of copyright ownership arises. Along with the eight categories of creative works that copyright protects, the law protects certain specialized works as well. More specifically it protects "work[s] made for hire." Section 101 of the Copyright Act details two kinds of works made for hire: (1) a work made by an employee within the scope of his employment; (2) a work made by a freelancer for a specific purpose recognized in the Copyright Act, and memorialized in a contract.[5]

The U.S. Supreme Court considered the work for hire doctrine in *Community for Creative Non-violence v. Reid*.[6] At issue in *CCN* was ownership of a sculpture commissioned from an artist by a nonprofit organization, as the parties failed to create a contract. As a preliminary issue, authorship and copyright usually rests with the creator of a work. When an employee creates a work within the scope of her employment, the employer holds the copyright. CCN argued that Reid, the artist, was an employee when he created the sculpture.

The Court disagreed, enumerating the characteristics of an employer–employee relationship within the scope of works for hire, none of which Reid fit. In *Aymes v. Bonelli*,[7] a works for hire case focused on the ownership of computer software, the Second Circuit refined these factors to include:

> (1) the hiring party's right to control the manner and means of creation; (2) the skill required; (3) the provision of employee benefits; (4) the tax treatment of the hired party; and (5) whether the hiring party has the right to assign additional projects to the hired party.[8]

The works for hire doctrine, then, has possible implications for those using social media in connection with their work. The scenario of an organization hiring an employee who uses his or her own social media would only give rise to the works for hire doctrine when there is a written contract between the parties. In the second situation, when social media is used as part of employment duties, the doctrine would dictate that if the employee were to leave the organization, the organization would retain the account, including the friends or followers with which it is associated.

Some journalists, so as not to involve themselves in the struggle over account ownership, have abandoned the accounts connected to their former employers. Sports journalists Brian Windhorst and Adam Rubin, for example, abandoned their former newspaper sports beat-connect accounts when they started working for ESPN. Others like Pat Forde and Michelle Beadle simply changed their Twitter account name, while retaining their same followers. But organizations have argued for ownership of Twitter accounts in court. The most famous case to date is *Phonedog v. Kravitz*, which involved a technology reporter who left his job at one publication to work for another, taking his corporate account with him, but changing the related Twitter handle. This case was not, however, brought under copyright law, but trade secret discussed in the next section.

Trade Secret

Indeed, ownership of friends lists or followers on a social media account has been the subject of more than one lawsuit. In all of these cases, employees separated from their companies, intending to take their social media accounts with them. In suing their former employees for ownership of these accounts and account connections, the organizations have claimed that the employee has violated trade secret law.

Trade secret law, predominantly governed by each individual state, is aimed at protecting the competitive advantage organizations have in secret, or secretive, information. This information can be embodied in chemical processes, machinery, and even client lists. Within the context of social media, friend lists and followers have been likened to client lists. For example, in *Phonedog v. Kravitz*,[9] a case that the parties settled in 2012, a company sued its former employee over ownership of a Twitter account under the California Uniform Trade Secret Act.[10] The company claimed that it owned both the employee's Twitter account name and the 17,000 followers connected to that account. The *Phonedog* court never reached the question of whether the list of followers should actually be protected under trade secret law. But other courts have considered whether social media connections should be thought of as trade secret, to differing results.

In *Christou v. Beatport*,[11] the Tenth Circuit Court of Appeals found that a man's MySpace profile and the friends list connected to it could be considered trade secrets. The case involved a former nightclub talent promoter who left his job and started his own nightclub and music promotion business using his former employer's online list of friends. The ex-employee argued that the social media list could not be a trade secret because it was public. The court was unpersuaded, instead deciding the case based on eight factors:

> (1) whether proper and reasonable steps were taken by the owner to protect the secrecy of the information; (2) whether access to the information was restricted; (3) whether employees knew customers' names from general experience; (4) whether customers commonly dealt with more than one supplier; (5) whether customer information

could be readily obtained from public directories; (6) whether
customer information is readily ascertainable from sources outside
the owner's business; (7) whether the owner of the customer list
expended great cost and effort over a considerable period of
time to develop the files; and (8) whether it would be difficult for a
competitor to duplicate the information.[12]

In contrast, a federal district court in Pennsylvania in *Eagle v. Morgan*
found that a publicly available list of connections was not the subject of
trade secret.[13] Linda Eagle and a colleague founded an online banking services company that was later bought by another organization. Her LinkedIn
account was used for marketing the company. A year after the purchase,
Eagle and other company officers were fired from the organization, which
maintained control over the LinkedIn account. Eagle regained access to
the account, and the company sued for trade secret misappropriation. The
court found that the company had not shown how LinkedIn connections,
and their information, were a competitive advantage. Although it is not
yet settled as to whether social media accounts and connections are trade
secrets, the implications of trade secret law for social media profiles could
be significant. If a company could demonstrate that the names and contact
information in its social media connections were of value, it may be able to
persuade a court to recognize trade secret. In fact, before the *Phonedog* case
settled, the company was asking for $340,000, or the number of followers
(17,000) valued at $2.50 each, times the amount of time that Kravitz had
used the Twitter account after leaving the company (eight months).[14]

Trademark and unfair competition

Trademark is a third area of intellectual property implicated in the use and
ownership of social media accounts. A trademark is "any word, name, symbol or device, or any combination thereof" used to identify the origin of
goods or services.[15] SM personas and accounts could, therefore, be considered akin to trademarks. Section 43(a) of the Lanham Act, along with
state law, protects trademarks from false descriptions, designations of origin,
and dilution. Public relations professional Jill E. Maremont, for instance,
filed a lawsuit against her former employer, Susan Fredman Design Group
(SFDG), claiming the company violated the Lanham Act when SFDG
employees made posts to her personal social media accounts, as well as
posted to the business social media account in her name.[16] Maremont was
unable to return to work where she ran the social media accounts for the
SFDG after being struck by a car. During the time she was convalescing,
she claimed that the business' employees posted to both her personal social
media account and the corporate account in her name.

The court found that Maremont could go forward with her Lanham act claims against her former employer.[17] Plaintiffs must prove three things to successfully win a trademark infringement or unfair competition suit under the Lanham Act: (1) a protectable mark exists, (2) the plaintiff owns the trademark, and (3) a consumer is likely to be confused.[18] Likelihood of confusion is a question of whether someone would believe that the good, service, or communication was coming from a particular source when it actually originated elsewhere. In her case against her former employer, Linda Eagle claimed that when she was locked out of her LinkedIn account the organization changed the name and photograph. Her current and potential customers were, therefore, rerouted to the changed profile. Eagle lost her Lanham Act case, however, because she failed to show confusion among her customers.

Patent

Patent, too, may provide a claim for those embroiled in a conflict over a social media account. Patents can be granted to anyone who invents or discovers "any new and useful process, machine, manufacture, or composition of matter . . ."[19] Social media accounts would, seemingly, not fall under the rubric of the things that could be patentable, although the actual platform and tools may be the subject of patent. Account users are not inventing or discovering anything new, but using the possibly patented inventions of others. Patent law does, however, offer a way of thinking about the relationship between employees and organizations with respect to ownership of social media accounts.

Shop rights are a well-established doctrine within patent law.[20] In shop rights, if an employee invents a patentable invention within the scope of their employment, or using the materials or other resources from their employer, their employer has an implied license to use that patent. This does not transfer ownership of the patent from the employee to the employer.[21] This means that the employing organization cannot sell or license the patent to other organizations. Within the context of social media accounts, then, an organization could argue that it has a shop right into the account of an employee. If recognized, this would allow the organization to access and use the account. Employers may also attempt to assert rights under the doctrine of "hired-to-invent," a state law doctrine similar to copyright's work for hire.[22]

APPROPRIATION AND RIGHT OF PUBLICITY

Similar to the property rights mentioned above, individuals may have common law rights to protect their SM personas. Two related claims of injury—appropriation and right of publicity—may provide remedies for the individuals seeking to assert ownership or access claims to SM accounts. Appropriation, also called misappropriation or commercialization, is one of the four common law privacy torts enumerated by Professor Prosser in 1964.[23] In general, appropriation is the use of someone' name or likeness for a commercial purpose without consent. Like the other invasion of privacy claims, appropriation is aimed at protecting or remedying an individual's shame and humiliation.

In *White v. Ortiz*, for example, the mother of mixed martial arts association owner Dana White sued a woman who posted under the Twitter handle "@RealJuneWhite."[24] The court found Ortiz's use of the handle was meant to capitalize on White's name to make it appear as though the tweets from the account were real. Further, the nature of the tweets from the account, which were to appear like true confessions about White's relationship with her children and other relatives, her mental health, and demeaning comments about other people exposed her to shame and humiliation. Of course *White* is not a case of in which someone has had their account taken over by another individual or organization. It does demonstrate, however, the kinds of appropriation claim possible with social media.

To be sure, an account like "@RealJuneWhite" is much different than those many Twitter accounts that attempt to be humorous takes on celebrity personalities and well-known businesses accounts. The account "@ BoredElonMusk," for example, posts innovations supposedly from the mind of the CEO of SpaceX and Tesla Motors. Twitter allows these kinds accounts under its rules, so long as the bio indicates that it is a parody. And parody is a defense against appropriation claims.

Unlike appropriation, which focuses on the motional and/or psychic harms of shame and humiliation, right of publicity aims at protecting an individual's economic interest in their name or likeness. In this way it is a property-style right like trademark. Unlike appropriation, which allows any plaintiff to sue for unauthorized use in their name or likeness, right of publicity applies only to those who have attained a certain level of fame or notoriety. An obvious example of this would be when an organization uses a celebrity's name or likeness in an advertising campaign without their permission. This happened in *Midler v. Ford Motor Co.*[25] in which the automobile manufacturer employed a Bette Midler sound-alike singer to perform for its commercial. Right of publicity can also inhere in nicknames[26] and catchphrases.[27] In *Hirsch v. SC Johnson & Son, Inc.*, for example, a famous football player was able to claim a right of publicity in the use of his nickname, "Crazylegs." In *Carson v. Here's Johnny Portable Toilets Inc.*, the famous comedian was able to protect his famous catchphrase from a company attempting to use the economic value in the phrase and connected references to sell a new brand of commode.

As alluded to in the nickname and catchphrase cases mentioned above, the right of publicity can also be found in images or likenesses that calls a person to mind. In *Motschenbacher v. RJ Reynolds Tobacco*,[28] for instance, the court found a valid right of publicity in a racecar driver's claim that a tobacco advertisement used his likeness. Although Motschenbacher's face was not visible, the use of a car that mirrored the one he drove was enough to be considered a use of his image. A more well-known case involved Vanna White of *Wheel of Fortune* fame. In *White v. Samsung Elec. Am. Inc.*,[29] White sued the electronics manufacturer for use her likeness in an advertisement. The ad contained a robot, wearing a blond wig and an evening gown, standing in front of a *Wheel of Fortune* word board. The court reasoned that those viewing the ad would think of White when they saw it. Similarly, in *Wendt v. Host Int'l*,[30] actors George Wendt and John Ratzenberger, otherwise known at Norm and Cliff on *Cheers*, were able to recover for right of publicity when a *Cheers*-themed bar used Norm and Cliff resembling robots.

The examples of right of publicity claims above would seemingly not be an issue for regular people using social media. But cases involving social media accounts may come out differently. In the *Maremont* case mentioned above, the court found that the Jill Maremont had demonstrated that she had a significant social media following and was well known in the public relations community. She, therefore, could sustain a right of publicity claim, although she would later fail to prove the injury. And the court in *Eagle* found that Linda Eagle's right of publicity had been violated when her former employer changed the password to her LinkedIn account, and altered the account to reflect the new CEO's information.[31]

Both appropriation and right of publicity are state law claims and not federal. Not all states, however, recognize either or both of these claims. It is important, then, to be aware of the law in which you reside to ensure protection.

THE CFAA AND EMPLOYEE DUTIES

When an organization hires an individual that employee is endowed with certain responsibilities. Many employees are hired under a contract. As a general matter, an employment contract is an agreement between parties detailing not only their assigned tasks, but also terms of employment, salary, and expectations related to intellectual property, among other things. For those using social media as part of their employment, the contract may explain how and to what extent the employee may use the SM account. The contract may also explain who controls and or owns the SM account.

Even though not always explicitly stated within a contract or terms of employment, employees have duties related to their employer. Of special concern is that of the duty of loyalty, or the requirement not to act in a way that places the organization's interests below that of the employee. Along with the traditional method of enforcing contracts and employment duties—the lawsuit—organizations turn to the Computer Fraud and Abuse Act[32] as a remedy for lack of loyalty. The CFAA, known as an anti-hacking statute, prohibits the unauthorized accessing of a computer. The law also punishes the unauthorized accessing of a computer with the intent to commit fraud. For either action, individuals and organizations can sue in a civil case to recover damages. Within the context of employees and social media, an employee may at one time had permission to access a SM account, once employment ended, so too did authorization.

A CFAA claim may be used in situation in which the positions are reversed, where an individual files a claim against their former employer for accessing a SM account. In *Eagle v. Morgan*, Linda Eagle claimed that her former employer violated the CFAA when it took over her LinkedIn account. A plaintiff has to demonstrate actual harm to recover under the CFAA. The *Eagle* court found that the kind of injury recognized under the law is narrow, including only those related to damage to a computer system.[33] Because Eagle could not demonstrate recognizable damages, she could not recover under the CFAA.

The damage threshold for the CFAA is $5,000.[34] An organization or individual must prove damages in this amount or they will not be able to win a claim under the CFAA. The law also includes criminal penalties of up to 20 years jail time for each separate claim. This has implications that relate, again, to the valuation of SM accounts and connections. Those asserting the CFAA in a case related to a SM account will have to prove the worth of the account, its related materials including friends/followers/connections, the potential connections and media. Though marketing and advertising organizations can offer estimated values for certain related social media materials, it may be difficult to prove damages in an exact amount. It would be more difficult to estimate the value of potential connections because they do not yet exist, and there is no guarantee that such connections will actually happen.

BEST PRACTICES

Though many of the claims above may not be successful against a former employee or organization, the act of having to mount a defense against the claims may be just as, if not more, professionally and financially devastating. A few best practices may be useful for helping to avoid many of the legal conflicts mentioned above. First, employees may want to keep their personal social media accounts separate from that used in connection with their job or within the scope of their employment. It is easy and convenient to use one account for connecting to others and distributing information on the Internet. The conflicts enumerated above, however, indicate that there can be negative consequences when the personal and professional are mixed.

Second, it is best that both employees and employers have a meeting of the minds as to ownership and control of social media accounts. This information can be detailed in the employment contract or other employee–employer agreement, and should be as descriptive as possible to avoid confusion in the event of separation or change in relationship. Of course, taking either, or both, of these measures is not a guarantee against a conflict over ownership and access of a social media account. These practices do, however, allow for organizations, and individuals, to discuss the implications of the use of social media for employment purposes. As the conflicts mentioned above indicate, because of a lack of legal bright line rules related to social media this area is unsettled, and continues to evolve with professional and financial consequences.

As a final matter, although the rhetoric surrounding social media accounts points to personal or organizational ownership, the terms of service for most platforms indicate that the social media site retains property rights individual accounts. These rights include the ability to boot usage policy violators from the site, as well as to allow users to reaccess their accounts after being hacked. In fact, in *Eagle v. Morgan* mentioned earlier, it was LinkedIn that allowed Linda Eagle to regain access to her profile after her former employer changed the password. Courts have also treated platforms as the actual owners of individual accounts. In *New York v. Harris*,[35] the New York state court ruled that Twitter had to turn over the tweets connected the account of Malcolm Harris, an activist being prosecuted for his role in Occupy Wall Street activities. Twitter had argued that users had ownership interests in their accounts. The court was unpersuaded.

State legislatures have, however, taken up the cause of employees, both actual and perspective, wishing to maintain control over their social media accounts. In 2012, Maryland became the first state to pass a law banning organizations from requesting or requiring that employees turn over passwords. Louisiana, New Hampshire, and Wisconsin, among others, followed suit, and similar laws are pending in many other states. The laws, framed as protecting employee privacy, indicate a recognition of personal ownership in social media accounts.

FREQUENTLY ASKED QUESTIONS

1. Are social media accounts considered property?

Yes. Social media accounts are considered property, although it is not always clear to whom, aside from the platform, the accounts belong. The accounts and the personalities connected to them have the attributes of many of the different kinds of intellectual property including copyright, trademark, trade secret, and patent. No court has said definitively whether a social media account and its related materials are a particular kind of intellectual property, but courts have noted the similarities. A ruling from a federal circuit court of appeals, in the absence of a ruling from the Supreme court, would provide a more definitive statement on whether and what kind of intellectual property exist in social media accounts.

2. May I use my social media account for work purposes?

It depends. Your employer may permit you to use your personal social media account for work purposes. You should, however, be careful of mixing personal and professional communications and responsibilities. It may be best to obtain a written list of expectations for the use of social media in your professional capacity.

3. May my employer access my social media accounts?

Maybe. If the social media account that you are using was created before or without respect to your employment, you may be considered the account owner. If your employer has placed you in charge of an account that the company has created for you to use within the scope of your employment, that account belongs to the organization. Because the account belongs to the organization, it can access it freely and without your permission. It may, therefore, change passwords and transfer control of the account to another employee. To leave little room for conflict, information about accessing social media accounts should be detailed in the employment contract or agreement.

4. What happens to my social media account if I leave my job?

This depends on to whom the account belongs. As mentioned above, if the account was created by the organization for use for organizational purposes, the account usually remains with the organization. If, however, you created the account outside the scope of your employment, you would retain the use of the account. Again, this detail may be described within the text of an employment contract or agreement.

5. How do I protect my social media from takeover by my employer?

Although it is convenient and easy to use your personal social media accounts to communicate information related to your professional position, it may be best to keep separate personal and professional accounts. Although this may take more work on your part, there can be little conflict about the scope and purpose of each account. This does not mean that there will be no overlap in content. It should be helpful, however, in sorting out to whom an account belongs.

NOTES

1 Alejandro Portes, Social Capital: Its Origins and Applications in Modern Sociology, in Eric L. Lesser, Knowledge and Social Capital, 43–76 (2000).
2 Carl Jung, Basic Writings,Vol. 300. Modern Library, 1959.
3 See Derek Armstrong and Kam wai Yu, The Persona Principle: How to Succeed in Business with Image Marketing. Simon and Schuster, 1997.
4 Yumi Hisanabe, Persona Marketing for Fujitsu Kids Site, Fujitsu Scientific and Technical Journal, 45(2), 210–218 (2009).
5 Copyright Act, 17 U.S.C. §101.
6 490 U.S. 730 (1989).
7 980 F. 2d 857 (2d Cir. 1992).
8 Id. at 861.
9 2011 US Dist LEXIS 129229 (2011)
10 California Civil Code section 3426.1
11 849 F. Supp. 2d 1055 (Dist. Col. 2012).
12 Id. at 1075 (quoting Hertz v. Luzenac Group, 576 F.3d 1103, 115 (10th Cir. 2009)).
13 Eagle v. Morgan, Civil Action No. 11–4303 (E.D. Pa. Dec. 22, 2011).
14 Phonedog v. Kravitz, No. C 11–03474 MEJ (N.D. Cal. Nov. 8, 2011).
15 15 U.S.C. § 1127 (2006).
16 Maremont v. Susan Fredman Design Group, Ltd., 772 F. Supp. 2d 967 (ND Ill. 2011).
17 Maremont's claim would later be dismissed for failure to provide proof of financial injury. Maremont v. Susan Fredman Design Group, Ltd., No. 10 C 7811 (ND Ill. Mar. 3, 2014).
18 A&H Sportswear, Inc. v. Victoria's Secret Stores, Inc., 237 F.3d 198, 210–11 (3d Cir. 2000).
19 35 USC § 101.
20 See Courtney J. Mitchell, Keep Your Friends Close: A Framework for Addressing Rights to Social Media Contacts, 67 Vand. L. Rev. 1459 (2014) for further discussion of shop rights and social media.
21 U.S. v. Dubilier Condenser Corp., 289 U.S. 178, 198 (1933).
22 Id. at 187. See also Paul M. Rivard, Protection of Business Investments in Human Capital: Shop Right and Related Doctrines, 79 J. Pat. & Trademark Off. Soc'y 753, 754-55 (1997).
23 William Prosser, Privacy. 48 Calif. L. Rev. 383, 389–92(1960).
24 White v. Ortiz, No. 13-cv-251-SM (D.N.H. Sept. 14, 2015).
25 849 F.2d 460 (9th Cir. 1988).
26 Hirsch v. SC Johnson & Son, Inc., 280 NW 2d 129 (WI 1979).
27 Carson v. Here's Johnny Portable Toilets Inc., 698 F.2d 831 (6th Cir. 1983).
28 498 F.2d 821 (6th Cir. 1974).
29 971 F.2d 1395 (9th Cir. 1992).
30 1995 U.S. App. LEXIS 5464, 1995 WL 115571 (9th Cir. 1995).
31 Eagle v. Morgan, Civil Action No. 11–4303 (E.D. Pa. Mar. 12, 2013).
32 18 U.S.C. §1030.
33 Eagle v. Morgan, Civil Action No. 11–4303 (Oct. 4, 2012) (citing Fontana v. Corry, No. Civ. A. 10-1685, 2011 WL 4473285, at 7 (WD Pa Aug. 30, 2011)).
34 18 U.S.C. §1030(a)(4).
35 Docket No. 2011NY080152 (N.Y. Crim. Ct. June 30, 2012).

CHAPTER 7

Government Information and Leaks

David Cuillier

University of Arizona School of Journalism

ABSTRACT

Facebook, Twitter, and other social media platforms provide the opportunity for government to communicate quickly and freely with citizens, but at the same time the technology provides new temptations for officials to conduct the public's business in secret. This chapter examines the implications of social media in government and public record laws. Also, social media outlets, such as WikiLeaks, offer the potential of quickly disseminating records, including classified documents, that the government doesn't want out. The chapter ends with best practices for government and information seekers in dealing with social media and public records.

More and more, the government by the people, for the people, is moving online. People don't just vote for a candidate anymore; they "like" him or her. They don't just listen to long political stump speeches; they read electronic snippets of 140 characters or less. They don't drive to City Hall to sit in a four-hour council meeting; they tune into podcasts.

Integration of social media in government communication introduces new wrinkles in the public's ability to know what its government is up to. Officials might conduct important business via text, or on private smartphones, with limited ability for the public to see the messages. Cities post information on a Facebook page but might let the messages expire, or remove them, if they turn out to be embarrassing. WikiLeaks and other sites allow for fast and easy dissemination of public records to the world, with or without the consent of government officials. In an era of social media, it would seem that government would be more transparent. Or is it just the opposite?

This chapter examines issues emerging as social media and the Internet change the way government information is disseminated, and the ability for journalists and citizens to access that information. On the one hand, the use of social media provides new avenues for public officials to engage citizens through e-government, such as broadcasting city council meetings live online with chat rooms, or allowing officials to debate and inform through Facebook and Twitter. However, the new technology provides challenges for ensuring the public's business via social media stays the public's business and complies with public record and open meeting laws.

For example, Twitter feeds sent by a government official regarding his or her official duties, even if sent on a private cell phone, would likely be considered a public record, according to some states' court rulings and the fundamental principles of freedom of information. But how does an agency record these transmissions and provide them for journalists and others who request them later? And what about the international dissemination of public records, including classified records, via the Internet and social media (e.g., WikiLeaks)? Can the U.S. government punish a U.S. newspaper for spreading classified documents online? These and other issues will be discussed in this chapter to explain the application of freedom of information laws to government and social media.

FREEDOM OF INFORMATION 1.0

The public's right to know what the government is up to is a centuries-old concept that spans the globe. Long before Facebook and Twitter, government established policies, laws, and common practices of communicating with its public through less electronic means—mainly paper.

The first known public records law was adopted in 1766 by Sweden and Finland, called the Freedom-of-Press and the Right-of-Access to Public Records Act.[1] The law required government officials to provide documents to citizens immediately and for free, and also created the world's first public records ombudsman to help people access their government (something the United States didn't do until 2009[2]). Now, more than 100 countries have such laws.

Access to government information in the United States started simple but developed into a complicated web of statutes, case law, and common practices. Originally, it was based on common law, assuming that people should have access to government information that it made sense for them to have; there was no need for statutes or court rulings, although that changed over time. In 1813, Congress created the Federal Depository Program to make sure people could access federal records from designated university libraries. The salaries of federal employees became public starting in 1816. Wisconsin adopted the first state law ensuring open records and meetings in 1849, and now every state has such laws. Congress enacted the Freedom of Information Act in 1966, and it continues to be updated every decade or so, including 1996 revisions requiring federal agencies to make certain records available electronically and online.[3] The Clery Act requires universities to post crime data,[4] and the Government in the Sunshine Act of 1976[5] requires some federal agencies to meet in public.

The basic premise of freedom of information laws, often called sunshine laws because they shed light on government, is that people need to know what their officials are doing in order to self-govern. Citizens want to know how their taxes are being spent. They want to make sure services and duties are carried out fairly, effectively, and honestly. They want to see how decisions are made by elected leaders so they can decide whether to re-elect them or find someone better. Access to public records and meetings is essential for democracy,[6] and some international courts are even ruling that access to government information is a fundamental human right.[7]

Under most of these laws, citizens have a right to look at any government records, including paper, audio, video, or electronic files, that show what the government is up to. In general, the government may keep some records, or parts of records, secret if the material contains information that would cause harm to the government or individuals. With paper records, the process has been relatively straightforward: Person walks up to counter, asks for record, clerk scuttles to filing cabinet, comes back to counter, shows record to person. Maybe the requester asks for a photocopy, pays 10 cents per page, and leaves. Sometimes the requester and official haggle over what should be public and what should be kept secret, blotting out the secret information with a Sharpie. Rarely are there hitches caused by the physical nature of a paper public record.

No longer is access that simple. The electronic nature of government records today—in databases and online—have created whole new issues. The U.S. Supreme Court has been reluctant to take on some of these matters, instead allowing lower courts to sort it out as technology develops. That's probably a good thing. When the nation's high court decides to take a case pertaining to electronic government records and technology, the outcomes are sometimes puzzling. For example, in the 1989 case *U.S. Department of Justice v. Reporters Committee*, the court decided that if a person wants to get criminal court records about someone, he or she can drive to various court houses and look up the paper files, but that person should not have access to the same information in one database because that would make it too easy.[8] Similarly, in the 2000 case *Reno v. Condon*, regarding states' rights, the justices viewed department of motor vehicle data as an "article of commerce," of little public-interest value and something to be bought and sold, like lumber.[9] Given the way the court understands electronic information and technology, it's probably best the law of social media and public information be hashed out at the state level to resolve disputes organically. As it turns out, that is exactly what is happening.

TEXTS AND EMAILS AS PUBLIC RECORDS

When email emerged as a useful communication device in the early 1990s, government officials found they could easily exchange information in secret without worrying about anyone seeing what they were writing. After all, emails aren't "written," right? They just disappear in some computer that no citizens can access, or flitter into cyberspace. Poof!

But eventually, state courts and legislatures made it clear that emails and text messages sent by public officials regarding public business must be made available to citizens just as if they were written on a piece of paper. Today, most state public record laws require that officials' work emails, texts, and other electronic communications be made available to citizens. This information has helped journalists expose problems in government. In 2008, for example, the *Detroit Free Press* and *Detroit News* sued for the text messages of then-Mayor Kwame Kilpatrick, and the resulting stories exposed corruption and perjury that resulted in Kilpatrick being sent to prison.

But even today, decades after the emergence of electronic messages, it's not simple or settled. Some government agencies have found several ways to avoid public scrutiny.

Deletion

Some government officials have simply avoided disclosure with the "delete" key. Former President George W. Bush deleted millions of official White House emails from 2003 through 2005.[10] In 2008, Texas Gov. Rick Perry developed a system to automatically delete emails every seven days, even though correspondence via paper had been kept for at least one year. Such deletions are flagrant violations of public record laws, or at least the intent of the laws, and can get public officials in hot water. Public records should be retained for a suitable amount of time, at least six months to a year depending on the nature of the record, and agencies should follow their retention policies.

Personal Devices

Some government officials have attempted to skirt the law by conducting work business on private computers or cell phones, instead of their work devices. The George W. Bush White House used email accounts through the Republican Party to conduct business.[11] When Sarah Palin was governor of Alaska, she used Yahoo accounts for state business to avoid scrutiny,[12] and governors in North Carolina, Iowa, Colorado, and other states followed suit. When Hillary Clinton was Secretary of State from 2009 to 2013 she sent and received more than 60,000 emails through a private server, and when exposed she deleted more than half of them, saying they were "personal and private."[13]

The courts have sometimes allowed for such practices, reasoning that the government agencies don't have possession of the messages so they can't be expected to cough them up. For example, in 2006, *The Dallas Morning News* had requested personal emails from city officials, including the mayor, relevant to a federal corruption investigation involving Dallas employees. The city refused to provide the emails, saying the messages didn't meet the definition of public records because the emails were sent on the mayor's personal BlackBerry. An appeals court ruled in favor of the city.[14]

However, the tide is turning, and a majority of state-level courts are realizing that the mode or ownership of the message isn't what matters; it's the content. In states such as Florida, Illinois, and Arkansas, if a public official sends an email or text message regarding public business on a personal smartphone or computer, then that message is subject to disclosure.[15] Likewise, courts in Arizona, Wisconsin, and elsewhere have acknowledged that messages that are purely personal can be kept secret, regardless of what type of device they are sent on, or the physical nature of the record. That makes sense. Public business is the public's business, and personal business can be kept secret. Movement is afoot at the federal level, as well, to clarify the issue. A federal ruling by the District of Columbia Circuit Court of Appeals in 2016 determined that federal agencies couldn't deny access to government emails maintained on private servers. "If a department head can deprive the citizens of their right to know what his department is up to by the simple expedient of maintaining his departmental emails on an account in an another domain, that purpose is hardly served," Judge David Sentelle wrote. "It would make as much sense to say that the department head could deprive requesters of hard-copy documents by leaving them in a file at his daughter's house and then claiming that they are under her control."[16]

Avoidance

Many government officials have simply instructed their employees to avoid using email for anything that could be embarrassing. In 2011, Florida Gov. Rick Scott told his staff to talk to him by phone instead of emailing. Unless the calls are recorded, those conversations can indeed be kept secret. Of course, it's not good management practice to conduct important business verbally without records. There are good reasons why humans learned to document their thoughts and communications.

Technical Barriers

Perhaps the most challenging barrier in accessing electronic messages, particularly tweets and texts, is how to physically archive and provide them to citizens. Is every public employee to download his or her texts daily, pick out the ones pertaining to public business, and save them to a central database for the public to see? As technology keeps changing, access gets more challenging. One solution is to require public employees do their agency business on work devices, which can be accessed more easily, and prohibit work communications on their personal equipment. Also, agencies will need to invest in technical solutions to archive tweets and messages, not to mention the online material that is linked from those messages.

Because Twitter itself does not provide a public archive of tweets, people seeking them may have to look elsewhere. In 2011, Twitter reached an agreement to provide full archives of public tweets to the Library of Congress, and federal agencies have been encouraged to retain their own social media postings through the National Archives and Records Administration.[17]

GOVERNMENT FACEBOOK AND TWEETS

Perhaps no politician knows the power of Twitter and Facebook more than Texas Gov. Rick Perry. While running for president in 2011–12, Perry used social media effectively, including having his son, Griffin, tweet like a hurricane, tossing out 140-character zingers about the other Republican nominees. Yet, the social media world is fickle, and volatile. In fall 2011, Perry blocked journalists he didn't like from his Twitter account. His spokesperson justified it by saying the account, with 35,000 followers, is personal and his to run how he wishes. In spring 2012, after Perry made a decision to cut funding for women's health programs, his Facebook page was deluged with more than 4,000 posts from women sarcastically seeking advice on their menstrual periods. The posts were removed.

Just how personal are these social media records, regarding a person who wanted to become president of the United States and sought the attention of all Americans? Government agencies are grappling with those issues and the legal terrain is still taking shape, but the same principles governing emails and other records apply: If it's the public's business then it should be public, regardless of the medium, and often regardless of where it is posted.

In 2009, the U.S. General Services Administration provided social media recommendations for federal agencies, making it clear that anything posted online is fair game for public scrutiny, particularly for those people in leadership positions. "Assume your thoughts are in the public domain and can be published or discussed in all forms of media. Have no expectation of privacy."[18] That is good advice for anyone, public official or not.

Many states have begun adopting social media policies. Washington state, for example, created guidelines in 2010 for social media use, making it clear that government officials should consider anything they write online regarding agency business to be subject to the state public records law.[19] The guidelines also state that it is the agency's responsibility to capture electronic copies of its social media records, using third-party tools to do so (e.g., TwInbox, Tweetake, SocialSafe, and Cloudpreservation).

North Carolina's agency guidelines for social media go a little further, recommending that public employees be wary of posting opinions, discussing areas outside of one's expertise, and committing the agency to an action. The guidelines make it clear that anything posted online in any forum may not be able to be "taken back" and that all are subject to the public records laws, including responses posted by citizens in response to an agency post. All privacy settings on social media sites are to be set to "public."[20]

It is unclear how moderating government social media sites will evolve, particularly regarding content issues and records retention. When a city employee deletes a comment deemed inappropriate on an agency Facebook page, that is essentially destroying a public record, or part of the record, before its time. The City of Seattle's social media policy, for example, states nine reasons for why the government can remove a post on its Facebook page—essentially censoring speech of citizens in a public forum.[21] Reasons include profanity, sexual content, advertisements, encouragement of illegal activity, content that promotes discrimination, comments not on topic, and comments supporting or opposing a political campaign. It is easy to see that discussions about medicinal marijuana, race, or city politics could lead to disagreement and potential suppression of protected speech and destruction of a public record.

So far, the case law regarding social media and public records is undeveloped. Only now are government agencies, journalists, and citizens beginning to realize that agency Facebook pages and tweets are public records. Most people don't even realize they are legally entitled to see such communications, but once they figure it out, litigation will ensue. As access disputes erupt and rulings are issued, no doubt the first place we will find out about it is in a status update.

WIKILEAKS: SPREADING DOCUMENTS ONLINE

In 2010, U.S. Army Private Bradley Manning made available to the public more than 250,000 classified documents regarding U.S. diplomatic relations with world leaders, the largest leak of top-secret material in history, dubbed "Cablegate" by some. He didn't need a box or U-Haul to transfer the records to WikiLeaks, the website that published the material. All he used was a rewritable CD labeled "Lady Gaga" while listening to her song "Telephone."

The fact that an Army private in Iraq could have unrestricted access to millions of classified government records and download them easily brought to light the new realities of electronic information dissemination. Despite worries from government officials, the information release resulted only in embarrassment of U.S. diplomats and no deaths of informants. Some people say the online information, spread via social media, actually helped spur revolution in the Arab world in 2011.[22] But nevertheless, if one person could do this, what could be released in the future that would cause harm?

Some would say Edward Snowden could have caused harm by his release of classified documents to the *Guardian* newspaper in 2013. The documents and resulting news coverage exposed widespread electronic surveillance by the U.S. government of its own citizens.[23] Was Snowden a patriot or traitor? Regardless of one's views, the leaks continued, including the 2016 disclosure of 11.5 million files in the Panama Papers disclosure, the largest in world history at 2.6 terabytes.[24]

These weren't the first time a government insider copied classified records and got them out to the public. In 1969, Daniel Ellsberg photocopied 7,000 pages of classified "Pentagon Papers" documents regarding the Vietnam War and provided them to the *New York Times*. Cablegate was different, though, in several respects. First, the volume of Cablegate records was enormous, equaling about 300 million words, compared to two million words in the Pentagon Papers. Second, the electronic nature of the records allowed fast worldwide dissemination to anyone with access to a computer. The Pentagon Papers were published in a newspaper and reprinted in a book.

Today, anyone can get a government document or database and pop it on the Internet for instant reading. Social media allows it to be spread quickly, from friend to friend, network to network. Following Cablegate, government officials expressed extreme concern about the potential danger of classified documents being easily spread online. Some called for the criminal prosecution of WikiLeaks founder Julian Assange and of the *New York Times* for printing some of the information, based on the Espionage Act of 1917.[25] Senator Joseph Lieberman said:

I certainly believe that WikiLeaks has violated the Espionage Act, but then what about the news organizations—including *The Times*—that accepted it and distributed it? To me, *The New York Times* has committed at least an act of bad citizenship, and whether they have committed a crime, I think that bears a very intensive inquiry by the Justice Department.[26]

While the government might have a case against the leaker, Manning, it is unlikely the Department of Justice could successfully prosecute Assange or editors of the *New York Times*. True, despite the First Amendment, the government does have some limited authority over publication, but to do so it must apply strict scrutiny, which means that a content-based restriction is OK only if it promotes a compelling interest and is the least restrictive means to further the interest. Certainly, protecting civilians and soldiers from enemies is a compelling interest. But the burden is on the government to make a strong case that publication would cause immediate harm.[27] In the case of Cablegate, nobody was killed or harmed, at least that has been reported. Because of that burden to show immediate harm from publication, no journalist has been prosecuted under the Espionage Act.

Because of the constitutional difficulty in prosecuting journalists, the government has instead focused its efforts on punishing leakers. In 2012, the Obama administration pursued the prosecution of six government leakers under the Espionage Act, more than any other president in U.S. history. Lucy Dalglish, former director of the Reporters Committee for Freedom of the Press, discussed the issue at an Aspen Institute summit with national security officials in 2011. The officials told her that Cablegate caused the government to institute a zero-tolerance policy on leaking information. If they couldn't stop journalists from printing information, or force reporters to reveal their anonymous sources, then they could scare government employees from giving it out. As one national security representative said: "We're not going to subpoena reporters in the future. We don't need to. We know who you're talking to."[28]

CONCLUSION: MODEL PRACTICES IN PUBLIC SOCIAL MEDIA

Social media provide exciting opportunities for the public to engage with its government, and politicians with their voters. As technology evolves and changes, so will the information dissemination practices of government agencies and information collection practices of journalists. Regardless of the technology or platform—Facebook, Snapchat, Twitter, Tumblr, Second Life, LinkedIn, or whatever new gizmo is invented—the same basic principles of transparency and accountability apply to government uses of social media.

Government Practices

Government agencies have an obligation to follow public record laws, even in cyberspace. But it can be tricky. Here are some best practices for making it work:

1. Assume anything posted online by a government employee regarding agency business could be subject to public record laws, whether it's on an official agency Facebook page, personal page, tweet or email, and whether it's sent from an agency-issued device or a personal device. Make that clear to all employees and the public. Government employees should not use personal cell phones or computers for their work communications. Avoid commingling public and personal conversations by using separate personal email accounts, Facebook pages, and cell phones for purely personal information.
2. Utilize software to collect and archive in real-time Facebook pages, email, tweets, and other social media records. Make the electronic files easily searchable, preferably online, and capture the materials linked from the agency communications—similar to saving the paper attachments referred to in a memo.
3. Social media records should be retained for a suitable amount of time, at least six months to a year depending on the nature of the record, and agencies should follow their retention policies by not prematurely deleting records.
4. Develop social media policies that clearly explain to employees and the public that the agency's social media communications, including posts by citizens, are considered public records and can be copied and shared with others.
5. If citizens are encouraged to share their thoughts on agency social media platforms, then agency moderators should be careful to remove only those writings that would be considered unprotected speech (advocating violence, obscenity, etc.). Removal of posts because they are unpopular or embarrassing to the agency could be considered a form of prior restraint.
6. High-ranking elected leaders should consider their Twitter accounts, Facebook pages, and other social media outlets available and open to all. Blocking specific journalists or other "undesirables" appears shady.

7. Governing bodies, such as city councils, should not use email, Twitter, or other online forums to discuss official matters without providing those messages to the public. Even when conversations are one-on-one, if a majority of the members are involved in such discussions, the communications can be construed as "serial meetings" and a violation of state open meeting laws.

Information-Gathering Practices

Journalists and citizens who want to keep an eye on government today need to do so with fingers on a keypad. Here are some suggestions for accessing government in the age of social media:

1. Encourage, nay, demand, that public agencies adopt the practices and policies listed above. Resources are tight in many government agencies, so urge elected leaders to dedicate more money toward social media and records retention.
2. If government agencies don't archive their social media posts, save them yourself. Record the mayor's tweets. Save Facebook posts, especially if they are removed later. Remember that sunshine laws do not apply to private organizations such as Twitter and Facebook, which are not obligated to provide public archives, so if you don't do the archiving, your only source may be the government agency.
3. When asking for government officials' emails, texts, or social media records, ask that they be provided electronically rather than paper printouts. It will save you copy fees and allow for easier keyword searching.
4. Learn the law of electronic public records. A great guide is provided by the Reporters Committee for Freedom of the Press at http://www.rcfp.org/access-electronic-communications.
5. When gathering information from government social media sites, be upfront about your identity. Don't hide behind pseudonyms. Disclose in your reports the source of the information you gather, and be careful who you friend. Apply the same ethical standards to social media as in any other information gathering.
6. Know that any communications you have with government could be considered a public record. Assume anything you post or type could be revealed publicly, so take appropriate precautions when communicating sensitive or potentially libelous information.
7. Carefully vet any information or documents leaked to you before disseminating them. That's what the *New York Times* did with the WikiLeaks Cablegate documents. They verified the information, and checked to make sure nobody would get hurt.

Social media will continue to evolve, with new platforms and exciting opportunities for people to communicate and discuss issues and events that affect their lives and communities. Regardless of the technology, the same basic principles should apply: Public business is the public's business. Any communications by government employees discussing what the government is up to, no matter the forum or machinery it is communicated upon, should be subject to public record laws. Online technologies have the potential of making government more transparent and accessible to the average person. That is what James Madison, the author of the Bill of Rights, would applaud, once he could figure out how to operate an iPad: "Knowledge will forever govern ignorance: And a people who mean to be their own Governors, must arm themselves with the power which knowledge gives."[29]

FREQUENTLY ASKED QUESTIONS

1. Are citizens entitled to see text messages, emails, and private messages sent on social networks by public officials?

In general, yes, if the messages pertain to public business. In most states, any electronic messages created by or possessed by a public employee regarding public business are subject to disclosure under public record laws. That usually includes messages sent on personal computers or smartphones, but it depends on the state. If a message is purely personal, though, the information is unlikely to be required to be made public, and public record laws allow for material to be kept hidden if it would harm national security or impede in some other government function.

2. Are government Facebook pages and their posts subject to public record laws and required to be made public?

In most cases, yes. If the purpose of the page or message is to convey what government is up to, and it is produced by government employees, then most state courts would consider them subject to public record laws. That would include any comments posted by citizens, and any videos or other materials incorporated in the page. It is likely that work-related comments posted on a high-ranking leader's *personal* Facebook page also might be subject to public record laws. Government agencies should develop systems to capture and archive their social media content, including the materials that are linked to from the page.

3. How does a journalist or citizen get to see text messages, emails, or Facebook posts written by government officials?

With much persistence. Emails on agency-provided accounts are relatively easy to get because most government agencies save them to a central server.

However, email messages sent on personal Yahoo or Gmail accounts can be more difficult to produce. That's why government employees shouldn't do government business on personal email accounts. Text messages, also, can be tricky. Ultimately, it is the responsibility, by law, of the government agency to figure out a way to archive these government communications and provide a way for citizens to see them or get copies. Put the onus on the agency to follow the law.

4. Are *my* emails, texts, and Facebook posts subject to public record laws?

Generally, no. What you communicate in your own time as a private citizen is your own business. You might make it "public" by posting something on a blog or Facebook page, but public records laws do not apply. There are exceptions, however. For example, if you communicate with a public official via email, text, or a post on his or her Facebook page, those communications might be subject to public record laws. Some jurisdictions, including federal agencies, blot out identities of people communicating with officials, but some don't. It's a good idea to assume that anything you write online could end up in the public sphere.

5. Can the government prosecute a journalist or anyone else for posting classified documents online?

The Espionage Act of 1917 suggests that unauthorized publication of classified documents could result in a fine, up to 10 years in prison, or both. However, no journalist has been prosecuted for publishing classified documents, and it is unlikely to happen unless the information is certain to cause immediate harm. If the government can make a strong case that the information will cause harm, then prior restraint or punishment might be allowed. Because it is difficult to show that, the government instead would likely go after the government employee who leaked the documents.

NOTES

1 For a brief history of the creation of this law, see Stephen Lamble, Freedom of Information, a Finnish Clergyman's Gift to Democracy, Freedom of Information Review, 97, 2–8 (2002). Also, find more information at the Anders Chydenius Foundation website, www.chydenius.net.

2 The Office of Government Information Services was created in 2009 through the Open Government Act. The agency, contained in the National Archives, assists citizens who seek public records from federal agencies, and mediates disputes between requesters and agencies. See https://ogis.archives.gov.

3 Electronic Freedom of Information Act of 1996 ("E-FOIA"), 5 U.S.C. § 552(a)(2) (A)–(E), 5 U.S.C. § 552(e)(2)(1996).

4 20 U.S.C. § 1092(f).

5　5 U.S.C. § 552b.

6　See Vincent Blasi, The Checking Value in First Amendment Theory, 2 Law & Soc. Inquiry 521, 609–610 (1977) (arguing that "the First Amendment may require that journalists have access as a general matter to some records"). See also Harold L. Cross, The People's Right to Know: Legal Access to Public Records and Proceedings (1953); Alexander Meiklejohn, Free Speech and its Relation to Self-Government (1948); Aimee C. Quinn, Keeping the Citizenry Informed: Early Congressional Printing and 21st Century Information Policy, 20 Gov't Info. Q. 281 (2003).

7　See Cheryl Ann Bishop, Access to Information as a Human Right (2012) (discusses rulings by the European Court of Human Rights and the Inter-American Court on Human Rights enunciating that access to government information is a human right based on the need to have information to express oneself).

8　U.S. Department of Justice v. Reporters Committee for Freedom of the Press, 489 U.S. 749, 780 (1989).

9　Reno v. Condon, 528 U.S. 141, 120S. Ct. 666, 145 L. Ed. 2d 587 (2000).

10　See the report, Citizens for Responsibility and Ethics in Washington, Without a Trace: The Story Behind the Missing White House E-Mails and the Violations of the Presidential Records Act (2010), http://www.scribd.com/doc/48889149/ Untold-Story-of-the-Bush-White-House-Emails (the documentation was a result of a settlement of two consolidated lawsuits, Nat'l Sec. Archive v. Executive Office of the President (D.D.C.), filed September 5, 2007, and CREW v. Executive Office of the President (D.D.C.), filed September 25, 2007).

11　CREW, Without a Trace.

12　Lisa Demer, Governor's Two E-mail Accounts Questioned, Anchorage Daily News, October 21, 2008.

13　Steven Lee Myers, F.B.I. Findings Damage Many of Hillary Clinton's Claims, N.Y. Times, July 5, 2016.

14　City of Dallas v. Dallas Morning News, LP, 281 S.W.3d 708 (Tex. App. – Dallas 2009).

15　See Joey Senat, Whose Business Is It: Is Public Business Conducted on Officials' Personal Electronic Devices Subject to State Open Record Laws? 19 Comm. Law & Pol'y 293 (2014); and Kyu Ho Youm, Access to Email and the Right of Privacy in the Workplace, in Charles Davis and David Cuillier, Transparency 2.0: Digital Data and Privacy in a Wired World 97–114 (2014).

16　Competitive Enterprise Institute v. Office of Science and Technology Policy, 2016 U.S. LEXIS 12357, 9 (D.C. Cir. 2016).

17　Emily Kopp & Jack Moore, Agencies Have 120 Days to Start Getting E-records in Shape, FederalNewsRadio.com, November 29, 2011, http://www.federal newsradio.com/?nid=85&sid=2648774.

18　General Services Administration, GSA Social Media Policy, CIO 2106.1 (2009), p. 2. Also, see the National Archives and Records Administration Best Practices for the Capture of Social Media Records, 2013, http://www.archives.gov/records-mgmt/ resources/socialmediacapture.pdf

19　Office of the Governor in Coordination with Multiple State Agencies and Contributors, Guidelines and Best Practices for Social Media Use in Washington State (2010).

20　North Carolina Office of the Governor, Best Practices for Social Media Usage in North Carolina (2009).

21 See City of Seattle, Social Media Use Policy, http://www.seattle.gov/pan/SocialMediaPolicy.htm.

22 See Bill Keller, Wikileaks, a Postscript, N.Y. Times, February 19, 2012, p. A19. Also, see Robert Mackey, Qaddafi Sees WikiLeaks Plot in Tunisia, N.Y. Times, January 17, 2011 (Colonel Qaddafi blames WikiLeaks for the uprisings in the Middle East).

23 Glenn Greenwald, No Place to Hide: Edward Snowden, the NSA, and the U.S. Surveillance State (2014).

24 See the Panama Papers reporting conducted by the International Consortium of Investigative Journalists, https://panamapapers.icij.org/

25 18 U.S.C. § 793 (2005).

26 Charlie Savage, U.S. Prosecutors Study WikiLeaks Prosecution, N.Y. Times, December 7, 2010, p. A-10.

27 See, e.g., New York Times Co. v. United States, 403 U.S. 713, 725 (1971) (Brennan, J., concurring) (rejecting as insufficient government's assertions that publication of Pentagon Papers "could," "might," or "may" prejudice the national interest); also, the Supreme Court has indicated that journalists can't be punished for publishing information that was provided to them, even if illegally obtained by a third party, see Bartnicki v. Vopper, 532 U.S. 514 (2001). For further discussion of this issue, see Congressional Research Service report 7–5700, Criminal Prohibitions on the Publication of Classified Defense Information, October 18, 2010, by Jennifer K. Elsea.

28 Lucy Dalglish, Lessons from Wye River, News Media & The Law, p. 1.

29 James Madison, Letter to William T. Barry, August 4, 1822. In James Madison: Writings (1999).

CHAPTER 8

Student Speech

Dan V. Kozlowski

Department of Communication
Saint Louis University

ABSTRACT

Social media now pervade the lives of students. This chapter explores existing cases and developing issues as the legal and school communities wrestle with how to handle students' social media speech, which is often created off campus but may have impact on campus. Confusion and uncertainty about social media and students' rights prevail, as the law has failed to catch up to the technology around it. Rather than outlawing social media use by students, educators are advised to encourage responsible, constructive uses.

More than 90% of teens report going online daily, including 24% who say they go online "almost constantly," according to a 2015 study from the Pew Research Center.[1] Facebook remains the most popular social media site among teens, the study found, but more than 70% of teens also report using more than one social network site; half of teens also use Instagram, for instance, and 40% use Snapchat.[2] It is fair to say that social media thus no doubt pervade the lives of students. And while these media give students the power to turn a performance at a school's sixth-grade music festival into fame and a viral video phenomenon (see Greyson Chance, whose 2010 cover of Lady Gaga's "Paparazzi" drew more than 55 million YouTube page views and launched his music career), social media also represent, in the words of one commentator, a school's "new bathroom wall"—a place where a student's "online postings . . . can destroy reputations, end relationships and intensify negative feelings."[3] School officials' attempts to regulate that virtual "bathroom wall" and to punish students for publishing on it constitute the all-important but still-unresolved quandary now facing student speech law:

How far does school authority reach? Can schools constitutionally punish students for speech they create and post online, even if they do so from off school grounds (which is typically the case)? Because the U.S. Supreme Court has not answered the question directly, lower courts have issued an array of often inconsistent, incongruent rulings. And, as one legal scholar has written, school authorities have filled the "judicial vacuum"[4] by seizing the opportunity for censorship, punishing students for Facebook posts, for example, or banning social media use by athletes entirely.

Indeed, instances of schools doling out discipline for social media speech occur constantly. An Indiana high school senior was expelled from school for a tweet he posted while at home, in the middle of the night, that opined on the myriad ways the F-word could be employed. The student insisted he posted using his personal computer, but he said the superintendent told him that, even if he did, when he later logged into Twitter with his school-issued laptop, the post could show up with a school IP address in the school's system that monitors tweets.[5] A Louisiana high school student sued his school after he was removed from an honors society and suspended from school for a Facebook post that criticized a teacher.[6] And in April 2015, a student was arrested at Oklahoma State University after he used Yik Yak to make threats about a school shooting.[7] Worried about the vitriol and hate that sometimes appears on Yik Yak, some colleges have moved to ban that app from their wifi networks entirely.

The list of examples could go on—and on, which is why scholars such as Clay Calvert have called the issue of how to treat students' online speech a "pervasive and pernicious First Amendment problem."[8] This chapter will trace existing cases and developing issues as the legal and school communities both wrestle with how to handle student speech in a culture that is defined by its always-evolving technology and media use.

STUDENT SPEECH AND THE U.S. SUPREME COURT

The U.S. Supreme Court has decided four cases that govern the First Amendment rights of public school students,[9] all within the last 50 years. In its first ruling, the 1969 case *Tinker v. Des Moines Independent Community School District*, the Court broadly supported student expression, famously declaring that "it can hardly be argued that either students or teachers shed their constitutional rights to freedom of speech or expression at the schoolhouse gate."[10] In the case, school officials suspended three students for wearing armbands in school to protest the Vietnam War. The Court ruled that students' speech could not be punished unless school officials reasonably conclude that the speech did, or would, "materially and substantially disrupt the work and discipline of the school."[11] And the Court indicated that standard should be interpreted stringently—even though the armbands caused "comments, warnings by other students, the poking of fun at [the students]," and even though a teacher said his lesson was "practically wrecked"[12] that day, the Court said the disruption caused by the armbands was not enough to justify censorship.

The Court's three subsequent student speech cases scaled back *Tinker's* protections. In *Bethel School District v. Fraser*, the Court upheld the suspension of a high school student who gave a "lewd"[13] speech laced with "pervasive sexual innuendo"[14] at a school assembly. Emphasizing that "schools must teach by example the shared values of a civilized social order,"[15] the Court sided with the school, concluding that the "First Amendment does not prevent the school officials from determining that to permit a vulgar and lewd speech such as [the student's] would undermine the school's basic educational mission."[16] Two years later, the Court held *Tinker* was inapplicable again, this time in a case involving a school-sponsored student newspaper. In the 1988 case *Hazelwood School District v. Kuhlmeier*, the Court ruled that educators could regulate school-sponsored student speech—curricular speech that bears "the imprimatur of the school"[17]—so long as their actions are "reasonably related to legitimate pedagogical concerns."[18]

In 2007, in *Morse v. Frederick*, the Court carved out another exception to *Tinker*: speech that school officials "reasonably regard as promoting illegal drug use."[19] The Court in *Morse* acknowledged that "there is some uncertainty at the outer boundaries as to when courts should apply school-speech precedents."[20] But the Court did nothing to resolve that uncertainty in *Morse*. Instead, the Court ruled that, even though the student in the case was across the street from the school, off school grounds, he was participating in a "school-sanctioned and school-supervised event"[21] when he held up his controversial BONG HiTS 4 JESUS banner as the Olympic Torch Relay passed in front of his high school. None of the Court's student speech cases have involved what it considered off-campus speech, then, and—with that lack of guidance from the Court—lower courts have offered differing rulings in cases interpreting how far administrators' arms can reach.

CONFUSION IN THE LOWER COURTS

The dilemma over whether schools can punish students for online speech they create off campus isn't new. The first federal court opinion to deal with the issue was decided back in 1998.[22] But the rise and ubiquity of social media have escalated both the number of disciplinary sanctions for such speech and the number of legal cases challenging punishment. Students, of course, have badmouthed teachers or school officials or other students for generations. Whereas before, though, students might have kept a diary or shared conversations involving those topics on the bus or over landline phones or at the shopping mall, now students can use social media tools to reach a wide audience rapidly.[23] And lower courts have struggled with how to respond.

Tracing the path of one relatively recent case nicely illustrates the degree of confusion. In *J.S. v. Blue Mountain School District*, a middle school student and her friend—on a weekend and on a home computer—created a fake MySpace profile as a parody of their principal. It included his photograph as well as "profanity-laced statements insinuating that he was a sex addict and pedophile."[24] In the words of the en banc Third Circuit Court of Appeals, "The profile contained crude content and vulgar language, ranging from nonsense and juvenile humor to profanity and shameful personal attacks aimed at the principal and his family."[25] The profile initially was accessible to anyone, but, the day after they created it, one of the students, known in the court proceedings as J.S., set the profile to "private" and limited access to about 20 students to whom she had granted "friend" status. The school's computers blocked access to MySpace, so no student ever viewed the profile while at school. Another student, however, told the principal about the profile and who had created it, and—at the principal's request—that student printed out a copy of the profile and brought it to him. The principal then suspended J.S. and her friend for 10 days.

J.S. sued, sending the case on a meandering journey through the federal courts. At the district court level, she lost. U.S. District Judge James Munley ruled that, even though the profile arguably did not cause any *Tinker*-level disruption, it was "vulgar, lewd, and potentially illegal speech that had an effect on campus."[26] The judge relied on *Fraser* and *Morse* and said that J.S. could be punished. In February 2010, a panel of the Third Circuit agreed—but for different reasons. The Third Circuit panel said that *Tinker* did govern the case and that the suspension was constitutional because the school could *forecast* disruption. "We hold that off-campus speech that causes or reasonably threatens to cause a substantial disruption of or material interference with a school need not satisfy any geographical technicality in order to be regulated pursuant to *Tinker*," Judge D. Michael Fisher wrote for the court. Because the profile accused the principal of having "interest or engagement in sexually inappropriate behavior and illegal conduct,"[27] the court said it was foreseeable that the profile would disrupt his work as principal and encourage others to question his demeanor and conduct.

Two months later, however, the Third Circuit vacated the panel opinion and ordered en banc review. And in June 2011, a divided en banc court of the Third Circuit ruled in favor of J.S. This time, an eight-judge majority ruled that it did not need to decide definitively if *Tinker* controlled the case because, even if it did, the profile caused no actual disruption, nor could the school reasonably forecast disruption. Although the court acknowledged that the profile was "indisputably vulgar," it ultimately ruled the speech "was so juvenile and nonsensical that no reasonable person could take its content seriously, and the record clearly demonstrates that no one did."[28] The court also categorically ruled that *Fraser* does not apply to off-campus speech. Five judges concurred in the case and wanted to go much further, though. The concurrence argued that *Tinker* should not apply to students' off-campus speech at all because "the First Amendment protects students engaging in off-campus speech to the same extent it protects speech by citizens in the community at large."[29]

Judge Fisher wrote in dissent this time, joined by five other judges. He argued again that *Tinker* applied and that disruption from the profile was reasonably foreseeable. Moreover, he chided the majority for adopting a rule that he thought was unworkable for schools. "[W]ith near-constant student access to social networking sites on and off campus, when offensive and malicious speech is directed at school officials and disseminated online to the student body, it is reasonable to anticipate an impact on the classroom environment," he argued.[30]

J.S. thus perfectly exemplifies disagreements the judiciary has had over when school authority begins, what standard to apply, and how to apply it. Judges, first, have differed about how, or when, speech even becomes eligible for on-campus punishment. Some courts confronting the issue have used what Mary-Rose Papandrea has called a "territorial approach"[31]— asking whether a student either used school computers or servers to create, share, or view the speech in question or whether someone actually brought hard copies of the speech to school.[32] Other courts, on the other hand, have said that schools have jurisdiction to regulate off-campus speech if it is "reasonably foreseeable"[33] that the speech will come to the attention of school officials, whether because the speech is directed or targeted at students or school officials or because it is about school generally.

Still other courts, though, have generally skipped over the threshold question of whether speech amounts to on-campus or off-campus expression and instead have just directly applied the Court's school speech precedents.[34] Courts have been especially willing to apply *Tinker* in cases involving off-campus, social media speech, with outcomes hinging on whether schools can persuade courts that speech either did, or would, create a material and substantial disruption at school. And different courts have seemingly required different levels of disruption, similar to what occurred in *J.S.*: a panel of the Third Circuit said that disruption was reasonably foreseeable, while the en banc majority disagreed. Social media obviously allow speech to spread fast, to a wide audience, at virtually any time, making the speech both easier for school officials to monitor than traditional oral or written speech and also easier for a whistleblower student to find and bring in.[35] "[W]ireless internet access, smart phones, tablet computers, social networking services like Facebook, and stream-of-consciousness communications via Twitter give an omnipresence to speech," one federal judge has written.[36] School officials argue that, given that "omnipresence," online speech inevitably finds its way to school and can thus be punished under *Tinker* because school officials can forecast disruption. Some courts also have loosely interpreted what amounts to an actual disruption at school. Those courts that have interpreted *Tinker*'s standard so leniently have thus made it easy for school officials to extend their reach off campus.

That was arguably the case in *Doninger v. Niehoff*, a Second Circuit decision involving a student blog post that disparaged school officials and encouraged readers to contact the superintendent in order "to piss her off more."[37] The student who wrote the blog, Avery Doninger, was frustrated about the scheduling of a band contest at school known as "Jamfest." Her blog post, which she wrote from home, called school administrators "douchebags" for canceling the event and encouraged students to contact the superintendent.[38] When the principal discovered the post, two weeks after it was written, she punished Doninger by barring her from running for senior class secretary. Doninger sued, seeking an injunction that prevented her discipline.

A panel of the Second Circuit held that *Tinker* applied and that the post created a risk of substantial disruption. The court first said that the language Doninger used in her post was "not only plainly offensive, but also potentially disruptive of efforts to resolve the ongoing controversy."[39] The school, moreover, argued that the post was misleading because school officials had informed Doninger that the event would be rescheduled rather than canceled. The Second Circuit thus said that Doninger used "at best misleading and at worst false" information in an effort to solicit more calls and emails.[40] And because rumors were already swirling at school about the status of the event when Doninger wrote on her blog, the court deferred to the school and concluded that "it was foreseeable in this context that school operations might well be disrupted further by the need to correct misinformation as a consequence of [the] post."[41]

Courts have been especially likely to rule against students when applying *Tinker* in cases involving threatening speech.[42] In the 2015 case *Bell v. Itawamba County School Board*,[43] for instance, a high school student posted to Facebook and YouTube a rap song he recorded that alleged two coaches at his school had improper contact with female students. The song included the lyrics "looking down girls shirts/drool running down your mouth/ you fucking with the wrong one/going to get a pistol down your mouth" and "middle fingers up if you can't stand that nigga/middle fingers up if you want to cap that nigga."[44] The student insisted the allegations about inappropriate behavior were true and that he wrote the song to "increase awareness of the situation,"[45] but school officials interpreted the lyrics as "threatening, harassing, and intimidating,"[46] and they thus suspended the student for seven days and transferred him to an alternative school for the remaining five weeks of the period.

The student sued. The Fifth Circuit Court of Appeals ruled[47] that because the student intended for his song to reach school, *Tinker* applied. "*Tinker* governs our analysis . . . when a student intentionally directs at the school community speech reasonably understood by school officials to threaten, harass, and intimidate a teacher, even when such speech originated, and was disseminated, off-campus without the use of school resources," the court wrote.[48] And the court ruled that the student's punishment was constitutional because "a substantial disruption reasonably could have been forecast" by school officials since the rap "pertained directly to events occurring at school, identified the two teachers by name, and was understood by one to threaten his safety and by neutral, third parties as threatening."[49]

In July 2011, the Fourth Circuit Court of Appeals faced a case involving speech not about, nor directed at, a teacher or school official—instead the incident at issue resulted from student speech targeting another student, amounting to what the court said was impermissible cyberbullying on MySpace.[50] In the case, high school senior Kara Kowalski created a discussion group on MySpace titled "S.A.S.H.," which she claimed was an acronym for "Students Against Sluts Herpes." The comments and pictures posted to the group, though, targeted one student, named Shay N., and one of the nearly two dozen students who joined the group at Kowalski's invitation said S.A.S.H. was actually an acronym for "Students Against Shay's Herpes."[51] Shay and her parents went to school officials the next day to report the site and file a harassment complaint. For creating a "hate website" in violation of a school policy against bullying, Kowalski received out-of-school suspension for five days and a 90-day social suspension, which prevented her from attending school events in which she was not a direct participant.[52]

The Fourth Circuit upheld the punishment. The court said Kowalski knew talk about the MySpace group would reach school and that thus the "nexus of Kowalski's speech to [the school's] pedagogical interests was sufficiently strong to justify" the school's actions under *Tinker*.[53] "Given the targeted, defamatory nature of Kowalski's speech, aimed at a fellow classmate, it created 'actual or nascent' substantial disorder and disruption in the school," Judge Paul Niemeyer wrote for the court.[54] He pointed out that Shay missed school in order to avoid further abuse. Moreover, the court ruled, "had the school not intervened, the potential for continuing and more serious harassment of Shay N. as well as other students was real."[55] The court said that "harassment and bullying is inappropriate" and that the First Amendment does not "hinder school administrators' good faith efforts to address the problem" of bullying generally.[56]

Not all students who have faced punishment for social media speech have lost their cases under *Tinker*, however. *J.S.*, of course, offers one example. In another case, a U.S. magistrate judge refused to dismiss a student's lawsuit against her school after she was punished for creating a Facebook group titled "Ms. Sarah Phelps is the worst teacher I've ever met."[57] The student deleted the group two days after it was created when three commenters on the page showed support for Phelps. The teacher herself never saw the group. Nevertheless, the principal learned of the group after it had been deleted, and he suspended the student for three days. U.S. Magistrate Judge Barry Garber said the student's lawsuit challenging the punishment could go forward because, under *Tinker*, there was no indication "that a well founded expectation of disruption was present."[58] In December 2010, the school settled with the student by agreeing to remove any record of her suspension and to pay her attorney's fees.[59]

And in *T.V. v. Smith-Green Community School*,[60] a district court ruled in favor of two high school students who were barred from participating in a quarter of their fall extracurricular activities—including volleyball games and a show choir performance—as punishment for posting pictures of themselves simulating sex acts with phallic-shaped lollipops. The students took the pictures during a slumber party over the summer and posted them on MySpace, Facebook, and Photobucket. A parent brought printouts of the pictures to the school superintendent and said they were causing "divisiveness" among the girls on the volleyball team.[61] The principal subsequently said the students violated a code of conduct that forbade students participating in extracurricular activities from bringing "discredit or dishonor upon yourself or your school."[62]

The students sued, and U.S. District Judge Philip Simon struck down the punishment. He assumed without deciding that *Tinker* controlled but ruled that the actual disruption in the case did not "come close" to meeting *Tinker's* standard.[63] "In sum, at most, this case involved two complaints from parents and some petty sniping among a group of 15 and 16 year olds. This can't be what the Supreme Court had in mind when it enunciated the 'substantial disruption' standard in *Tinker*," Simon wrote.[64] He concluded that the school also did not demonstrate any factual basis to justify that officials reasonably forecast disruption. Even though the speech at issue in the case amounted to "crass foolishness,"[65] Simon said the First Amendment forbids any attempt at line drawing between worthy and unworthy speech. Moreover, Simon also ruled that the school's code of conduct was unconstitutionally vague and overbroad. A school's code cannot nullify students' First Amendment rights, and Simon said that the code at issue here poorly defined the subjective terms "discredit" and "dishonor," and the code was overbroad because it potentially could be applied to a variety of constitutionally protected out-of-school student conduct.[66]

SOCIAL MEDIA AND COLLEGE STUDENTS

The court cases discussed so far have all involved middle or high school students, but college students also have found themselves embroiled in legal disputes over their social media speech. In *Yoder v. University of Louisville*,[67] for instance, a federal judge ruled that a former nursing student, Nina Yoder, effectively waived her First Amendment rights when she signed a consent form as part of a childbearing course that required her to follow a mother through the birthing process. The form, which was signed by both Yoder and the mother she followed, provided that any information shared with the student "will be presented in written or oral form to the student's instructor only."[68] After Yoder witnessed the mother's labor and delivery, though, she wrote a blog post on her MySpace page about the experience. Although she did not reveal any information that specifically identified the mother or her family, Yoder's post described, "in intimate detail," what took place, including "medical treatment the birth-mother received, such as an epidural," along with other health-related issues.[69] One of Yoder's classmates told the course's instructor about the post, and the instructor then told School of Nursing administrators, who decided to dismiss Yoder from school. U.S. District Judge Charles Simpson III upheld the punishment, ruling that the school had legitimate reasons for having patients and students sign the consent form, and "because Yoder herself agreed not to publicly disseminate the information she posted on the internet, she is not entitled to now claim that she had a constitutional right to do so."[70]

In another example, in a much-publicized case Minnesota courts ruled that a college student could be punished for her Facebook posts. In *Tatro v. University of Minnesota*, Amanda Tatro, a student in the mortuary science department, was punished for a series of Facebook posts she made to her wall over two months in late 2009. In one post, she wrote that she "gets to play, I mean dissect, Bernie today"—which was the name she had given to the donated cadaver on which she was working.[71] In another post, she wrote that she wanted to use an embalming tool "to stab a certain someone in the throat . . . [P]erhaps I will spend the evening updating my 'Death List #5' and making friends with the crematory guy."[72] The comments worried a fellow mortuary science student, who reported them to university officials. The officials notified university police, who conducted an investigation but determined no crime had been committed and Tatro could return to class. The university, though, instead filed a formal complaint against Tatro, alleging she violated the school's student conduct code by engaging in "threatening, harassing, or assaultive conduct" and by engaging in conduct "contrary to university rules related to the mortuary-science program."[73] A panel of the campus committee on student behavior agreed that Tatro violated the code. As punishment, she was given a failing grade in the course and required to enroll in an ethics course, write a letter of apology, and complete a psychiatric evaluation. She also was placed on academic probation for the remainder of her undergraduate career.

Tatro's attorney argued that *Tinker* should not apply to a university student at all, particularly in a case involving off-campus speech. The Minnesota Court of Appeals disagreed, though. Citing a recent Third Circuit decision that applied *Tinker* in the university setting, the Minnesota court reasoned that *Tinker* controlled the case but "what constitutes a substantial disruption in a primary school may look very different in a university."[74] The court nevertheless arguably leniently applied *Tinker* and sided with the school. Tatro said she jokingly was referring to her ex-boyfriend when she wrote about stabbing someone, and police determined that she posed no threat. Even so, the court said "the fact that the university's concerns were later assuaged does not diminish the substantial nature of the disruption that Tatro's conduct caused or the university's need to respond to the disruptive expression."[75] Tatro then appealed to the Minnesota Supreme Court, which also upheld her punishment—but on a different ground. The state supreme court concluded that Tatro's posts violated the rules for her mortuary science program. "[W]e hold that a university does not violate the free speech rights of a student enrolled in a professional program, when the university imposes sanctions for Facebook posts that violate academic program rules that are narrowly tailored and directly related to established professional conduct standards," the court wrote.[76] The court emphasized what it said were the unique circumstances of a case that involved "a program that gives students access to donated human cadavers and requires a high degree of sensitivity."[77]

Tinker protected a college student from discipline for his online speech in *Murakowski v. University of Delaware*. There, a student's "sophomoric, immature, crude and highly offensive" essays—some of which referenced violence and sexual abuse—that he posted on a website he created led to his suspension.[78] The website, maintained on the university's server, came to the attention of school authorities after two students complained about the student and said they had visited his website and felt "uneasy and fearful around him."[79] U.S. Magistrate Judge Mary Pat Thynge ruled that, although the writings contained "graphic descriptions of violent behavior," they did not "evidence a serious expression of intent to inflict harm" to specific individuals.[80] The court also ruled that the complaints did not amount to a substantial disruption, nor had the university presented evidence that demonstrated it reasonably could forecast disruption. The suspension was thus unconstitutional.

PRIVACY AND SOCIAL MEDIA

An emerging, though still largely unlitigated, area of controversy involves student privacy on social media. Issues surrounding the monitoring of student athletes have been especially visible. In one high-profile incident, for instance, a top high school football player saw an elite university withdraw its scholarship offer to him after the school discovered the student had used racial and sexual slurs in his tweets.[81] Schools say such offensive speech risks damaging both students' reputations and the school's image, so to curb any controversy some colleges have adopted policies that, among other things, require their student athletes to "friend" either a coach or a compliance officer.[82] For example, a University of North Carolina social media policy requires that "each team must identify at least one coach or administrator who is responsible for having access to and regularly monitoring the content of team members' social networking sites and postings."[83] The policy emphasizes to students that playing for the school "is a privilege, not a right."[84] The university adopted the policy, in part, in response to an NCAA investigation of the school that found a former UNC football player had tweeted about expensive purchases, revealing improper contact with an agent.[85]

Other schools have relied on software packages—offered by companies such as Varsity Monitor and UDiligence—that automate the monitoring of athletes' social media use. The *St. Louis Post-Dispatch* reported that, as of February 2012, about three dozen colleges were already using UDiligence's program, including the University of Missouri's football team.[86] According to the *Post-Dispatch*, the program "searches for key words in tweets, blogs, comments on Facebook and photo captions that could be considered objectionable or raise a red flag."[87] UDiligence provides each school with a list of words, from which schools can add or subtract. Players then download an app to each of their social media accounts, giving UDiligence permission to monitor them—which involves a daily scan of the accounts and an email sent to the student and a school administrator if any of the key words appear. The company charges $1,500 a team or $8,000 a school. "It's not a gotcha tool, it's a mentoring tool," the CEO of the company told the *Post-Dispatch*.[88] Privacy advocates have decried the programs, however, as violating the privacy rights of both student athletes and the athletes' "friends" on social media.

Also alarming student speech advocates, some college coaches have instituted outright bans on social media use—banning social media generally or focusing specifically on Twitter. In recent seasons, coaches at Boise State, Mississippi State, Texas Tech, New Mexico State, Kansas, and South Carolina, among other places, have barred student athletes from using Twitter.[89] The bans have frequently involved football or men's basketball programs, but in January 2012, UNC women's basketball coach Sylvia Hatchell also instituted a Twitter ban for her players.[90] To date, none of the bans has been challenged in court. Commentators, though, have questioned their legality.[91] Rather than punishing students for specific tweets—critical comments about the coaching staff, for instance, which the coach might argue could cause a disruption[92]—the outright bans impose a blanket prior restraint that extends into the athletes' private lives, encompassing speech about their activities and interests off the field and away from school. The bans also necessarily prevent student athletes from using social media to discuss political or social issues, and protecting political speech has long represented a core concern of the First Amendment.

Issues other than those surrounding college athletes have also raised privacy concerns. For example, in March 2012, a sixth-grade student in Minnesota sued her school district, claiming, among other things, that her Fourth Amendment rights were violated when school officials demanded that she give them her Facebook password and they then searched her account—without a warrant—while she was in the room.[93] In that same month, a school district investigation revealed that a Florida high school teacher undertook a series of questionable actions aimed to determine whether students had made disparaging comments about her on Facebook. The teacher reportedly called a student to the front of the classroom and told her to sign into her Facebook account on the teacher's personal cell phone.[94] According to news coverage of the incident, the teacher also "gave a small group of students a list with red marks next to the names of those suspected of making comments. She asked them to review Facebook accounts and write 'ok' next to those who did not write anything negative."[95] The school superintendent found the teacher's behavior "very troubling" and suspended her.[96]

Another privacy controversy involves attempts to regulate social media interactions between students and teachers. School officials and legislators have insisted guidelines and restrictions serve to keep students safe from educators who misuse social media. Although administrators recognize that the vast majority of teachers use social media properly, examples do exist of teachers engaging in inappropriate contact that blurs teacher–student boundaries.[97] And in extreme cases, educators have been arrested for sexual misconduct—for relationships that law enforcement officials say began with online communication.[98]

But strict regulations banning social media interactions entirely have faced pushback from teachers. Missouri, for instance, passed a state law in 2011 that provided, in part, "No teacher shall establish, maintain, or use a nonwork-related Internet site which allows exclusive access with a current or former student."[99] The law, among other things, presumably would have thus forbidden teachers from "friending" students on Facebook. Teachers criticized the law, saying they used social media as a valuable pedagogical tool and to engage students. The state teachers union sued, and in August 2011 a judge issued an injunction that barred the law from going into effect. The judge said the breadth of the prohibition was "staggering" and that it would have "a chilling effect on speech."[100] On the heels of the injunction, legislators dropped the ban and instead ordered school districts to develop their own policies.

GUIDANCE AND BEST PRACTICES

Confusion and uncertainty about social media and students' rights obviously prevail, as the law has failed to catch up to the technology around it. Absent a Supreme Court decision providing clarity, educators would be wise not to be so quick to censor and punish. Such overreactions invite negative attention and miss an opportunity to teach—about free speech, about tolerance, and about civility.

In November 2011, for instance, a Kansas high school senior on a field trip to the state capitol tweeted: "Just made mean comments at gov. brownback and told him he sucked, in person #heblowsalot." The student, Emma Sullivan, was frustrated at Brownback, the Kansas governor, for cutting arts funding in schools, but the tweet was untrue—she had not actually spoken to him. Members of the governor's social media staff saw the tweet and alerted program managers leading the Youth in Government trip Sullivan was on. The program mangers then told the student's principal, who demanded that she apologize. Sullivan refused, and the incident quickly became a national story. Her Twitter account had around 60 followers at the time of the controversial tweet; once the story attracted national attention, her followers rocketed to more than 11,000.[101] Within a week, the principal backed off the demand that she apologize. As Ken Paulson of the First Amendment Center wrote at the time, "[E]fforts to punish her for her free expression backfired on every adult involved."[102] Brownback even issued a statement, apologizing for his staff's overreaction. "Freedom of speech is among our most treasured freedoms," he said.[103]

Sullivan's tweet itself—occurring at an off-campus, school-sanctioned event—certainly did not cause any *Tinker*-level disruption. The controversy that ensued instead was brought on by the social media staff's monitoring, and then by the principal's readiness to punish a student for criticizing her governor. That temptation to monitor and punish is hard for school officials to resist. Western Kentucky University, for instance, attracted media attention in 2012 for its aggressive monitoring of social media.[104] The school persuaded Twitter to briefly shut down an account parodying the university, and the university's president used Facebook to scold students for social media etiquette, telling them that employers "can and will track ways in which prospective employees have used social media. We, at WKU, track such things as well."[105] One student who said school officials had rebuked her friends for their social media posts told a reporter, "I don't ever criticize the school on Twitter because I don't want an ordeal made."[106]

But discouraging criticism of government and encouraging self-censorship rather than voicing complaints are not lessons we want schools to embrace. School officials instead should handle off-campus, social media speech with the legal remedies already available for off-campus speech generally: If the speech is libelous, for instance, school officials can sue. If the speech communicates a serious intent to commit violence against a particular person or group, it can be punished as a true threat. If a school becomes aware of cyberbullying that is "sufficiently severe, pervasive, or persistent as to interfere with or limit a student's ability to participate in or benefit from the services, activities or opportunities offered by a school," the speech may constitute harassment.[107] But if the speech is criticism or parody or inflammatory in general—whether crude or sophisticated, juvenile or mature—schools are better off resisting punishment. Obviously no school officials will be thrilled at discovering a vulgar social media profile parodying them. Arguably the best approach to social media, though, is not to punish or ban but instead to educate, to teach social media literacy, talking with students—and students' parents—about the positives and negatives of social media and about the possible consequences and impact of social media speech (for students and for those whom they write about). Schools, in other words, can emphasize the importance of civility, of treating others—even those with whom we disagree—respectfully, and of using social media, and First Amendment rights, responsibly.[108]

Fear of social media instead has led school officials to impulsively punish students (backed by lenient applications of *Tinker* by some lower courts), to monitor their social media use, and to ban social media entirely inside many K-12 schools. When used appropriately, though, social media tools can help educators reach students on their own terms. Armed with that perspective, in April 2012 a coalition of education and technology advocates put forth a series of recommendations "aimed at rebooting school technology policies."[109] The recommendations, in part, called for K-12 schools to move away from blanket bans on cell phones and social networking sites inside schools and instead to adopt a "responsible-use policy . . . that emphasizes education and treats the student as a person responsible for ethical and healthy use of the Internet and mobile devices."[110]

Student Media

Given social media's popularity for students, student media advisers, at both the high school and college level, should encourage their staffs to embrace social media as a reporting tool. Courts have yet to grapple with cases generated from social media use by student journalists working for school-affiliated media. Presumably how school officials could regulate a Facebook page created as a way for a high school student newspaper to distribute news, for instance, or a tweet by a student reporter breaking news for that publication, would depend on the legal categorization of the student media outlet. School-sponsored media are governed by *Hazelwood* and can be censored if school officials point to a legitimate pedagogical concern. Student media designated—either by policy or practice—as public forums for student expression, where student editors make their own content decisions, are instead governed by *Tinker*. It remains an open question whether *Hazelwood* applies at all to college media. A controversial 2005 Seventh Circuit decision said it did,[111] but other courts have ruled that college media are free from *Hazelwood*'s constraints. No matter the outlet, advisers should push their staffs to consider developing social media guidelines that encourage responsible use and professionalism when using social media to represent their publication.[112]

Research conducted by the Knight Foundation has shown that students who work on student media are more aware and more supportive of First Amendment rights. That research has also now found that as students' social media use grows generally, so too does their support for free expression.[113] By championing social media, then, schools are better preparing students for civic life.

FREQUENTLY ASKED QUESTIONS

1. Can K-12 public schools ban students' social media use at school?

Yes. Although outright bans on cell phones and all social media use during the school day might not be the best pedagogical policy, schools can constitutionally bar students from accessing social media while at school. The bans, schools say, are reasonable content-neutral policies put in place to protect the learning environment from distractions.

2. Can schools punish students for speech they create using social media off campus, away from school?

Right now it depends—on the court, on the standard the court applies, on how the court applies that standard, and on the speech at issue. The Supreme Court has not answered the question, and confusion thus pervades the lower courts. Many of those lower courts have applied *Tinker* and have seemingly required different levels of disruption. The *J.S. v. Blue Mountain School District* case offers striking evidence of the confusion: The district court said a student's MySpace parody profile could be punished under *Fraser* and *Morse*; a panel of the Third Circuit instead said that *Tinker* applied and that the student could be punished because the school could reasonably forecast disruption; while the en banc Third Circuit ruled that, even if *Tinker* did apply, no disruption occurred, nor could the school forecast disruption. Three decisions involving the same case, with three different rationales.

3. Is a college student's off-campus, social media speech treated with a different legal standard than speech from a middle or high school student?

Not necessarily, according to some recent court decisions. Although the Supreme Court ruled in 1972 that the First Amendment applies with "[no] less force on college campuses than in the community at large,"[114] lower courts have applied *Tinker* to cases involving college students' social media speech. And in *Yoder*, a federal judge ruled that a college student effectively waived her First Amendment rights when she signed a consent form as part of a childbearing course, which meant that she could thus be dismissed from school for her MySpace blog that described the labor and delivery she witnessed.

4. Can schools ban student athletes from using social media entirely?

That's unresolved. Coaches have instituted social media bans, particularly bans on using Twitter, at several universities in recent years. None of the bans has been challenged in court. In a 1995 case involving student athletes' privacy, the Supreme Court did say that students "who voluntarily participate in school athletics have reason to expect intrusions upon normal rights and privileges."[115] The outright bans on social media use, though, impose a blanket prior restraint that extends far into the athletes' private lives.

5. What will it take to resolve the confusion and uncertainty?

A Supreme Court ruling. The Court so far has denied cert when it has been asked to hear student speech cases involving social media. But given the inconsistencies in the lower courts, and given how frequently social media cases now arise, the Court will likely weigh in soon.

NOTES

1 Amanda Lenhart, Teens, Social Media & Technology Overview 2015, http://www. pewinternet.org/2015/04/09/teens-social-media-technology-2015/
2 Id.
3 Evie Blad, Networking Web Sites Enable New Generation of Bullies, Ark. Democrat-Gazette, April 6, 2008, at A1.
4 Clay Calvert, Punishing Public School Students for Bashing Principals, Teachers and Classmates in Cyberspace: The Speech Issue the Supreme Court Must Now Resolve, 7 First Amend. L. Rev. 210, 219 (2009).
5 See Emily Summars, Ind. Senior Says He was Expelled for Tweeting Profanity at Home, Student Press L. Ctr., March 29, 2012, http://www.splc.org/news/news flash.asp?id=2358.
6 See Nicole Hill, La. Student Sues After Being Punished for Facebook Status, Student Press L. Ctr., October 26, 2011, http://www.splc.org/news/newsflash.asp?id=2288.
7 Rebecca Cantrell, Oklahoma State Student Arrested for Making "Threats of Mass Violence," KFOR.com, April 21, 2015, http://kfor.com/2015/04/21/oklahoma-state-student-arrested-for-making-threats-of-mass-violence/.
8 Calvert, supra note 4 at 211.
9 The First Amendment does not apply to private schools because they are not government agencies. Private school students could possibly find relief, though, either in state constitutions or state laws or in claiming school censorship amounts to a breach of the guidelines or rules established by the private school itself—if those guidelines or rules promise protections for free speech. See generally Legal Guide for the Private School Press, Student Press L. Ctr., http://www.splc.org/article/2002/12/legal-guide-for-the-private-school-press_1201
10 393 U.S. 503, 506 (1969).
11 Id. at 513.
12 Id. at 517 (Black, J., dissenting).
13 478 U.S. 675, 677 (1986).
14 Id. at 683.
15 Id.
16 Id. at 685.
17 484 U.S. 260, 271 (1988).
18 Id. at 273.
19 551 U.S. 393, 408 (2007).
20 Id. at 401.
21 Id. at 396.
22 See Beussink v. Woodland R-IV Sch. Dist., 30 F. Supp. 2d 1175 (E.D. Mo. 1998).

23 See generally Mary-Rose Papandrea, Student Speech Rights in the Digital Age, 60 Fla. L. Rev. 1027, 1036–1037 (2008).

24 593 F.3d 286, 290 (3rd Cir. 2010), rev'd en banc, 650 F.3d 915 (3rd Cir. 2011).

25 650 F.3d 915, 920 (3rd Cir. 2011).

26 2008 U.S. Dist. LEXIS 72685, 18 (M.D. Pa. 2008).

27 593 F.3d 286, 308 (3rd Cir. 2010), rev'd en banc, 650 F.3d 915 (3rd Cir. 2011).

28 650 F.3d 915, 929 (3rd Cir. 2011).

29 Id. at 936 (Smith, J., concurring).

30 Id. at 950–951 (Fisher, J., dissenting).

31 Papandrea, supra note 23 at 1056.

32 See, e.g., J.S. v. Bethlehem Area Sch. Dist., 569 Pa. 638, 668 (Pa. 2002) ("We hold that where speech that is aimed at a specific school and/or its personnel is brought onto the school campus or accessed at school by its originator, the speech will be considered on-campus speech").

33 Wisniewski v. Weedsport Cent. Sch. Dist., 494 F.3d 34, 39 (2nd Cir. 2007) ("[I]t was reasonably foreseeable that the IM icon would come to the attention of school authorities and the teacher whom the icon depicted being shot"). See also D.J.M. v. Hannibal Pub. Sch. Dist., 647 F.3d 754, 766 (8th Cir. 2011) ("[I]t was reasonably foreseeable that D.J.M.'s threats about shooting specific students in school would be brought to the attention of school authorities and create a risk of substantial disruption within the school environment"); J.C. v. Beverly Hills Unified Sch. Dist., 711 F. Supp. 2d 1094, 1108 (C.D. Cal. 2010) ("Several cases have applied Tinker where speech published or transmitted via the Internet subsequently comes to the attention of school administrators, even where there is no evidence that students accessed the speech while at school").

34 Papandrea, supra note 23 at 1064.

35 See Calvert, supra note 4 at 235.

36 Layshock v. Hermitage Sch. Dist., 650 F.3d 205, 220–221 (3rd Cir. 2011) (Jordan, J., concurring). The judge continued, "Modern communications technology, for all its positive applications, can be a potent tool for distraction and fomenting disruption." Id. at 222.

37 Doninger v. Niehoff, 527 F.3d 41, 45 (2nd Cir. 2008).

38 Id.

39 Id. at 50–51.

40 Id. at 51.

41 Id. After being denied the injunction, Doninger continued her case in court and argued that she deserved monetary damages because she was denied her First Amendment right to criticize school officials. In 2011 a different Second Circuit panel ruled that it did not need to decide whether her punishment in fact violated the First Amendment because the law surrounding off-campus speech is so unsettled that the school officials were entitled to qualified immunity. See Doninger v. Niehoff, 642 F.3d 334 (2nd Cir. 2011).

42 This is generally true in all student speech cases, not just those involving social media. See generally Calvert, supra note 4 at 243–244.

43 799 F.3d 379 (5th Cir. 2015).

44 Id. at 384.

45 Id. at 386.

46 Id. at 383.

47 A Fifth Circuit panel had actually ruled in favor of the student in December 2014, but the full Fifth Circuit subsequently vacated that panel opinion and ordered en banc review.

48 799 F.3d at 396.

49 Id. at 398–99. *See also* O.Z. v. Bd. of Tr. of the Long Beach Unified Sch. Dist., 2008 U.S. Dist. LEXIS 110409, 11 (C.D. Cal. 2008) (upholding the transfer of a student as punishment for a slide show she posted to YouTube that depicted the killing of her English teacher because "although O.Z. created the slide show off-campus, it created a foreseeable risk of disruption within the school").

50 Kowalski v. Berkeley County Sch., 652 F.3d 565 (4th Cir. 2011). In extreme instances in recent years, students have committed suicide as a result of bullying from their peers, some of which occurred online. See, e.g., Martin Finucane, DA Defends Light Sentences in Phoebe Prince Case, Boston Globe, May 5, 2011, http://www. boston. com/news/local/breaking_news/2011/05/two_more_teens.html.

51 For example, one student uploaded a picture of himself and a friend holding their noses while displaying a sign that read "Shay Has Herpes." 652 F.3d at 568.

52 Id. at 568–569.

53 Id. at 573.

54 Id. at 574 (internal quotations and citations omitted).

55 Id.

56 Id. at 577. But see J.C. v. Beverly Hills Unified Sch. Dist., 711 F. Supp. 2d 1094, 1122 (C.D. Cal. 2010) (striking down a student's punishment for posting a video to YouTube that demeaned another student because the court "cannot uphold school discipline of student speech simply because young persons are unpredictable or immature, or because, in general, teenagers are emotionally fragile and may often fight over hurtful comments").

57 Evans v. Bayer, 684 F. Supp. 2d 1365, 1367 (S.D. Fla. 2010).

58 Id. at 1373.

59 See David L. Hudson, School Learns Lesson in Facebook Case, First Amendment Ctr., December 29, 2010, http://www.firstamendmentcenter.org/school-learns-lesson-in-facebook-case.

60 807 F. Supp. 2d 767 (N.D. Ind. 2011).

61 Id. at 5.

62 Id. at 7.

63 Id. at 35.

64 Id. at 38.

65 Id. at 41.

66 Id. at 51–56.

67 2012 U.S. Dist. LEXIS 45264 (W.D. Ky. 2012).

68 Id. at 3.

69 Id. at 17.

70 Id. See also Snyder v. Millersville University, where a judge upheld the removal of a university student, Stacey Snyder, from a student teaching placement at a local high school. The punishment kept her from obtaining teacher certification. The judge ruled that Snyder was more akin to a teacher—a public employee—than a student given that she did not take university classes during the placement and instead was responsible for curriculum planning, grading, and attending faculty meetings at the high school. She could thus be punished, in part, for her MySpace postings that

referenced the school and her students and for a picture that showed her drinking since the posts did not discuss matters of public concern but instead "raised only personal matters." 2008 U.S. Dist. LEXIS 97943, 42 (E.D. Pa. 2008).

71 800 N.W.2d 811, 814 (Minn. Ct. App. 2011).

72 Id.

73 Id. at 815.

74 Id. at 821. The court cited DeJohn v. Temple University, 537 F.3d 301 (3rd Cir. 2008).

75 800 N.W.2d at 822.

76 Tatro v. Univ. of Minnesota, 816 N.W.2d 509, 521 (Minn. 2012).

77 Id. at 524.

78 575 F. Supp. 2d 571, 590 (D. Del. 2008).

79 Id. at 578.

80 Id. at 590.

81 See Nick Glunt, Expulsion Over Raunchy Tweets May Cost High School Football Star His College Dream, Student Press L. Ctr., January 23, 2012, http://www. splc. org/wordpress/?p=3109. The student subsequently accepted a scholarship offer from the University of Colorado.

82 At least a dozen states have passed laws that limit colleges' ability to gain access to their students' social media postings. The laws generally forbid colleges "from requiring students or prospective students to provide passwords or otherwise allow access to private social media accounts." The laws do not prohibit schools from monitoring publicly available social media information, though. Denielle Burl, Youndy C. Cook, and Margaret Wu, Social Media, Anonymous Speech and When Social Media Becomes the Crisis, The National Association of College and University Attorneys (2015), http://www.nacua.org/securedocuments/programs/June2015/8E_15_6_63.pdf.

83 The University of North Carolina at Chapel Hill, Department of Athletics, Policy on Student-Athlete Social Networking and Media Use (2011), http://grfx. cstv. com/photos/schools/unc/genrel/auto_pdf/2011-12/misc_non_event/Social NetworkingPolicy.pdf.

84 Id.

85 See Bob Sullivan, Govt. Agencies, Colleges Demand Applicants' Facebook Passwords, The Redtape Chronicles (March 6, 2012), http://redtape.msnbc.msn. com/_ news/2012/03/06/10585353-govt-agencies-colleges-demand-applicants-facebook-passwords.

86 See Kathleen Nelson, Services Monitor Athletes on Facebook, Other Sites, St. Louis Post-Dispatch, February 1, 2012, http://www.stltoday.com/sports/college/mizzou/services-monitor-athletes-on-facebook-other-sites/article_8e6517ba-e78d-5dfe-83ba-30d673042dfb.html. Although the monitoring programs presumably could be applied broadly to a range of students, to this point schools have generally limited their use to student athletes.

87 Id.

88 Id.

89 See generally Eric Robinson, Intentional Grounding: Can Public Colleges Limit Athletes' Tweets? Citizen Media Law Project (November 9, 2010), http://www. citmedialaw.org/blog/2010/intentional-grounding-can-public-colleges-limit-athletes-tweets.

90 See Michael Lananna, Sylvia Hatchell Bans UNC Women's Basketball Team's Twitter Use, The Daily Tar Heel, January 27, 2012, http://www.dailytarheel.com/ index. php/article/2012/01/sylvia_hatchell_bans_womens_teams_twitter_use.

91 See, e.g., Robinson, supra note 88. But see Mary Margaret "Meg" Penrose, Free Speech Versus Free Education, 1 Miss. Sports L. Rev. 1, 94 (2011) (arguing that "athletic departments should feel confident in regulating or banning their student-athletes' use of social media").

92 See, e.g., Terry Hutchens, IU DB Andre Kates now suspended indefinitely, Indystar.com (October 31, 2010), http://blogs.indystar.com/hoosiersinsider/2010/ 10/31/iu-db-andre-kates-now-suspended-indefinitely/ (Indiana University football player suspended for tweets critical of the coaching staff). In the high school setting, courts have upheld punishment of athletes under Tinker for speech that criticized coaches and sought to undermine their authority. See, e.g., Lowery v. Euverard, 497 F.3d 584 (6th Cir. 2007).

93 See Emily Summars, Lawsuit Claims Minn. School Officials Demanded Sixth-grader's Facebook Password, Student Press L. Ctr., March 7, 2012, http://www. splc. org/news/newsflash.asp?id=2344.

94 See Jeffrey Solochek, Pasco Teacher Accused of Policing Students' Facebook Comments, Tampa Bay Times, March 22, 2012, http://www.tampabay.com/news/ education/ k12/pasco-teacher-accused-of-policing-students-facebook-comments/ 1221093.

95 Id.

96 Id.

97 See Jennifer Preston, Rules to Stop Pupil and Teacher From Getting Too Social Online, N.Y. Times, December 17, 2011, http://www.nytimes.com/2011/12/ 18/ business/media/rules-to-limit-how-teachers-and-students-interact-online.html.

98 Id. ("In Sacramento, a 37-year-old high school band director pleaded guilty to sexual misconduct stemming from his relationship with a 16-year-old female student; her Facebook page had more than 1,200 private messages from him, some about massages").

99 S.B. 54, 96th General Assembly, 1st Regular Sess. (Mo. 2011).

100 Mo. State Teachers Ass'n v. Mo., No. 11AC-CC00553 (Cir. Ct. Cole County Aug. 2011).

101 See Nicole Hill, School District Won't Make Kan. Student Apologize for Tweet Against Governor, Student Press L. Ctr., November 28, 2011, http://www.splc.org/ news/newsflash.asp?id=2302.

102 Ken Paulson, Tweet Backlash: Kan. Officials Learn Lesson About Free Speech, First Amendment Ctr., November 28, 2011, http://www.firstamendmentcenter.org/ tweet-backlash-kan-officials-learn-lesson-about-free-speech.

103 Id.

104 See, e.g., Ky. School Aggressively Fights Twitter Criticism, Fox News.com (February 27, 2012), http://www.foxnews.com/us/2012/02/27/ky-school-aggressively-fights-twitter-criticism/.

105 Id.

106 Id.

107 See Department of Education, "Dear Colleague" Letter Re Bullying (October 26, 2010), http://www.nacua.org/documents/DearColleagueLetter_Bullying.pdf.

108 See, e.g., Denielle Burl, From Tinker to Twitter: Managing Student Speech on Social Media, 9 NACUA Notes (2011), http://www.studentaffairs.uconn.edu/docs/ risk_mgt/nacua5.pdf (advising that the best way to prevent student misuse of social

media is to "fight speech with speech"); Neal Hutchens, You Can't Post That . . . Or Can You? Legal Issues Related to College and University Students' Online Speech, 49 J. of Student Aff. Res. and Prac. 1, 13 (2012) (arguing that "colleges and universities should engage students more broadly and deeply regarding issues related to their online expression"); Papandrea, supra note 23 at 1098 (arguing that "the primary approach that schools should take to most digital speech is not to punish their students, but to educate their students about how to use digital media responsibly").

109 Frank LoMonte, In "Making Progress" Report, Education Leaders Call for a Reboot of Schools' Restrictive Technology Policies, Student Press L. Ctr., April 11, 2012, http://www.splc.org/wordpress/?p=3508.

110 Making Progress: Rethinking State and School District Policies Concerning Mobile Technologies and Social Media (2012), http://www.splc.org/pdf/making_progress_2012.pdf.

111 Hosty v. Carter, 412 F.3d 731 (7th Cir. 2005).

112 See, e.g., Nick Dean, Living Social: College Newsrooms Revisiting Ethics Policies for the Twitter Generation, 32 Student Press L. Ctr. Rep. 30 (2011), http://www.splc.org/news/report_detail.asp?id=1611&edition=56.

113 Knight Foundation, Future of the First Amendment (2011), http://www.knight foundation.org/media/uploads/article_pdfs/Future-of-the-First-Amendment-2011-full.pdf.

114 Healy v. James, 408 U.S. 169, 180 (1972).

115 Vernonia Sch. Dist. v. Acton, 515 U.S. 646, 657 (1995).

CHAPTER 9

Obscenity, Revenge Pornography, and Cyberbullying

Amy Kristin Sanders

Northwestern University in Qatar

ABSTRACT

The rise of the Internet brought about new challenges in the regulation of undesirable sexually explicit content in the United States. At the core of these challenges is our nation's fundamental belief in the protection of expression under the First Amendment. Increased use of electronic communication devices and social media, however, transformed these challenges into everyday concerns for employers, parents, and communicators— looking to limit the exchange and receipt of sexual photos, text messages, and other content. This chapter examines the legal implications of instantaneous communication in this context, including cyberbullying, revenge pornography, and the exchange of indecent and obscene images and text.

As social media has grown, so too has its power to spread harm. Revenge pornography, which traces its roots to notorious website IsAnyoneUp. com, has made headlines worldwide as victims grapple with the consequences of having their sexually explicit images spread across the Internet. Similarly, recent research suggests that online harassment—from revenge pornography to cyberbullying—has become a way of life in cyberspace. According to an October 2014 study by the Pew Research Center, nearly three-fourths of adult Internet users have witnessed someone being harassed online while 40% report they've experienced it themselves.[1] Whether it's adults intimidating children or former lovers sharing scanty photos without permission, the law and the courts have been ill-prepared to deal with the increase in hostility that social media has made a regular part of our everyday lives.

The development of electronic communication technology and social media tools opened the door for criminal and civil litigation in a variety of areas including defamation, privacy, and intellectual property, as this book has suggested. Many of the early developments in cyberspace law related to the availability and regulation of sexually explicit content on the Internet. In 2004, one researcher testified before Congress, likening Internet pornography to illegal drugs:

> The [I]nternet is a perfect drug delivery system because you are anonymous, aroused and have role models for these behaviors. To have [a] drug pumped into your house 24/7, free, and children know how to use it better than grown-ups know how to use it. [I]t's a perfect delivery system if we want to have a whole generation of young addicts who will never have the drug out of their mind.[2]

Congressional interest in regulating sexually explicit content—including obscenity and pornography—on the Internet pre-dates the development of social media and even the aforementioned 2004 legislative hearing.[3] However, those efforts largely inform current attempts to proscribe cyberbullying and the transmission of sexually explicit content resulting from the use of social media.

After a basic introduction to the regulation of obscenity and indecency, this chapter provides an overview of early legislation that attempted to stem the tide of sexually explicit content on the Internet. Particular attention will be paid to early legislative effort that resulted in litigation culminating in the U.S. Supreme Court. Next, the recent attempts to regulate revenge pornography, or the practice of maliciously posting sexually explicit photographs of another person, is explored. The discussion focuses on several prominent cases, including what is believed to be the first conviction under a law specifically aimed at revenge pornography. The chapter then addresses cyberbullying, including an update on the status of legislation designed to curtail the practice. Finally, the chapter concludes by highlighting related areas of legal concern that are likely to develop in the future.

REGULATING SEXUALLY EXPLICIT SPEECH OFFLINE AND ONLINE

The U.S. Supreme Court set the stage for the regulation of obscene and indecent expression long before the Internet arrived in our homes. Nearly 60 years ago in *Roth v. United States*,[4] Justice William Brennan, writing for a six-justice majority, clearly enunciated the Court's belief that obscene speech fell outside the protection of the First Amendment:

> The dispositive question is whether obscenity is utterance within
> the area of protected speech and press. Although this is the first
> time the question has been squarely presented to this Court, either
> under the First Amendment or under the Fourteenth Amendment,
> expressions found in numerous opinions indicate that this Court
> has always assumed that obscenity is not protected by the
> freedoms of speech and press.[5]

He went on, noting that as far back as 1942, the Court acknowledged in
Chaplinsky v. New Hampshire the permissible regulation of sexually explicit
speech rising to the level of obscenity.[6]

Shortly after the *Roth* decision, however, consensus broke down on the
Court as to what standard should be used to determine whether speech was
obscene. It was during this time period that Justice Potter Stewart, when
describing obscenity, made his oft-repeated remark:

> I shall not today attempt further to define the kinds of material I
> understand to be embraced within that shorthand description;
> and perhaps I could never succeed in intelligibly doing so. But I
> know it when I see it, and the motion picture involved in this case
> is not that.[7]

Obscenity law remained in a state of disarray, with the Court deciding
cases on an almost ad-hoc basis until 1973.[8]

In that year, a 5–4 majority in *Miller v. California* agreed upon the standard currently used to determine whether expression should be considered obscene and outside the scope of First Amendment protection.[9] The
Supreme Court vacated a California criminal conviction under the state's
obscenity statute, ruling that the First Amendment required a three-part
showing for speech to be considered obscene:

> (a) whether the average person, applying contemporary community
> standards would find that the work, taken as a whole, appeals to
> the prurient interest; (b) whether the work depicts or describes, in a
> patently offensive way, sexual conduct specifically defined by the
> applicable state law; and (c) whether the work, taken as a whole,
> lacks serious literary, artistic, political, or scientific value.[10]

The ruling served to cement the Court's approach to obscenity regulation,
and the *Miller* test has returned to the forefront as Congress has attempted to
legislate expression occurring on the Internet and via social media.

Legislative efforts to regulate sexually explicit expression on the Internet
have not solely been based on obscenity's status outside the scope of First

Amendment protection. In fact, a number of legislative attempts have tried to curtail indecent speech and pornography as well. Such a regulatory approach would have limited the rights of Internet speakers in much the same way the Court limited the rights of broadcasters in its 1978 ruling in *FCC v. Pacifica*.[11] There, a majority of the Court upheld the FCC's right to sanction broadcasters for airing indecent content, in part based on the notion that broadcast television and radio were pervasive and uniquely accessible to children.[12] As a result, the FCC has the authority to fine broadcasters who air indecent content outside the Safe Harbor hours of 10 p.m. to 6 a.m.

Indecency, however, remained a concept reserved solely for broadcast media throughout much of the 1980s and 1990s. Print publishers and cable operators were not subject to the FCC's regulations, which prohibited the broadcast of "language that describes, in terms patently offensive as measured by contemporary community standards for the broadcast medium, sexual or excretory activities and organs, at times of the day when there is a reasonable risk that children may be in the audience."[13] However, that changed when President Bill Clinton signed the Telecommunications Act of 1996[14] into law.

The Telecommunications Act of 1996 represented the first comprehensive overhaul of telecommunication policy since the 1934 Communications Act, and it attempted to solidify the Internet's place within the FCC's regulatory authority.[15] Contained within the Act's 128 pages was Title V, targeting obscenity and violence in various telecommunication media, including the Internet. Title V, also known as the Communications Decency Act, was of particular interest to those concerned about freedom of expression because Section 223 criminalized the knowing transmission of obscene or indecent material to recipients under 18.[16]

On the day President Clinton signed the law, the American Civil Liberties Union and 19 additional plaintiffs challenged Section 223 of the Communications Decency Act in federal court,[17] laying the groundwork for the U.S. Supreme Court's first decision[18] in the area of cyberspace law. In the case, the ACLU argued that two of the CDA's provisions designed to protect minors from harmful material on the Internet were unconstitutional.[19] After the issuance of a temporary restraining order, a three-judge panel in U.S. District Court made a lengthy finding of fact before issuing a preliminary injunction that prevented the government from enforcing the provisions against material claimed to be indecent under §223(a)(1)(B) or any material under §223(d). Based on a special provision in the statute, the government appealed the District Court decision directly to the U.S. Supreme Court.

Justice Stevens, writing for the majority in *ACLU v. Reno*, penned an opinion that laid the foundation for the Court's subsequent jurisprudence in the realm of cyberspace and electronic communication. Observing that the rules of traditional media should not automatically be applied to the Internet, Justice Stevens opined:

> Neither before nor after the enactment of the CDA have the vast democratic fora of the Internet been subject to the type of government supervision and regulation that has attended the broadcast industry. Moreover, the Internet is not as "invasive" as radio or television.[20]

Distinguishing the Internet from the regulations permitted in broadcast, Justice Stevens noted that the Court need not be bound by the *Pacifica* ruling.[21] Section 223(a)(1)(B), the opinion asserted, was more akin to regulations the Court had struck down in a 1989 case involving the prohibition of sexually oriented commercial telephone messages.[22] In *Sable Communications*, the Court ruled that a provision in the Communications Act that prohibited the transmission of both obscene and indecent dial-a-porn messages was unconstitutional as to the indecent content, which was entitled to some First Amendment protection.[23] Relying heavily on *Pacifica*'s reasoning that broadcast is uniquely pervasive, the Court distinguished commercial messages transmitted via the telephone:

> In contrast to public displays, unsolicited mailings and other means of expression which the recipient has no meaningful opportunity to avoid, the dial-it medium requires the listener to take affirmative steps to receive the communication. There is no "captive audience" problem here; callers will generally not be unwilling listeners . . . Unlike an unexpected outburst on a radio broadcast, the message received by one who places a call to a dial-a-porn service is not so invasive or surprising that it prevents an unwilling listener from avoiding exposure to it.[24]

Justice Stevens also observed that the scarcity rationale used by Congress to justify the regulation of broadcast and embraced by the Court in *Red Lion Broadcasting v. FCC*[25] simply did not apply in the Internet context.[26] In all reality, the Court likened the Internet more to the print medium, establishing a jurisprudential approach that would make content regulation extremely difficult.[27]

In addition to the hands-off regulatory approach that seemed to be embraced by the Court in *Reno*, the majority took issue with the breadth of the CDA's restrictions on speech. Foreshadowed by Justice Stevens' discussion of *Sable*, the majority held both provisions to be unconstitutionally overbroad.

The majority found troubling the statute's restriction on "indecent" content as well as its prohibition on "patently offensive" material—neither of which were defined in the legislation. Both terms, Justice Stevens wrote, could be interpreted to include within their sweep content that adults possessed a First Amendment right to access:

> We are persuaded that the CDA lacks the precision that the First Amendment requires when a statute regulates the content of speech. In order to deny minors access to potentially harmful speech, the CDA effectively suppresses a large amount of speech that adults have a constitutional right to receive and to address to one another. That burden on adult speech is unacceptable if less restrictive alternatives would be at least as effective in achieving the legitimate purpose that the statute was enacted to serve.[28]

The Court further noted the breadth of application of the CDA's provisions.[29] As written, the statute applied to all transmissions of material harmful to minors—commercial or otherwise. No exceptions were made for non-profit entities, individuals, or educational institutions, leaving within the provisions' scope non-pornographic materials that may have educational or other social value.

On the heels of the loss in *Reno*, legislators returned to the drawing board in an attempt to craft a new statute that could address the Court's concerns. As a result, the Child Online Protection Act[30] (COPA) was enacted in October 1998.[31] It prohibited:

> any person from "knowingly and with knowledge of the character of the material, in interstate or foreign commerce by means of the World Wide Web, mak[ing] any communication for commercial purposes that is available to any minor and that includes any material that is harmful to minors."[32]

Taking cue from the Court's decision in *Reno*, legislators attempted to draft COPA in a more narrow fashion, making three distinct changes. First, the new provision applied only to World Wide Web content whereas the CDA provisions applied to all expression via the Internet, including email.[33] Second, COPA was limited to communication for commercial purposes, meaning educational or other non-profit communication would be exempted from its criminal penalties. Finally, lawmakers reworked the CDA prohibition on "indecent" and "patently offensive" speech—terms that had doomed the legislation in the Supreme Court—by substituting in the phrase "material harmful to minors" which was drawn from a previous

Supreme Court case, *New York v. Ferber*[34] and defining the term using a test similar to the *Miller* test.

One month prior to COPA taking effect, free speech advocates, including the ACLU, challenged the legislation in court, claiming it violated the First Amendment.[35] After winning an initial injunction against COPA, the ACLU was victorious when the Third Circuit ruled the use of "community standards" to define "material harmful to minors" was overbroad.[36] However, the U.S. Supreme Court in 2002 rejected this reasoning, and the case returned to the Third Circuit.[37] Hearing the case a second time, the Third Circuit once again struck down the law as unconstitutional, finding it limited adults' rights to access content to which they had a constitutional right.[38] In 2004, the U.S. Supreme Court again heard *Ashcroft v. ACLU*, ruling this time that the law was likely to be unconstitutional and noting the ability of filtering software to serve as an alternative to more harsh restrictions.[39] After a re-hearing at the District Court, where a permanent injunction was issued, the Third Circuit upheld that decision, effectively killing COPA.[40]

After the ACLU's victories in both cases, it seemed the government was at a loss to regulate sexually explicit content on the Internet, adding support to the colloquial references to the Internet as the Wild West. On the heels of the government's early losses in *Reno* and *Ashcroft*, Congress was busy drafting additional legislation aimed to protect children from sexually explicit Internet content. The Children's Internet Protection Act (CIPA), signed into law in 2000, took a different approach than its predecessors. Instead of tackling all Internet use, CIPA focused on two key providers of Internet access to children: schools and libraries. Although Congress could not force all school and library boards to require the use of filtering software on their Internet stations, it could condition funding through its E-Rate program on their installation. Given the large number of schools and libraries that were dependent on the funding, the legislation swept broadly across the country.

In response, the American Library Association sued, claiming CIPA required librarians to violate patrons' constitutional rights by blocking access to protected speech. In 2002, a three-judge panel in U.S. District Court agreed with the librarians group, ruling that less restrictive means—including supervision by librarians—would better achieve the government's objective without infringing on patrons' First Amendment rights. The U.S. Supreme Court, in a 6–3 vote, overruled the lower court decision, characterizing CIPA not as a speech restriction but instead as a condition of participating in a government funding program—which libraries were not required to do.[41]

The government's victory in *U.S. v. American Library Association* empowered lawmakers, who have introduced numerous pieces of legislation involving minors and sexually explicit speech on the Internet since the Court's 2003 decision. Legislation that would require schools and libraries to protect children from sexual predators when using social networking and chat sites has been introduced in Congress a number of times—though never being passed by both chambers. Known as the Deleting Online Predators Act (DOPA), the legislation would have limited access to a wide range of websites based on its broad definition of "social networking site."[42]

Several states, including Georgia, North Carolina, and Illinois, have attempted to take similar actions to protect children using the Internet. Typically, these laws take one of two forms. The first group of laws— similar to the proposed Illinois Social Networking Prohibition Act— impose restrictions on libraries and schools, mandating limitations on what students can access or prohibiting the access of certain sites altogether. The second type—more akin to the North Carolina Protect Children From Sexual Predators Act enacted in 2008[43]—place the onus on social networking sites by punishing those that allow minors to create profiles without parental consent and requiring the site allow parents full ability to monitor their children's profiles.

The constitutionality of these types of laws is questionable. In early 2012, a U.S. District Court in Louisiana struck down a recently enacted state law that prohibited registered sex offenders whose crimes involved children from using or accessing social networking sites, chat rooms, and peer-to-peer networks.[44] In the decision, the court noted the statute was both unconstitutionally overbroad and vague:

> Although the Act is intended to promote the legitimate and compelling state interest of protecting minors from [I]nternet predators, the near total ban on [I]nternet access imposed by the Act unreasonably restricts many ordinary activities that have become important to everyday life in today's world. The sweeping restrictions on the use of the [I]nternet for purposes completely unrelated to the activities sought to be banned by the Act impose severe and unwarranted restraints on constitutionally protected speech.

Cases dealing with similar restrictions have been heard in several states, including Nebraska, where a federal court held that three sections of the state's sex offender registration law that dealt with restrictions on Internet usage appeared to be unconstitutional, which suggests lawmakers will have a hard time legislating in this area.[45]

One of the biggest issues social media sites face is the desire to attract young users while balancing the risks facing those users. In October 2013,

Facebook announced it was loosening privacy restrictions that had previously been placed on teens aged 13–17. Under its new policy, it has allowed teens to share their posts publicly to anyone on the Internet. Previously, teen content would only be shared within friends' circles. Critics denounced this decision, citing instances of cyberbullying and online harassment and claiming that Facebook had made the decision to lure in new sources of revenue based on advertisers' ability to reach these young consumers and see their data. Facebook, however, defended its actions by saying that it was allowing teens the opportunity to be heard more broadly in the world. Facebook continues its under-13 ban, largely out of a desire to steer clear of the Children's Online Privacy Protection Act (COPPA), which took effect in the U.S. in 1998 and was strengthened in 2013.[46] COPPA requires that commercial websites directed at children under 13 who wish to collect personal information must engage in several privacy protection measures. These measures include: posting privacy policies, providing parents with notice of their site's information practices and verifying parental consent before collecting personal information from children. COPPA's requirements are far-reaching, not only affecting websites and services that directly target children under 13, but also covering sites and services aimed a general audience where the site has "actual knowledge" it is collecting information from children under 13.

THE PUBLIC'S REVENGE—CRACKING DOWN ON REVENGE PORNOGRAPHY WEBSITES

Recent studies suggest adults and children alike are using their mobile devices to take, share or receive sexually explicit messages and photos. A 2013 study by McAfee[47] found that half of respondents admitted to such practices and a full 30% admit to cyberstalking their former lovers on social media. The same study suggested that one in ten exes threatened to reveal intimate photos, and that 60% of those who threatened to do so actually followed through by posting the images online.

Legal scholars have suggested numerous approaches to combatting revenge pornography, from civil to criminal approaches. Victims have tried to pursue civil litigation based on a theory of invasion of privacy, but that approach has been largely unsuccessful in the courts. Similar attempts based on a contract law theory have also come under scrutiny as these relationships often fail to be based on explicit agreements. Although a copyright-based claim is more likely to succeed, research suggests that at least one-fifth of revenge porn photos are not "selfies," meaning that the copyright would not be held by the victim. As a result, a number of legislatures in the U.S.

and around the world have been applying criminal law theories in an attempt to quell revenge pornography.

Notorious revenge porn king Hunter Moore, of IsAnyoneUp.com fame, will spend more than two years in prison after being sentenced in December 2015. His sentence, which includes three additional years of supervised probation and a $2,000 fine, was part of a negotiated plea deal in which Moore pleaded guilty to two charges, unauthorized access to a private computer and aggravated identity theft, after several years of running his notorious revenge porn website.[48]

Moore's case demonstrates the challenges associated with taking down purveyors of revenge porn using criminal law. He, and other well-known defendants, often plead guilty to, or are convicted of, crimes not covered by the revenge porn laws that have been passed by more than half of U.S. states. Instead, they often are sentenced under fraud, identity theft or other laws unrelated to the sexually explicit nature of the photos they post.

Even in states that have revenge porn laws—such as California—routine offenders like Kevin Bollaert, who operated revenge porn site UGotPosted as well as another website where users had to pay to get their photographs removed, are prosecuted under other laws. California Attorney General Kamala Harris said the minor penalties available under California's law were enough to get justice for what Bollaert had done. As a result, he was found guilty on 6 counts of extortion as well as 21 counts of identity theft, for which he was sentenced to 18 years in prison and restitution payments totaling $450,000.[49]

Other concerns remain as well. Chief among them is the paltry sentences often associated with the crime, which in California and many other states amounts to a mere misdemeanor. In what was heralded as the first conviction under California's revenge porn law—which took effect in October 2013 and criminalizes the distribution of nude or explicit photos or videos of someone without their consent—the defendant, Noe Iniguez, posted a topless photo of an ex-girlfriend to her employer's Facebook account and posted messages urging that she be fired because she was a "drunk" and a "slut."[50] For his actions, Iniguez was sentenced to a year in jail. Additional prosecutions have also occurred against website operators who are attempting to extort money from revenge porn victims.

TLK 2 ME DURTY—STEMMING THE TIDE OF SEXTING

A Pennsylvania high school math teacher made headlines after he was charged with sending a teenage student sexually explicit pictures followed by a video of himself performing a sex act. What started out as a Facebook friendship between a 26-year-old teacher and 17-year-old student resulted in the teacher facing charges of sending sexual materials to a minor and corruption of a minor, both misdemeanors. Court records revealed a history of two-way contact, and the student admitted to sending sexually explicit nude photos to the teacher after receiving some from him. As a result of his actions, the teacher was suspended from teaching while he faced trial, but could be allowed back in the classroom if acquitted of the charges.

The case in Pennsylvania represents only the tip of the sexting iceberg—albeit one of the most concerning types of sexting situations. With the increased availability of sexually explicit content on the Internet, it should come as no surprise that individuals quickly began sending and receiving pornographic emails, text messages and photos using their mobile devices. Programs like Snapchat, where messages "disappear" within X seconds, only furthered the clandestine practice of sharing sexually explicit content. Four distinct situations emerge within the law in relation to sexting: sexting between consenting adults, sexting between two adults where one does not consent, sexting between an adult and a minor child, and sexting between two minor children.

Traditionally, prosecutors have used a number of existing laws to address sexting where one adult sends another unwilling adult pornographic or nude messages. These could include harassment, stalking, and similar criminal statutes. In a most interesting development, attorneys and legal scholars are divided about whether criminal statutes could be used to prosecute a person who records the audio of his neighbors engaged in sexual relations and then posts the sound file to the Internet. A post to the user-generated news site Reddit drew significant attention after the poster mentioned a friend had recorded his neighbors' noisy encounter and uploaded the audio to SoundCloud.[51] Prosecutors looking to bring a case might be able to turn to the Electronic Communications Privacy Act (ECPA), a federal law that is designed to protect the transfer of information through wire, radio, electromagnetic, photoelectronic or photooptical communications systems. Although the chance of a successful federal prosecution is slim, it isn't clear it wouldn't be possible. Even withstanding ECPA, a number of state laws, which vary from state to state, could apply. These would include wiretapping laws, communication privacy statutes similar to ECPA and possibly any statutory privacy protections. To further complicate the issue, the aggrieved couple might be able to sue civilly based on the state's common law privacy torts or a trespass if the recorder entered onto private property. Whether a court would allow the use of these existing statutes and common law torts in this way is unclear.

Courts have been willing to use existing statutes to deal with sexting that occurs between an adult and a minor child—whether the child consented or not. Often these might include prostitution, child sexual abuse, or misconduct statutes.

More disturbing than sexual indiscretions involving adults is the rise in the practice of sexting among "consenting" minors—a practice the law has struggled to combat. A 2014 study conducted by researchers at Drexel University found that 54% of college students reported sending sexually explicit text messages or photos before they were 18 years old.[52] These reports, along with stories in the media about "collect the sexts" challenges going on in schools, suggest the need for additional education to make students aware of the risks of sexting. Research suggests that when students are made aware that sexting often falls under child pornography laws, they are less likely to engage in the practice once they have been made aware of the harsh sanctions.

Additionally, lawmakers across the United States have responded to these media reports as well, often attempting to pass legislation prohibiting various forms of sexting. According to the Cyberbullying Research Center, 20 states had passed sexting laws by July 2015.[53] All 20 laws address minors sending sexually explicit messages, and 18 of them address minors receiving the messages. Some states have even made it a felony for minors to engage in sexting, akin to how sexting is often handled using existing child pornography laws.

Although most legislation aims to prohibit the sending of sexually explicit, nude or partially nude text and photos messages, two states have taken a different approach. In Arizona, SB 1219 would require cellular providers to offer parents the right to view their children's text messages when issuing new contracts. At the time of publication, it remained in committee. In South Carolina, HB 4555 would give parents the right to review messages sent or received with the minor's device, and it would not allow minors to have access to text services without providing consent for parents and guardians to review the messages. At the time of publication, it remained in committee.

If school districts or other employers try to restrict personal communication among employees and other consenting adults, other challenges would likely arise. Given the emphasis on freedom of speech in the United States, courts are likely to find policies that prohibit communication completely to be unconstitutional, even for teachers who deal with minors. Policies related to texting and other social media will have a better chance of withstanding judicial scrutiny if they are limited in scope—addressing only sexually explicit communication, for example. Further, policies that attempt to restrict communication between parties over the age of 18 will no doubt face higher scrutiny. Employers who attempt to block access during working hours are likely to have more success with their policies than those who attempt a blanket prohibition that would include employees' personal time. Regardless of the effort taken by employers, any social media policy put in place by a government body will face significant obstacles based on its potential to chill speech.

BANISHING THE BULLY FROM THE BEDROOM

The fact pattern has become all too familiar. A young person—often a pre-teen or teenager—commits suicide after being the target of online harassment. Cyberbullying—the name for online harassment most often used when minors are the victims—rose to the public purview in a 2006 case involving a mother, Lori Drew, whom prosecutors alleged created a MySpace profile impersonating "Josh Evans" in order to befriend one of her daughter's female classmates.[54] After deceiving 13-year-old Megan Meier into believing Evans liked her, prosecutors argued that Drew (acting under her cyberpersona) then told her the world would be a better place without her. Afterward, Meier hanged herself in her bedroom. Although state prosecutors wanted to charge Drew with a crime, there was no federal cyberbullying statute to rely on. After being charged with four felony counts of unauthorized computer access under the federal Computer Fraud and Abuse Act (CFAA), a jury found Drew guilty of three lesser charges. In July 2009, a federal judge overturned the jury verdict, acquitting Drew of all charges.

Although teasing and other forms of bullying have been around as long as there have been schoolyards for the bullies to occupy, cyberbullying cases like the one involving Lori Drew present an entirely new set of challenges. Initially, one of the most difficult challenges posed was a definitional one. Even if lawmakers were to come to a consensus as to what constituted cyberbullying, regulating expressive activities without violating the First Amendment presented a further challenge. Add to that the complex nature of regulating on-campus/off-campus activities and the plot thickens. Finally, even with laws in place, cyberbullying that goes unreported cannot be prohibited. All of these factors combine to create an environment in which most of the undesirable behavior goes unpunished.

Child psychologists and educators in the United States often have little difficulty defining cyberbullying, and even though they may not all agree on the exact terms of a single definition, the similarities are striking. One of the first definitions of cyberbullying is attributed to Canadian teacher Bill Belsey, who started Bullying.org. Belsey defines it as "the use of information and communication technologies to support deliberate, repeated, and hostile behaviour by an individual or group, that is intended to harm others." Most definitions include a number of these requirements, including the desire to harm, the use of technology to communicate, and deliberate contact. Other organizations limit cyberbullying to cases involving victims who are minors. StopCyberbullying.Org has one of the narrowest definitions of cyberbullying:

> Cyberbullying is when a child, preteen or teen is tormented, threatened, harassed, humiliated, embarrassed or otherwise targeted by another child, preteen or teen using the Internet, interactive and digital technologies or mobile phones. It has to have a minor on both sides, or at least have been instigated by a minor against another minor.

Although there may be minor differences in the various definitions, those in education and healthcare largely agree on the primary characteristics of the behavior.

Despite the nearly universal agreement as to the types of undesirable behavior that constitutes cyberbullying among health and education professional, a larger disagreement resulted among lawmakers, who were tasked with defining the type of conduct their states desired to punish. Given the expressive nature of the conduct at issue, lawmakers have had a particularly difficult task. This is because the First Amendment to the U.S. Constitution provides a certain amount of protection for expression—and even children attending school are not completely without these protections.[55] Thus, when drafting statutes to curtail cyberbullying, lawmakers must walk the fine line between prohibiting the conduct they seek to regulate and running afoul of the First Amendment.

The constitutional challenges have not stopped lawmakers in their efforts. As of January 2016, all 50 states have laws in place to address bullying, but only 23 of those include cyberbullying-specific provisions, according to the Cyberbullying Research Center. In addition, three more states have proposed legislation to address cyberbullying. More than 95% of the current laws do include prohibitions on electronic harassment, which depending on how each state has defined the term, could include revenge pornography, sexting, and cyberbullying. Of the laws in place, only 36% provide for a criminal penalty while a full 90% allow the school to sanction students instead.

The protections in various states run the gamut—from Montana's hands-off approach to Arkansas' attempt to restrict an enormous amount of student activity. Montana represents the outlier—having been the last state to pass a cyberbullying law in 2015. Even then, Montana's law merely defines cyberbullying; it does not create any obligation on the part of schools to draft policies. This suggests any punishment for cyberbullying must be the result of prosecution under the state's criminal statute prohibiting electronic harassment.

Most states, however, fall somewhere in between. Nearly all states require the school district to establish a policy but also allow the school district to sanction students. Far fewer allow the regulation of off-campus activity or criminal penalties. Nearly all of the states have enacted or updated their laws in the past five years, and they will not come without legal challenges.

In addition to state laws, legislation has been proposed at the federal level. At the time of publication, though, no federal law specifically prohibited cyberbullying. In 2009, lawmakers introduced the Megan Meier Cyberbullying Prevention Act (HR 1966), which would have criminalized "any communication, with the intent to coerce, intimidate, harass, or cause substantial emotional distress to a person, using electronic means to support severe, repeated, and hostile behavior" that was transmitted between states. Under the bill, violators faced up to two years in prison or a fine. Although subcommittee hearings were held in late 2009, the bill never made it to the House floor.

Similar legislation—the Tyler Clementi Higher Education Anti-Harassment Act—was introduced in 2011 after Rutgers University freshman Tyler Clementi committed suicide after being harassed online by another college student. The legislation (HR 1048) mandated that universities who receive federal funds must implement a policy that prohibits harassment of students based on race, color, national origin, sex, disability, sexual orientation, gender identity, or religion. Although the bill was referred to committee in 2011, it never made it to the House floor.

To date, most legal challenges have resulted when school districts have attempted to sanction students for assaultive speech aimed at teachers and administrators. In those cases, courts are less likely to consider the conduct cyberbullying or harassment and often uphold the students' free speech rights to maintain their websites or make their online postings.

REPLY HAZY, TRY AGAIN: PREDICTING THE FUTURE OF LIABILITY

As Internet communication and social media proliferate as part of our everyday lives, so too will the legal changes resulting from electronic communication and online conduct. Most courts are struggling to decide whether to apply traditional laws to new forms of communication or wait for lawmakers to create specific laws addressing social media and other emerging technologies. In general, the most successful prosecutions have occurred using traditional laws that target conduct instead of expression, but that hasn't stopped legislatures from attempting to craft bills addressing revenge pornography, sexting, and cyberbullying. Particularly when the harms involve children, members of the public initially seem more willing to curtail constitutional free speech rights in the name of protecting minors. However, the calculus grows more complicated when restrictions target consenting adults or create sweeping prohibitions on all forms of online communication.

Additionally, the changing relationship between employers and employees has impacted the notion of what a person can rightfully do in his or her private life. One only needs to follow the news to unearth examples of employees—often professors or teachers in particular—who have been reprimanded for their electronic communication or social media use. The law is murky—at best—with regard to the actions employers can and cannot take, and a number of factors complicate the inquiry. Should it matter whether the employer issued the communication device? What about if the employee used a personal device while at the employer's place of business? Does it matter if it was after hours? Should some employees—teachers, for example—be held to a higher standard because they are viewed as role models and interact with children? One thing is clear: Judges and lawmakers face an uphill battle addressing these important issues.

Whether and how to regulate electronic communication and social media use in the workplace and schools also raises a number of constitutional issues, including the First Amendment. As Congress' history of regulation in the area of sexually explicit speech on the Internet suggests, legislation will likely result in significant scrutiny from the courts and must be drafted with the utmost care to be found constitutional. Based on the Court's opinion in *Reno*, it seems unlikely the justices will be willing to constrain speech online any more than they would offline.

What is clear is that social media policies dealing with sexually explicit communication or bullying/harassment must be tightly worded to clearly define the types of conduct to be regulated. The policies should differentiate between conduct involving minors and conduct involving adults given that courts would be more likely—though not guaranteed—to support incidental restrictions on speech aimed at protecting minors. Policies aimed at adults should clearly address professional versus personal conduct, including appropriate use of employer-provided communication devices. Enforcement of these types of policies should be done uniformly and with a high level of documentation. When possible, action should be taken under existing laws aimed to curtail undesirable conduct—stalking, harassment, and sexual misconduct statutes—that have already withstood constitutional scrutiny.

Not only must Congress and employers worry about outcomes in the court of law, they also must be concerned with an even more unpredictable jury: the court of public opinion. As news stories surface of employers spying on employees and inappropriately using social media to screen applicants, employers must be cautious about the effects of the publicity on the next generation of employees and consumers. Policies made by executives who came of age in the pre-Internet era are likely to strike prospective Millennial generation employees as antiquated and overbearing.

Further, the gaps in law surrounding social media and its uses suggest it is incumbent upon sites like Facebook, Instagram, Twitter, and Periscope to set their own standards of conduct. Although they have largely attempted to do so through Terms of Service and Privacy Policy agreements, the language in those agreements remains obscure and tedious for the average user. But, as many users know, the language in those agreements is often obscure and tedious for the non-legal mind. Some improvements have been made, including Facebook's Community Standards, which tries to spell out in lay terms what kind of conduct will be permitted on the social media site. The challenge for all of these sites is not only to lay out what is impermissible in concrete enough terms that users can understand but to also do so in a manner that creates a policy that is adaptable as the technology and its uses change.

This challenge is not a particularly novel one. The same task was expected of CompuServe and Prodigy when the Internet was in its youth. In fact, the example serves to remind us that multiple paths are possible. Prodigy, for example, set out to become the family friendly portal—policing its site for offensive content to encourage parents to allow their children to use its services. Today, the law specifically allows social media sites the flexibility to choose whether to filter out "offensive" content—sexually explicit photos or profanity-laden posts—without fear of legal retribution by the posters. An upstart competitor to Facebook or YouTube, for example, might choose to carve out a niche by following the trail Prodigy attempted to blaze in the 1990s. Sites could create family-specific games, video channels, and more, where parents could allow their children to spend time without fear of what content might appear.

It is the users themselves, however, who wield the most influential card in the deck. Public outcry has caused a number of businesses to rethink certain policies or practices, and social media companies are not immune to the court of public opinion. In this case, users truly vote with their clicks of the mouse—choosing to accept Terms of Service and Privacy Policy language when they log in. Evidence suggests that social media sites are listening—at least when the outrage is large enough—and making changes with regard to their services in some instances.

FREQUENTLY ASKED QUESTIONS

1. Can I get in trouble for posting sexually explicit photographs on a social media site?

Facebook—like most social media sites—expressly prohibits the sharing of content it labels "pornographic." In its Community Standards section, you will find language that suggests users can have their content removed or be blocked from using the service if they violate the standards, which include posting pornographic content and violating copyright terms, among other things. Further, because Facebook is not a government entity, the First Amendment will not protect your right to post content to the site—pornographic or otherwise. The law does not require Facebook to allow you to use its site to post any or all of the content you wish. In addition, any sexually explicit content that rises to the level of obscenity, as defined by state law, could be regulated because obscene speech falls outside the scope of First Amendment protection.

2. Does the First Amendment protect use of foul language on Twitter?

Like Facebook, Twitter also need not follow the First Amendment. Therefore, it has the legal right to make rules about permissible content on its site. Interestingly, although Twitter's Rules make mention of a number of restricted areas, including threats, copyright, trademark, and pornography, they make no mention of profane language—suggesting that your taste in language is for you to decide.

3. Can my employer examine my mobile device or email for indecent or obscene materials?

In light of the *Quon* case, it would seem that employers have the right to examine employer-issued devices, including cell phones and laptops—particularly if they are doing so with probable cause or in accordance with a standard procedure. A smart employee should think twice about using an employer-issued device to engage in any conduct that would violate the employer's rules. Although it might seem extreme, employees would be wise to act as though they have no right to privacy with regard to employer-provided devices, email, and landline phone service. Similarly, an employer would be wise to establish rules and regulations for acceptable use of technology both at, and away from, the workplace to inform their employees as to what is permissible.

4. If a user makes an offensive post about me or tags me in an inappropriate photograph on Facebook, can I demand that the post or photograph be removed?

Under Section 230 of the Communications Decency Act, you are unlikely to be able to demand that Facebook remove unwanted content about you. However, you may well have a cause of action against the specific user who posted the content—if it defamatory or violated your privacy, for example. Even if you succeed in getting the content removed from one site, there is no guarantee that it has not been archived or may re-appear on another site. The soundest course of action is often simply to ask the poster to remove the offending content.

5. What kinds of social media activities are most likely to lead to criminal charges?

Users of social media can face criminal charges for their expression, particularly if the speech is not protected by the First Amendment. In most states, this means speech that amounts to obscenity, true threats, incitement, fighting words, and false advertising. Additionally, the rise of live-streaming video apps has increased the likelihood that someone who shares live content of a criminal act could be held liable as an accessory to that crime. In April 2016, an 18-year-old woman was charged with four felony counts, including rape and kidnapping for live-streaming her friend's rape on Periscope.[56] However, the U.S. Supreme Court overturned the conviction of a Pennsylvania man who posted violent messages on Facebook after a split with his wife.[57] In *Elonis v. United States*, the Court ruled a conviction could not stand based on negligence alone. It ruled the government needed to show a higher level of intent for criminal conviction. As a result, the Court has clearly indicated that social media does not merit a lower level of intent than similar activities carried out off-line.

NOTES

1 Aarti Shahani, Live-Streaming of Alleged Rape Shows Challenges of Flagging Video in Real Time, NPR.org, April 19, 2016, http://www.npr.org/sections/alltechconsidered/2016/04/19/474783485/live-streaming-of-alleged-rape-shows-challenges-of-flagging-video-in-real-time

2 The Science Behind Pornography Addiction: Hearing Before the Subcommittee on Science, Technology and Space of the S. Comm. on Commerce, 108th Cong. (2004) (statement of Mary Anne Layden, co-director of the Sexual Trauma and Psychopathology Program at the University of Pennsylvania's Center for Cognitive Therapy).

3 See Communications Decency Act of 1996, 47 U.S.C. §223 (1997).

4 354 U.S. 476 (1957).

5 Id. at 481.

6 Id. at 485 (quoting Chaplinsky v. State of New Hampshire, 315 U.S. 568, 571–572 (1942)).

7 Jacobellis v. Ohio, 378 U.S. 184, 197 (1964) (Stewart, J., concurring).

8 See, e.g., Jacobellis, 378 U.S. at 184; Memoirs v. Massachusetts, 383 U.S. 413 (1966); Interstate Circuit v. Dallas, 390 U.S. 676 (1968).

9 413 U.S. 15 (1973).

10 Id.

11 438 U.S. 726 (1978).

12 Id. at 748–749.

13 Id. at 732 (quoting 56 F. C. C. 2d, at 98).

14 P.L. No. 104-104, 110 Stat. 56 (1996).

15 For more information on the Telecommunications Act of 1996, see Telecommunications Act of 1996, http://transition.fcc.gov/telecom.html.

16 47 U.S.C. §223(1)(a).

17 929 F. Supp. 824 (E.D. Pa. 1996).

18 Reno v. ACLU, 521 U.S. 844 (1997).

19 The lawsuit specifically challenged §223(a)(1)(B), which criminalizes the "knowing" transmission of "obscene or indecent" messages to any recipient under 18 years of age and §223(d) prohibits the "knowin[g]" sending or displaying to a person under 18 of any message "that, in context, depicts or describes, in terms patently offensive as measured by contemporary community standards, sexual or excretory activities or organs."

20 Reno, 521 U.S. at 868–869.

21 Id.

22 Sable Communications of Cal., Inc. v. FCC, 492 U.S. 115 (1989).

23 Id. at 128.

24 Id.

25 Red Lion Broadcasting v. FCC, 397 U.S. 367 (1969).

26 Reno, 581 U.S. at 866–867.

27 Id.

28 Id.

29 Id.

30 Pub. L. No. 105-277, 112 Stat. 2681-736 (1998).

31 Child Online Protection Act, 47 U.S. §231.

32 47 U.S. §231(a)(1). "Whoever knowingly and with knowledge of the character of the material, in interstate or foreign commerce by means of the World Wide Web, makes any communication for commercial purposes that is available to any minor and that includes any material that is harmful to minors shall be fined not more than $50,000, imprisoned not more than 6 months, or both."

33 Id.

34 458 U.S. 747 (1982).

35 American Civil Liberties Union v. Reno, 31 F. Supp. 2d 473 (E.D. Pa. 1999).

36 American Civil Liberties Union v. Reno, 217 F.3d 162 (3d. Cir. 2000).

37 Ashcroft v. American Civil Liberties Union, 535 U.S. 564 (2002).

38 American Civil Liberties Union v. Ashcroft, 322 F.3d 240 (3d. Cir. 2003).

39 Ashcroft v. American Civil Liberties Union, 542 U.S. 656 (2004).

40 American Civil Liberties Union v. Mukasey, 534 F.3d 181 (3d. Cir. 2008).

41 U.S. v. American Library Ass'n, Inc., 539 U.S. 194 (2003).

42 Deleting Online Predators Act of 2006, H.R. 5319.

43 Senate Bill 132 / S.L. 2008-218 (signed in law August 16, 2008).

44 Doe v. Jindal, 2012 U.S. Dist. LEXIS 19841 (M.D. La. 2012).

45 Doe v. Nebraska, 734 F. Supp. 2d 882 (D. Neb. 2010).

46 Federal Trade Commission, Children's Online Privacy Protection Rule: Not Just for Kids' Sites (April 2013), https://www.ftc.gov/tips-advice/business-center/guidance/childrens-online-privacy-protection-rule-not-just-kids-sites

47 McAfee, Love, Relationships & Technology, Nov. 17, 2014, http://promos.mcafee.com/offer.aspx?id=605436&culture=en-us&affid=0&cid=140624

48 Abby Ohlheiser, Revenge Porn Purveyor Hunter Moore Is Sentenced to Prison, Washington Post, Dec. 3, 2015, https://www.washingtonpost.com/news/the-intersect/wp/2015/12/03/revenge-porn-purveyor-hunter-moore-is-sentenced-to-prison/

49 Allie Conti, Will Giving Kevin Bollaert 18 Years in Prison Finally End Revenge Porn?, Vice, April 6, 2015, http://www.vice.com/read/is-giving-kevin-bollaert-18-years-enough-to-finally-end-revenge-porn-406

50 Veronica Rocha, Revenge Porn Conviction Is First Under California Law, L.A. Times, Dec. 4, 2014, http://www.latimes.com/local/crime/la-me-1204-revenge-porn-20141205-story.html

51 Helen A.S. Popkin, Is It Illegal to Record and Post Noisy Neighbors Having Sex?, MSNBC.com, May 19, 2012.

52 Randye Hoder, Study Finds Most Teens Sext Before They're 18, Time, July 3, 2014, http://time.com/2948467/chances-are-your-teen-is-sexting/

53 Sameer Hinduja & Justin W. Patchkin, State Sexting Laws, Cyberbullying Research Center (2015), http://cyberbullying.org/state-sexting-laws.pdf

54 Kim Zetter, Judge Acquits Lori Drew in Cyberbullying Case, Overrules Jury, Wired. com, July 2, 2009.

55 Tinker v. Des Moines Indep. Sch. Dist., 393 U.S. 503, 506 (1969).

56 Shahani, supra note 1.

57 Ariane De Vogue, SCOTUS Rules in Favor of Man Convicted of Posting Threatening Messages on Facebook, CNN.com, June 1, 2015, at http://www.cnn.com/2015/06/01/politics/supreme-court-elonis-facebook-ruling/

CHAPTER 10

Social Media Use in Courtrooms

Cathy Packer

University of North Carolina at Chapel Hill
School of Media and Journalism

ABSTRACT

News reporters want to blog and tweet from courtrooms. Jurors are blogging and tweeting about cases and searching the Internet for information about cases they sit on, including the applicable laws and the parties involved. This chapter examines how the rules governing the use of cameras in the courtroom apply to computers and smartphones; how courts are handling juror issues; the implications of federal, state, and local rules on courtroom technology use; and what rights journalists have to use social media to cover trials.

The recent explosion of social media use, combined with the proliferation of smartphones, tablets, and other small computers, is presenting new challenges to state and federal court judges whose duty it is to ensure the fairness of court proceedings. Americans now go everywhere with phones in hand, including to court, and they are accustomed to constantly communicating with family, friends, and colleagues. Therefore, courts must grapple with issues such as whether reporters should be permitted to blog or tweet news and commentary from the courtroom and whether a juror—or even an attorney or a judge—who comments about a case on her Facebook page or uses Google to conduct a bit of independent research has deprived a defendant of a fair trial.

This chapter outlines the major case precedents on access to courtrooms and then surveys the current state of the law on reporters' use of social media in federal and state courts, the law on juror use of social media, and the problems that arise when judges and attorneys use social media.

ACCESS TO COURTROOMS

Some of the strongest First Amendment opinions ever written by the U.S. Supreme Court established the rights of journalists and citizens to attend judicial proceedings and to report on those proceedings. Most famously, Chief Justice Warren E. Burger wrote for the Court in *Richmond Newspapers Inc. v. Virginia* (1980):

> We hold that the right to attend criminal trials is implicit in the guarantees of the First Amendment; without the freedom to attend such trials, which people have exercised for centuries, important aspects of freedom of speech and "of the press could be eviscerated."[1]

The Court held that criminal trials in state and federal courts are presumptively open, and, in subsequent cases, the Supreme Court or lower courts ruled that most criminal and civil judicial proceedings could be closed only upon the showing of a compelling government interest and that any closure had to be "narrowly tailored to serve that interest."[2] Four years earlier, in *Nebraska Press Association v. Stuart*, the Supreme Court had ruled that prior restraints on media coverage of judicial proceedings are allowed only as a last resort to ensure the fair trial guaranteed to criminal defendants by the Sixth Amendment.[3]

In those cases, the Supreme Court clearly articulated how courtroom access serves the public interest. The Court said open courts promote confidence in the fair administration of justice and have a "significant community therapeutic value . . . providing an outlet for community concern, hostility, and emotion."[4] Access to courtrooms also serves as a check on government power, helping to ensure that defendants receive fair trials.[5] The Court observed that the public receives most of its information about the judicial process from reporters. The media "contribute to public understanding of the rule of law and to comprehension of the functioning of the entire criminal justice system," the Court said.[6]

Today journalists have the right to attend trials and most other judicial proceedings and to report on what they see and hear in courtrooms. There are only a few exceptions, including grand jury proceedings, some juvenile proceedings, and involuntary commitment and adoption proceedings. However, the Supreme Court has had very little to say about what technology journalists can use in courtrooms. In the absence of guidance from the Supreme Court, the *Richmond Newspapers* decision recognizing a right of access to criminal trials has been interpreted by lower courts as guaranteeing a right to bring to court only the most rudimentary and unobtrusive newsgathering tools—a notebook or sketchbook, pencil or pen. Several federal courts have ruled explicitly that the media's First Amendment right to attend criminal trials does not include a right to record or televise those trials.[7]

Television was once a new technology that raised difficult questions about its use in courtrooms. In the 1930s, when television was new, the Supreme Court began hearing cases in which criminal defendants claimed to have been denied their Sixth Amendment rights to a fair trial because the presence of television reporters and their equipment in the courtroom caused physical and psychological disruptions.[8] In several high-profile cases, the Court granted the defendants new trials.[9] In those cases, the Court decried courtrooms with multiple, large cameras; microphones on the judge's bench and aimed at the jury box and counsel tables; and cables snaking across the floor. All of that deprived criminal defendants of "that judicial serenity and calm to which [they are] entitled."[10]

By the mid-1970s, only two states allowed cameras in their courtrooms, and there were no cameras in federal courts. However, communication technology continued to change, with bulky television cameras being replaced by smaller, less obtrusive cameras. Consequently, the rules governing the use of communication technology in courtrooms changed, too. In *Chandler v. Florida* (1981), the Court ruled that the presence of cameras in courtrooms does not automatically violate criminal defendants' Sixth Amendment rights to a trial by an impartial jury and that states were free to experiment with allowing cameras in court.[11] Today, all states allow cameras in at least some of their courtrooms. The federal courts have been more resistant, and currently cameras are allowed only in two federal circuits and in three federal district courts on an experimental basis.

Federal and state courts are just beginning to figure out how, if at all, these legal rules apply to reporters and others who want to use smartphones, tablets, and laptop computers to report on courtroom proceedings. The Reporters Committee on Freedom of the Press reported in 2011: "Tweeting from the courtroom is *de rigueur* nowadays among courts reporters. It's a fast growing trend, especially in competitive markets."[12] In the 2012 trial of Dr. Conrad Murray concerning the death of Michael Jackson, for example, tweeting was permitted in court, and one local news station sent out nearly 1,900 tweets to 3,000 followers.[13] However, the Reporters Committee reported in 2015 that there still is no broad consensus about whether to permit journalists to tweet and blog from state courts. Decisions usually are made on a case-by-case basis.[14]

Jurors' use of smartphones, computers, and the Internet creates a somewhat different legal problem. The problem is that jurors are supposed to arrive at a verdict based solely on the evidence presented in court—not based on a Google search performed on a smartphone or a Facebook discussion. Jurors' independent research or communication related to a case can result in a defendant being denied his Sixth Amendment right to trial by an impartial jury and result in a mistrial—what some call a "Google mistrial"[15] or a "digital misadventure."[16] This has put pressure on judges to find a way to control jurors' use of smartphones and other devices that link them to the Internet.

Recently some judges also have had to find ways to control criminal defendants' use of social media. For example, in a 2016 case involving the bankruptcy of the rapper known as 50 Cent, a U.S. Bankruptcy Court judge banned 50 Cent from carrying electronic devices into the courtroom or the adjoining conference room after the rapper posted photos from court on Instagram. 50 Cent had posted a photo of himself in the conference room eating M&Ms with $100 bills stuffed in the waistband of his pants. The judge said the photo showed 50 Cent was not taking the case seriously.[17]

When judges and attorneys use social media to communicate about cases, they also risk interfering with the fair administration of justice. They risk running afoul of their professional codes of ethics, too.

In 1965, the Supreme Court predicted that "[t]he ever-advancing techniques of public communication and the adjustment of the public to its presence may bring about a change in the effect of telecasting upon the fairness of criminal trials."[18] How judges are dealing with the very latest techniques of public communication is the subject of the subsequent sections of this chapter.

SOCIAL MEDIA IN FEDERAL COURTS

In 2009, a federal court judge for the first time specifically granted permission for a journalist to use a smartphone to report on a trial from the courtroom.[19] The order, which enabled a *Wichita* (Kan.) *Eagle* reporter to tweet updates on a racketeering trial, was based on Federal Rule of Criminal Procedure 57(b). That rule says a judge may regulate his courtroom in any manner consistent with federal law and judicial rules, giving federal judges broad discretion to regulate courtroom affairs. The judge in this case reasoned that allowing reporters to tweet about the case would open the judicial process to the public, which would lead to greater public understanding of the judicial process.[20]

That same year, another U.S. district court judge denied a request from a reporter for the *Columbus* (Ga.) *Ledger-Enquirer* to be allowed to use a smartphone to tweet during a criminal trial.[21] The judge ruled that Rule 53 of the Federal Rules of Criminal Procedure—the rule that bans photography and broadcasting in most federal courtrooms—also prohibits tweeting from the courtroom.[22]

As these two cases suggest, federal judges differ in their views on whether reporters should be allowed to use smartphones, tablets, or other small computers in federal court. Overall, however, most federal courts remain opposed to allowing social media—or any form of photography or audio recording—in the courtroom, especially in criminal courts. Federal courts often ban reporters and other spectators from bringing phones, tablets, or other small computers into their courthouses, not just into their courtrooms.[23] However, there are exceptions. One federal judge banned the use of computers and cell phones in the courtroom but allowed reporters to step outside the courtroom to tweet or blog in the hallway.[24] Another judge allowed a reporter covering a fraud trial to tweet from the back of the courtroom where her typing would not be distracting.[25]

The conflicting federal rules and practices raise several intriguing questions. What are the rules that currently govern reporters' use of smartphones, tablets, and other small computers in federal courtrooms? Do the use of smartphones, tablets, and other small computers in courtrooms serve the values the U.S. Supreme Court said it was protecting when it granted media and public access to courtrooms? Or do these new technologies create physical and psychological disruptions similar to those that have been the bases for banning cameras from courtrooms for decades? First, it is helpful to review the federal rules governing this topic.

Federal Criminal Courts and Rule 53

Rule 53 has kept most cameras, smartphones, tablets, and other small computers out of the hands of reporters in federal criminal courtrooms. Rule 53 says in part, "[T]he court must not permit the taking of photographs in the courtroom during judicial proceedings or the broadcasting of judicial proceedings from the courtroom." The judge who did not allow a reporter to tweet in a U.S. district court in Georgia used a dictionary definition of broadcasting to determine that tweeting was a form of broadcasting. The judge observed that the definition of broadcasting "includes 'casting or scattering in all directions' and 'the act of making widely known.' . . . It cannot be reasonably disputed that 'twittering,' as previously described, would result in casting to the general public and thus making widely known the trial proceedings."[26]

The district court judge also ruled that, as previously established by federal courts, Rule 53 did not violate the media's First Amendment right of access to attend criminal trials. He explained:

> The press certainly has a right of access to observe criminal trials,
> just as members of the public have the right to attend criminal trials.
> In this case, the press will be able to attend, listen and report on
> the proceedings. No restriction is being placed upon their legitimate
> right of access to the proceedings.[27]

Tweeting, however, was out of the question.

The Federal Rules of Criminal Procedure are written by the Judicial Conference of the United States. The Judicial Conference is a body of federal court judges responsible for making policy regarding the administration of the federal courts. Rule 53 was enacted in 1946. It was rewritten in 2002 to remove a reference to "radio" but leave the word "broadcasting." The Judicial Conference's Advisory Committee on Rules of Criminal Procedure said it viewed the change as "one that accords with judicial interpretation applying the current rule to other forms of broadcasting and functionally equivalent means."[28] This suggests the question for the federal judges is whether tweeting or blogging are "functionally equivalent" to broadcasting. In practice, it means judges have broad discretion over how or whether to regulate the use of new media technologies in their courtrooms.

Federal Civil Courts

Reporters and the public have a strong right of access to federal civil courts, just as they do to criminal courts. Furthermore, there is no federal civil court equivalent to Rule 53 to bar the broadcasting of civil proceedings. In practice, camera access to federal civil courts remains very limited, although there are frequent reports of federal judges allowing reporters to tweet and blog during civil court proceedings.

Since 1996, Judicial Conference policy has been to allow circuit courts to determine when cameras are permitted in their civil courtrooms. As a result, cameras are allowed during oral arguments in the U.S. Courts of Appeals for the Second and Ninth Circuits. The Conference also has conducted several experiments with cameras in courtrooms. In 2011, for example, the Judicial Conference began a three-year project to evaluate the effects of cameras on civil trials in 14 federal districts.[29] However, the project resulted in no policy change. The experiment continues in three district courts.

While these forays into televising court proceedings dealt only with cameras—not with smartphones, tablets, or other small computers—they do suggest that federal courts' interest in allowing communication technologies to be used in their courtrooms is not strong.

Local Federal Court Rules and Their Application

The Judicial Conference has left it to individual courts to decide how to implement the Conference's rules on technology in the courtroom. Each federal court posts its local rules online,[30] and those rules vary in ways that are both interesting and significant. For example, the rule adopted by the U.S. District Court for the Middle District of North Carolina says, "Radio, television, Internet broadcasting and the use of photographic, electronic, or mechanical reproduction or recording equipment is prohibited in courtrooms or their environs. 'Environs' is defined to mean the courtrooms, the offices of the Judges, Clerk, probation officers, or any corridor connecting or adjacent thereto."[31] In that district, a lawyer needs special permission to bring an electronic device into the courtroom, and the device may not be used to record or broadcast the proceedings.[32]

The U.S. District Court for the Middle District of Alabama has a somewhat more lenient local rule that says cell phones and laptop computers "without photographic, video or audio recording capabilities" may be possessed in the courtroom by members of the press, court personnel, and attorneys. Laptop computers can be used in the courtroom, but cell phones must be turned off. Cell phones can be used outside the courtroom.[33]

The U.S. District Court for the District of Connecticut has a local rule on laptops and another on cell phones, but both speak only to whether phones and laptops can be brought into the courthouse—not whether they can be used in court.[34] The laptop rule is that laptops are prohibited in the courthouse except for use by attorneys, court personnel, and "[o]ther individuals permitted by the Court." The cell phone policy is similar, allowing attorneys, police, jurors, and court personnel—and "[o]ther individuals permitted by the Court"—to bring cell phones into the courthouse. Other people have their cell phones collected by the U.S. Marshals Service as they enter the courthouse.

Clearly some courts are resistant to the mere presence of smartphones and computers in the courthouse. Other courts tolerate the presence of the devices in the courtroom but not their use. And there is growing anecdotal evidence that some courts are allowing them to be used. Federal court judges who view blogging and tweeting as forms of broadcasting logically will be more resistant to allowing smartphones and laptops to be used in the courtroom. Judges who see the newer technologies as smaller and quieter than television cameras, and thus less physically and psychologically disruptive, might allow their use while continuing to ban traditional broadcasting of court proceedings. However, it is difficult for an outside observer to assess how federal court rules actually are applied and why or how often reporters are allowed to tweet and blog from court. Judges' decisions on these matters most often do not result in written court opinions. Instead the evidence is largely anecdotal and based on news reports.

One federal court case that illustrates the confusion in the federal courts created by the new communication technologies involved the U.S. district court trial on the challenge to Proposition 8, California's constitutional amendment outlawing same-sex marriages in the state. In 2010, the U.S. Supreme Court ruled that the district court could not allow the broadcasting of the courtroom proceedings as part of a pilot project because the court had failed to give proper public notice and opportunity for comment on the pilot program.[35] Meanwhile, the proceedings were covered live by hundreds of news companies using Twitter, Facebook, and blogs from the courtroom gallery.[36] The Supreme Court did not comment on that.

Congress on Access to Federal Courts

Beginning in 2005, members of the U.S. Congress repeatedly have introduced bills that would let federal court judges decide whether to allow cameras and other electronic media in their courtrooms. The law would invalidate federal Rule 53, the rule that has kept cameras out of most federal criminal courtrooms. However, while the Senate and House judiciary committees both have passed versions of these "Sunshine in the Courtroom" bills, the bills never have come up for a vote of the full House or Senate.

Two recent bills—one in the House and one in the Senate—are both called the Sunshine in the Courtroom Act of 2015. The name of the proposed legislation is a reference to former U.S. Supreme Court Justice Louis Brandeis' statement that "sunlight is said to be the best of disinfectants."[37] The bills say, in part, that a presiding federal court judge "may, at the discretion of that judge, permit the photographing, electronic recording, broadcasting, or televising to the public of any court proceeding over which that judge presides."[38] The bills also provide that some facets of judicial proceedings, such as the faces of jurors, cannot be photographed.

Is it not clear what effect, if any, such a law would have on activities such as blogging and tweeting from the courtroom. However, it is interesting to note that during a 2007 House Judiciary Committee hearing on one of the Sunshine in the Courtroom bills, a U.S. attorney from Oklahoma expressed concern that "broadcasts now in the modern world do not just include major networks or Court TV or C-SPAN, but also include, of course, bloggers and all kinds of Web sites and all kinds of unique other delivery mechanisms."[39] Whether tweeting and other social networking posts are, in fact, forms of broadcasting is a question that might have to be addressed by Congress as well as by the courts.

SOCIAL MEDIA IN STATE COURTS

Since the U.S. Supreme Court paved the way for the opening of courtroom doors to cameras and recordings devices in 1981, each state has adopted its own rules governing cameras in courtrooms. Some states allow cameras only in their appellate courts, some allow cameras only with the consent of the parties involved in the judicial proceeding, most limit the number of cameras allowed in the courtroom at one time, and most allow broad judicial discretion. A 2014 survey of judges and court personnel across the nation found that 37% of courts had adopted social media policies,[40] which indicates progress in dealing with social media in courtrooms but leaves most judges with little guidance when deciding whether to allow new technologies to be used in court. On a more encouraging note, the 2014 survey found that judges and other court officials' attitudes are improving. Court officials were more supportive of allowing the media to send electronic messages from the courtroom than they were when they were surveyed a year earlier. The number of survey respondents who objected fell from 66 to 46%. A complete list of the state court rules on the use of television cameras, still cameras, audio-recording devices and, in some cases, smartphones and laptop computers, is available on the website of the Radio Television Digital News Association.[41] Also, the Reporters Committee on Freedom of the Press has a website that indicates most states have no rules regarding social media in courtrooms.[42] But the lack of rules does not mean reporters and others will not be allowed to tweet or blog from court. It means those activities are allowed at the discretion of the presiding judge.

A 2011 study of how Wisconsin judges are applying their camera-in-the-courtroom guidelines to online media observed that some of the debate in state courts across the nation focuses not on what recording devices should be allowed in the courtroom but on who should be allowed to use them.[43] For example, in 2010 an independent blogger was not allowed to photograph and audio record a public divorce proceeding in an Ohio courtroom because the judge determined the blogger was not a member of the media—unlike Channel 5 News, the judge said. The blogger said her work would be published on the Internet, but the judge was not persuaded.[44]

Another issue that has arisen in state courts is how rules that limit the number of cameras or recording devices that can be used in a courtroom at one time apply when dozens of people want to use their smartphones or laptops at the same time. For example, in 2010 a Florida judge banned blogging in the courtroom during a murder trial. He first explained that Florida's 1979 cameras-in-the-courtroom rule did not address laptop communication. After his order was quickly reversed by an appeals court, the judge said a photographer for one news outlet and a blogger for another could be in the courtroom at the same time but they could not use their equipment—a camera and a laptop computer—at the same time. A video camera already was in the courtroom, and only two devices were allowed.[45]

The author of the Wisconsin study also noted that most television stations pool their video feeds, so restrictions on the numbers of cameras allowed in a courtroom are not problematic for them. However, the author expressed concern that "[a] blogger who simply wishes to record on a hand-held device . . . may lack the tools and know-how to contribute to or partake from the established media pool."[46]

The study of the Wisconsin courts also found that judges were most concerned that nothing disrupted the court proceedings—including the sound of typing on a laptop.[47] For example, the judge presiding over the 2012 trial of the man accused of killing the family of singer/actress Jennifer Hudson told reporters they could not tweet or post on Facebook from inside the courtroom. According to a court spokesman, the judge "didn't want constant typing on cell phones to distract jurors and other courtroom participants."[48]

Other judges seem to think the use of new technology is not distracting. For example, a U.S. district court judge in Kansas has been quoted as saying that he did not "see any difference between this and a journalist sitting there taking notes."[49] And scholars commonly note that typing on a smartphone or laptop computer is less distracting that having reporters repeatedly leaving the courtroom to post the news.

In at least one case, a reporter's tweet from a courtroom has resulted in a mistrial. In a 2012 case in Kansas, a judge ordered a mistrial in a murder case after a reporter tweeted a courtroom photo that included the profile of a juror. That photo violated a Kansas Supreme Court rule that prohibited the photographing of individual jurors—a common rule in state courts. The publisher of the *Topeka Capital-Journal* apologized for his reporter's tweet, and the murder trial was to be rescheduled.[50]

Prior Restraints

In a couple of state court cases involving blogging and tweeting reporters, the legal issue was not access to courtrooms but prior restraint on media coverage of judicial proceedings. Prior restraints on the media are considered by the U.S. Supreme Court to be "the most serious and least tolerable infringement on First Amendment Rights"[51] and thus rarely are allowed to be used to control media coverage of judicial proceedings.

In early 2012, a Texas trial court judge ordered the media covering a capital murder trial not to report on any court proceedings that occurred in open court when the jury was not present. The court order, which listed 19 rules to be followed, led the newspaper to remove a number of blog posts and tweets that already had been published. Those blog posts and tweets reported on testimony given outside the jury's presence, the judge's ruling on motions from the prosecution and defense, and an informal admonishment by the judge of two attorneys in the case. The order said the restrictions were put in place "to ensure due and proper administration of justice."[52] The order was quickly revised on appeal to allow the media to report everything that happened in open court regardless of whether the jury was present. The posts that had been removed then were republished.[53]

In 2010, a *Pittsburgh Press-Gazette* reporter posted more than 1,000 tweets while covering a criminal case involving a former state representative and several other state employees. She tweeted about the atmosphere in the courtroom and witness testimony, among other topics.[54] The criminal defendants had moved to ban that reporter and others in the courtroom from "using any and all social networking systems to electronically publish testimony during trial." The defendants argued that tweeting violated a state judicial rule that prohibited "advanced communication technology" transmissions from the courtroom and would have informed sequestered witnesses about events in the courtroom. The court denied the motion, in part because it would have constituted an unconstitutional prior restraint on the media. The court did not address the meaning of the state judicial rule in question.[55]

JURORS AND THEIR DIGITAL MISADVENTURES

Googling and tweeting jurors have received much more attention—and criticism—than tweeting courtroom news reporters. The scholarly and popular media contain many reports of jurors conducting their own research or tweeting or posting messages on Facebook about the cases they are deciding. Such activities can result in the dismissal of a juror or a mistrial.[56]

For example, in April 2012, the jury foreman in a second-degree murder trial in California used Wikipedia and nolo.com to research the difference between second-degree murder and manslaughter. A deputy sheriff cleaning the jury room at the end of the trial found printouts from those websites and reported his findings to the judge. The judge said the jury foreman disobeyed instructions not to conduct independent research. Declaring a mistrial, the judge said, "We tell jurors time and time again not to go to the internet and this case is a textbook example of why. The internet is a morass of misinformation. And it is wrong."[57]

In addition to sometimes being wrong, information jurors find on their own can be incomplete or outdated. It also might be information that has been purposely excluded from a case, such a record of a criminal defendant's prior convictions.[58]

Judges declare mistrials when they determine that the trial was not fair. In the American criminal justice system, defendants' right to a fair trial is firmly rooted in their Sixth Amendment right to a trial by an impartial jury. An impartial jury is one that reaches a verdict based solely on the evidence presented in court, not on evidence jurors gather from other jurors or from outside the courtroom. In both criminal and civil cases, each piece of evidence and all testimony are evaluated by the parties to the case. Only evidence that meets the standards established by the rules of evidence is presented to the jury.[59] Sometimes the evidence presented to the jury is unclear or incomplete. Even in those cases, jurors are instructed to decide the case based only on the evidence presented. They can make reasonable inferences, but they are not allowed to do research.

Jurors' use of social media and other Internet services can jeopardize a fair trial when a juror conducts independent research either before being selected for a jury or during a trial. When a judge discovers a juror has engaged in such research, the judge decides whether the activity was prejudicial. When juror research is directly related to an issue of fact in a trial, is shared with other jurors, and causes a jury to vote differently than it would have without the information, a mistrial is likely.[60] For example, the Oklahoma Court of Appeals ruled that a mistrial was warranted in a medical negligence case in which a juror conducted Internet and other research. The juror used the Internet to research a medical procedure, medications taken by the plaintiff, and a court case similar to the one being tried. The juror, who was a nurse, said she also consulted nursing care plans she possessed. The juror said she communicated some but not all of that information to the other jurors.[61] The court affirmed the decision to order a mistrial because, it said, "there is no doubt" that the information about the similar court case "had a direct bearing upon a key issue in plaintiffs' theory and proof of negligence."[62]

The case law clearly suggests that not all juror research is prejudicial, however. It generally is not prejudicial if the research is not shared with the other jurors.[63] For example, in a 2002 civil case in a California state court, a juror used the Internet to research the meaning of the word "negligence." The state appeals court ruled that research was not prejudicial. The court found no evidence that the juror's research either confused the jury as a whole or prejudiced the jury in favor of one party or the other.[64]

Problems also arise when jurors use social media to share information and opinions about cases on which they are serving with other jurors, parties to the case, or others. For example, in 2011, a Texas juror tried to "friend" the defendant in the civil car-accident case on which he was serving, and he discussed the case on his Facebook page. The defendant in the case reported the friend request to her lawyer. As a result, the juror was dismissed from the jury, and the trial continued with 11 jurors. The juror was charged with and pleaded guilty to four counts of contempt of court, for which he was sentenced to two days of community service. The juror's lawyer said:

> It is a reflection of the times. Most everyone has smartphones now. They can hop on at almost anytime. And there's a lot of down time in jury duty, so what most people do is hop on their phone. But the rules are there for a reason.[65]

The state of Texas recently had added new rules barring jurors from discussing cases on social networking sites.[66]

There is some disagreement about how many jurors are conducting online research about cases or using social media to communicate about cases. In 2014, the Federal Judicial Center surveyed federal district court judges about their experiences with jurors using social media during trials and deliberations.[67] Of the 494 judges who responded to the survey, only 33 judges—about 7%—reported having detected jurors using social media. According to the survey results, most of the problems with jurors using social media during trials involved the use of Facebook. The most common complaints from judges were that jurors divulged confidential information about a case or attempted to communicate directly with participants in the case. The judges reported no instances in which a juror's use of social media resulted in a mistrial. Rather, judges reported that their most common response was to caution the juror against using social media and allow him to remain on the jury. Some 96% of the judges said they routinely take precautionary steps to ensure that jurors no not use social media in their courtrooms. The most common precaution, they said, was explaining to jurors, in plain language, the reason for the social media ban.

In contrast to the Federal Judicial Center survey results, others have observed that one can search online and find countless tweets posted by jurors. Almost all of them are inconsequential observations or complaints like "There was a run on salads and yogurt at the cafeteria. I ended up with a dry chicken sandwich. #juryduty" or "Day 4. Hour 5. Captain's Log: We sat through a heartbreaking testimony by a 9 year old. It is SO real on these streets. I'm spent. #JuryDuty" or "I don't know why I'm always so disappointed in courtrooms #JuryDuty is just not like TV."[68] Judges generally have found that a juror who posts online comments about a case like these but does not receive information about the case from others does not prejudice the trial.[69]

Long before the Internet, judges had to control juror use of newspapers, television, and radio to ensure jurors did not read, view, or hear about the case they were charged with deciding. They also worked to discourage jurors from talking about their cases with each other before deliberations began or with other people before the trial was concluded. Jury instructions have been the most common methods of dealing with these problems. Jury instructions are the oral instructions a judge gives to members of the jury at any point during the trial but most commonly at the beginning of the trial and at the beginning of deliberations.

Since 2009, scholars have been calling for judges to update their jury instructions to specifically address juror use of computers for Internet research and communication through social media sites such as Twitter and Facebook. They encourage judges to deal with today's jurors by writing instructions that specify which technologies jurors are prohibited from using and when. Most courts allow jurors to bring their mobile devices to court for use during breaks, and today's jurors, in their lives outside court, are accustomed to immediately researching the answer to any question that comes to mind and to sharing their thoughts online throughout the day.

In 2012, a federal Judicial Conference committee issued updated model jury instructions that federal judges can use to help prevent the improper use of cell phones and Internet by jurors to communicate about cases on which they serve or to investigate cases. The new instructions provide detailed explanations of the consequences of social media use during a trial, along with repeated reminders of the ban on social media usage. The jury instructions also list the technologies that are not to be used. The instructions say: "You may not communicate with anyone about the case on your cell phone, through e-mail, Blackberry, iPhone, text messaging, or on Twitter, through any blog or website, including Facebook, Google+, My Space, LinkedIn, or YouTube. You may not use any similar technology of social media, even if I have not specifically mentioned it here."[70]

Two-thirds of the states also have rewritten their jury instructions to specifically restrict Internet research.[71] Some states have dealt with the Googling and tweeting jurors by forbidding jurors from bringing their cell phones to court.[72]

SOCIAL MEDIA USE BY JUDGES AND ATTORNEYS

Judges increasingly use social media to communicate with friends and family and, in states in which they are elected, as a campaign tool.[73] Attorneys conduct online research for their cases and often have websites on which they advertise their legal practices. There even are jury-selection apps for smartphones, tablets, and computers that help lawyers organize information about prospective jurors for use during jury selection.[74] While such uses of social media generally do not interfere with the judicial process, social media use by judges and attorneys sometimes does interfere with a fair trial or detract from the dignity of the court.

The federal courts and most state courts adhere to rules of judicial and attorney behavior based on the American Bar Association's Model Code of Judicial Conduct[75] and Model Rules of Professional Conduct.[76] Both sets of rules have provisions that, while not specifically addressing social media use, clearly govern such activities. The Code of Judicial Conduct, for example, provides that a judge must disqualify himself from presiding over any proceeding in which his impartiality "might reasonably be questioned," including instances in which the judge has made a public statement outside of court that "commits or appears to commit the judge to reach a particular result or rule in a particular way in the proceeding or controversy."[77] Those public statements would include tweets and Facebook posts. A dozen of the rules governing attorneys similarly can be applied to their use of social media.[78]

Some states have begun offering guidelines for judges' social media use. Ohio's guidelines, for example, instruct judges to maintain dignity in every online posting, not to post online comments about any case before the judge or before any other judge, not to view the social networking sites of those who are parties to a case or who are witnesses, and not to offer legal advice online.[79]

State judicial ethics boards can investigate and recommend punishment for judges who violate judicial ethics codes.[80] For example, in 2009 a North Carolina trial court judge was reprimanded by the state Judicial Standards Commission for having an inappropriate Facebook relationship with an attorney and the attorney's client in a child-custody case before his court. The judge posted on his Facebook page the opinion that he had "two good parents to choose from" and used Google to find information about the mother. He found poems on the mother's website, and he read one of the poems in court. He said the poem gave him "hope for the kids" and convinced him the mother "was not as bitter as he first thought." The Judicial Standards Commission ruled that the judge's behavior "constitute[d] conduct prejudicial to the administration of justice that brings the judicial office into disrepute." The Commission specifically objected to the judge's *ex parte* (outside the courtroom) communications with an attorney in a case before the court and to the fact the judge had been influenced by his own online research, which was not entered into evidence.[81]

LOOKING FORWARD

Social media use in courtrooms is a new and rapidly developing area of the law. Professional communicators and others are advised to pay close attention to developments in their local courts, including the possible adoption of new court rules governing social media and judicial decisions regarding whether smartphones, tablets, and computers can be brought into the courthouse or the courtroom, and, if they are, when they can be used.

Journalists are encouraged to make their voices heard as courts decide how to deal with social media use. Judges who still are uncomfortable with television cameras in court cannot be expected to quickly embrace social media. However, if judges can be convinced that smartphones, tablets, and laptop computers are not as physically and psychologically disruptive as traditional television cameras, they very well might agree that those new technologies can be used in court. Also, professional communicators can argue that social media serve the values that have prompted judges to keep most courtrooms open to the public throughout U.S. history. Social media are the 21st-century means of ensuring that justice is administered fairly, that the public has confidence in the courts, that the public understands the workings of the judicial system, and that communities have outlets for their emotions.

Journalists should report and editorialize on these issues. They also should attempt to become part of the decision-making process by, whenever possible, discussing with judges the use of social media to report from courtrooms.

These discussions should be in both formal and informal settings, individually and with journalistic and judicial professional organizations.

An important issue that apparently has not been addressed is whether citizens will have the same rights to blog or tweet from court as traditional journalists. Who is a reporter in this age of citizen journalism? Professional communicators should weigh in on this issue.

Meanwhile, journalists and others must take responsibility for learning the rules that govern social media use in the courts they cover.

FREQUENTLY ASKED QUESTIONS

1. Can judges forbid citizens or journalists from bringing smartphones or computers into courthouses or courtrooms? If people are allowed to bring their communication devices into the courtroom, does that mean they can use them there?

Courts can and often do forbid people from bringing smartphones or computers into the courthouse. Some courts allow the devices to be brought into the courtroom but do not allow them to be used there. Other courts allow the use of social networking sites such as Twitter in the courtroom. The rules on what technology you can bring to court and whether you can use it there vary from court to court and even from trial to trial. Judges have the authority to decide these matters.

Even if you are allowed to bring a smartphone into a courthouse, though, you may not be able to use it—or to use social networking sites such as Twitter—depending on the judge's rules for such usage.

2. Don't these restrictions violate the First Amendment?

No, because while you do have a strong First Amendment right to be in the courtroom, that right does not include the right to use cameras or recording equipment—or smartphones, tablets, or laptop computers. Many courts have found the use of cameras or recording equipment in the courtroom to be physically and psychologically disruptive, jeopardizing the fair administration of justice.

3. Is "friending" a juror on Facebook during a trial a good newsgathering strategy?

No. This could result in the dismissal of the juror or a mistrial. Judges routinely admonish jurors that they are not to discuss the case with anyone while the case is under way.

4. Can I tweet from my smartphone if the judge can't see me?

No. That's at least unethical and might well be illegal. You could be found in contempt of court. However, once you have posted a tweet, a judge probably cannot make you delete the post without running afoul of the very strong legal rules against prior restraints on the press.

5. Then what should I do?

Ask court officials what media use is allowed, and, if you don't like the answer, try to reason with the judge. Find out what spaces may be fair game, such as courthouse halls or just outside the building, for social networking communications. Also, work with your local professional organizations to encourage your local courts to adopt rules that allow you to use social media to report on courtroom proceedings.

NOTES

1   448 U.S. 555, 580 (1980) (quoting Branzburg v. Hayes, 408 U.S. 665, 681 (1972)).
2   Globe Newspaper Co. v. Superior Court, 457 U.S. 596, 607 (1982); see also Press-Enterprise Co. v. Riverside Cnty. Superior Court, 464 U.S. 501 (1984); Publicker Indus. v. Cohen, 733 F.2d 1059 (3d Cir. 1984).
3   Nebraska Press Ass'n v. Stuart, 427 U.S. 539 (1976).
4   Richmond Newspapers, 448 U.S. at 570–571.
5   Id. at 595–596 (Brennan, J., concurring).
6   Nebraska Press Ass'n, 427 U.S. at 587 (Brennan, J., concurring).
7   See, e.g., United States v. Moussaoui, 205 F.R.D. 183 (E.D.Va. 2002); United States v. Hastings, 695 F.2d 1278 (11th Cir. 1983).
8   Estes v. Texas, 381 U.S. 532, 541 (1965).
9   See, e.g., id.; Sheppard v. Maxwell, 384 U.S. 333 (1966).
10 Estes, 381 U.S. at 536.
11 449 U.S. 560 (1981).
12 Nicole Lozare, More Reporters Tweeting from Courtroom: High-Profile Trials Can Increase Reporters' Followers by Thousands, News Media & The Law, Fall 2011, at 6.
13 Bruce Carton, Is Tweeting From the Courtroom by Reporters Too Distracting for Jurors?, Legal Blog Watch, April 6, 2012, http://legalblogwatch.typepad.com/legal_blog_watch/2012/04/is-tweeting-from-the-courtroom-by-reporters-too-distracting-for-jurors.html.
14 Tom Isler, Tweeting from Courts Still Slow in Catching On, News Media & The Law, Spring 2015, at 3.
15 John Schwartz, As Jurors Turn to Web, Mistrials are Popping Up, N.Y. Times, March 17, 2009, http://www.nytimes.com/2009/03/18/us/18juries.html?pagewantedall. This might be the first time the term was used.
16 Hilary Hylton, Tweeting in the Jury Box: A Danger to Fair Trials?, Time Online, December 29, 2009, http://content.time.com/time/nation/article/0,8599,1948971,00.html.
17 Angus Walker, Judge Bans 50 Cent from Having Electronics in the Courtroom, hotnewhiphop.com (April 7, 2016), http://www.hotnewhiphop.com/judge-bans-50-cent-from-having-electronics-in-the-courtroom-news.20976.html.
18 Estes, 381 U.S. at 551–552.
19 Ahnalese Rushman, Courtroom Coverage in 140 Characters, News Media & The Law, Spring 2009, at 28.

20 Id.

21 United States v. Shelnutt, No. 4:09–CR–14, 2009 WL 3681827 (M.D. Ga. Nov 2, 2009).

22 Id. at *1.

23 Rushman, supra note 17.

24 Id.

25 Id.; see also, Lozare, supra note 12.

26 Shelnutt, 2009 WL 3681827 at *1.

27 Id. at *2.

28 Fed. R. Crim. P. 53 advisory committee's note to 2002 amendment.

29 Rosemary Lane, Lights, Camera and Some Action: The Movement to Expand Cameras into Federal Courtrooms Gets a Few Boosts, News Media & The Law, Fall 2010, at 33.

30 See Court Website Links, http://www.uscourts.gov/about-federal-courts/federal-courts-public/court-website-links (last visited May 11, 2016).

31 Local Rule 83.7 (U.S. Dist. Ct. for M.D.N.C.), http://www.ncmd.uscourts.gov/sites/ncmd/files/CIV_LR.pdf (last visited May 11, 2016).

32 Id.

33 Photography, Broadcasting, Recording and Electronic Devices (U.S. Dist. Ct. for M.D. Ala.), http://www.almd.uscourts.gov/general-orders/general-order-re-photography-broadcasting-recording-and-electronic-devices.

34 Courthouse Security Policies (U.S. Dist. Ct. for D.Conn), http://www.ctd.uscourts.gov/courthouse-security-policies-0.

35 Hollingsworth v. Perry, 558 U.S. 183 (2010).

36 Matthew E. Feinberg, The Prop 8 Decision and Courtroom Drama in the YouTube Age: Why Camera Use Should be Permitted in Courtrooms During High-Profile Cases, 17 Cardozo J.L. & Gender 33, 61 (2010) (citing Hollingsworth, 130 S.Ct. at 719).

37 Louis D. Brandeis, What Publicity Can Do, Harper's Weekly, December 20, 1913, available at https://louisville.edu/law/library/special-collections/the-louis-d.-brandeis-collection/other-peoples-money-chapter-v.

38 Sunshine in the Courtroom Act, H.R. 917, 114th Cong. Sec. 2(b)(1)(A) and Sec. 2(b)(2)(A)(i) (2015); Sunshine in the Courtroom Act, S. 783, 114th Cong. Sec. 2(b)(1)(A) and Sec. 2(b)(2)(A)(i) (2015).

39 Sunshine in the Courtroom Act of 2007: Hearing on H.R. 2128 Before the H. Comm. on the Judiciary, 110th Cong. 125 (2007) (testimony of John C. Richter, U.S. Att'y).

40 Conf. of Court Pub. Info. Officers, New Media Survey 3 (2014), http://ccpio.org/publications/reports/. See, e.g., Md. Rules, Rule 16-110, Cell Phones; Other Electronic Devices; Cameras (Thomson Reuters 2012) (ordering that cell phones must be turned off in the courtroom); Ark. Amin. Order 6(d)(7), Broadcasting, Recording, or Photographing in the Courtroom (2010) (ordering that "[e]lectronic devices shall not be used in the courtroom to broadcast, record, photograph, e-mail, blog, tweet, text, post, or transmit by any other means except as may be allowed by the court"), http://courts.arkansas.gov/rules-and-administrative-orders/administrative-orders.

41 Radio Television Digital News Association, Cameras in the Court: A State-By-State Guide, http://www.rtdna.org/content/cameras-in-court (last visited May 11, 2016).

42 Reporters Committee for Freedom of the Press, Open Court Compendium, http://www.rcfp.org/open-courts-compendium (last visited May 11, 2016).

43 Stacy Blasiola, Say "Cheese!" Cameras and Bloggers in Wisconsin's Courtrooms, 1 Reynolds Courts & Media L.J. 197 (2011).

44 Id. at 197 (citing Ohio ex. rel. Macfarlane v. Common Court of Pleas, No. 10-1771 (Ohio order December 15, 2010)).

45   Id. at 197, 203; see also, Steve Patterson, Appeals Court Tosses Court-Blogging Order Against Jacksonville.com, Jacksonville.com (January 20, 2010), http://jacksonville. com/news/metro/2010-01-20/story/appeals_court_tosses_court_blogging_order_ against_jacksonvillecom#izxx1s2mn8jCO.

46   Id. at 209.

47   Id. at 207.

48   Carton, supra note 13.

49   Adriana C. Cervantes, Note, Will Twitter Be Following You in the Courtroom? Why Reporters Should Be Allowed to Broadcast During Courtroom Proceedings, 33 Hastings Comm/Ent L.J. 133, 148 (2010) (citing Lynne Marek, What Is that Reporter Doing in Court? "Twittering", The National Law Journal March 16, 2009.

50   Rachel Bunn, Reporter's Tweeted Photo of Juror Leads Judge to Declare Mistrial in Murder Prosecution, Reporters Committee for Freedom of the Press (April 16, 2012), http://www.rcfp.org/browse-media-law-resources/news/reporters-tweeted-photo-juror-leads-judge-declare-mistrial-murder-pr.

51   Nebraska Press Ass'n v. Stuart, 427 U. S. 539, 559 (1976).

52   Dianna Hunt, Judge Restricts Reporting on Capital Murder Trial in Fort Worth, Fort Worth Star-Telegram (January 6, 2012).

53   Rachel Bunn, Texas Judge Limits Media Coverage of Murder Trial (January 10, 2012), http://www.rcfp.org/browse-media-law-resources/news/texas-judge-limits-media-coverage-murder-trial.

54   Mark L. Tamburri, Thomas M. Pohl, & M. Patrick Yingling, A Little Bird Told Me About the Trial: Revising Court Rules to Allow Reporting from the Courtroom Via Twitter, 15 BNA Electronic Com. & L. Rep. 1415 (September 15, 2010), available at http://papers.ssrn.com/sol3/papers.cfm?abstract_id=1888025.

55   Id. (citing Pa. R. Crim. P. 112; Order Denying Joint Motion To Bar The Use Of Advanced Technology [Twitter] From Trial, Commonwealth v. Veon, No. CP-22-CR-4656-2008 (Pa. C.P. Dauphin January 25, 2010)).

56   Fed. R. Evid. 606(b) (mandating a new trial if the jury has uncovered prejudicial information on its own. The judge determines whether there is a "reasonable possibility" that the outside research altered the verdict).

57   Sontaya Rose, Juror Misconduct in Fresno County Led to a Mistrial, abc30.com (April 20, 2012), http://abc30.com/archive/8630153/.

58   Timothy J. Fallon, Mistrial in 140 Characters or Less? How the Internet and Social Networking are Undermining the American Jury System and What Can Be Done to Fix It, 38 Hofstra L. Rev. 935, 939 (2010).

59   Judge Dennis M. Sweeney (Ret.), Worlds Collide: The Digital Native Enters the Jury Box, 1 Reynolds Courts & Media L.J. 121, 129 (2011).

60   Id. at 174, 175.

61   Thompson v. Krantz, 137 P.3d 693, 697 (Okla. Civ. App. 2006).

62   Id. at 698.

63   Gareth S. Lacy, Untangling the Web: How Courts Should Respond to Juries Using the Internet for Research, 1 Reynolds Courts & Media L.J. 169, 175 (2011).

64   Id. (citing Real v. Wal Mart Stores, Inc., No. B145819, 2002 WL 80664 (Cal. App. Dist. January 22, 2002)).

65   Eva-Marie Ayala, Tarrant County Juror Sentenced to Community Service for Trying to "Friend" Defendant on Facebook, Fort Worth Star-Telegram.com (August 28, 2011), http://www.tdcaa.com/issues/tarrant-county-juror-sentenced-community-service-trying-friend-defendant-facebook.

66   Id.

67 Meghan Dunn, Jurors' and Attorneys' Use of Social Media During Voir Dire, Trials, and Deliberations: A Report to the Judicial Conference Committee on Court Administration and Case Management, Federal Judicial Center (May 1, 2014), http://www.fjc.gov/library/fjc_catalog.nsf.

68 Joe Palazzolo, Law Blog: Court Tweets: Volume One, Wall St. J. (January 26, 2012), http://blogs.wsj.com/law/2012/01/26/court-tweets-volume-one/.

69 See, e.g., United States v. Fumo, CR No. 06-319, 2009 WL 1688482 (E.D. Pa. June 17, 2009) (finding a juror's postings on Twitter and Facebook during a trial were innocuous and not grounds for a mistrial).

70 Judicial Conference Committee on Court Administration and Case Management, Proposed Model Jury Instructions: The Use of Electronic Technology to Conduct Research on or Communicate about a Case (June 2012), http://www.uscourts.gov/news/2012/08/21/revised-jury-instructions-hope-deter-juror-use-social-media-during-trial.)

71 Lacy, supra note 61 at 176.

72 See, e.g., Tresa Baldas, For Jurors in Michigan, No Tweeting (or Texting, or Googling) Allowed, Nat'l L.J. Online (July 1, 2009); Anita Ramasastry, FindLaw.com Legal Commentary: Why Courts Need to Ban Jurors' Electronic Communications Devices (August 11, 2009), http://writ.news.findlaw.com/ramasastry/20090811.html.

73 See Conf. of Ct. Public Info. Officers, New Media Survey (2014), http://ccpio.org/publications/reports/.

74 See, e.g., Ken Broda-Brahm, Is It Time for the iPad to Replace Paper Notes in Voir Dire?, The Jury Expert (March 30, 2011), http://www.thejuryexpert.com/2011/03/is-it-time-for-the-ipad-to-replace-paper-notes-in-voir-dire/ (reviewing iJuror and Jury Duty, two jury-selection apps for the iPad).

75 See Genelle I. Belmas, That's What "Friend" Is For? Judges, Social Networks and Standards for Recusal, 1 Reynolds Courts & Media L.J. 147, 155 (2011) (discussing Model Code of Jud. Conduct R. 2.11 (2007)).

76 Model Rules of Prof'l Conduct (2011).

77 Model Code of Jud. Conduct R. 2.11 (2007).

78 See Angela O'Brien, Note, Are Attorneys and Judges One Tweet, Blog or Friend Request Away from Facing a Disciplinary Committee?, 11 Loy. J. Pub. Int. L. 511 (2010).

79 Ohio B. Commr's of Grievances & Discip. Opinion 2010-7 (December 3, 2010), available at www.supremecourt.ohio.gov/Boards/BOC/Advisory_Opinions/2010/Op_10-007.doc.

80 For example, the North Carolina Judicial Standards Commission receives written complaints about judicial behavior from citizens, investigates those complaints, and, where appropriate, recommends to the state Supreme Court that the judge be disciplined. See The North Carolina Court System, Judicial Standards Commission, http://www.nccourts.org/Courts/CRS/Councils/JudicialStandards/Default.asp (last visited May 13, 2016).

81 Public Reprimand B. Carlton Terry Jr. District Court Judge, Inquiry No. 08-234, N.C. Jud. Stds. Comm. (April 1, 2009), http://www.aoc.state.nc.us/www/public/coa/jsc/publicreprimands/jsc08-234.pdf; see also, Belmas, supra note 73 at 156–157.

CHAPTER 11

Social Media Policies for Journalists

Daxton R. "Chip" Stewart

Bob Schieffer College of Communication
Texas Christian University

ABSTRACT

As social media tools have become prevalent ways for people to share and connect, journalists have increasingly incorporated these tools into their daily practice. However, the rapid expansion of social media tools has presented challenges for journalists and for news organizations as they seek to engage and inform their audiences while adhering to long held professional norms. This chapter reviews social media policies of several print, online, and broadcast journalism institutions to find common themes and concerns. Major issues addressed in this chapter include transparency, balancing the personal and the professional, maintaining confidentiality, rules for friending and following, intellectual property matters, and breaking news on social media.

The president was in what he thought was an off-the-record discussion with a pool of White House reporters. Less than a week before, Kanye West had famously interrupted country music star Taylor Swift's speech during the Video Music Awards, and a reporter from CNBC casually asked what President Obama thought about West's outburst. An ABC employee, listening on a shared live feed of the discussion, circulated Obama's slightly crude response, and soon after, Nightline co-anchor Terry Moran sent out the following on Twitter: "Pres. Obama just called Kanye West a 'jackass' for his outburst at VMAs when Taylor Swift won. Now THAT's presidential."

Before ABC officials could respond or make a decision regarding whether this should be published, the damage was done. Moran had more than one million followers on Twitter, the microblog site created in 2006 that allows users to share information through "tweets" 140 characters or less in length. Even though Moran later deleted the tweet, the word was out. ABC was widely condemned for its lack of professionalism in the matter, and the network soon issued an apology, noting that its "employees prematurely tweeted a portion of (Obama's) remarks that turned out to be from an off-the-record portion of the interview. This was done before our editorial process had been completed. That was wrong."[1]

Social media tools present great opportunities for communicators, including news media professionals, to engage with the audience in ways impossible just a decade ago. However, the benefits social media allow communicators are tempered by the risks inherent in tools that allow messages to be sent immediately and spread rapidly. Further, laws and professional ethics policies drafted with a 20th-century understanding of mass media may not be in tune with communication tools that emerge, develop, spread, and change constantly.

In the aforementioned situation involving the rogue tweet of a Nightline co-anchor, the statement by ABC News concluded with the following: "We apologize to the White House and CNBC and are taking steps to ensure that it will not happen again."[2] But what steps can media organizations take to prevent embarrassing, unprofessional, or even illegal behavior when its employees use social media tools?

Several news media organizations have developed guidelines and policies for employee use of social media. These have been catalogued and discussed by professionals,[3] and there is no shortage of blog posts about social media risks and best practices warehoused at sites such as socialmediagovernance. com. However, social media policies have not yet been subjected to any greater academic scrutiny in light of the legal and ethical demands of the journalism field. The purpose of this chapter is to build understanding of social media policies in this context, cataloguing the chief concerns of journalists and outlining best practices in developing such policies.

Despite such risks, journalists cannot avoid engaging their audiences through social media. News media companies have incorporated social media into their plans, trying to build online followings as print circulation and broadcast audiences have dwindled. Facebook and Twitter have become essential publishing platforms for journalists, with nearly every newsroom employing a social media editor of some kind.[4] As Snapchat has grown in popularity, particularly among younger audiences, journalists have also begun to explore the platform's possibilities for news, with the New York Times, Buzzfeed, ESPN, the Wall Street Journal, CNN, Fusion, NPR and more establishing a presence.[5]

The widespread use of social media by journalists has triggered most news companies and professional organizations to develop guidelines for best practices, either in their codes of ethics or in stand-alone social media policies. When the Society of Professional Journalists (SPJ) revised its Code of Ethics in 2014, it attempted to make it clear that the principles applied to all forms of communication by journalists, encouraging "use in its practice by all people in all media."[6] Two other major professional groups—the Radio Television Digital News Association (RTDNA) and the American Society of News Editors (ASNE)—have issued guidelines for social media use. However, these have come under fire from several critics who have worked to build community engagement for news media.

In this chapter, the policies of news media companies and professional organizations are reviewed to examine how they define social media tools and determine how guidelines about them should apply, the main topics the policies addressed, and themes regarding the way these organizations advised practitioners to handle the particular challenges of social media. The views of critics who have found these policies to be too restrictive are also presented. The chapter concludes with best practices for designing social media policies for journalists in light of the policies discussed and the previous chapters of this book.

DEFINITIONS AND DESCRIPTIONS OF SOCIAL MEDIA

To provide a foundation for designing best practices for journalists using social media, the way journalism organizations define and describe social media was examined first.

Most journalism organizations reviewed—including the American Society of News Editors, the Associated Press, the *Austin American-Statesman*, the British Broadcasting Corporation (BBC), ESPN, the *Los Angeles Times*, National Public Radio, the *New York Times*, Politico, Reuters, the Radio Television Digital News Association (RTDNA), the *Roanoke Times*, and the *Washington Post*—list specific tools such as Facebook and Twitter in their social media policies. The *New York Times* specifically mentioned LinkedIn, a SNS aimed at connecting professionals.

The tone of the policies and guidelines was generally accepting of the fact that social media had emerged and should be dealt with according to usual newsroom standards. When the Associated Press updated its guidelines in 2011, it moved away from a more restrictive policy to one that encourages all of its journalists to have accounts on social media sites because they have become "an essential tool for AP reporters to gather news and share links to our published work."[7]

The necessity of dealing with social media issues is perhaps best summarized with the following opening passage from the RTDNA guidelines:

Social media and blogs are important elements of journalism. They narrow the distance between journalists and the public. They encourage lively, immediate and spirited discussion. They can be vital news-gathering and news-delivery tools. As a journalist you should uphold the same professional and ethical standards of fairness, accuracy, truthfulness, transparency and independence when using social media as you do on air and on all digital news platforms.[8]

One issue that has arisen is not just what qualifies as social media, but also to whom the guidelines should apply. In 2012, for example, a freelance writer for the *New York Times* engaged in an "insulting and profane" tirade on Twitter against author Jennifer Weiner. The *Times'* associate managing editor for standards, in a company-wide email, made it clear that its social media guidelines "also apply to freelancers in connection with their work for *The Times*." Ultimately, the *Times* suspended the freelance writer from column writing duties for four weeks.[9]

MAJOR THEMES FROM JOURNALISM SOCIAL MEDIA POLICIES

The most comprehensive effort to date to build a social media policy for news organizations was completed by ASNE in 2011, when its Ethics and Values Committee issued its "10 Best Practices for Social Media." The guide includes references to 18 other social media policies from news organizations, and included the following 10 guidelines:

1. Traditional ethics rules still apply online.
2. Assume everything you write online will become public.
3. Use social media to engage with readers, but professionally.
4. Break news on your website, not Twitter.
5. Beware of perceptions.
6. Independently authenticate anything found on a social networking site.
7. Always identify yourself as a journalist.
8. Social networks are tools, not toys.
9. Be transparent and admit when you're wrong online.
10. Keep internal deliberations confidential.[10]

Embedded in these 10 guidelines are several themes common to other social media policies for journalists. These themes include transparency, friending matters, clearance and review, sourcing, balancing personal and private matters, confidentiality, and intellectual property concerns. Each is discussed briefly below.

Transparency

The SPJ Code of Ethics calls for journalists to identify sources when possible and to "avoid undercover or other surreptitious methods of gathering information" in most situations.[11] This call for openness in reporting methods is reflected in the social media policies as well, most of which demand that journalists identify themselves as journalists in two particular circumstances. First, they should always identify themselves as journalists who are representing a particular organization before posting comments or updates on social media sites, blogs, or while commenting on other news stories. As National Public Radio notes:

> Just as we do in the "real" world, we identify ourselves as NPR journalists when we are working online. So, if as part of our work we are posting comments, asking questions, tweeting, retweeting, blogging, Facebooking or doing anything on social media or other online forums, we clearly identify ourselves and that we work for NPR. We do not use pseudonyms when doing such work.[12]

The RTDNA extends this to avatars and forbids anonymous blogging, and Reuters extends it to chat rooms.

Second, journalists should also be transparent about who they are when they contact potential sources for reporting purposes. The *Wall Street Journal* requires that its employees never "us(e) a false name when you're acting on behalf of your Dow Jones publication or service" and always self-identify as a reporter for the *Journal* when gathering information for a story.[13]

Friending and Following

Journalists are called to "act independently" under the SPJ Code of Ethics, in particular by avoiding conflicts of interest, "real or perceived." This concern is at the heart of statements in nearly every news organization social media policy reviewed in this study, reflected by specific guidelines for who can be added to a list of "friends" or what organizations or movements journalists can become a "fan" or "follower" of. Journalists are warned to be careful in who they associate with online for fear of compromising their appearance of independence and neutrality.

First, becoming a "friend" of a source or subject of coverage invites risk. The *New York Times* 2009 policy asked, for example, if reporters can write about someone who is a friend on a SNS before concluding:

> In general, being a "friend" of someone on Facebook is almost
> meaningless and does not signify the kind of relationship that could
> pose a conflict of interest for a reporter or editor writing about that
> person. But if a "friend" is really a personal friend, it would.[14]

The *Wall Street Journal* requires approval by an editor before a source who may demand confidentiality can be added as a friend. "Openly 'friending' sources is akin to publicly publishing your Rolodex,"[15] according to the *Journal*'s policy. Issues can also arise in newsrooms between managers and employees who may be "friends" in social media. The AP says that managers "should not issue friend requests to subordinates, since that could be awkward for employees. It's fine if employees want to initiate the friend process with their bosses."[16]

Second, becoming a friend of a person involved in a controversial issue, or becoming a fan of a movement, may present issues. Reuters notes that its duty to be "responsible, fair and impartial" may be compromised when journalists "'like' a post or adopt a 'badge' or join a 'cause,'" though it defers to the judgment of individual journalists to handle this as circumstances dictate.[17] NPR forbids its reporters from advocating "for political or other polarizing issues online," a policy that extends to using social media "to express personal views . . . that you could not write for the air or post on NPR.org."[18] The *Roanoke Times*, however, is more flexible, advising caution and consistency:

> You may sign up for a group or become a "fan" of something,
> perhaps even to get story ideas, but others could construe that as
> bias toward a business or organization that the newspaper covers.
> If you follow a group or account that represents one side of a
> controversial issue, seek out the group that represents the other
> side and follow them as well . . . Manage your friends carefully.
> Having one source on your friends list but not another is easily
> construed as bias. Be consistent: Accept no sources or people you
> cover as friends, or welcome them all.[19]

Clearance and Review

News organizations generally require journalists to receive clearance from editors or managers before engaging in social media or releasing news items publicly. While most policies were less formal—as NPR advises, "when in doubt, consult with your editor"—others required specific clearances.[20]

ESPN, for example, requires employees to receive permission from supervisors before "engaging in any form of social networking dealing with sports."[21] Similarly, the Roanoke Times requires employees who blog to "notify their immediate supervisor that they have or regularly participate on/contribute to a blog, and talk through any potential conflicts of interests or complications."[22]

Sourcing

The SPJ Code of Ethics requires journalists to "test the accuracy of information from all sources," a demand that can be challenging when reporters use social media tools to engage with sources. A healthy skepticism of sources contacted or uncovered through social media tools is built into many of the news organizations' social media policies.

The RTDNA treats information found on social media sites as similar to "scanner traffic or phone tips,"[23] which must be confirmed independently. Similarly, the Roanoke Times notes that "Facebook and MySpace are not a substitute for actual interviews by phone or in person, or other means of information gathering, and should not be solely relied upon," instead requiring offline confirmation and verification of claims made through these sites.[24]

The Associated Press and the Los Angeles Times specifically extended requirements of verification and authentication to retweeting items found on Twitter. As the AP notes: "Sources discovered [on social networks] should be vetted in the same way as those found by any other means."[25]

Personal vs. Professional

The primary concern expressed in social media policies of news organizations was blurring of the line between a journalist's personal life and his or her professional life. Several policies, such as those of the Los Angeles Times and NPR, suggest that journalists assume that there is no divide between one's professional life and one's personal life. "[E]verything you write or receive on a social media site is public," as NPR notes.[26]

NPR and the New York Times extend this caution to reporters expressing personal opinions, in a similar manner to concerns about following or becoming a "fan" of a political person or movement mentioned above. As the Times notes, "Anything you post online can and might be publicly disseminated, and can be twisted to be used against you by those who wish you or The Times ill—whether it's text, photographs, or video."[27] The AP notes that expressions of opinion "may damage the AP's reputation as an unbiased source of news" and thus employees should avoid "declaring their views on contentious public issues in any public forum" such as social media.[28]

Reuters says its policy is "not to muzzle anyone," but it recommends that employees should "identify ourselves as Reuters journalists and declare that we speak for ourselves, not for Reuters."[29] The *Roanoke Times* is similarly less restrictive, instead suggesting that social media posts "be crafted with concern for how they might reflect on our news products or our reputation for fairness and professionalism."[30]

Confidentiality

Several social media policies demand that journalists avoid revealing confidential information. The AP forbids "(p)osting AP proprietary or confidential material,"[31] while the *Wall Street Journal* advises journalists to avoid discussing "articles that haven't been published, meetings you've attended or plan to attend with staff or sources, or interviews that you've conducted."[32]

Intellectual Property

While a concern about intellectual property rights was not common in these social media policies, they were noted in different ways in a few policies. The *Roanoke Times* and NPR both made it clear that the company owned copyrights on the materials created by its employees and that employees should not violate those rights on social media. As NPR notes, linking to stories on NPR.org is fine, but employees

> may not repost NPR copyrighted material to social networks without prior permission. For example, it is o.k. to link from your blog or Facebook profile to a story of yours on the NPR site, but you should not copy the full text or audio onto a personal site or Web page.[33]

The BBC expressed similar concerns about using creative works elsewhere on the web, encouraging its employees to make sure the BBC has the "necessary rights to any content we put on a third-party site" and that the company is "aware of, and comfortable with, the site's own terms and conditions," which may limit uses to personal or non-commercial purposes.[34]

CRITIQUES OF JOURNALISM SOCIAL MEDIA POLICIES

After the ASNE issued its guidelines—which largely include the themes discussed above—the response from the digital journalism community was swift and hardly complimentary. Steve Buttry, formerly the director of community engagement and social media for the Journal Register Company and a widely-respected news editor, said the ASNE guidelines reflected a fear of social media—"Their need to control remains an impediment to innovation"—and called the underlying policies used as sources "far more fearful and restrictive than they should be."[35] Joy Mayer, a longtime journalism teacher who specializes in audience engagement, noted that there were some good things in the guidelines, but that it also included some "real missteps."[36]

The major critiques of the aforementioned policies particularly targeted two topics: Friending policies and handling breaking news.

Who's a Friend?

The ASNE guidelines caution journalists about whom they follow on Twitter and whom they select as friends on Facebook. This warning came under the heading "Beware of Perceptions," which Buttry said was overly cautious. "The tone of fear and restriction here and in the lengthy discussion of 'friends' is unnecessary," Buttry wrote. "I don't think journalists need more here than simple advice to consider appearances when sharing links and using social media to connect with sources."[37]

Similarly, Mayer expressed concern that such a policy would restrict experimentation among editors. Further, she said that in the discussion of this guideline the ASNE suggests that journalists who friend sources and should then hide their friend lists contradicted another important tenet—transparency.

Breaking News

The most controversial of the ASNE best practices was the call to "break news on your website, not on Twitter." The ASNE policy calls for balance between "getting the information out" and "waiting for a story to move through the editorial pipeline," but it favors holding back breaking news from Twitter because it may damage the "main value" of social media—driving traffic to the news organization's website.[38] This practice was mirrored later in the year when ESPN announced similar guidelines for its employees.[39]

Mayer said she was "horrified" when she first read of the ASNE's policy because it undercut journalists' ability to be "a relevant, quick part of ongoing conversations."[40] Buttry said this guidance was "as foolish as the silly old newspaper fear of 'scooping ourselves' by publishing stories online before they have been in print."[41]

While both Buttry and Mayer said some caution is warranted in breaking news situations, particularly when there are details that need to checked for accuracy, they thought this policy would make it more difficult for journalists to take advantage of the positive aspects of social media—using it as a tool for community engagement, crowdsourcing, and verifying information gleaned from social media users. Buttry offered the example of NPR's Andy Carvin, who would often retweet unconfirmed information from sources during times of strife in the Middle East, but would raise questions and ask his Twitter followers "to help verify and refute" facts streaming in from his various sources.[42]

BEST PRACTICES FOR DEVELOPING SOCIAL MEDIA POLICIES

John Paton, CEO of Digital First Media, once stated his three employee rules for using social media as follows:

"1.
 2.
 3."[43]

This minimalist approach—one that trusts journalists to make responsible decisions while using social media—is the antithesis of the reality for news organizations. In general, news media social media guidelines for employees seem to be quite restrictive, both in terms of what kinds of social media tools are typically used and how they should be used. Critics have rightly assailed these policies as damaging to the essential nature of social media tools. However, the policies from both perspectives so far seem to avoid addressing the legal challenges presented by these tools.

Journalism organizations mostly focused on Facebook and Twitter, and the policies about these seem largely concerned with protecting the organization's status as an objective, neutral reporter of the news. This is to be expected considering the ethical demands of the field. However, it can also be unnecessarily limiting. One of the great benefits of social media tools is enhancing interconnectivity with the audience, and the journalism organization policies seem to inhibit the ability of journalists to engage the audience in this manner. When organizations such as the *New York Times* and NPR do not allow journalists besides those in the business of providing opinions to blog about personal or political matters, it limits how the audience understands who journalists are and what they do. This policy may detract from, rather than enhance, transparency. If journalists cannot publicly "friend" some people or become fans or followers of their organizations, the audience may be left in the dark as to their motivations and affiliations.

Beyond transparency matters, the social media policies for journalists reviewed in this chapter have several weaknesses. For one, they do not specifically address several very important concerns of professionals. For journalism organizations, the rogue tweet of President Obama's off-the-record aside still seems likely to occur. While the policies mention using social media posts as sources of information and seeking clearances for breaking news, handling informal comments and items perhaps not suited for publication may fall in between the cracks of these policies. Further, journalism organizations should approach social media in a more expansive and inclusive manner, recognizing sites beyond Facebook and Twitter.

Location-based applications (such as Foursquare) and review sites (such as Yelp) were rarely mentioned in the policies, suggesting that journalists have either found little use for these tools or are unsure of dealing with any possible dangers they present. As social media tools develop, the social media policies should adapt to handle them. Broad statements of principles that guide engagement through social media tools can help practitioners, but specific advice for different sites is of value as well. These policies should be constantly updated.

Overall, the social media policy debate amongst journalists shows that while individual news organizations have developed social media policies that provide guidance to practitioners, there is much more work to be done to ensure that communicators understand the benefits and risks of the broad array of social media tools. Professional organizations such as SPJ and RTDNA should continue to revise and update their guidelines to make sure they are in line with current technology and the best practices in the field.

FREQUENTLY ASKED QUESTIONS

What Are the Five Things Every Social Media Policy for Journalists Should Address?

1. Transparency

Transparency is a hallmark of journalism. Professional standards require journalists to be honest about who they are and their methods, and deception is strongly discouraged. As such, journalism organizations should require employees to use their real names and to disclose their affiliations when using social media for work purposes. For example, a Twitter account used by J. Jonah Jameson for the *Daily Bugle* should be something along the lines of "JJJameson_DB" or should otherwise include a note that Jameson works for the *Bugle* in his profile information. He should not skulk about using pseudonyms, either on Twitter or while commenting on stories on Facebook or elsewhere.

One of the great strengths of social tools is that they allow interaction with citizens. While citizens may hide behind false profiles or comment anonymously, journalists should not respond in kind, instead promoting honest communication and accountability to the public.

2. Friending and Following

Journalism organizations should make clear what the rules are for journalists who use social media accounts, both in their professional and in their private activities. However, such guidelines should provide some flexibility for journalists to maintain a private life in which they can participate meaningfully in democracy, culture, and relationships.

While fairness and objectivity are noted professional standards for journalists, these concepts have flaws, as noted by Bill Kovach and Tom Rosenstiel in their manifesto, *Elements of Journalism*.[44] More important, they argue, is independence from faction and avoiding conflict of interests. As such, journalists should be able to friend or follow whoever they wish, as long as they remain independent from those friends or causes and are transparent about any connections they may have. One possible policy would be urging journalists to maintain separate professional and private accounts—one for business, one for personal connections. However, even then, skeptical members of the public or subjects of coverage may uncover the journalist's private account, leading to potential embarrassment for his or her organization.

To avoid the appearance of conflict of interest or bias, once a journalist follows or friends one side of a cause, he or she should look to follow/friend other sides as well. And, perhaps most essentially, journalists should make clear in their profiles that personal statements are their own and not representative of their employer's thoughts.

3. Intellectual Property

Intellectual property matters—particularly copyright—present some of the greatest challenges for journalists using social tools. Journalism organizations should ensure that employees are of the mindset that anything not created by the organization needs permission from the copyright holder before it can be republished.

This means that hosting photographs, YouTube videos, and text from sites other than your own are all potentially dangerous. True, news reporting is one of the categories protected by the fair use doctrine (see Chapter 4), but because news is a commercial use, and because photographs and videos are typically used in full, there is a strong likelihood that republishing them for news purposes does not qualify as fair use. Using trademarks is another matter—logos and such used for news reporting purposes has stronger protection under the Federal Trademark Anti-Dilution Act—but still, journalism organizations should be cautious of such uses without permission.

Therefore, journalism organizations should get in the habit of asking permission to use the works of others. Social media guidelines should establish a process for seeking permission and confirming that it has been granted. And when in doubt, journalists should seek the aid of their attorneys before publishing something that could cost the organization damages for infringement.

4. Sharing and Retweeting

The culture of social media is one of sharing, and journalists should recognize this for effective use of social tools. However, the culture of sharing does not automatically mean sharing has strong legal protections.

First, before posting the video, audio, or words of another person, journalists should consider potential intellectual property and copyright issues (see Intellectual Property, above and in Chapter 4). Then, journalists should provide proper attribution for the source of the shared material. If a reporter hears a news tip or breaking story from another organization, he or she should note the source in the social media post—for example, by using the HT ("hat tip") notation in Twitter.

The easiest and most widely accepted form of acknowledgment is the hyperlink. Journalism organizations should take advantage of linking to provide both background to their stories and credit where it is due.

Another very easy way to share information gathered by or stated by others on Twitter is the retweet, which has caused headaches for several news organizations such as the Associated Press, which generally discourages retweeting as a form of reporting. Retweeting is Twitter's form of sharing—either a link, a photo, a video, or even a tip or snippet of information provided by citizens. The culture of social media makes it clear that retweeting is not an endorsement, or even a statement that the underlying information is truthful. It's more of a "heads up" to the audience—though if a journalist has doubts about the veracity of a statement, or if it is yet to be independently confirmed, the journalist certainly should make this clear in the process of sharing.

Nothing in the law makes retweeting particularly dangerous for news organizations—Section 230 of the Communications Decency Act provides a robust shield against defamation and other tort actions for republishing the posts of others online (see Chapter 2). The greater concerns are accuracy and timeliness, both of which can be handled through proper use of social tools.

5. Breaking News

There is simply no legal justification for the notion that journalists should avoid breaking news via social media. If a journalist is confident in the facts and sourcing enough to publish, the consequences for error will likely be the same for publication online as it would be if the statement were made in broadcast or print.

While caution may be urged—for example, contentious issues or factual discrepancies should be cleared by an editor or lawyer before publishing on Twitter—journalists should feel comfortable publishing on a social platform. Twitter and Facebook are tools for publishing, not their own publications. News organizations may very well have strategic or financial considerations in mind when establishing a "no breaking news on Twitter" rule, but the law should be no more barrier for publishing online than it is offline.

Further, publications via social media have the opportunity to be corrected in real time. Previous social media posts can be deleted, though this may interfere with the goal of transparency. Instead, social media posts can include updates and corrections to steer the audience to accurate, updated information.

In short, if a news organization isn't comfortable publishing something, it shouldn't. The platform for publishing makes very little difference in the eyes of the law.

NOTES

1 Clint Hendler, Pinning Down the "Jackass" Tale, Columbia Journalism Rev., September 18, 2009, http://www.cjr.org/transparency/pinning_down_the_jackass_tale.php.
2 Id.
3 Pamela J. Podger, The Limits of Control, Am. Journalism Rev., August/September 2009, 32.
4 Melanie Stone, Social Media Editors in the Newsroom: What the Job Is Really Like, MediaShift, March 17, 2014, http://mediashift.org/2014/03/social-media-editors-in-the-newsroom-what-the-job-is-really-like/
5 See Talya Minsberg, Snapchat: A New Mobile Challenge for Storytelling, N.Y. Times, May 18, 2015, http://www.nytimes.com/times-insider/2015/05/18/snapchat-a-new-mobile-challenge-for-storytelling/?_r=0; Joseph Lichterman, Snapchat Stories: Here's How 6 News Orgs Are Thinking about the Chat App, NiemanLab, February 23, 2015, http://www.niemanlab.org/2015/02/snapchat-stories-heres-how-6-news-orgs-are-thinking-about-the-chat-app/.
6 Society of Professional Journalists, SPJ Code of Ethics (2014), http://www.spj.org/ethicscode.asp.
7 Associated Press, Social Media Guidelines for AP Employees 1 (2015), http://www.ap.org/Images/Social-Media-Guidelines_tcm28-9832.pdf.

8 Radio Television Digital News Association, Ethics: Social Media and Blogging Guidelines (2012), http://www.rtdna.org/pages/media_items/social-media-and-blogging-guidelines1915.php.

9 Margaret Sullivan, After an Outburst on Twitter, The Times Reinforces Its Social Media Guidelines, N.Y. Times, October 17, 2012, http://publiceditor.blogs.nytimes.com/2012/10/17/after-an-outburst-on-twitter-the-times-reinforces-its-social-media-guidelines/.

10 James Hohmann & the 2010–2011 ASNE Ethics and Values Committee, 10 Best Practices for Social Media: Helpful Guidelines for News Organizations 3 (May 2011), http://asne.org/portals/0/publications/public/10_best_practices_for_social_media.pdf.

11 Society of Professional Journalists, supra note 6.

12 National Public Radio, NPR Ethics Handbook: Social Media (2012), http://ethics.npr.org/tag/social-media/.

13 J.D. Lasica, Wall Street Journal's Social Media Policy, SocialMedia.biz, May 14, 2009, http://www.socialmedia.biz/social-media-policies/wall-street-journals-social-media-policy/.

14 The *New York Times* policy was an internal memo circulated by standards editor Craig Whitney and sent to Poynter.org in 2009. J.D. Lasica, New York Times Social Media Policy, SocialMedia.biz, January 19, 2009, http://www.socialmedia.biz/social-media-policies/new-york-times-social-media-policy/. It is unclear whether the *Times* still employs this policy; in 2011, Liz Heron, the *Times'* social media editor, said the company's policy was basically "use common sense and don't be stupid." Noah Davis, The New York Times Social Media Strategy Boils Down To "Don't Be Stupid," Business Insider, May 23, 2011, http://articles.businessinsider.com/2011-05-23/entertainment/29997911_1_facebook-chat-code-common-sense.

15 Lasica, supra note 13.

16 Associated Press, supra note 7 at 3.

17 Reuters Handbook of Journalism, Reporting from the Internet and Using Social Media (2016), http://handbook.reuters.com/index.php/Reporting_From_the_Internet_And_Using_Social_Media.

18 National Public Radio, supra note 12.

19 The Roanoke Times, Professional Standards and Content Policies, July 21, 2015, http://www.roanoke.com/site/professional_standards.html

20 National Public Radio, supra note 12.

21 ESPN, Social Networking for Talent and Reporters (2011), http://www.espnfrontrow.com/wp-content/uploads/2011/08/social-networking-v2-2011.pdf.

22 Roanoke Times, supra note 19.

23 Radio Television Digital News Association, supra note 8.

24 Roanoke Times, supra note 19.

25 Associated Press, supra note 7.

26 National Public Radio, supra note 12.

27 Lasica, supra note 13.

28 Associated Press, supra note 7 at 1.

29 Reuters, supra note 17.

30 Roanoke Times, supra note 19.

31 Associated Press, supra note 7.

32 Lasica, supra note 13.

33 National Public Radio, supra note 12.

34 British Broadcasting Corporation, Social Networking, Microblogs and other Third Party Websites: BBC Use (2012), http://www.bbc.co.uk/editorialguidelines/page/guidance-blogs-bbc-full#social-media-representatives.

35 Steve Buttry, ASNE Offers Good Advice on Social Media, But Too Much Fear and Not Really "Best Practices," The Buttry Diary, May 12, 2011, http://stevebuttry.wordpress.com/2011/05/12/asne-offers-good-advice-on-social-media-but-too-much-fear-and-not-really-best-practices/.

36 Joy Mayer, Good advice interspersed with real missteps in ASNE's social media best practices, Donald W. Reynolds Journalism Institute, May 12, 2011, http://www.thankthis.com/r/Q606Fq6aT02bsRvwnIATaQ:3g_zM1ILVq4ae7L6eEAi_vBm-skW_D5s7sIp-cNxZRsA.

37 Buttry, supra note 35.

38 Hohmann, supra note 10 at 8.

39 ESPN, supra note 21.

40 Mayer, supra note 36.

41 Buttry, supra note 35.

42 Id.

43 John Paton, JRC Employee Rules for Using Social Media, Digital First, April 30, 2011, http://jxpaton.wordpress.com/2011/04/30/jrc-employee-rules-for-using-social-media/.

44 See Bill Kovach & Tom Rosenstiel, Elements of Journalism (2007).

CHAPTER 12

Social Media Policies for Advertising and Public Relations

Holly Kathleen Hall

Arkansas State University

ABSTRACT

The increasing use of social media strategies and tactics in advertising and public relations leave some feeling a loss of control—leaders and managers are losing some control over what employees, consumers, and others say about their organization. But all control is not lost. After a number of brand-damaging incidents, more and more public relations practitioners are recommending and drafting policies and guidelines for the appropriate use of social media. Particular areas of attention include the importance of transparency and the need to disclose any conflicts of interest in order to avoid deception or manipulation of relationships with consumers and respecting privacy.

Organizations are increasingly discovering they need to be utilizing social media strategies and tactics in their public relations plans and campaigns. With the definition of social media comprising "a group of Internet-based applications that . . . allow the creation and exchange of user-generated content," many companies are feeling some loss of control over the conversation and grappling with the power shift to the consumer.[1] However, all power is not lost. After a number of brand-damaging incidents, more and more organizations are drafting policies and guidelines for the appropriate use of social media.

While many companies already have general communication policies in place, such as how to handle media interviews, social media presents some unique challenges. Particular areas of attention include the importance of transparency and the need to disclose any conflicts of interest in order to avoid deception or manipulation of relationships with consumers, as well as issues regarding privacy and the boundaries of labor laws. This chapter will address those concerns as well as examine successful and unsuccessful policies, and provide a framework for drafting effective and dynamic social media guidelines. Every company and campaign is unique and will differ on what is appropriate, in some respects. Yet, there are some standard principles that can be applied universally.

USES OF SOCIAL MEDIA IN THE PUBLIC RELATIONS INDUSTRY

The appeal of social media in public relations is multifaceted. Social media can provide instantaneous feedback from consumers or potential consumers and an unparalleled level of engagement with audiences. Social media is less about selling products and more about helping solve consumers' problems, whereby the organization's brand and reputation is enhanced and the organization positions itself as the trusted expert in their particular area. This new communication dynamic also means a lot of the power and access to data has transferred from the organization (or the mass media) to the consumer. Alex Bogusky, co-founder of Crispin Porter + Bogusky likened the shift to the once powerful notion of secret ingredients: "I think of the obsolete notion of secret ingredients in food. Remember secret ingredients? Secret ingredients point to the old power. The new power is in transparency."[2]

When social media programs are executed well, the benefits to the brand can be exponential. When implemented incorrectly, the consequences range from no translation to the bottom line to big time losses and a brand that is irreparably damaged; from the loss of one or two customers to thousands of customers; from the loss of one or two ill-thinking employees to a major lawsuit against the entire organization. And that means money damages and attorneys' fees in addition to a tarnished reputation. With so much at stake, organizations are increasingly implementing and reviewing social media policies, with a 20% increase in the number of organizations implementing policies between 2013 and 2014.[3]

We're Losing Control!

"On the one hand, there's a lot of demand for the business to be out on social media, and there's a lot of need to be out there—but on the other hand, you don't want to do anything to destroy the reputation or change it in ways you really can't control," said Doug Chia, assistant general counsel for Johnson & Johnson. "Once you're out on social media, the expectations for transparency are much higher than they otherwise are."[4]

One of the issues associated with the loss of control is that some people feel too comfortable being extremely transparent. As chief counsel for the Pennsylvania School Boards Association puts it, "The thing about social media that seems to lead to difficulties . . . is that people tend to say and reveal things about themselves . . . that years ago, they wouldn't say in a roomful of friends, and yet they feel comfortable writing about it online."[5]

Hence, there is a litany of social media mishaps that provide solid proof of the need for social media policies. Take, for example, the Domino's Pizza employees who weren't afraid to video themselves and post the video on YouTube displaying numerous health code violations while preparing food in the most lewd manner possible.[6] Other instances of over-sharing tend to deal with disgruntled employees who air their grievances on a social medium and, many times, face the consequences from a slap on the wrist to being fired. Often, because of the novelty of the first few social media–legal cases, there is much publicity and it usually does not reflect positively on the organization.

Despite the lessons of recent years, the statistics showing how many companies actually have social media policies are dismal. One study from 2010 showed 29% of American companies have drafted some formal guidelines for their employees.[7] Peter Vogel, a Dallas attorney and Internet expert, gave speeches to chief information officers in Atlanta, Boston, and Philadelphia in 2010 in which he asked how many of the companies represented had social media policies. The estimate of the response was in the range of 10 to 15%.[8] Another study from eMarketer noted the rate of companies without social media policies in early 2010 was at 69%.[9] A 2014 study reported the figure at 80%.[10] Whatever the true number is, the fact remains that countless organizations remain unprotected and are at risk. While many people continue to envision the Internet as a great unenforced marketplace or Wild West where all kinds of misbehavior is perfectly acceptable, the medium is actually developing "certain customs, ethical standards and unspoken social interactions."[11]

The inability to control the message in the marketplace is the major reason cited as to why some organizations outright forbid their employees from using social media altogether. This is an impractical approach for companies who need the level of engagement and the data that social media can provide. Instead, strategic communicators should draft social media policies that, as Lansons head of digital Simon Sanders noted, "set the boundaries of what can be said and offer guidelines on how it can be said. As much as they restrict, they also enable and empower, giving freedom within a framework."[12]

Without that framework, some kind of harm is very probable. We need only look to a few examples to see the kind of damage a single tweet can do. In March 2011, an employee of New Media Strategies, the agency responsible for Chrysler's consumer-facing Twitter account, tweeted, "I find it ironic that Detroit is known as the #motorcity and yet no one here knows how to f***ing drive." Chrysler dropped the agency, fearing the resulting firestorm from the tweet would impair their relationship with the Motor City.[13] Around the same time, attention turned to the aftermath of the earthquake and tsunami in Japan. Gilbert Gottfried, the voice of the Aflac duck, posted a stream of jokes on his Twitter feed related to the tragedy. In addition to displaying incredible insensitivity, Gottfried's actions had the potential to destroy 75% of Aflac's revenue, which came from Japan. The company soon announced the duck would be voiced by a new actor.[14] Technology company LG attempted to poke fun at Apple in 2014 when complaints poured in to the iPhone maker regarding the "bendability" of its new iPhone 6. The tweet from the LG France account stated, "Our smartphones don't bend, they are naturally curved ;)." That seems innocuous enough. The problem? The tweet was sent from an iPhone and the joke therefore backfired on LG.[15]

And what of the companies who actually have policies in place? A 2010 survey of 261 companies revealed 20% of them took action against an employee for policy violations.[16] A 2014 survey shows a significant increase of over 70% of businesses taking some kind of disciplinary action against an employee for social media misuse, compared to 35% from the same survey in 2013.[17] However, companies actually have to monitor social media and be aware of their policies. In a 2010 poll conducted by Deloitte, one-fifth of respondents claimed their organization does not monitor their social media. Data from 2014 indicates 36% of employers actively block access to social media.[18] Garter, Inc., an information technology and research advisory company, predicted that in 2015 the percentage of employers monitoring employee social media accounts would rise to 60%.[19] If the organization is not monitoring and is involved later with a lawsuit dealing with social media, it can be problematic in terms of finding and handing over data during the discovery process.

So, policy or no policy, how do you know if you are at risk? As far back as 2007, Michael Wiley, head of digital strategy at Edelman, cautioned organizations to "adapt or die" and that "those who fail to stay abreast of change in today's 'conversation society' do so at their own risk." He offered a list of questions to ask yourself to gauge whether your organization is at risk or missing the social media boat:

"Who is telling our story?" and "What is the narrative?" The days
of monolithic message ownership are long gone . . . Do you
have a digital and/or social media newsroom? Are your websites
RSS-enabled? . . . Do you have a search engine optimization
strategy? Do you have an employee-centric social media policy?
If your answer to any of these questions is "no", you are missing
opportunities and taking unnecessary risks.[20]

So, are you at risk? What is the likelihood of a Domino's, Chrysler, or
Aflac-type incident in your organization? The key is to participate in the
social media conversation. Provide employees the opportunity to contribute
in those spaces. Give them the freedom. But, provide them with the tools
and principles to guide them in this new environment.

LEGAL CASES AND CONSIDERATIONS

One of the aspects making social media policy development so challenging is
that many times the drafters feel compelled to touch on every aspect of laws
or regulations that might be implicated. This is, obviously, an impossible
task. Some of the most pressing areas of the law that should be considered in
the policy development phase include intellectual property considerations,
labor/union issues, defamation, harassment, privacy, and obscenity.

One of the most interesting legal issues to watch in recent years is how
the U.S. courts have dealt with privacy (see Chapter 3). Three cases in
particular are viewed as groundbreaking. In *Pietrylo v. Hillstone Restaurant
Group*, a federal district court in New Jersey found the restaurant group
liable for violating the Stored Communications Act.[21] Two employees of
the restaurant group developed a password-protected MySpace page in
which they aired their grievances about their employment. A manager
learned of the site and asked for the log-in ID and password. One of the
employees provided the information and the two creators of the site were
fired "for damaging employee morale and for violating the restaurant's
'core values.'"[22] During the trial, the employee stated she felt she had been
coerced into providing the ID and password. The court felt the restaurant
group was at fault; that the managers had not been authorized to view
the site. Had this been a non-password protected site, the outcome might
have been different.

In *Stengart v. Loving Care Agency*, a home health employee used her com-
pany-provided laptop to access her Yahoo! mail account to communicate
with her attorney regarding issues with her work situation.[23] Again, this
was a personal, password-protected site and the court felt this employee
had a certain expectation of privacy in emails to her attorney. This case

also incorporated the aspect of attorney–client privilege. So, does this mean companies cannot monitor workplace computers? Not necessarily. The New Jersey Supreme Court opinion stated:

> Our conclusion that Stengart had an expectation of privacy in e-mails with her lawyer does not mean that employers cannot monitor or regulate the use of workplace computers. Companies can adopt and enforce lawful policies relating to computer use to protect the assets, reputation, and productivity of a business and to ensure compliance with legitimate corporate policies . . . But employers have no need or basis to read specific contents of personal, privileged, attorney-client communications in order to enforce corporate policy.[24]

Perhaps the most fascinating decision was in *City of Ontario v. Quon*. In this case, the city of Ontario, California, combed through an employee's text messages from his city-issued pager to see how many messages were personal or work-related due to overage fees that were being assessed to the city. The legal issue at hand was whether this search violated the Fourth Amendment. The Supreme Court refused to decide whether or not Mr. Quon had a reasonable expectation of privacy. While the Court held the city did not violate Mr. Quon's privacy, the justices acted with an abundance of restraint regarding privacy expectations and new technologies, urging prudence regarding emerging technology and stating:

> Cell phone and text message communications are so pervasive that some persons may consider them to be essential means or necessary instruments for self-expression, even self-identification. That might strengthen the case for an expectation of privacy. On the other hand, the ubiquity of those devices has made them generally affordable, so one could counter that employees who need cell phones . . . could purchase and pay for their own. And employer policies concerning communications will of course shape the reasonable expectations of their employees, especially to the extent that such policies are clearly communicated.[25]

While the absence of a sudden and perhaps inflexible decision from the court was welcome, the case also leaves many questions unanswered for employers and employees alike. The key takeaway from these privacy cases seems to be: Employers need to have a policy in place that specifically and clearly outlines the level of privacy employees can expect in their workplace. And any employer searches conducted of employee sites or content should be done for legitimate business reasons. When courts are determining if an employee had a reasonable expectation of privacy, any employer policy or terms of service-type document will likely be examined to assist in characterizing what is reasonable.[26]

Somewhere in the middle, the right of the employer to protect his or her enterprise collides with the right of an employee to exercise speech that might very well be protected by the National Labor Relations Act, which applies to union and non-union employees. Under the act, employees should be allowed to discuss online "wages, hours, or terms or conditions of employment."[27] So, employers have to determine the fine line between working condition discussions, for example, and disparaging the company's leaders.

The first groundbreaking case relating to workers and social media dealt with an employee of a Connecticut ambulance service who criticized her employer on Facebook, using several vulgarities in ridiculing her supervisor. Regardless, the National Labor Relations Board (NLRB) labeled her speech under the "working conditions" discussion category.[28] In February 2011, the parties settled, leaving the question open as to the range of speech allowed to employees in social media policies. The company did agree to revise its rules, recognizing they were too broad. The case does demonstrate, however, that the NLRB is willing to fight for employees' rights in this area, despite the vulgarities and mocking that may be involved in an employees' postings.[29] Between 2013 and 2014, hundreds of actions were brought by employees under the heading of unfair labor practices regarding the enforcement and maintenance of social media policies. Most of these cases do not go to trial and are settled after the NLRB issues a complaint and the company agrees to modify its social media policy.[30]

In April 2011, the NLRB filed a complaint against Reuters news service after a Reuters reporter, Deborah Zabarenko, sent a Tweet stating, "One way to make this the best place to work is to deal honestly with Guild members." She was verbally scolded over what she considered to be free speech. Reuters did have a policy in place, which it believed to be clear and understandable. Reuters decided to settle and changed its social media policy, recognizing the right of its employees to engage in online discussions about workplace issues.[31]

In May 2011, the NLRB sided with a BMW employee who posted criticisms of his employer on Facebook. The employee was asked and agreed to remove the postings, yet was subsequently let go. The NLRB maintained the discussions qualified as "protected concerted activity."[32] In September 2011, an administrative law judge for the NLRB agreed with the NLRB's position and said BMW had "an overly broad policy about employee speech."[33]

One conclusion we can draw about social media and labor issues is that employers simply cannot have a blanket policy stating employees cannot talk about their organizations. Companies have to be specific about the type of speech that is and is not protected. Speech that has as its purpose improving working conditions including critique of supervisors, should be protected to be in compliance with labor laws, including the National Labor Relations Act (NLRA), and any federal and state laws such as Sarbanes Oxley and whistleblower statutes which would protect employees who complain about working conditions or bring potential fraud to light. Speech that simply defames or insults supervisors would most likely not be protected.

ETHICAL CONSIDERATIONS

The instantaneous, sometimes brutally honest feedback and high level of engagement from consumers stems from organizations that are open and transparent in their social media efforts. What is transparency in the context of social media? Sharlyn Lauby, president of Internal Talent Management defines it like this: "Transparency is about being open, honest, and accountable. It's about responsibility. People are listening to you and making evaluations and decisions based upon what you say."[34] Andy Sernovitz, organizer of BlogWell events, believes transparency is vital: "The number one issue around ethics comes down to disclosure – being honest about your true identity . . . Almost every social media scandal involving brands boils down to a lack of disclosure. The blogosphere expects to know your motivations."[35] The disclosure statement can be shockingly simple. Sernovitz recommends this statement to help disconnect the company views from the individual: "I work for X, and this is my personal opinion."[36]

Sometimes it is not that a person is trying to dupe someone into believing he or she is someone else, rather they omit information that then leaves a false impression. For example, during one of the points at which Facebook revised their terms of service, but barely communicated the change, suspicion and doubt among Facebook users rose.[37] The lesson: even if you aren't purposefully trying to deceive, a less-than-high level of disclosure and transparency can be just as damaging.

Due to those instances, however, when consumers did not know, for example, that someone was being paid by a company to blog about their products, the Federal Trade Commission (FTC) enacted new guides in 2009 prompting disclosure of any such arrangements (see Chapter 5). The guides were revised in 2013 to provide examples and more detail for digital endorsements.[38] The same level of transparency should be in effect for situations where a company has hired a third party to produce social media content, such as blogs, on their behalf. Though that kind of disclosure is not yet required, one could argue that the failure to disclose the true author of those materials is misleading. Without that disclosure, won't consumers think they are truly interacting with someone at the company; not the company's advertising or public relations agency? The FTC is responsible for protecting consumers from misleading or deceptive information, including omissions. While their general philosophy maintains that online communications are subject to the same regulations and principles as traditional media, the FTC finds itself having to step in and carve out specific policies and recommendations for online commercial speech. In addition to the FTC, there are also many groups actively self-regulating.

The Word of Mouth Marketing Association (WOMMA) is a well-respected trade organization that represents the social media industry. WOMMA's code of conduct attempts to guide appropriate behavior in the social media sphere. Of the eight listed standards in the code, the first five are all about disclosure: disclosure of relationships, identity, compensation, being honest in communications, and being compliant with the FTC guides mentioned previously.[39]

A group called SocialMedia.org provides a "Disclosure Best Practices Toolkit" to help organizations "learn the appropriate and transparent ways to interact with blogs, bloggers, and the people who interact with them."[40] The first checklist echoes WOMMA's suggestions, encouraging disclosure of identity, relationships, and compliance with appropriate laws. In addition, it recommends clear disclosure of involvement on all blogs produced by their company or agencies and specifically prohibits the use of pseudonyms or unclear aliases.

Another subject area within transparency is the level of honesty organizations allow within their own ranks. How much dissent and criticism does your company allow without an individual facing discipline or being fired? Alex Bogusky supports a kind of radical transparency: "When you allow people to be transparent within the company construct, then the company gets a soul. It's not the company's soul. It's the soul of every individual that works there. They no longer have to check who they are at the door and reclaim themselves on the way home."[41] It's a philosophy that may not be readily embraced by many organizations, but some healthy organizations welcome some of that rebellious spirit and conflict in order to take the brutal feedback and use it to strengthen the company.

Companies continue to struggle to find the appropriate balance. As Edelman director of strategy Stefan Stern described the considerations, "If social media are to have any energy or vitality to them, employees should feel free to speak openly about their work and experiences . . . But they should always remember that they are employees, and anything they say could be taken as a semi-official company statement."[42] So, how do you encourage, but caution employees without chilling speech? It begins with employees being confident and knowing what the boundaries are. Vogel recommends beginning the process with your existing employee handbook—many of the foundational elements will most likely already be there such as conflict of interest, trade secrets, and anti-harassment policies. They all should apply to the social media realm. Keep the verbiage simple and clear. And proactively encourage social media use by employees, but provide training and guidance.

Lessons can be learned from organizations that began with too restrictive social media policies. The ambulance company case previously discussed involved a company policy that prohibited employees from discussing practically anything about the organization online. There is a high likelihood that such a policy would run afoul of the First Amendment. A union representing teachers in Santa Rosa County, Florida, threatened a lawsuit over the county's "overly restrictive social media policy" in 2010.[43] The policy was a classic illustration of the "thou shalt not" litany. Far from encouraging social media use, it listed with great legal flair all the risks and liabilities associated with social media and email use.

The assumed standard-bearer for an association to guide best practices in public relations social media use, the Public Relations Society of America (PRSA) offers a rather unwieldy 25-page policy for PRSA social media use. While comprehensive, the sheer size of the policy discourages a basic understanding of PRSA's social media use philosophy or beliefs. This demonstrates again the need for conciseness, which in turn leads to understanding. The policy includes sections dealing with communicating via social media, the "rules" of participation, information on measurement, and a specific policy on blogging. Specific legal areas of concern such as copyright, antitrust, and trademark are mentioned. Ethics are alluded to briefly via a referral to the overall PRSA Code of Ethics, which does include provisions such as transparency and disclosure of information.[44]

Organizations who have "done it right" provide some guidance in drafting social media policies. Generally well-regarded policies include those from Kodak, Coca-Cola, Kaiser Permanente, GM, Best Buy, Ogilvy PR, Hill and Knowlton, the British Broadcasting Corporation (BBC), and IBM. The strength of Kodak's policy is in its ability to briefly educate employees on the purpose of different platforms to guide them in their decision as to which format will be of the greatest engagement benefit. Likewise, Coca-Cola aims to educate its employees on the Coca-Cola brand, ensuring that messages stay brand-consistent.[45] As an antithesis to the 25-page PRSA policy, Best Buy offers its no-nonsense, one-page "Be smart. Be respectful. Be human" guidelines.[46] The simplicity and clarity of Best Buy's policy should be emulated by others. The beauty of the BBC policy is in its attempt to foster "conversations" instead of "broadcasting messages," and IBM urges users to "try to add value" by providing "worthwhile information and perspective."[47] General Motors' strength is hardwiring the need for transparency into its policy.[48]

These are examples of some of the principles that can be universally incorporated into any social media policy. Every organization is unique and will have to decide what kind of social media usage will be appropriate and effective. Organizations can begin the policy formulation process by bringing the right team together to set the stage. Mario Sundar, formerly of LinkedIn, advocates bringing in "your most active social media employees to collaborate," which accomplishes two objectives: you have the knowledge base of these social media savvy employees and you have a set of social media evangelists to encourage appropriate social media use.[49] Think about including people from representative areas such as human resources, technology, public relations, and marketing. Once the actual content-crafting begins, consider the can-dos rather than the thou-shalt-nots in order to nurture social media practices. If further clarifications are needed on acceptable use, provide brief illustrations and examples of what is appropriate, rather than tacking on additional "don'ts" or augmenting the policy with legalese.

Suggested content areas can include transparency/disclosure, tone, level of engagement, and liabilities. Some would advise that policies need to "stress the potential reach and impact of information sent over the Internet" as a caution and even require employees to sign forms stating their awareness of workplace equipment monitoring.[50]

While PRSA's own social media policy is lengthy, their toolkit for building a social media policy is a helpful and concise four pages. One particularly valuable piece of advice notes that policies surrounding social media "should morph and grow as social media use and tools evolve, and as an organization forges ahead in the social media landscape and interacts with stakeholders in new ways." PRSA recommends taking a new look at social media policies on an annual basis. In this ever-changing world of social media, it is important to not back the organization into a corner with the policy.

Recognize that social media can also be a powerful and effective tool during a crisis. However, policies and guidelines are needed here, too. If social media is mishandled, it can compound the crisis. Nestlé in 2010 provides an example of how social media made a crisis situation go from bad to worse. Greenpeace called out Nestlé for its use of palm oil, which Greenpeace claimed was obtained in such a way that it harmed rainforests. Consumers began to voice their discontent with this finding through social media. Nestlé was present and engaged. They were monitoring what was being said and they began to respond. So far, so good. Unfortunately, Nestlé's reactions "became problematic when responses lost professionalism and instead became defensive and, at times, juvenile."[51] The lesson learned? Make sure, especially in a crisis, to get the tone right and, like any good crisis communication situation, have a plan. Make sure the employee(s) responding on social media channels know the appropriate framework, tenor, and boundaries.

CONCLUSION

In the end, we are left with this question: Has social media really changed the landscape, or are we just reiterating and expanding existing policies to fit a new medium? As Johnson & Johnson's Doug Chia said, "Social media hasn't changed anything . . . People are blabbing insider information when they're not supposed to. They have been for years."[52] As an HR consultant put it, "It's no different than parents saying to their teenager, 'The stuff you put on Facebook will come back to haunt you in 10 years when you're looking or a job.' You wouldn't scream expletives about your boss, so don't post it."[53] It does seem, however, that there is a singular and unprecedented emphasis on disclosure, transparency, and privacy in social media use and policy development and that courts are still grappling with the unique labor-free speech issues social media presents. Solid policies will be dynamic, touch on transparency and expected privacy levels and do so in a clear, concise, comprehensible way.

No matter the policy or its content, it is worthless if an organization does not adequately train and educate its staff and seek numerous opportunities to communicate the policy's substance. The policy needs to be highly visible, dynamic, understandable, and employee-centric. Laws in this area will continue to evolve; so will social media policies. Is there risk for an organization that uses social media? Yes. Is there potential liability? Yes. Will a good social media policy protect an organization from every possible harm? No. Social media policies are not a cure-all. They are, however, essential. And they need to be well-constructed and administered. Every organization will differ on what they believe is appropriate. But, all organizations should have guidelines, principles, goals, or statements—something that provides a framework, but also freedom.

FREQUENTLY ASKED QUESTIONS

What Are the Five Things Every Social Media Policy for Strategic Communication Should Address?

1. Transparency

Every policy needs to address certain facets of the transparency principle: That you are who you say you are and that the content you write is your opinion. Use the simple statement "I work for X and this is my personal opinion." It is also a necessity that you clearly disclose if you are being given any money, products, or services by an organization you may choose to write about. The statement can be as straightforward as "Company X gave me this product to try."

2. Privacy

Employers can monitor employee social media use—to a degree. Employees will have an expectation of privacy in passwords and areas such as their communications with their attorney. It is vital that employers specifically and clearly state the level of privacy employees can expect in their workplace and as they are working with clients. Something as simple as a Foursquare check-in for a meeting at a client's workplace could be in contradiction to the "Safeguarding Confidences" provision of the PRSA Code of Ethics by revealing the name of a client who may wish to remain private.

3. Employee Control

The National Labor Relations Board seems very willing and eager to step in and fight for an employee's right to express themselves freely on social media sites if the speech relates to working conditions and terms of employment. It is important for employers to realize their policies should not overly-restrict speech, such as including a blanket statement asking employees not to post content about their work, or else they potentially run afoul of the NLRA, Sarbanes-Oxley and other federal and state laws. With this freedom also comes the need for employer responsibility and employee expectations in any monitoring of the conversations taking place. Define the hours and the depth of monitoring taking place.

4. Intellectual Property

While materials are increasingly available and simple to copy online, it is important to give credit where it is due and to ask permission before using someone else's content such as photographs, videos, and logos. Strategic Communicators working for a specific client should also actively monitor the web for suspicious uses of the client's brand for nefarious purposes, such as online impersonation or setting up fake accounts (see Chapter 4).

5. Tone

When the actual policy-crafting begins, approach the discussion with a "here's what we can do" viewpoint rather than creating a catalog of "thou-shalt-nots" to cultivate appropriate social media practices. Provide illustrations to demonstrate acceptable online behavior and discourage negative tone-of-voice and online battles or fights, which can be brand-damaging.

NOTES

1 Andreas M. Kaplan & Michael Haenlein, Users of the World, Unite! 61 Business Horizons (2010).

2 Nutrition Business Journal, Corporations, You Could Be Losing Your Power, Jan. 1, 2011, http://newhope360.com/managing-your-business/bogusky-corporations-could-be-losing-their-power.

3 Proskauer, Social Media in the Workplace Around the World 3.0, April 29, 2014, http://www.proskauer.com/files/uploads/social-media-in-the-workplace-2014.pdf.

4 Melissa Klein Aguilar, Experts Speak on Using Social Media for Good, Compliance Week, June 20, 2010, http://www.complianceweek.com/pages/login.aspx?returl=/experts-speak-on-using-social-media-for-good/article/186783/&pagetypeid=28&articleid=186783&accesslevel=2&expireddays=0&accessAndPrice=0.

5 Adrienne Lu, How Far Can Schools Go in Regulating Teachers' Social Media Use?, Philadelphia Inquirer, March 14, 2011.

6 See Stephanie Clifford, Video Prank at Domino's Taints Brand, N.Y. Times, April 16, 2009, http://www.nytimes.com/2009/04/16/business/media/16dominos.html.

7 Dallas Lawrence, Six Terrific Examples of Social Media Policies for Employees; Smart Companies Stress Education, Transparency, Legal Liability, and Company Goals and Values, Ragan's Report, May 2010, http://www.ragan.com/Main/Articles/6_terrific_examples_of_social_media_policies_for_e_40774.aspx.

8 Cheryl Hall, Don't Have Social Media Guidelines? Get Some. Dallas Morning News, November 21, 2010, http://www.dallasnews.com/business/columnists/cheryl-hall/20101121-cheryl-hall-don_t-have-social-media-guidelines-for-company-then-get-some.ece.

9 Jason Falls, What Every Company Should Know About Social Media Policy, Social Media Explorer, February 3, 2010, http://www.socialmediaexplorer.com/social-media-marketing/what-every-company-should-know-about-social-media-policy/.

10 Proskauer, supra note 3

11 J.D. Lasica, Ethical Guidelines for Talking with Your Customers, SocialMedia.biz, February 16, 2010, http://www.socialmedia.biz/2010/02/16/ethical-guidelines-for-talking-with-your-customers/.

12 PR Week UK, Social Media – What's Your Policy?, November 19, 2010, http://www.prweek.com/uk/features/1041541/.

13 Stuart Elliot, When the Marketing Reach of Social Media Backfires, N.Y. Times, March 16, 2011, http://www.nytimes.com/2011/03/16/business/media/16adco.html.

14 Id.

15 Rebecca Borison, The Top 10 Social Media Fails of 2014, Inc., Dec. 10, 2014, http://www.inc.com/rebecca-borison/top-10-social-media-fails-2014.html.

16 Rita Pyrillis, Companies Grapple with Viral Vents, 89 Workforce Management 6, 6–8 (December 15, 2010).

17 Proskauer, supra note 3

18 Id.

19 Gartner, Gartner Says Monitoring Employee Behavior in Digital Environments Is Rising, May 29, 2012, http://www.gartner.com/newsroom/id/2028215.

20 Michael Wiley, Edelman – Beyond the Buzz: Adapt or Die, PR Week UK, December 7, 2007, http://www.prweek.com/uk/news/772522/Digital-Essays-Edelman—Beyond-buzz-adapt-die/?DCMP=ILC-SEARCH.

21 Pietrylo v. Hillstone Restaurant Group d/b/a Houston's, United States District Court, District of New Jersey, Civil Case No. 2:06-cv-5754-FSH-PS.

22 Brian Hall, Court Upholds Jury Verdict in Pietrylo v. Hillstone Restaurant Group, Employer Law Report, October 19, 2009, http://www.employerlawreport.com/2009/10/articles/workplace-privacy/court-upholds-jury-verdict-in-pietrylo-v-hillstone-restaurant-group/#axzz24I04aHO1.

23 Stengart v. Loving Care Agency, Inc., 990 A.2d 650 (2010).

24 Id.

25 City of Ontario v. Quon, 560 U.S. 746 (2010).

26 Lukowski v. County of Seneca, 2009 WL 467075 (W.D.N.Y. 2009) (finding that the "terms of service agreements between customers and businesses have been considered relevant to characterization of privacy interests").

27 323 N.L.R.B. 244, 1997.

28 Steven Greenhouse, Company Accused of Firing Over Facebook Post, N.Y. Times, November 8, 2010, http://www.nytimes.com/2010/11/09/business/09facebook.html.

29 Philip L. Gordon, Settlement in NLRB's AMR/Facebook Case Contains Message for Employers about Social Media Policies, Workplace Privacy Counsel, February 8, 2011, http://privacyblog.littler.com/2011/02/articles/social-networking-1/settlement-in-nlrbs-amrfacebook-case-contains-message-for-employers-about-social-mediapolicies/.

30 Proskauer, supra note 3

31 Michael Grubbs & Patrick Scully, Back and Forth with the NLRB on Social Media, September 1, 2011, ShermanHoward.com, http://shermanhoward.com/NewsAndEvents/View/1B3CC7DE-5056-9125-63F98B49F10AF963/.

32 See Karl Knauz Motors, Inc., N.L.R.B. A.L.J. No. 13-CA-46452 (2011).

33 Ameet Sachdev, Judge Backs Car Dealer that Fired Employee over Facebook Post, Chicago Trib., October 1, 2011, http://articles.chicagotribune.com/2011-10-01/business/ct-biz-1001-nlrb-20111001_1_facebook-post-karl-knauz-bmw-dealership.

34 Sharlyn Lauby, 5 Ways to Make Your Business More Transparent, Mashable, September 30, 2009, http://mashable.com/2009/09/30/business-transparency/.

35 Lasica, supra note 11.

36 Id.

37 Grubbs & Scully, supra note 31.

38 Federal Trade Commission, How to Make Effective Disclosures in Digital Advertising, March 2013, https://www.ftc.gov/sites/default/files/attachments/press-releases/ftc-staff-revises-online-advertising-disclosure-guidelines/130312dotcomdisclosures.pdf.

39 Word of Mouth Marketing Association, Code of Ethics and Standards of Conduct for the Word of Mouth Marketing Association (2009), http://womma.org/ethics/code/.

40 Disclosure Best Practices Toolkit (2012), http://www.socialmedia.org/disclosure/.

41 Nutrition Business Journal, supra note 2.

42 Supra at note 12.

43 Sarah Evans, Restrictive Nine-Page Social Media Policy Leads to Lawsuit. Employment Law in the Digital Age, August 30, 2010, http://www.lawhed.com/social-media/nine-page-social-media-policy-leads-lawsuit/.

44 PRSA Social Media Policy (2012), http://www.prsa.org/AboutPRSA/Guidelines Logos/SocialMediaPolicy/.

45 Supra at note 7.

46 Best Buy Social Media Policy (2012), http://forums.bestbuy.com/t5/Welcome-News/Best-Buy-Social-Media-Policy/td-p/20492.

47 Chris Lake, 16 Social Media Guidelines Used by Real Companies, EConsultancy. com, December 2, 2009, http://econsultancy.com/us/blog/5049-16-social-media-guidelines-used-by-real-companies.

48 Lawrence, supra note 7.

49 Tiffany Black, How to Write a Social Media Policy, Inc., May 27, 2010, http://www.inc.com/guides/2010/05/writing-a-social-media-policy.html.

50 Keisha-Ann G. Gray, Responding to Criticism on the Web, HREOnline.com, November 2, 2009, http://www.hreonline.com/HRE/story.jsp?storyId=282114 288.

51 PR Week UK, supra note 12.

52 Aguilar, supra note 4.

53 Pyrillis, supra note 16.

CHAPTER 13

The Future of Discourse in Online Spaces

Jared Schroeder

Southern Methodist University

ABSTRACT

As more and more of the discourse in democratic society—the very information exchanges that shape our understandings of important issues—shifts to social media and other networked communication tools, questions arise regarding the ownership of virtual spaces, the nature of our selective relationships with others online, and the place of artificially intelligent and corporate communicators amidst our conversations. This chapter explores emerging questions regarding the differing characteristics between physical public forums and virtual spaces, the capability individuals have to limit the spectrum of ideas they encounter, and the legal and social concerns that arise when non-human communicators insert themselves into our interactions.

Individuals are increasingly likely to express themselves using social media. Whether they are angered or inspired by a politician, political movement, or fellow citizen's comment, people have gotten into the habit of whipping out their mobile device or sitting down in front of their computer and tapping or typing exactly what they are thinking. Such a habit is evidenced in Twitter users surpassing 500 million tweets per day and Snapchat reaching 400 million "snaps" every 24 hours.[1] Social media users are not simply posting about what they had for dinner or funny cat videos, they are engaging in discussions about political candidates and social issues that are important to them and others in society.[2] The emergence of social media, as well as the development and maturation of other network-based communication tools such as blogs, message boards, and comments sections, during the first part of the 21st century has raised important questions about the future of generally free expression and discourse in democratic society. Indeed, it is not much of a stretch to contend that social media have come to occupy, practically, if not legally, the idealized public spaces that have been at the heart of how legal scholars and philosophers have understood communication in a democratic society since, as the Supreme Court has consistently stated, "time out of mind."[3] Individuals' tendency to adopt social media as a 21st-century embodiment of the 20th-century soapbox, a place upon which they can stand up amidst a crowd and communicate ideas and grievances about a range of issues, raises important and largely unanswered questions about the future of discourse in a democratic society. Among these questions are: What are the limits of expression within corporately controlled and individually curated virtual communication spaces, such as social media platforms, as public forums, and what role will artificially intelligent speakers, often referred to as "bots," play in online discourse?

These questions have arisen as a result of the massive expansion and adoption of networked communication technologies. As sociologist Manuel Castells explained, the emergence of the network era during the waning years of the 20th century is fundamentally unique to other eras in history because it is based on *information* itself.[4] The industrial revolution, for example, produced massive, widespread economic, social, and political change as manufacturing technologies and fossil fuels altered the way people lived. The network era has brought similar shifts to how people live, but the changes are being multiplied by the information-based foundation of the era. Castells concluded that, "What characterizes the current technological revolution is not the centrality of knowledge and information, but the application of such knowledge and information to knowledge generation . . . in a cumulative feedback loop between innovation and the uses of innovation."[5] A part of this fundamentally information-based revolution is the fact that the ability to communicate messages to audiences no longer remains in the hands of those who own printing presses or broadcast television licenses, as was the case as the primary understandings regarding First Amendment law developed during the 20th century.

Discussion regarding networked technology's potential as democratizing force in communication within society arose before the participatory nature of Web 2.0, which started in 2004, had been realized. Justice John Paul Stevens, in the seminal case regarding freedom of expression online, identified networked technologies as "vast democratic fora" and tools that can make "any person with a phone line . . . a town crier with a voice that resonates farther than it could from any soapbox."[6] Scholars shared similar perspectives regarding the potential networked technologies held to free individuals from the limitations imposed by traditional media gatekeepers, and to allow a purer version of the marketplace of ideas than was physically possible when Justice Oliver Wendell Holmes wrote the popular theory of the First Amendment into the Supreme Court's lexicon in 1919.[7] Now, two decades after the Court's ruling in *Reno v. ACLU* and nearly a century after Justice Holmes's discussion of the "free trade in ideas" in his dissent in *Abrams v. United States*,[8] the unknown potential within the "vast democratic fora" that Justice Stevens and others could only speculate about has come into clearer focus. With that clearer focus have come new, or at least revised, questions about the future of discourse in democratic society. The emergence of social media and other network-based communication tools raise new questions about the carefully developed philosophical and legal precedents regarding the nature of discourse among free individuals in public forums. These questions are especially pertinent as the fourth-generation of networked communication approaches, an era that scholars have concluded will be characterized by involved, interactive relationships between humans and machines.[9] For these reasons, the roots of these questions stretch in several directions, many of which have been carefully considered in the preceding chapters. Looking forward, these questions share a common concern about the future of a central element of democracy— discourse—and the ability of individuals to send and receive information in order that citizens can conduct discourse and be self-governing.

SOCIAL MEDIA AS A FAUX PUBLIC FORUM

When individuals engage with others using social media, or other online tools that allow similar interactions, such as comments sections or message boards, they browse messages left by others, respond to messages, or create messages. In other words, they commonly engage in ongoing, a-synchronous, or real-time interactions. In this sense, networked communication technologies can be seen as embodying, and even substantially improving upon, many of the characteristics of interactions that take place in traditional physical public forums. A part of that improvement addresses the accessibility of potentially mass communication tools by citizens. Relatively cheap smartphone and other computing technology, along with general accessibility to the Internet, have made it far easier for individuals to step into discussions in virtual spaces than was ever possible in physical public spaces. As a result of this and other changes, social media have moved from a trendy new tool for teens and college students to communicate to a part of every day life for more than two-thirds of Americans—all in about a 10-year span.[10] About 90% of young adults, those between 18 and 29 years old, take advantage of the accessibility of social media as tools for expression. Indeed, social media have become a dominant form of self-expression, and a powerful tool for news organizations to reach audiences and for persuasive messages, such as advertisements, to use self-disclosed and online tracking data to target just the right potential customers.[11] The interactive nature of social media and other network-based communication tools, such as message boards and comments sections, allow all of these speakers, big and small, to do more than communicate one-way messages, as was dominant with 20th-century forms of media.[12] These emergent tools allow interactivity. Social media sites are structured to allow interaction and, not surprisingly, they have become massively popular virtual discussion spaces for discussions ranging Justin Bieber's hair to presidential politics.

The second, and related, key perceived improvement networked communication tools make upon traditional spaces is that online messages can instantaneously reach individuals nearly anywhere in the world, thus in many ways mitigating two of communication's oldest problems—space and time. Nearly every advancement in media-related technology has sought to improve the speed at which information reaches audiences. The Internet, for the most part, has ended that progression. The power to send instantaneous messages across great distances has allowed for the creation of virtual communities, which allow individuals who in the past would have remained ideologically or geographically isolated because of limitations they faced in their ability to connect meaningfully with others to find connections and reinforcement from others who are online.[13] Such characteristics enhance the potential for discourse among individuals who share common ideas, concerns, or interests online. Crucial differences, however, remain between traditional public forums and virtual forums, including the matter of who owns online spaces, the homogeneous nature of online relationships as they compare to interpersonal interactions, and the growing impact of non-human speakers.

OWNERSHIP OF VIRTUAL SPACES

The traditional public forums the Supreme Court and philosophers have identified as intrinsically necessary for discourse in democratic society are shared *public* spaces, those owned by the people and maintained by the government on behalf of the public. For spaces such as these, the courts have constructed a relatively strong set of legal precedents that justify the widest possible scope of protection on the basis of the freedoms contained within the First Amendment.[14] Though the Supreme Court has qualified the time, place, and manner of the expression in such forums at times,[15] justices have generally found public spaces are held "in trust for public use"[16] and characterized them as being associated with "free exercise and expressive activities."[17] Chief Justice John Roberts, in writing for a unanimous

Court in the abortion protest case *McCullen v Coakley* in 2014, reiterated the Court's ardent support of relatively unfettered discourse in public spaces by contending that, "petitioners wish to converse with their fellow citizens about an important subject on the public streets and sidewalks—sites that have hosted discussions about the issues of the day throughout history."[18] To protect discourse in such spaces, the courts have used the intermediate scrutiny test, which requires that any time, place, and manner restriction on expression in a public space must not be content-based, cannot halt all avenues through which the ideas can be communicated, must align with a valid government interest in restraining the expression, and must be narrowly tailored to fit with the government interest and not go beyond it to limit other forms of expression.[19]

Such carefully crafted protections against limitations on expression do not yet exist in virtual spaces. Unlike traditional, physical public forums, those spaces that the Court has clearly identified as shared, protected spaces for discourse, virtual spaces are owned by corporations and almost uniformly require users to agree to a code of conduct through terms of service agreements drafted by the companies that have created the space. This difference does not automatically mean that virtual public forum-like spaces, such as Twitter, offer no protection against limitations on expression. Facebook creator Mark Zuckerberg has spoken publicly about his support of free speech.[20] Google has pages on its company website that are devoted to advocating free expression on the Internet.[21] The difference in the ownership of virtual spaces does mean, however, that such corporations are not required to follow the laws and legal precedents that have been carefully constructed for physical public forums with the First Amendment as their guide. Twitter, for example, revised its code of conduct in 2015 to justify more expansive understandings of harassment and intimidation, thus broadening the range of speech that is not protected on the social media outlet.[22] Aside from creating and interpreting its own rules for expression, Twitter also raised questions about its policies when it temporarily deleted British journalist Guy Adams' account during the London Olympics in 2012.[23] Adams had harshly criticized NBC's Olympics coverage on Twitter, eventually posting the email address of one of NBC's executives. NBC and Twitter had formed a business partnership during the games. Public backlash over the corporation's actions drove Twitter to ultimately apologize for its actions and reinstate the account.[24] Importantly, the corporations that own social media platforms decide, with their interests in mind, the amount of expression that will be allowed. Such allowances are generally outlined in codes of conduct or community guidelines. These agreements, a requirement before using a social media platform, generally state that users cannot: "defame, stalk, bully, abuse, harass, threaten, impersonate or intimidate" others, as Instagram's terms of use document outlines.[25] While in certain circumstances similar speech in physical public forums might also face limitations, any such restriction must align with the First Amendment and a long line of related legal precedents that generally halt government limitations on expression unless they represent a valid time, place, or manner restriction.[26]

In 1984, for example, Gregory Lee Johnson burned an American flag in protest outside of the Republican National Convention in Dallas. While no one was harmed, many said they were offended by Johnson's actions.[27] Johnson was arrested under a state statute, but the Supreme Court ultimately confirmed the state court's decision to overturn his conviction, concluding that the bedrock principle of the First Amendment is "that the government may not simply prohibit the expression of an idea simply because society finds the idea itself offensive or disagreeable."[28] While it is not possible to burn a physical flag in a virtual space, it is reasonable to conclude that ideas that are interpreted as offensive or disquieting by those who use or moderate social media spaces can easily be removed in the name of keeping the peace and with the backing of the outlet's code of conduct. Such a tendency to seek peace by suppressing or punishing speech that is offensive to individuals in physical spaces has, for the most part, been halted by Supreme Court precedents like the one in *Johnson*. The Supreme Court upheld a man's right to where a jacket that read "Fuck the Draft" in a courthouse and the right of members of the Ku Klux Klan to burn a cross in protest of the government.[29] Similar actions in virtual spaces, such as Facebook or Instagram, would likely, according to the wording of the various codes of conduct, lead to the deletion of the communicator's account.

Importantly, those who own the popular, community-creating spaces online can limit speech without any concern about First Amendment protections. Corporations that host online forums, such as Facebook and YouTube, employ people who seek out harassing and offensive messages.[30] Such moderators do not have to align their decisions with First Amendment principles. Snapchat's community guidelines, for example, state that the company will "remove the offending content or terminate your account" if a person violates the rules.[31] Instagram's decision to delete any image that includes nudity, even if it is an artistic or creative work, drew the social media platform into the "Free the Nipple" campaign regarding gender equality in 2014.[32] Instagram has deleted topless images posted by celebrities, such as Chelsea Handler, Miley Cyrus, and Rihanna, leading to criticism that it is a double standard that men can be topless on Instagram but women cannot do so without violating the community standards. Handler posted a topless photo of herself that parodied a popular picture of Russian President Vladimir Putin shirtless on horseback. When the photo was removed for violating Instagram's standards, she tweeted, "Taking this down is sexist.

I have every right to show I have a better body than Putin."[33] Instagram has not backed down from its nudity policy, making the guidelines stricter in April 2015.[34] Twitter outlines that indirect threats, harassment, "hateful conduct," and other actions are grounds for accounts to be deactivated or removed.[35] In 2016, Twitter announced that, after meetings with government officials, it had deleted tens of thousands of accounts that were thought to be connected with terrorism.[36] While such a decision might thwart terroristic efforts, it raises questions about the criteria the company uses to delete such vast swaths of accounts. In short, First Amendment protections generally have historically been understood as protecting individual expression in public forums from limitation by the government. Social media companies have different legal requirements than the government. As corporations, they face few legal hurdles in halting speech that they or others find disagreeable. The marketplace of ideas, in the instance of social media, can be compared to trying to conduct discourse in a Wal-Mart. The property owner is generally happy for you to frequent the establishment, but might remove you if your ideas are unpopular or potentially damaging to their business enterprise. While this may be an oversimplification, since many social media outlets have been outspoken in their beliefs in freedom of expression, the fact remains that platforms such as Twitter and Instagram have removed speakers who communicate unpopular ideas.[37] Such a dynamic is substantially different than the underlying ideas behind the public-forum concept, raising concerns about the future of discourse in a democratic society, when such interaction substantially takes place on social media.

ECHO-CHAMBERS, HOMOGENEITY, AND SELF-PRESENTATION

The ways social media systems are constructed provide another discourse-influencing difference between traditional, physical public forums and online spaces. While social media interfaces vary, most allow users to curate how they wish to present themselves and who can and cannot see their information and communicate with them. Facebook, for example, is based on "friend" requests. Twitter and Instagram are based on followers. Since social media allow users to draw only those who they wish to connect with into their networks, delete or block messages they do not wish to encounter, and remove those who they dislike, individuals can limit the range of ideas they encounter while, at same time, selecting how they seek to present themselves. As Sherry Turkle, a pioneer in studying the impacts of networked-based communication explained, "Our networked life allows us to hide from each other, even as we are tethered to each other."[38] Such capabilities differ substantially from those that are inherent in traditional public forums, where physical presence tends to limit individuals' abilities to construct strategically beneficial profiles of themselves and provides those with differing views generally equal rights to be present within the physical space. Protestors from Westboro Baptist Church, with their "God Hates Fags" and "Thank God for Dead Soldiers" messages at military funerals and other emotional moments, for example, have a right to communicate their beliefs regarding the sin of the nation and God's wrath on public property, as the Supreme Court concluded in *Snyder v. Phelps*.[39] Chief Justice Roberts, in writing for the Court, explained, "Westboro believes that America is morally flawed; many Americans might feel the same about Westboro. Westboro's funeral picketing is certainly hurtful and its contribution to public discourse may be negligible. But Westboro addressed matters of public import on public property."[40] The Patriot Guard Riders who attend military funerals to counter-protest Westboro's message have a similar right to gather on public property and express ideas.[41] Neither protest group has the right to "unfriend" or "unfollow" the other group while they share a public space. They must, to some extent, tolerate each other. Others who are in the same physical area, those who are not a part of either group, also encounter the ideas communicated by both groups, without the ability to screen them out, while in a public forum.

The approach that has been developed regarding expression in physical public forums is based on the assumption that, though speech at times can be hurtful and offensive, more expression, rather than less, is the best way for discourse to occur in democratic society.[42] This understanding regarding the expression of popular as well as unpopular ideas was at the heart of Justice Louis Brandeis's concurring opinion in the case of a member of the communist party who was brought up on California Criminal Syndicalism charges 1927.[43] Justice Brandeis contended that, "If there be time to expose through discussion the falsehood and fallacies, to avert the evil by the processes of education, the remedy to be applied is more speech, not enforced silence."[44] The value in individuals in society encountering a wide spectrum of ideas also aligns with the marketplace of ideas approach to the First Amendment, which assumes that, when rational individuals are left free to evaluate the full spectrum of ideas, the truth will emerge and false ideas will fall aside.[45] This was the thinking put forth by John Milton in 1644, in his argument against the British government's licensing system, as well as the idea behind Justice Oliver Wendell Holmes's employment of the metaphor when he introduced it into the Court's thinking in 1919.[46] Justice Holmes wrote that "the ultimate good desired is better reached by free trade in ideas—that the best test of truth is the power of the thought to get itself accepted in the competition of the market, and that truth is the only ground upon which their wishes safely can be carried out."[47] These assumptions about discourse in democratic society have underpinned the construction of legal understandings regarding traditional public forums.[48]

The growing place of networked communication platforms as spaces for discourse in the lives of citizens raises questions about the power individuals have to curate their marketplace—both in how they present themselves and in the ideas they encounter.[49] Both potentially distort the spectrum of points of view that those who are connected via networked technology encounter each day. People tend to curate a particular version of themselves on social media, creating an online version that may or may not align with who they are in real life. Turkle wrote that, "We can write the Facebook profile that pleases us. We can edit our messages until they project the self we want to be. And we can keep things short and sweet."[50] In fact, scholars have found that people use social media as tools for self-affirmation to offset the myriad frustrations that are caused by the far less controlled encounters that occur in their physical environments each day and to strategically promote themselves.[51] Such calculated presentations of self raise questions about the potential for social media to embody the characteristics of traditional public forums because individuals are able to manipulate how they present their identities differently than they can in the physical realm. In doing so, they influence and exercise power over the range and types of messages they and others discuss within their networks of self-chosen connections.

Furthermore, while social-media, in their functionality, have the *potential* to be used as public forums, they can easily become private forums, echo chambers where individuals receive only affirmation and reinforcement regarding their existing understandings. Legal scholar Cass Sunstein listed this as among his concerns for democracy in the network era, contending that members of democratic society must have unplanned encounters with a diversity of ideas and individuals.[52] He argued that when individuals fragment in groups with like-minded individuals, "diverse groups will tend to polarize in a way that can breed extremism and even hatred and violence."[53] Castells raised a similar concern when he recognized that the ideological fragmentation that networked technologies allow can lead individuals to struggle to understand the viewpoints of others. He found that when we curate our networked identities, "social groups and individuals become alienated from each other, and see the other as a stranger, eventually as a threat. In this process, social fragmentation spreads, as identities become more specific and increasingly difficult to share."[54] These characteristics of social media diverge substantially with the make-ups of physical public forums, where individuals cannot "unfollow" a speaker whose ideas do not align with their own. They also cannot block or delete unpopular responses to their own ideas.

Overall, the selective, fragmentary nature of social media and other networked communication tools make it difficult for them to be used as a replacement for physical, traditional public forums. The voices individuals are connected with in their self-composed networks tend toward homogeneity.[55] In some ways, there is nothing new about the fact that people often interact most with those who are similar to them, whether the interactions are in-person or online. People have always formed "ego networks," which scholars define as a series of social connections between an individual, the "ego," and others, known as "alters."[56] The emergence of networked technologies, however, has vastly expanded the capabilities individuals have to encounter others and to select who they communicate with. Though individuals do not always exclusively construct networks of like-minded people, generally a person shares enough in common, whether in the form of strong or weak ties, to create some level of connection within his or her ego network.[57] Similarly, when a person encounters a perspective that is disagreeable, he or she has the choice of whether they seek to respond with their own thoughts, remain silent, or disband the connection with the person within their ego network. Two of those options run in parallel with the structure of traditional, physical public forums. A person walking down the street can choose to address or ignore another person who expresses an idea. The third option, however, gives individuals the power to limit the range of ideas they encounter within the virtual space they occupy.

ORGANIZATIONAL AND NON-HUMAN SPEAKERS IN ONLINE SPACES

Not all of the ideas expressed within individuals' social networks originate from citizens who seek to express an idea or respond to a message communicated by another person. Artificially intelligent account-holders, often called "bots" or "chatbots" and corporate, governmental, and other persuasive speakers increasingly occupy prominent roles in online spaces, raising questions about how discourse will function in social media and other networked communication tools in the future.[58] Microsoft and other corporations are authoring software to make it easier for individuals to create bots, which are forms of artificial intelligence that can replicate human conversation.[59] Bots, once set in motion, communicate messages on their own, posting whenever their code tells them to interact with certain users that trigger their attention. Google created a chatbot in 2015 that was programmed to debate the meaning of life.[60] Microsoft gained substantial attention in spring 2016 when it briefly introduced Tay, a bot that was designed to learn about conversation by interacting with people on

Twitter.[61] The experiment lasted 24 hours, with the corporation quickly taking the experimental bot offline because Tay, @TayTweets, almost instantly learned how to be a foul-mouthed racist from its interactions with others on social media. Microsoft has also been in the news because it is producing software that allows users to create chatbots for Twitter, Skype, and Slack, making it far easier for people without programming skills to create artificially intelligent entities online.[62]

While technology developers continue to experiment with and improve upon artificial intelligence applications for social media and other forms of networked communication, hundreds of millions of bots already populate online spaces. Twitter has recognized that tens of millions of accounts, possibly nearing 10% of all registered users on the popular social media site, are bots.[63] Similarly, Instagram has purged millions of accounts in an attempt to cull the number of non-human actors operating within the social media outlet's system.[64] Some of the non-human accounts are more run-of-the-mill "spambots," whose messages are often easily identifiable by most social media users. Chatbots, however, can be more difficult to identify. Piles of Buzzfeed-style, list-based articles already provide tips on how humans can figure out if they are interacting with a bot, rather than a person.[65] One such list suggests social media users should be suspicious of overly formal responses and, quite helpfully, also look out for overly informal answers, when communicating online.[66] Some chatbot creators do not attempt to hide that the artificially intelligent social media accounts they have created are not real people, such as the @brainpickings bot on Twitter, which has nearly 150,000 followers and is automated to tweet out links to the Brain Pickings blog. Many other bot-based accounts have also become popular, garnering thousands of followers, such as @oliviataters and @autocompletejok on Twitter. @autocompletejok creates knock-knock jokes by using Google's autocomplete tool. @oliviataters seeks to emulate the language of teenage girls, and is capable of replying to those who follow it. The bot once had an extended, three-bot conversation on Twitter that included Bank of America's customer service bot.[67] Olivia Taters' posts often include circular logic, political commentary, emojis, and a lot of foul language. It posted, "My family hid eggs with money in the yard and me and kaya were literally behind america, look now," for example, in March 2016. Some bots are programmed to engage individuals, often when they use certain key words. So, when Not Keith Calder, a fake account for a British film producer, engaged Olivia Taters, the two began triggering each other's response programming, creating a nonsensical interaction. The Not Keith Calder bot tweeted, for example, "I just saw two Parks and Rec."[68] Olivia Taters responded, "Rec are so adorable." The exchange continued, picking up the third party, Bank of America's customer service bot. Not

Keith Calder tweeted, "It has two different BOA branches trying to get a temporary debit card." Bank of America responded, "Hello, were you able to get the problem resolved? If not, I'd like to help." Quite logically, Not Keith Calder responded: "Why do people break up?"[69]

While the nonsensical, three-way conversation among a group of artificially intelligent computer programs on Twitter made for plenty of snarky commentary online, later in the conversation Bank of America's bot asked the Not Keith Calder bot if it needed assistance with its banking and the bot responded, "BofA_Help Have you seen them kiss?," the recognition that a growing number of speakers in virtual spaces are not human is an important one when considering that social media outlets have increasingly been utilized by citizens as places to share ideas and conduct discourse. Can bots be programmed to generate human-like responses to major political issues and be set to trigger each time a tweet is found that states certain key words? In 2014, during the Gamergate scandal surrounding male enthusiasts' resistance to women in the video-game industry, a Twitter bot was created to simulate conversations with those discussing the controversy.[70] Eliza, a chatbot on Twitter with the handle @ElizaRBarr, uses a decades old artificial intelligence computer program to simulate conversation.[71] The bot was programmed to respond to anyone who used the #gamergate hashtag with simple questions, such as "tell me more about that" or "That's interesting, please continue." The bot succeeded in engrossing many of those who took to social media to attack women in video games in endless conversation loops with what they thought was a person, but was actually an artificially intelligent Twitter account.[72] A scenario such as this, when a person finds himself arguing about technology, gender roles, economics, and other concerns with a bot, could easily slide into more central roles in the nation's discourse. This example, and the use of chatbots in customer service, seems to indicate that some small adjustments to programming could make it easy for an army of political bots to occupy social media spaces during coming election cycles, all along engaging citizens in pseudo debates. Customer service chatbots are already responding to discussions on message boards and online forums.[73] If a person engages with a bot, and likely does not knowing they are doing so, and that artificially intelligent account is capable of responding to basic arguments about a major political issue, such as gun control or abortion, does the ensuing exchange between voting, rights-bearing citizen and computer entity qualify as discourse? Such questions are only likely to intensify as the process of creating such communication tools becomes more accessible to people who do not have computer-programming skills. The Microsoft Bot Framework boasts that users can "build and connect intelligent bots to interact with your users naturally wherever they are."[74]

Unlike previously discussed concerns regarding ownership and homo-geneity, aspects which have at least some parallels to historical questions and concerns regarding physical public forums, no clear comparison exists between the growing army of artificial speakers that are programmed to insert themselves into online discussions and physical conversations. It is also noteworthy, though outside the focus of this chapter, that the increas-ing presence of non-human communicators online raises many questions about how the courts will handle instances when bots defame people, invade their privacy or post obscene content. Who is responsible when a bot defames someone, and how would the negligence and actual malice standards be evaluated? Who owns the copyright on a bot-created work? In regard to physical public forums, the closest comparison to the artifi-cial intelligence phenomenon in virtual spaces, essentially the presence of non-human speakers within discourse in online spaces, is the long his-tory of those who seek to influence public opinion by inserting persuasive messages into discourse in traditional public forums. Importantly, while foundational thinkers have long considered the impact of persuasive mes-sages on discourse in traditional forums, online spaces carry substantial, almost built-in inclusions of persuasive messages, in the forms of bots and tools such as carefully targeted marketing, advertising, and public relations, that have not, historically, been nearly as integrated into traditional public spaces.[75] In other words, governmental actors, interest groups, and corpo-rations have long worked to influence the development of public opinion, but the tools that are available in virtual spaces are more robust and are more naturally integrated into the tools of discourse than those that have been at their disposal in physical spaces.

German philosopher Jürgen Habermas' conceptualization of the public sphere, and the theory of communicative action he developed afterward, both hinge upon the requirement that private people have the freedom to willingly and meaningfully come together to address the problems and issues that face society.[76] Similarly, American philosopher John Dewey concluded that, "I am inclined to believe that the heart and final guarantee of democ-racy is in free gatherings of neighbors on the street corner to discuss back and forth what is read in uncensored news of the day, and in gatherings of friends in the living rooms of houses and apartments to converse freely with one another."[77] The public sphere, to Habermas, was indeed the "sphere of public authority," an idealized space that, in American legal terms aligns closely with the concept of a public forum.[78] Habermas expressed substantial concern that the intrusions of government or persuasive messages into the public sphere would damage and distort the ability of free individuals to gather for the purpose of discourse and, ultimately, the formation of *public* opinion, which has the potential to substantially influence the actions of political actors.[79] Importantly, Habermas' theory of communicative action envisions a two-level structure regarding identity and society.[80] The system level includes government and corporations, which are primarily artificial social creations. The second level, the "lifeworld," represents family and traditional, organic formations with society. In Habermas' thinking, the first level, the state and corporations, must not hinder the ability of the second-level institutions in society, because it was on the second level that the public sphere, the space of individuals come together to form a public, resides.

Habermas contends that democratic society requires that free individuals, and not governmental, business, or other persuasive parties, gather to conduct discourse and solve problems in society. He found that the "colonization" of the lifeworld of individuals by such purposive, goal-oriented communicative interests undermines the ability of citizens to conduct the type of discourse in its original, purest sense.[81] In terms of online spaces, the architecture of social media and other network-based communication tools lend themselves to substantial influence from purposive forces. Importantly, they do so in ways that are different than how such forms of communication might function in physical spaces. First, as noted earlier, online spaces are owned by corporations, which play a role in who can and cannot speak and what can be communicated. Also, online communicators often invite persuasive communication from the government, corporations, or other interest groups into virtual spaces by linking, liking, sharing, or retweeting. In many social media outlets, affirmative steps such as these act as an invitation for that organization to "colonize" a person's social media space. "Liking" an interest group on Facebook, such at the National Rifle Association, can lead to that organization's posts to be visible on the user's wall, as well as friends of that user's walls. The group is essentially invited, if not into the forum, at least into the lobby of the forum. Thirdly, those who seek to communicate persuasive messages to targeted online groups of individuals know far more about those who they seek to reach than a similar group in a physical space would. The amount of personal information individuals disclose in online spaces (discussed in Chapter 3) allows organizations to target messages to specific audiences. During the 2016 presidential primaries, Senator Ted Cruz hired a group to compile profiles on potential voters using millions of Facebook accounts, for example.[82] When groups organize to protest in public forums, others in the physical space generally are not aware of many of the details people disclose to those within social networks and, in many cases, people who are not linked at all. A glance at a LinkedIn profile or a person's Twitter stream can provide substantial information that a physical meeting on the street would not disclose. For these reasons, discussions in online spaces are substantially more susceptible to persuasive messages than physical forums.

The Black Lives Matter movement, for example, which originated in 2012 after shooting death of Trayvon Martin, and the ultimate acquittal of the shooter, George Zimmerman, leveraged networked communication tools to create a national movement.[83] The #blacklivesmatter hashtag became a powerful unifying tool, allowing anyone who commented on the issue, reposted news or comments, provided links, or expressed ideas to have a common way of connecting their ideas across a variety of social media platforms. The hashtag, along with #Ferguson, became particularly powerful after the protests in Ferguson, Missouri, in 2014 after the shooting death of Michael Brown, an unarmed black teenager, by a white police officer.[84] Protestors, in real time, posted audio, video, photographs, and text of locations for protests, police activities, and traditional media coverage, all for anyone in the world to see. The movement's use of networked technology tools, particularly the #blacklivesmatter hashtag, allowed it to spread nationally and immediately in ways that physical-forum-based efforts could not have done. The nature of online spaces also allowed individuals to gather more information about fellow protestors and counter protestors. Unlike in physical forums, the depth of knowledge individuals could garner about each other was amplified by networked communication tools.

FIVE THINGS FOR PROFESSIONAL COMMUNICATORS TO THINK ABOUT

1. If a social media outlet, such as Twitter, becomes crucial to your ability to do your job, what type of impact would it have if your account were suddenly cancelled because of a perceived violation of the code of conduct? What power do the corporations that own virtual spaces have to eliminate certain perspectives from the marketplace of ideas?

2. With increasing amounts of political discourse occurring in virtual spaces, is there any hope that the courts will eventually recognize virtual spaces as having the same or similar First Amendment protections as those provided for traditional public spaces? How could this be workable in light of the corporate, rather than public, ownership of online spaces? How could these spaces remaining private and corporately held limit the ability of reporters to gather information?

3. How does the ability individuals have to determine the range of ideas they encounter in virtual spaces create challenges for journalists? How can journalists use social media tools to try to reach the broadest spectrum of individuals? Does the fragmentary nature of networked communities harm democratic discourse?

4. The Associated Press and other news organizations are already using bots to generate basic news reports. Public relations practitioners and other communicators might also begin to employ different types of artificial intelligence to help send and comment on messages. Should non-human entities still receive the same freedom of expression rights as human communicators? Should the decision rest on *who* communicates the message or *what* the content of the message is about?

5. Who owns the copyright on works that are composed by bots? If a bot generates haikus for an advertising or public relations campaign, can anyone gather the haikus and publish them in a book without getting permission? Who would have the right to provide the permission to use the output from the bot's programming?

NOTES

1 Jordan Crook, Snapchat Sees More Daily Photos than Facebook, TechCrunch, November 13, 2013, http://techcrunch.com/2013/11/19/snapchat-reportedly-sees-more-daily-photos-than-facebook/; Twitter Usage Statistics, Internet Live Stats (2016), http://www.internetlivestats.com/twitter-statistics/.

2 Patrick R. Miller et al., Talking Politics on Facebook: Network Centrality and Political Discussion Practices in Social Media, 68 Pol. Research Q. 1, 1 (2015). Politics Fact Sheet, Pew Research Center, November 14, 2012, http://www.pewinternet.org/fact-sheets/politics-fact-sheet/.

3 McCullen v. Coakley, 134 S. Ct. 2518, 2529 (2014) (quoting Pleasant Grove City v. Summum, 555 U.S. 460, 469).

4 Manuel Castells, The Rise of the Network Society, 28–30 (2000).

5 Id. at 31.

6 Reno v. ACLU, 521 U.S. 844, 870 (1997).

7 Yochai Benkler, The Wealth of Networks: How Social Production Transforms Markets and Freedom 9 (2006); Henry Jenkins, Convergence Culture: Where Old and New Media Collide 25–28 (2006); Clay Shirky, Here Comes Everybody: The Power of Organizing Without Organizations 70–74 (2008); Cass R. Sunstein, Republic 2.0: Revenge of the Blogs 7–9 (2007).

8 Abrams v. United States, 250 U.S. 616, 630 (1919) (Holmes, J., dissenting).

9 Sareh Aghaei et al., Evolution of the World Wide Web: From Web 1.0 to Web 4.0, 3 Int'l J. of Web & Semantic Tech. 1, 8 (2012); Younghee Noh, Imagining Library 4.0: Creating a Model for Future Libraries, 41 J. of Academic Librarianship 786, 788 (2015).

10 Drew Perrin, Social Media Usage: 2005–2015, Pew Research Center, October 8, 2015, http://www.pewinternet.org/2015/10/08/social-networking-usage-2005–2015/

11 José van Dijck, 'You Have One Identity': Performing the Self on Facebook and LinkedIn, 35 Media, Culture, & Society 199, 201–204 (2013).

12 Manuel Castells, Communication Power 54–57 (2009).

13 Jenkins, supra note 7, at 26–27; Shirky, supra note 7, 83–86; Sunstein, supra note 7, 44–45.

14 See Hague v. Committee for Industrial Organization, 307 U.S. 496 (1939); Schneider v. State, 308 U.S. 147 (1939); Police Department of the City of Chicago v. Mosley, 408 U.S. 92 (1972); Southeastern Promotions v. Conrad, 420 U.S. 546 (1975); National Socialist Party v. Village of Skokie, 432 U.S. 43 (1977); Snyder v. Phelps, 562 U.S. 443 (2011), for examples.

15 See Kovacs v. Cooper, 336 U.S. 77 (1949); Grayned v. Rockford, 408 U.S. 104 (1972); United States v. Kokinda, 497 U.S. 720 (1990); Lee v. International Society for Krishna Consciousness, 505 U.S. 830 (1992), for example.

16 Hague, 307 U.S. at 514.

17 United States v. Grace, 461 U.S. 171, 177 (1983).

18 McCullen v. Coakley, 134 S. Ct. 2518, 2541 (2014).

19 Ashutosh Bhagwat, The Test That Ate Everything: Intermediate Scrutiny in First Amendment Jurisprudence, 2007 U. Ill. L. Rev. 783, 788–789 (2007).

20 Alex Hern, Mark Zuckerberg Says He Believes in Freedom of Speech. Does Facebook?, The Guardian, January 12, 2015, http://www.theguardian.com/world/2015/jan/12/mark-zuckerberg-freedom-speech-facebook.

21 Free Expression, Google (2016), https://www.google.com/intl/en/takeaction/free-expression/.

22 Fighting Abuse to Protect Freedom of Expression, Twitter, December 30, 2015, https://blog.twitter.com/2015/fighting-abuse-to-protect-freedom-of-expression-au. Emily Bell, Twitter Tackles Free Speech Conundrum, The Guardian, January 10, 2016, http://www.theguardian.com/media/2016/jan/10/twitter-free-speech-rules-hostile-behaviour.

23 Katie Rogers, Twitter "Sorry" for Suspending Guy Adams as NBC Withdraws Complaint, The Guardian, July 31, 2012, https://www.theguardian.com/technology/2012/jul/31/guy-adams-twitter-growing-pains.

24 Alex Macgillivray, Our Approach to Trust & Safety, and Private Information, Twitter, July 31, 2012, https://blog.twitter.com/2012/our-approach-to-trust-safety-and-private-information.

25 Terms of Service, Instagram (2016), https://help.instagram.com/478745558852511.

26 See Hague v. Committee for Industrial Organization, 307 U.S. 496 (1939); Schneider v. State, 308 U.S. 147 (1939); Police Department of the City of Chicago v. Mosley, 408 U.S. 92 (1972); Southeastern Promotions v. Conrad, 420 U.S. 546 (1975); National Socialist Party v. Village of Skokie, 432 U.S. 43 (1977); Snyder v. Phelps, 562 U.S. 443 (2011), for example.

27 Texas v. Johnson, 491 U.S. 397, 399 (1989).

28 Id. at 414.

29 Cohen v. California, 403 U.S. 15 (1971); Brandenburg v. Ohio, 395 U.S. 444 (1969).

30 Jeffrey Rosen, The Deciders: The Future of Privacy and Free Speech in the Age of Facebook and Google, 80 Fordham L. Rev. 1525, 1536 (2011–2012); Miguel Helft, Facebook Wrestles with Free Speech and Civility, New York Times, December 12, 2010, http://www.nytimes.com/2010/12/13/technology/13facebook.html?_r=0.

31 Community Guidelines, Snapchat (2016), https://support.snapchat.com/en-US/a/guidelines.

32 What Is Free the Nipple, Free the Nipple: How Far Will You Go for Equality (2016), http://freethenipple.com/.

33 Nadine Saad, Chelsea Handler Leaves Instagram after It Nixes Her Topless Pic, Los Angeles Times, October 31, 2014, http://www.latimes.com/entertainment/gossip/la-et-mg-chelsea-handler-topless-photo-instagram-20141031-htmlstory.html.

34 Andrea Chang, Instagram Updates User Guidelines with More Details, Stricter Tone, Los Angeles Times, April 17, 2015, http://www.latimes.com/business/technology/la-fi-tn-instagram-guidelines-20150417-story.html; Community Guidelines, Instagram (2016), https://help.instagram.com/477434105621119/.

35 The Twitter Rules, Twitter Help Center (2016), https://support.twitter.com/articles/18311.

36 Paresh Dave & Brian Bennett, Twitter Offers New, Though Limited, Evidence that It's Driving Terrorists Away, Los Angeles Times, February 5, 2016, http://www.latimes.com/business/technology/la-fi-tn-twitter-terrorism-20160205-story.html.

37 Dave & Bennett, supra note 36.

38 Sherry Turkle, Alone Together: Why We Expect More from Technology and Less from Each Other 1 (2011).

39 562 U.S. 443 (2011).

40 Id. at 460.

41 Anna Zwierz Messar, Balancing Freedom of Speech with the Right to Privacy: How to Legally Cope with the Funeral Protest Problem, 28 Pace L. Rev. 101, 120 (2007–2008); Michael E. Ruane, Bikers Protest Westboro Baptist Demonstrators at Arlington Burial, Washington Post, October 4, 2010, http://www.washingtonpost.com/wp-dyn/content/article/2010/10/04/AR2010100406662.html.

42 Snyder, 562 U.S. at 456–457.

43 Whitney v. California, 274 U.S. 357, 377 (1927) (Brandeis, J., concurring).

44 Id.

45 Cass R. Sunstein, The First Amendment in Cyberspace, 104 Yale L. J. 1757, 1760 (1995).

46 Michael Mendle, De Facto Freedom, De Facto Authority: Press and Parliament, 1640–1643, 38 The Hist. J. 307, 330–32 (1995); John Milton, Areopagitica and of Education 40–41 (George H. Sabine ed., Harlan Davidson 1951); Abrams v. United States, 250 U.S. 616, 630 (1919) (Holmes, J., dissenting).

47 Id. at 630 (Holmes, J., dissenting).

48 See Bakery & Pastry Drivers v. Wohl, 315 U.S. 769, 776 (1942) (Douglas, J., concurring); Amalgamated Food Employees v. Logan Valley Plaza, 391 U.S. 308, 323 (1968); Hill v. Colorado, 530 U.S. 703, 778 (2000) (Scalia, J., dissenting), for example.

49 Van Dijck, supra note 11, at 201–204.

50 Turkle, supra note 38, at 12.

51 Catalina L. Toma & Jeffrey T. Hancock, Self-Affirmation Underlies Facebook Use, 39 Personality and Social Psychology Bulletin 321, 329 (2013); Van Dijck, supra note 11, at 210.

52 Sunstein, supra note 7, at 5–7.

53 Id. at 44.

54 Castells, supra note 4, at 3.

55 Sunstein, supra note 7, at 104–105; Castells, supra note 12, at 36–37.

56 David Knoke, Networks of Political Action: Toward Theory Construction, 68 Soc. Forces 1041, 1043 (1989–1990).

57 Miller et al., supra note 2, at 12.

58 Tetyana Lokot & Nicholas Diakopoulos, News Bots: Automating News and Information Dissemination on Twitter, 3 Digital Journalism 1, 1–2 (2015).

59 Jennifer Hill et al., Real Conversations with Artificial Intelligence: A Comparison Between Human-Human Online Conversations and Human-Chatbot Conversations, 49 Computers in Human Behavior, 245, 246 (2015).

60 Cade Metz, Google Made a Chatbot That Debates the Meaning of Life, Wired, June 26, 2015, http://www.wired.com/2015/06/google-made-chatbot-debates-meaning-life/.

61 Daniel Victor, Microsoft Created a Twitter Bot to Learn from Users. It Quickly Became a Racist Jerk, N.Y. Times, March 24, 2016, http://www.nytimes.com/2016/03/25/technology/microsoft-created-a-twitter-bot-to-learn-from-users-it-quickly-became-a-racist-jerk.html.

62 Rob Marvin, Microsoft Brings AI, Bots to Business Chat, PC Magazine, March 30, 2016, http://www.pcmag.com/news/343333/microsoft-brings-ai-bots-to-business-chat.

63 Zachary M. Seward, Twitter Admits That as Many as 23 Million of Its Active Users Are Automated, Quartz, August 11, 2014, http://qz.com/248063/twitter-admits-that-as-many-as-23-million-of-its-active-users-are-actually-bots/.

64 Deepa Seetharaman, Fake Accounts Still Plague Instagram Despite Purge, Study Finds, Wall Street Journal, June 30, 2015, http://blogs.wsj.com/digits/2015/06/30/fake-accounts-still-plague-instagram-despite-purge-study-finds/

65 Sam Weiner, 12 Signs Your Tinder Match Might Be a Bot, Buzzfeed, July 7, 2015, http://www.buzzfeed.com/samweiner/12-signs-your-tinder-match-might-be-a-bot#.pwMLAwoob; Esther Inglis-Arkell, 10 Tricks That Chatbots Use to Make You Believe They're Human, io9, April 13, 2012, http://io9.gizmodo.com/5901579/10-tricks-that-chatbots-use-to-make-you-believe-theyre-human.

66 Joseph Rauch, How to Tell if You're Talking to a Bot: The Complete Guide to Chatbots, Talkspace, January 22, 2016, http://www.talkspace.com/blog/2016/01/how-to-tell-if-youre-talking-to-a-bot-the-complete-guide-to-chatbots/.

67 Alexis C. Madrigal, That Time 2 Bots Were Talking, and Bank of America Butted In, The Atlantic, July 7, 2014, http://www.theatlantic.com/technology/archive/2014/07/that-time-2-bots-were-talking-and-bank-of-america-butted-in/374023/.

68 Id.

69 Id.

70 Ian Steadman, The Ultimate Weapon against GamerGate Time-Waster: A 1960s Chat Bot That Wastes Their Time, NewStatesman, October 15, 2014, http://www.newstatesman.com/future-proof/2014/10/ultimate-weapon-against-gamergate-time-wasters-1960s-chat-bot-wastes-their-time.

71 See, Joseph Weizenbaum, ELIZA, A Computer Program for the Study of Natural Language Communication between Man and Machine, 9 Comm. Of the ACM 36 (1966), which discusses the original computer chat program.

72 Steadman, supra note 70.

73 Marty Swant, Why Brands from Barbie to Uber Are so Hot on Chatbots: Are Automated Messaging Platforms the New Customer Service Reps, Adweek, April 3, 2016, http://www.adweek.com/news/technology/why-brands-barbie-uber-are-so-hot-chatbots-170577.

74 Microsoft Bot Framework, Microsoft, https://dev.botframework.com/.

75 José van Dijck, The Culture of Connectivity: A Critical History of Social Media 36–40 (2013).

76 Jurgen Habermas, On the Pragmatics of Communication 24 (1998).

77 John Dewey, Creative Democracy – The Task Before Us, in The Essential Dewey Vol. 1, 342 (Larry A. Hickman & Thomas M. Alexander, eds., 1998)

78 Jurgen Habermas, The Structural Transformation of the Public Sphere 18 (Thomas Burger & Frederick Lawrence, trans., 1999)

79 Id. at 141–142; Jürgen Habermas, The Theory of Communicative Action Vol. 2 350–351 (1984).

80 Lasse Thomassen, The Derrida–Habermas Reader 1 (2006); Peter Dews, Autonomy & Solidarity: Interviews with Jürgen Habermas 1 (1992).

81 Habermas, supra note 79, at 354–356.

82 Harry Davies, Ted Cruz Using Firm That Harvested Data on Millions of Unwitting Facebook Users, The Guardian, December, 11, 2015, http://www.theguardian.com/us-news/2015/dec/11/senator-ted-cruz-president-campaign-facebook-user-data.

83 About the Black Lives Matter Network, Black Lives Matter (2016), http://blacklivesmatter.com/about/.

84 Deen Freelon et al., Beyond the Hashtag: #Ferguson, #Blacklivesmatter, and the Online Struggle for Offline Justice 5 (2016); Scott Neuman, Ferguson Timeline: Grief, Anger, and Tension, NPR, November 24, 2014, http://www.npr.org/sections/thetwo-way/2014/11/24/364103735/ferguson-timeline-grief-anger-and-tension.

Contributors

Courtney A. Barclay, Ph.D., J.D., is an assistant professor at Jacksonville University. She teaches courses in strategic communications, media law, and social media. Her research on developing legal policies for consumer protections in the online and mobile environments has been published in law reviews including *Media Law and Policy* and *Computer Law & Security Review*. She also served as clerk and visiting scholar at the Electronic Privacy Information Center.

David Cuillier, Ph.D., is director and associate professor at the University of Arizona School of Journalism and is a former president and freedom of information chair for the Society of Professional Journalists. He was a newspaper reporter and editor in the Pacific Northwest before entering academia, and now teaches courses in access to public records and data journalism. He is co-author with Charles N. Davis of *The Art of Access: Strategies for Acquiring Public Records* and *Transparency 2.0: Digital Data and Privacy in a Wired World*.

Holly Kathleen Hall, J.D., is an associate professor of strategic communication at Arkansas State University teaching classes in media law and ethics, public relations, and social media. She has published in *Visual Communications Quarterly*, *Communication Law and Policy*, and contributed chapters regarding social media to four books. Prior to joining the faculty at Arkansas State, Hall worked in public relations for 10 years and is Accredited in Public Relations by the Public Relations Society of America.

Woodrow Hartzog, J.D., Ph.D., LL.M., is the W. Stancil Starnes Professor of Law at the Cumberland School of Law at Samford University and an Affiliate Scholar at the Center for Internet and Society at Stanford Law School. His research on privacy, media, and robotics has been or is scheduled to be published in numerous law reviews and peer-reviewed publications such as the *Yale Law Journal, Columbia Law Review, California Law Review*, and *Michigan Law Review*, and popular publications such as *The Guardian, Wired, The Atlantic, CNN* and *BBC*. His book, *Privacy's Blueprint: The Battle to Control the Design of New Technologies*, is under contract with Harvard University Press.

Jennifer Jacobs Henderson, Ph.D., is a professor and chair of the Department of Communication at Trinity University in San Antonio, Texas. Her research addresses issues of media law, the ethics of media, and the use of participatory cultures for political and social action. She is co-editor of the 2012 Routledge *Participatory Cultures Handbook*. Her recent chapter in *The Rise of the Transtexts* (2016) proposes a new copyright scheme to accommodate increasingly common remixed and transmedia narratives.

Dan Kozlowski, Ph.D., is an associate professor in the Department of Communication at Saint Louis University, where he teaches free expression and a variety of journalism and media courses. He also holds a secondary appointment in SLU's School of Law. His work has appeared in *Communication Law and Policy*, *Journalism & Mass Communication Quarterly*, *Free Speech Yearbook*, *The International Encyclopedia of Communication*, and other journals. His research interests include student speech rights, judicial decision-making, comparative law, and journalism and culture. He received his master's degree from Saint Louis University and his doctorate from the University of North Carolina at Chapel Hill. Before entering academia, he worked professionally as a copy editor and page designer for a community newspaper in Missouri and as a sports producer and production assistant for a local TV news station in New York City.

Jasmine E. McNealy is an assistant professor of Telecommunication at the University of Florida College of Journalism and Communications. She studies information, communication, and technology with a view toward influencing law and policy. Her research focuses on privacy, online media, communities, and culture. She has been published or accepted for publication in both social science and legal journals including the *First Amendment Law Review*, *Newspaper Research Journal*, and *Communication Law & Policy*.

Kathleen K. Olson, J.D., Ph.D., is an associate professor at Lehigh University in Bethlehem, Pennsylvania. She has worked as an attorney and copy editor and helped create the online version of the *Austin American-Statesman* in Austin, Texas. Her research focuses on intellectual property issues, including copyright and the right of publicity, and is the co-author of *Mass Communication Law in Pennsylvania*.

Cathy Packer, Ph.D., is the W. Horace Carter Distinguished Professor in the School of Media and Communication at the University of North Carolina at Chapel Hill. She is co-director of the UNC Center for Media Law and Policy and co-editor of the N.C. Media Law Handbook. A former newspaper reporter, she teaches courses in media law and Internet law to undergraduate and graduate students.

Amy Kristin Sanders, J.D., Ph.D., is an associate professor in residence at Northwestern University in Qatar. Along with T. Barton Carter and Marc A. Franklin, she is the author of the widely recognized casebook

First Amendment and the Fourth Estate: The Law of Mass Media. A licensed attorney and award-winning journalist, Sanders regularly serves as an expert witness in legal proceedings and a consultant for Fortune 500 companies and national telecommunications regulators. In addition, she has authored more than a dozen scholarly articles in numerous law and mass communication journals. Before joining the professoriate, Sanders worked as a copy editor and page designer for the *Gainesville* (Fla.) *Sun*, a New York Times Co. newspaper. She earned a Ph.D. in mass communication law from the University of Florida. Her MA in professional journalism and her Juris Doctorate are from the University of Iowa.

Jared Schroeder, Ph.D., is an assistant professor in the Division of Journalism at Southern Methodist University. His research focuses on legal questions that have emerged regarding discourse in democratic society during a time when social media and other network-based tools have become a crucial part of how individuals communicate. His work draws from legal and philosophical sources to consider questions about how 21st-century communication concerns can be resolved in light of legal principles and precedents that are decades if not centuries old. Dr. Schroeder was a journalist for several years before earning his doctorate at the University of Oklahoma. He teaches courses in communication law and journalism history.

Derigan Silver, Ph.D. is an associate professor in the Department of Media, Film and Journalism Studies at the University of Denver, and he is an adjunct professor in the Sturm College of Law. He teaches graduate and undergraduate courses on the First Amendment, media law, Internet law, and political communication. He has published scholarly articles on originalism, defamation law, social architecture theory, access to terrorism trials, national security law, and student expression. His first book, *National Security in the Courts: The Need for Secrecy v. the Requirements of Transparency*, was published in 2010. He is also the author of a chapter in the widely used media law textbook, *Communication and the Law.*

Daxton R. "Chip" Stewart, Ph.D,. J.D., LL.M., is an associate professor of journalism in the Bob Schieffer College of Communication at Texas Christian University. He has more than 15 years of professional experience in news media and public relations and was licensed as an attorney in Texas and Missouri after earning his law degree from the University of Texas. Dr. Stewart's master's and doctorate in journalism are from the University of Missouri, where he focused on media law while working as an editor and columnist at the *Columbia Missourian*. He has served as the editor-in-chief of *Dispute Resolution Magazine*, the quarterly publication of the American Bar Association's Section of Dispute Resolution, and is one of the founding editors of *Community Journalism*, an online, peer-reviewed academic journal that launched in 2012.

Index